WALT DISNEY'S

MICKEY MOUSE

THE ULTIMATE HISTORY

EDITED BY

Daniel Kothenschulte

TEXT BY

J.B. Kaufman & David Gerstein

DESIGN BY

Anna-Tina Kessler

DIRECTED AND PRODUCED BY

Benedikt Taschen

TASCHEN

"I only hope that we never lose sight of one thing—that it was all started by a mouse."

WALT DISNEY, OCTOBER 27, 1954

IT'S HARD TO BELIEVE, but most of us have never lived in a world without Mickey Mouse in it. From the moment he made his first appearance, the little scamp with the outsized personality and a mind full of mischief has been an enduring symbol of optimism, wholesome fun, and "can-do" spirit. For millions around the world, Mickey is Disney, which is fitting because he's the very heart and soul of our company.

His birth is the stuff of legend, giving rise to a robust Mickey mythology over the years—much of it perfectly plausible and some of it probably true. What we know for absolute certain is that he was born of hope and determination following a personal and professional betrayal that broke Walt Disney's heart and threatened the very existence of his animation studio: the loss of Oswald the Lucky Rabbit. Just when all seemed lost, Mickey bounded onto the screen full of brio and bravado, whistling a happy tune in *Steamboat Willie*. Animation would never be the same. Neither would The Walt Disney Company.

Ninety years later our company looks a lot different. So does Mickey. He's evolved with the times; drawing inspiration from every era to refine his look, expand his reach, and embrace new technology to stay connected with his friends and fans around the world. But at heart he still is the same irresistibly irreverent and irrepressible spirit he's always been. Some things never change.

One of the great joys of being CEO of Disney is watching new generations of people all over the world discover Mickey for the first time. It's usually love at first sight, just like it was for the rest of us.

We respond to his infinite kindness and loyal friendship. We enjoy his happy-go-lucky nature, his insouciance, and his resilience, which comes in handy given his uncanny knack for getting himself into all sorts of predicaments. Generations have watched him ingeniously turn problems into possibilities, using the power of optimism to transform obstacles into opportunities. We appreciate his sense of wonder and adventure, which invites the child in each of us to come out and play, and we revere him as an enduring, direct connection to our founder, Walt Disney.

The world loves Mickey for many reasons, most of all because he never fails to make us smile, and the world is a better place for that!

—BOB IGER

SONKEN-GALAMBA CORPORATION
KANSAS CITY, KANSAS
Sept. 29, 1930
Mr. Walt Disney,
Hollywood, Calif.
Dear Walt: I am enclosing herewith a clipping which appeared in the Kansas City paper this morning, which of course we are all very proud to note.
Suppose you will remember the good time we had at Chicago when I came up to visit you from Great Lakes.
Hope some day you will be able to draw Mickey Mouse in the role of a "junk man".
Yours
August 12, 1930
Dear Mr. Disney
HOLLYWOOD
CALIFORNIA

INTRODUCTION

A Mouse of a Thousand Faces

In 1981, a Disney film crew went to visit Andy Warhol. "They asked me who my favorite Disney character was," Warhol noted in his diary, "and I said, 'Minnie Mouse, because she can get me close to Mickey.'"[1]

Even without this kind of introduction, millions of people on earth, probably billions, feel pretty close to Mickey. No movie star, and almost no other cultural product of the modern era, has taken root in our collective consciousness to this extent. How has Mickey managed to retain his popularity for more than 90 years, continuing to enchant generation upon generation?

His present-day vitality, however, is the result of a process of perpetual change, while simultaneously and consistently returning to his roots. Like no other visual creation of the 20th century, Mickey Mouse has become part of our daily lives without his own creative evolution ever being interrupted. His cultural history is a story of countless artistic impulses that continually revitalize his persona. Anyone writing a book on the history of Mickey Mouse, like David Gerstein and J.B. Kaufman have done on these subsequent pages following years of archival research, must traverse the ages and, just as in the cartoon *Thru the Mirror*, will encounter many Mickeys through the looking glass.

Despite this constant change, Mickey always reflects his own story. Since 1929, the Disney studio has celebrated every single one of his birthdays. The notes from a story conference

Previous A 1930 publicity photograph documents how the soaring popularity of Mickey Mouse resulted in an explosive intake of fan mail — and demand for consumer products. Walt and Roy so loved the doll designed by seamstress Charlotte Clark that they set it as the standard against which all subsequent Mickey Mouses were to be measured.

Disney legend John Hench painted Mickey's 25th birthday portrait in 1953. Respected by Walt as one of the studio's most gifted artists, Hench was appointed Mickey's official portraitist and worked for the Walt Disney Company for nearly 65 years.

Walt Disney poses as a teletype operator in an early 1930s publicity photograph. At a time when Mickey's popularity was exploding, somebody had to take care of the hundreds of requests reaching the Mouse every day.

A French stock poster kept the audience guessing what exact Mickey Mouse title they were about to see. The art, by Floyd Gottfredson and Al Taliaferro, was repurposed from 1931 publicity drawings and the 1932 daily comic strip serial "The Great Orphanage Robbery."

from June 27, 1939, document how rapidly and dramatically Walt Disney's quality requirements for Mickey Mouse films had increased. That Tuesday afternoon, together with his colleagues Riley Thomson and David Hand, Walt revisited early Mickey cartoons for a planned compilation movie, which was going to be called *Mickey's Revival Party*. While each cartoon had been a worldwide success in its own right, there was hardly a scene Walt still considered worth watching: "We could plunk anything in those days and the audience liked it," he blurts out at *Mickey's Choo Choo*. "Look at the drawing. And the ink on it! [Minnie playing the violin]. Isn't that sound bad? You don't realize it."[2]

All the praise these films had received just a few short years earlier appears to have been forgotten in this situation. And this despite the fact that one of the most influential books on the history of film of the time, Paul Rotha's *The Film till Now*, described *Mickey's Choo Choo* as a "masterpiece." In the book, film critic Rotha also gives us an idea of the immense artistic appreciation his colleagues had for Disney's films as early as the 1930s: "To many writers at the moment, the Disney cartoons are the most witty and satisfying productions of modern cinema."[3]

The Mickey craze of the early 1930s is one of media history's greatest phenomena and plays an important part in our book. This period also marked the heyday of elaborate Mickey merchandise which, nowadays, is among the most sought-after Disney memorabilia. With his iconic design, perfected by Fred Moore, Mickey cut a rather dashing figure, as dynamic as Streamline Art Deco. Some Mickey fans who grew up with him in this era were dismayed to see that the studio would consider changing a design which, in their eyes, was simply perfect. Artist Maurice

IMAGED BY HERITAGE AUCTIONS, HA.COM

MICKEY MOUSE MAGAZINE

PUBLISHED BY KAY KAMEN, INC.
BY PERMISSION WALT DISNEY ENTERPRISES, LTD

August 1933 | EDITED BY HAL HORNE | Vol. 1 No. 8

Happy Days!

Sendak, whose character Max in *Where the Wild Things Are* was based on Mickey, declared: "That golden-age Mickey metamorphosed, alas, into less original forms at the end of his first decade."

But Walt Disney would not have become known as a perpetual innovator had he not chosen to evolve his most famous creation. And yet the story of linear progression, which is how Mickey's biography is often laid out, does not do justice to the numerous, often parallel, developments. It is more akin to the famous images of Mickey from different eras, passing the animator's pencil from one to the next.

As early as 1930, seamstress and doll designer Charlotte Clark had introduced the world to a Mickey with three-dimensional ears. In his films, however, their flatness was regarded as essential to his appearance. To some critics they represented a visible interface between drawing and film space, showing the miracle of animation with particular clarity. As writer John Updike later put it, "These ears properly belong not to the three-dimensional space but to an ideal realm of notation, of symbolization, of cartoon resilience and indestructibility."[4]

When *Steamboat Willie* premiered on November 18, 1928, animated movies had already been around for three decades; Walt Disney, however, had been making them since 1921. Felix the Cat or Disney's own Oswald had been successful, but it was Mickey who managed to become one with the audience's perception of this art form. The synchronized sounds that seemed to come directly from the figures on the screen and the music that determined the entire flow of the film — these attractions might quickly lose their novelty factor. Not so with Mickey. In his 1934 song "You're the Top," Cole Porter mentions Mickey's name in the same breath as the Colosseum and the *Mona Lisa*.

In January 1933 Disney's marketing executive Kay Kamen created a small publication called *Mickey Mouse Magazine*, containing stories, articles, gags, games, and poems. Over the years a variety of different sizes were tried out, until finally in 1940 the magazine reached comic-book size — and was renamed *Walt Disney's Comics and Stories*.

Two years before Mickey's network radio debut, he made a "broadcast" in this 1930 promotional drawing by Win Smith, seen here as part of a Disney studio New Year's greeting in *Moving Picture Review* and *Theatre Management* magazine.

Published in 1938 by Whitman, *Mickey Mouse Has a Party* was another storybook marketed as a school reader. Its cover artwork shows Mickey and Minnie in the company of Toby Tortoise and other characters from Disney's Silly Symphony series.

In 1935 a stock poster sheet proudly announced to U.S. audiences that Mickey's black-and-white years were over. After producing his Silly Symphony cartoons in Technicolor since 1932, Walt was finally given the budget by United Artists to let Mickey enter the realm of glorious three-strip color. Only his shoes had not yet found their ultimate shade.

The world of art and design was quick to recognize Mickey's physiognomy, created using simple circular shapes, as a paradigm of reduction and abstraction seldom attained. "Mickey's head is to be drawn as a circle, or better as a ball, with the features placed on this ball," Fred Moore wrote in his instructions on a model sheet, admittedly making it sound easier than it was, "the ears to be drawn as two 'not quite' circles, overlapping slightly into this ball."[5]

Mickey himself became the modernists' darling. A 1936 press release by the New York Museum of Modern Art even called him "the world's best-loved Surrealist," claiming "If Mickey Mouse in his peregrinations does not cavort in the 'omnipotence of the dream' and 'in the absence of all control exercised by the reason,' then no one does or can."[6]

Walt Disney kept his distance from such bold interpretations, as he famously explained to Aldous Huxley: "We just try to make a good picture. And then the professors come along and tell us what we do."[7]

Among the few early cultural critics who assessed the Mickey phenomenon independently of its technical innovation was philosopher Walter Benjamin, who noted in 1931: "So the explanation for the huge popularity of these films is not mechanization, their form; nor is it a misunderstanding. It is simply the fact that the public recognizes its own life in them."

IMAGED BY HERITAGE AUCTIONS, HA.COM

Reviewers who had not yet come to terms with the demise of the silent movie, with its own visual language, celebrated Mickey as a new Chaplin—and Walt agreed with them: "I think that we were rather indebted to Charlie Chaplin for the idea," he confirms in 1931. "We thought of a tiny bit of a mouse that would have something of the wistfulness of Chaplin... a little fellow trying to do the best he could."[8] Although in later interviews Disney put Mickey's comic potential into perspective and likened him to a different comedian: "I compared him to Harold

Tooker - Moore Lithograph Co., Inc. 136 W. 52nd St., New York

Printed in U. S. A.

The nostalgia boom, which brought back Mickey Mouse films and images from an earlier time, also generated some new merchandising ideas of its own. This colorful Mickey Mouse telephone from the 1970s was an actual working instrument and came in both dial and push-button models.

Lloyd. Mickey in himself wasn't funny, he was cute. So the situation had to make Mickey funny."[9]

In his later films Mickey was to mature from a rebellious country boy into more of an elegant everyman. The real role model, however, was a third side of his identity: "The amazing mouse was indeed Walt's alter ego, echoing the personality traits, mores, outlook on life, and ideas of his boss," animator Frank Thomas recalled. "He acted out Walt's fantasies in a remarkably personal way."[10]

John Hench, designated as Mickey's official portrait artist by Walt, confirmed this: "In a way he was the personification of Walt. He had Walt's optimism. We couldn't have known Mickey any better if he was really a small boy running around the studio every day."[11]

In the United Nations archives in Geneva, a historical Mickey Mouse flag attests to the esteem in which he was held by the League of Nations at the time. According to a 1934 press release, the member states voted unanimously to make Mickey a member.[12] In an era characterized by depression and political unrest, Mickey was considered a peaceful citizen of the world and Floyd Gottfredson's comic-strip adventures gave him the opportunity to also explore this world, be it by airplane, submarine, or even on camelback. After World War II, Italian artist Romano Scarpa continued in Gottfredson's vein, followed by other international artists and authors entering into dialogue with Americans Carl Fallberg or Paul Murry. In the comics, Mickey, the hero of all genres, is fully transformed into "Cosmopolitan Mickey," as David Gerstein dubs him in this volume.

In the 1980s, Mickey's return to the big screen in *Mickey's Christmas Carol* (1983) and *Who Framed Roger Rabbit* (1988) paved the way for a thriving era of new animated movies now known as the "Disney Renaissance." During that time, Mickey was also part of a reawakened historical consciousness when it came to animated movies. In 1991, his

portrait adorned the *Fantasia* home video release, which sold 14.2 million copies despite only being available for 50 days—more than any other VHS tape before. The new medium, the LaserDisc, made his black-and-white movies available once again.

For Andreas Deja, who animated him, among others, in the bold short *Runaway Brain*, it is impossible to bring Mickey to life without referencing his earlier manifestations: "The hardest thing about animating Mickey . . . is that the whole world knows him and how he behaves. You really have to go back and study the old shorts to find out what these characters are all about. It's not just how he looks or moves, but what is in his soul that makes him so incredibly appealing."[13]

The TV episodes that have been produced by Paul Rudish since 2013 have revived the anarchic humor of the early films, using the modern digital techniques of Toon Boom and Flash animation.

Colored pencil study for *Mickey and Claudius the Bee*, a story which was abandoned before reaching the production stage. The story crew's enthusiasm for this plotline grew from their interest in exploring the insects' fascinating, complex lifestyle. In late 1939, story man Bob Carr even proposed an alternate version of the story with Donald as lead player—but like the Mickey version, it ultimately buzzed off.

On June 11, 2013, director Lauren MacMullan surprised the audience at the Annecy International Animated Film Festival in France with an ostensible archive find from 1928. It was the premiere of *Get a Horse!*, the subsequently Oscar-nominated homage to the art of the first Disney animators, convincingly framed as an unearthed treasure. In his long career, Mickey has frequently rescued his beloved Minnie from captivity, but no barrier ever seemed as impregnable as the screen itself. In this spectacular short, the screen divides the two-dimensional realm of the early animated movies and the three-dimensional realm of computer animation.

In a rare historical arc, we witness the return of an aspect of Mickey Mouse held in particularly high esteem by his early avant-garde admirers: a boyish naturalness, an anarchic spirit willing to challenge the boundaries of filmic reality.

Ninety years after the premiere of *Steamboat Willie*, the world's most persistent movie star seems to be as present as ever before. The story of these 90 years of Mickey, the countless facets of his immeasurably rich and complex development, will be the subject of the following pages. Let Andy Warhol's wish be our command: let's get close to Mickey.

—Daniel Kothenschulte

A detailed, inventive 1932 greeting card from Hall Brothers, today's Hallmark, invites the birthday celebrant to share screen credit with a beloved screen idol—and maybe to identify with the little Mickey in the picture, attending the screening with a mother-like Minnie.

This iconic image of Walt and Mickey, attributed to Hollywood photographer Tom Collins, was snapped circa 1931.

MICKE

THE GOLDEN AGE

LONDON COUNTY COUNCIL ELECTION 1931
POLLING DAY: THURSDAY, MARCH 5 — 8 AM TO 8 PM
VOTE FOR
MOUSTARDIER
AND RAY THE
MUNICIPAL REFORM CANDIDATES
MOUSTARDIER
RAY
MOUSTARDIER
RAY
Western Electric
SOUND SYSTEM

CHAPTER ONE

A Mouse Is Born

Walt Disney had a lifelong habit of turning failures into resounding successes. Mickey Mouse, conceived in desperation and born of necessity in 1928, is by far the most spectacular example. After nearly five years of dogged hard work in Hollywood, Walt had finally begun to achieve a modest success as a producer of animated cartoons—only to see his starring character, Oswald the Lucky Rabbit, taken from him by an unscrupulous distributor. Walt, clinging to his precarious foothold, needed a substitute character in a hurry, and Mickey Mouse was the substitute. Brought to the screen in haste, Mickey survived the unlikely circumstances of his birth. By the end of 1928 he was beginning to attract attention; within one year he was an established favorite of delighted audiences in America and abroad; within five years he was an international sensation. Today, Mickey Mouse remains the most beloved and widely recognized cartoon character of all time.

The story of Mickey's birth was one of the pivotal events in Walt's life, and has been related in numerous accounts.[1] Walt, nearing completion of his first year's series of Oswald cartoons, had gone to New York in late February 1928 to meet with his distributor and negotiate a new contract for the second series. He was in for an unpleasant surprise. Charles Mintz, essentially a middleman between Walt and Universal Pictures (which distributed the Oswalds), was looking to take over production of the series himself, at a new studio managed by Mintz's

Previous This fall 1931 marketing model sheet is mostly comprised of comic strip poses by Floyd Gottfredson (and, occasionally, Ub Iwerks), reinked for the sheet by Al Taliaferro.

February 26, 1931: During a London County Council election campaign run by Sir W. Ray, *The Barnyard Battle* is shown on a small screen in a city street. The sign says "Vote for Moustardier and Ray."

Mickey poses for a publicity picture with the two men who brought him to life: Walt Disney and Ub Iwerks. This image is part of a group of studio photos that can be concisely dated, thanks to the specific staffers present and absent, between December 19, 1929 and January 17, 1930.

A precious historical document: the earliest known sketches for the character who would become Mickey Mouse (as well as a formative Minnie). This tantalizing page of sketches reportedly emerged from a meeting between Walt, Roy, Ub Iwerks, and Les Clark on Walt's return from New York in March 1928.

brother-in-law George Winkler. Behind Walt's back, Mintz had approached the Disney animators with job offers, and several of them—with the notable exception of master animator Ub Iwerks—had accepted. Because Universal owned the rights to Oswald, Mintz's move was ethically dubious but technically legal. Walt's choices were to lose his character, his release, and much of his staff, or to submit to Mintz's authority and work for him as an employee. There's reason to believe that Mintz expected Walt to knuckle under and accept his terms, but Walt instinctively rebelled at that idea. Instead, he relinquished Oswald. On March 13, Walt and his wife Lillian boarded the train for the fateful trip back to California.

That transcontinental trip has long since become the stuff of legend. Somewhere between New York and Los Angeles, Mickey Mouse was born. In later years, both Walt and Lilly would tell the stories again and again: the inspiration Walt derived from a mouse that had visited his Kansas City studio, years earlier; his initial suggestion to call the new character Mortimer Mouse and Lilly's instant dislike of the name, so that the mouse was christened Mickey as a second choice. (In subsequent years, as we'll see, the Disney studio would apply the name Mortimer to other mouse characters as a kind of running in-joke.) Other influences came into play too; one was Walt's admiration for animation pioneer Paul Terry, who regularly filled his cartoons with mice. Ub Iwerks and comic strip artist Floyd Gottfredson would later cite period cartoonist Clifton Meek, whose mouse drawings appeared in newspapers and magazines in the 1910s and '20s and clearly influenced some of the early Mickey designs.[2]

On arrival in Los Angeles, Walt immediately repaired to the little Disney studio on Hyperion Avenue and went into a huddle with his brother Roy, Ub Iwerks, and Les Clark, another animator who had elected to remain loyal. From that meeting emerged a cryptic page of mouse drawings and a plan: Mickey would be the new Disney character and would be copyrighted, trademarked, and wholly owned by the Disney studio. Never again would Walt leave himself vulnerable to a hostile takeover. The Mouse's personality was

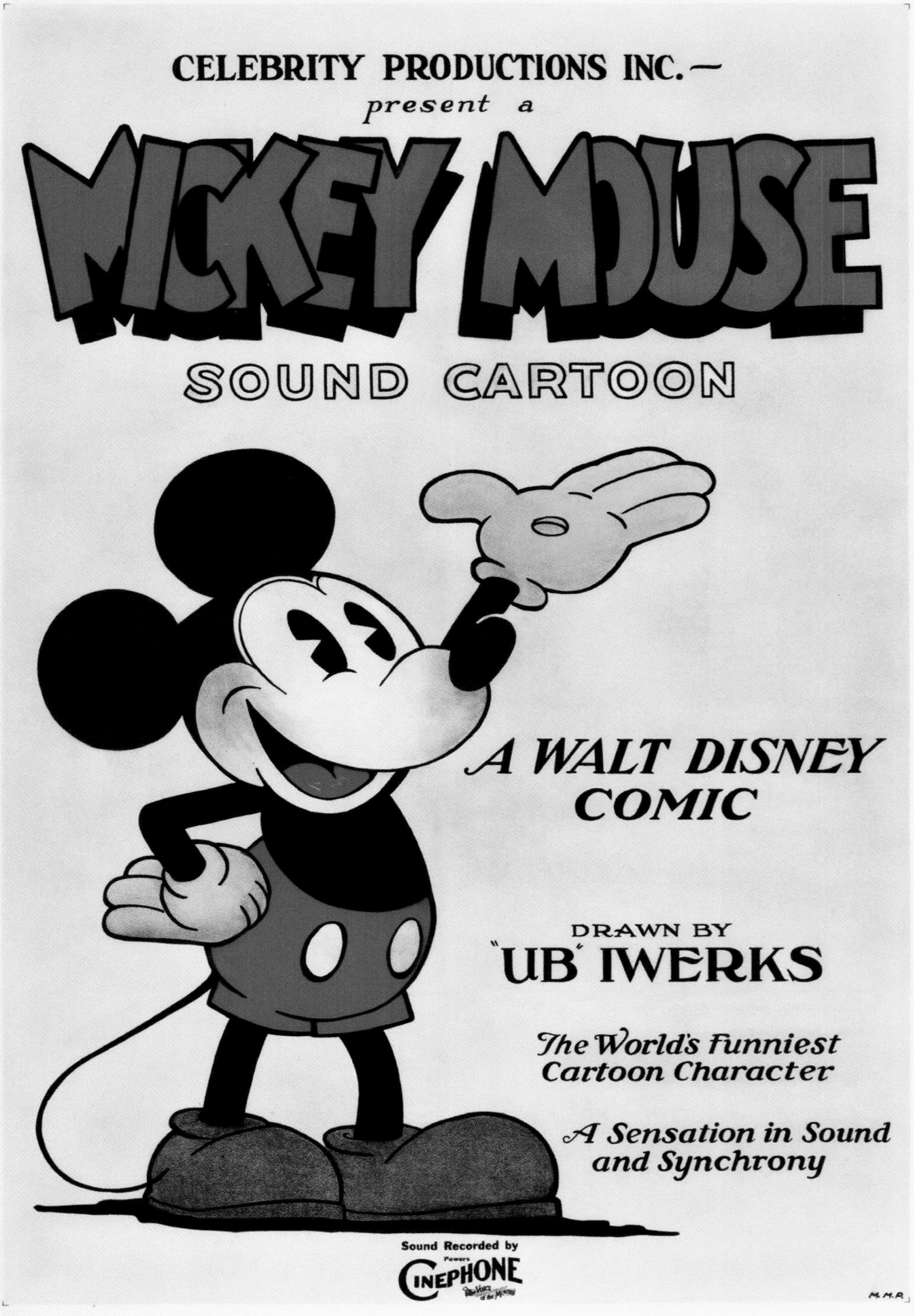
CELEBRITY PRODUCTIONS INC.—
present a
MICKEY MOUSE
SOUND CARTOON
A WALT DISNEY
COMIC
DRAWN BY
"UB" IWERKS
The World's Funniest
Cartoon Character
A Sensation in Sound
and Synchrony
Sound Recorded by
Powers
CINEPHONE

planned along ambitious lines: Walt saw him as a character with a touch of Chaplin in his makeup; Iwerks thought more in terms of Douglas Fairbanks. ("[Mickey] was always an adventurous character," Iwerks later told an interviewer. "I thought of him in that respect, and I had him do naturally the sort of thing Doug Fairbanks would do."[3]) But, most importantly, Mickey had to be brought to the screen *right away*. There was no time to lose.

This stock poster announces a new release by Celebrity Productions, a separate entity formed by Powers in the autumn of 1929 to handle distribution of the Disney cartoons. Note the credit to Ub Iwerks, and the importance of sound as a selling point for the Mickey Mouse cartoons.

Walt poses for a publicity shot to promote the *Mickey Mouse* newspaper comic strip.

THE FIRST FILMS (1928-1929)

PLANE CRAZY

Walt's choice of an aviation-centered story for his first Mouse picture is hardly surprising; aviation was nothing less than a national craze in the late 1920s. Charles Lindbergh's historic New York-Paris flight in the spring of 1927 had ignited a new wave of interest, and flying mania had been reflected in popular entertainment, including both feature-length films and animated cartoons — one of them, Oswald the Lucky Rabbit's *The Ocean Hop* (1927), produced by Walt himself. Small wonder that he now returned to that same contemporary obsession. Early in March 1928, Ub Iwerks went to work on the inaugural cartoon in the new series, *Plane Crazy*, and Mickey Mouse began his career by taking to the skies.

The Mickey who appears in *Plane Crazy* is still in a formative state: no shoes, no gloves, and a stick-like, goggle-eyed appearance that facilitates fast animation, but has yet to evolve into his familiar self. Even the cartoon convention of four fingers per hand (including the thumb) is not fully settled; Mickey's hands alternate in his earliest films between four fingers and five, sometimes within a single scene. His personality, too, is rudimentary; Mickey in *Plane Crazy* is simply an energetic, quick-witted, sometimes mischievous cartoon mouse, notably lacking in calm or introspection despite being cast as a Lindbergh-inspired dreamer. Once he manages (on his second attempt) to get a plane airborne, he loses interest and becomes easily distracted by the charms of his passenger, Minnie Mouse — likewise making *her* first screen appearance — with disastrous results. Supporting characters in *Plane Crazy* include a dachshund whose long, pliable body serves as an engine for Mickey's first plane, and a passing cow chased by the second. This cow has sometimes been cited as a prototype for the later Clarabelle, but she is non-humanized and unnamed in *Plane Crazy*.

Because the defecting animators were still present in the studio completing the last of the Disney Oswalds under the old contract, *Plane Crazy* was produced mostly in secret. Iwerks was sequestered in a separate room. He worked in isolation, animating the entire picture singlehandedly (with the aid of one imminent defector, staff artist Ben Clopton, according to some accounts).[4] Iwerks's heavy animation burden was somewhat lightened by plenty of cycles and repeats. But, on the other hand, he also included an opening crowd scene — one of the most tedious kinds of animation, this one featuring no fewer than seven simultaneous lines of action. Iwerks was not only a skilled animator, but an exceptionally fast worker: he animated this entire one-reel cartoon in a matter of weeks, reportedly producing as many as 700 drawings in a single day. His prodigious output has been enshrined in legend.[5]

And the legend doesn't end there. The making of the first Mickey Mouse cartoon would be remembered as a significant historic occasion in any case, but that cloak of secrecy has given the story an added aura of romance in Disney lore. While Iwerks labored privately over the pencil animation, Walt set up benches in his garage at home so that his wife, Lillian, his sister-in-law Hazel Sewell, and Roy's wife, Edna, could ink and paint the cels. Studio cameraman Mike Marcus returned to the studio at night, after the other animators had gone home, to shoot the finished scenes. By early May 1928, while the last Oswald titles were still in progress, *Plane Crazy* was finished and ready for showing; a preview reportedly took place at a local theater around May 15. Walt duly registered the name "Mickey Mouse" as a trademark and filed a copyright on *Plane Crazy*, both under his own name.

Opposite and following page Story sketches for the first Mickey Mouse cartoon, *Plane Crazy*. The introduction of the storyboard, with its separate movable drawings, was still years in the future; at this time Disney story sketches were grouped together on a page, comic-strip style. Note the scene that will later be cut, and other visual details changed in the finished film. Note, too, the attention to scene footage and other technical details.

"PLANE CRAZY"
#1
3 1/2"
HOW TO FLY
ACE OF ACES
LINDY
HOW TO FLY

7
PAN
8
9
OUT
10
11
12

Main title for the sound version of *Plane Crazy*, released to theaters in 1929. This was the stock title card for the Powers series, and plainly postdates the film itself; like much publicity art from the Powers era, the art adds frills to Mickey's and Minnie's wardrobes that didn't appear in the films until much later, if at all. Mickey not only wears gloves, shoes, and *striped* shorts, but also carries a hat and cane; Minnie, too, is overdressed here.

A recreated *Plane Crazy* cel setup dating from the mid-1930s, when scenes from the film were mocked up for use in publicity and special presentations by Disney licensing representative Kay Kamen.

IMAGED BY HERITAGE AUCTIONS, HA.COM

THE GALLOPIN' GAUCHO

Upon *Plane Crazy*'s completion, Walt and Roy immediately set to work trying to sell their new series, using the film as a sample reel. Walt's idea this time was that the Disney studio would eliminate the middleman and contract directly with a major studio to distribute the series. Meanwhile, the studio immediately began production on Mickey's second picture, *The Gallopin' Gaucho*. This time there was no veil of secrecy, since the defecting animators had made their departure, and Iwerks worked openly with the remaining Disney animation staff: Les Clark, Johnny Cannon, and Wilfred Jackson. This picture highlighted the Douglas Fairbanks facet of Mickey's nascent personality. In fact, the Fairbanks connection was unmistakably obvious, since the real Douglas Fairbanks had starred in a spectacular feature, *The Gaucho*, only the previous autumn. *The Gallopin' Gaucho* saluted the Fairbanks picture and lampooned it at the same time: Mickey appeared in an Argentine setting and engaged in bold, devil-may-care adventures, all the while essaying impossible cartoon gags (using his tail as a lasso) and struggling with ludicrous problems (including his steed, an ostrich).

Minnie rejoined Mickey in the cast of *The Gallopin' Gaucho*, and both were menaced by a huge, hulking bully whom we accept in retrospect as Pete (aka Peg Leg Pete), Mickey's perennial nemesis. In fact, Pete's roots were already well established in the Disney universe: a bear named Pete (with several aliases, including "Putrid Pete" as well as "Peg Leg Pete") had been introduced in the Alice Comedies in 1925 and had served as an all-purpose villain in later Alice pictures and in the Oswald the Lucky Rabbit series. When Universal took over the Oswald cartoons, Pete continued to appear in them and was still recognizably a bear. This new villain in the early Mickey pictures was a distinct creature, and for more than a year was never identified by name. Finally, in the *Mickey Mouse* newspaper comic strip—after initially introducing the character as "Terrible Tom"—Walt himself identified him as Peg Leg Pete in April 1930,[6] and this time the name stuck. Disney fans have known him as "Pete" ever since, and he remains the same hefty brute who first kidnapped Minnie in *The Gallopin' Gaucho*.

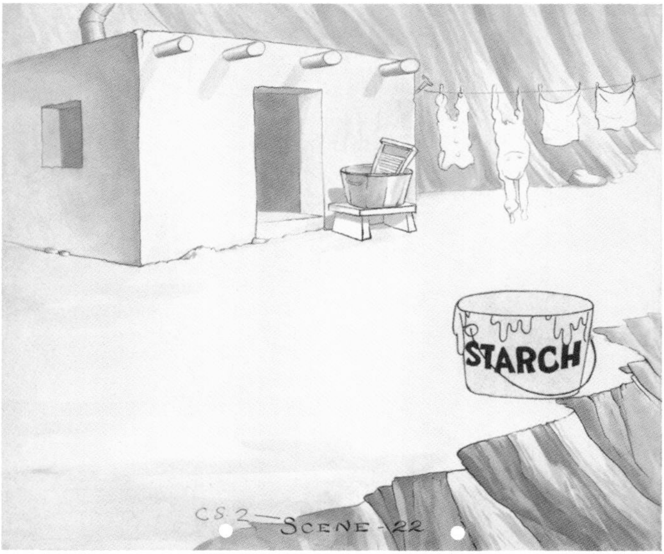

This *Gallopin' Gaucho* background painting unmistakably plants a key prop: the bucket of starch.

A story sketch page for *The Gallopin' Gaucho*: Mickey rides boldly across the pampas, then stops at the cantina to refresh himself and romance the lovely Minnie.

GALLOPING GAUCHO # 2
CANTINO ARGENTINO
REWARDO
100 PESOS EL GAUCHO
CLOSER

(1)

-Main Title-

Orchestra starts playing opening verses of ' Steamboat Bill ', as soon as title flashes on.

The orchestration can be so arrainged that many variations may be included before the title fades out.

It would be best if the music was arrainged so that the end of a verse would end at the end of the title...... and a new verse start at beginning of the first scene.

Scene # 1.
Opening effect of black foliage passing by in front of camera gradually getting thinner until full scene is revealed

Action......Old side'wheel river steamboat paddleing down stream. The two smoke stacks work up and down alternately.... shooting black chunks of smoke out as they shoot up....smoke makes stacks bulge out as it goes up and out. (16 drawing cycle) 12 Ft. from opening, the Three whistles on top of cabin squat down before they whistle tune ' TA--DA-DE-DA-DA---DA-DA-'....2 Ft. of action after whistle and cut.

Scene # 2.
Close up of Mickey in cabin of wheel'house, keeping time to last two measures of verse of ' steamboat Bill '. With gesture he starts whistleing the chorus in perfect time to music....his body keeping time with every other beat while his shoulders and foot keep time with each beat. At the end of every two measures he twirls wheel which makes a ratchet sound as it spins. He takes in breath at proper time according to music. When he finishes last measure he reaches up and pulls on whistle cord above his head. (Use FIFE to imitate his whistle)

The first page of the *Steamboat Willie* script reveals the meticulous care with which Walt and his team planned the synchronization of sound and picture.

An iconic moment in animation history: Mickey toots the whistle in *Steamboat Willie*, announcing his presence as a *sound* cartoon character.

STEAMBOAT WILLIE

Partway through production of *The Gallopin' Gaucho* occurred a momentous occasion: Walt decided to try making a cartoon with synchronized sound. The Mickey Mouse series had started, like the Alice Comedies and the adventures of Oswald, as a series of silent cartoons; now Walt conceived the idea of adding sound. In 1928 this was an inspired notion, for talking pictures were enjoying a surge of popularity in the movie industry at large. Sound films had actually existed, in one form or another, for several decades without causing much excitement; most audiences merely tolerated them as a novelty. A combination of circumstances in the late 1920s changed all that, and suddenly the talkies were a craze. Practically overnight, the major movie studios were scrambling to equip for sound production and add dialogue, sound effects, and songs to their pictures.

Now Walt proposed a similar innovation in his animated cartoons, and again, this was not *quite* a new idea; other producers had added sound to their cartoons as early as four years previously. But watching a cartoon while simultaneously listening to sounds is one thing; watching a cartoon character who actually seems to be *producing* those sounds is something very different. What Walt had in mind was an unprecedented new illusion.

If the making of *Plane Crazy* has long been celebrated in Disney lore, the making of *Steamboat Willie* has become downright mythic. The film actually began with a test: the now-iconic opening scene in which Mickey pilots the boat down the river, whistling the chorus of the song "Steamboat Bill." After animating, inking and painting, and photographing this scene, the team staged what has become a fabled experiment: Roy projected the scene on a bedsheet "screen" from outside a studio window while Walt and the artists, watching the picture, provided music and sound effects through a makeshift speaker system. The object of the test was to see whether the illusion would be convincing, whether Mickey would really appear to be whistling and producing other sounds. Today we take such an illusion for granted; in 1928 it was such an innovation that no one was sure whether it would work. Happily, it did. "I've never been so thrilled in my life," Iwerks later recalled. "That evening proved that an idea could be made to work."[7]

Amid the excitement over sound, another innovation is sometimes overlooked: in animating this test, Iwerks—after weeks of experimenting with the character's appearance—finally settled on the definitive character design of Mickey Mouse. If his initial concern had been to avoid the characteristic look of Oswald the Lucky Rabbit, that concern was now eroding, outweighed by the necessity of crafting an engaging star character for the new series. In this scene Mickey has lost much of his original stick-figure appearance and gained something of Oswald's rounded, appealing look. He is still missing his gloves, and some other minor refinements that will appear in time, but the design of his face, with large black eyes set directly in the mask of his face, is established here and will remain the classic Mickey design for the first decade of his screen life.

The test completed, Iwerks returned to the unfinished *The Gallopin' Gaucho* and animated the remaining scenes. (This brought about an interesting side effect: Mickey's appearance changes in the course of *The Gallopin' Gaucho*—not an uncommon occurrence in some studios' cartoons, but practically unheard of in Disney films. In the early scenes he is still the goggle-eyed, stick-figure Mickey of *Plane Crazy*, but he now wears shoes and his eyes are beginning to evolve. By film's end he has become, essentially, the familiar Mickey Mouse who is still beloved today.) Now Walt had two silent Mickey Mouse cartoons to show, but he was completely taken with the idea of sound and was focusing all his attention on the film that would become *Steamboat Willie*. That experimental test became the opening scene of the picture, and Walt and his artists concocted new scenes with continuing action. Knowing that the convincing illusion of sound would depend on precise synchronization, they devised a system that would guarantee a tight link between cartoon action and music—*if* the action was planned, and the music recorded, according to a strict predetermined rhythm.

By the end of August the picture portion of *Steamboat Willie* was finished, and Walt and his team (notably the newly hired Wilfred Jackson, who had some rudimentary knowledge of music) had cobbled together a workable musical score. Now it remained to record the soundtrack. Unable to find recording facilities in Hollywood that were available to independent producers, Walt decided to take the film to New York and find a way to record the soundtrack there. Packing the print and the written score, he boarded a train for the cross-country trip.

Walt had planned this trip with his customary foresight: en route to New York, he stopped in Kansas City to see Carl Stalling, the theater organist he had known in his Laugh-O-gram days. Stalling, intrigued with Walt's new sound cartoon venture, agreed to compose musical scores for the already-completed *Plane Crazy* and *The Gallopin' Gaucho*. Walt left prints of the two films with him, and arranged for Stalling to join him later in New York.

Walt's New York visit in the autumn of 1928 lasted approximately three months and was one of the decisive events of his career. He had set himself *two* challenging goals: to secure access to a sound-recording process and use it to record a soundtrack for *Steamboat Willie*, and then, armed with this innovative cartoon, to use it to secure a distribution contract for the Mickey series — without surrendering his independence. Ultimately he realized both of these goals by contracting with Pat Powers, a film-industry veteran whose methods were colorful but not always scrupulous. Within two years the Disneys would find it necessary to sever their ties with Powers, but in 1928 he was genuinely helpful to Walt and provided the crucial opening he had been seeking.

One of Powers's enterprises was a sound recording process called Powers Cinephone. This was an optical-track system that operated on essentially the same principles as other processes, but in the chaotic world of talking pictures in 1928, Powers was attempting to sell it as a separate proprietary product. In Walt's proposed series of sound cartoons, Powers saw an opportunity to promote his own interests. After some negotiation, Walt committed the Disney studio to Powers Cinephone and arranged to record the *Steamboat Willie* soundtrack at Powers's facility. Powers recruited a sound-effects crew and an orchestra led by conductor Carl Edouarde, while Walt himself provided miscellaneous vocal effects. The first recording session, on September 15, was *almost* satisfactory, but the sound effects were poorly synchronized — and Walt knew the success of his film would depend on that convincing illusion. After further practice and adjustments, a second session was held on Sunday, September 30. This time the recording was successful; music, voices, and sound effects all synchronized perfectly with the picture on the screen. Walt's sound cartoon was a reality at last.

In November it was given its first public showing. On a program with the sound feature *Gang War* (1928; dir. Bert Glennon), *Steamboat Willie* opened at New York's Colony Theatre on Sunday, November 18, 1928 — a date that is immortalized today as the anniversary of Mickey's debut (as well as Minnie's). As Walt had foreseen, audiences and critics were delighted with the convincing illusion that Mickey and Minnie were making noises and performing music. "Giggles came so fast at the Colony they were stumbling over each other," said *Variety*. "With most of the animated cartoons qualifying as a pain in the neck it's a signal tribute to this particular one."[8]

The enthusiasm of those early audiences is easy to understand; seen today, *Steamboat Willie* still delights the viewer. Having forged an innovative bond between action and music, Walt places it at the center of his sound cartoon: not using music as an adjunct to the action, but making it integral to the gags. Mickey and Minnie improvise their performance using animals, kitchen utensils, and other found objects as fanciful "instruments" — a visual/aural fantasy uniquely suited to animated cartoons, built on a clever illusion that was, in 1928, an absolute novelty to movie audiences. Minnie is dismayed when a goat eats her "Turkey in the Straw" sheet music; Mickey promptly opens the goat's mouth, Minnie turns his tail like the crank of a hand organ, and, with perfect cartoon logic, the tune begins to issue from the goat's mouth! (Surprisingly, Walt had used precisely the same gag earlier in the year in an Oswald cartoon, *Rival Romeos*, despite the absence of sound.) As the music continues, Mickey extracts further "melody" from a yowling cat, a honking goose, and squealing piglets. In his hands, pots and pans become percussion instruments, and a cow's teeth double as a xylophone. Some of these gags would soon become clichés through incessant imitation, but in November 1928 they were fresh and delightful.

It has often been remarked that Walt himself, from the beginning, provided Mickey's voice on the film soundtrack. Mickey does emit some miscellaneous vocal sounds in *Steamboat Willie*, but speaks no actual dialogue; and Minnie's dialogue is restricted to her signature line: "Yoo hoo!" Pete, too, produces some threatening growls but no real

The finished scene in *Steamboat Willie* conforms very closely to this story sketch.

Mickey, the deck hand, is abused by Pete as the steamboat captain in this Iwerks animation drawing.

Ordered below by the captain, Mickey lands on the soap in this original animation drawing.

A background painting of Podunk Landing, where the steamboat stops to take on cargo.

words. The one character who has an actual line of dialogue is the boat's parrot, whose voice is also provided by Walt — and whose words are barely intelligible! The bird delivers the same wisecrack twice in the film, and Mickey seems infuriated both times. Generations of Disney fans have listened to the parrot over and over, trying to decipher the insult; as animator Mark Kausler revealed, the exposure sheet clarifies it as "Hope you don't feel hurt, big boy," a modified quote from Ida Cox's 1927 blues hit "Worn Down Daddy," in which a woman mocks her hapless boyfriend.[9] In the meantime, contrary to the legend, Walt was not immediately established as the voice of Mickey in subsequent cartoons. According to Carl Stalling, several studio hands, himself included, took turns in the role. For a time in the 1930s, the expat Italian nobleman Count Gaetano Mazzaglia Cutelli, a Hollywood-based sound effects expert, claimed that he too had provided Mickey's voice. A later memo from Walt indicates that Cutelli did indeed provide some early voices for the studio, though Walt never specifically cites Mickey's voice as one of them.[10]

Steamboat Willie's place in history is so inextricably linked to sound that it is sometimes forgotten that Walt also produced a silent version. In late 1928 some American theaters were still not wired for sound, and the enterprising producer had to be prepared to offer both sound and silent versions of new films. This was apparently an afterthought for Walt, and he cut a separate print for the silent version during his New York stay. Shipping it back to the studio in California, he suggested that Ub and the others add "noise marks and musical notes" to key scenes: "Maybe it is possible to put noise marks on chickens cackling and [the] cow mooing."[11] The present authors are unaware of any surviving prints of the silent version.

Steamboat Willie's status as a test case — an independently recorded film, played on Western Electric equipment with perfectly acceptable results, and with none of the dire technical consequences that Western Electric had threatened — helped to attract additional attention in November 1928. Word of this innovative new cartoon was spreading by mid-December, and distributors were starting to contact the Powers office in New York to sign contracts. Walt was not about to lose this momentum; he and his staff were already at work on new cartoons.

Minnie, having missed the boat, runs along the bank in Iwerks's animation drawing for *Steamboat Willie*. One of Iwerks's assistants was Wilfred Jackson, who would later become a top Disney director. In later years Jackson recalled that Iwerks delegated another Minnie scene to him, letting him animate it by himself. Jackson remembered this as his first full animation assignment.

THE BARN DANCE

Even before leaving California, Walt had started work on the fourth Mouse picture — planned expressly for sound, as a follow-up to *Steamboat Willie*. By the time he entrained for New York in September 1928, the first part of *The Barn Dance* was already planned in some detail, and Iwerks and the other animators were ready to start work on it. As Walt pursued his fortunes in New York, most of his letters to the studio were concerned with the search for a sound system, the recording of *Steamboat Willie*, and his efforts to establish a distribution deal, but periodically he returned to *The Barn Dance*. His criticism and direction of the animation, and discussion of story ideas for the second part of the film — comments which would ordinarily have been delivered in person — were here conveyed by correspondence. These letters form a precious historical sidelight on Walt's production process in 1928, and have been documented elsewhere.[12]

Meanwhile, Carl Stalling arrived in New York late in October with his completed scores for *Plane Crazy* and *The Gallopin' Gaucho*, and he and Walt started making arrangements with Powers to record them. By December, animation for *The Barn Dance* was completed, and all three cartoons recorded and ready for release to theaters.

The Barn Dance is a worthy follow-up to *Steamboat Willie*, equally delightful in its own way. Walt's constant exhortations to his colleagues ("Try not to use the old gags if it is possible to put in a new one — that's the way we discover new gags, by trying something different"[13]) result in a fresh, funny, lively cartoon. Here Mickey and Pete are romantic rivals, each set on escorting Minnie to the barn dance. As in several Oswald shorts with a similar situation, the first part of the picture is staged at the girlfriend's house, established as such when we see bloomers drawn in from a second-story clothesline.

Like *Steamboat Willie*, *The Barn Dance* was *planned* as a sound film from the start, and once again sound is an integral part of the gags. Mickey, having no such fancy amenity as a horn on his horse-drawn buggy, grabs a passing duck and squeezes it to produce a "honk" sound effect. And the second part of the cartoon, the dance itself, offers another extended opportunity to synchronize action with music.

Mickey's personality, too, is further established in *The Barn Dance*. When he and Minnie arrive at the dance, we learn — by way of an inventive visual device, as Mickey's feet grow to monstrous dimensions and tread on Minnie's legs, stretching one of them far out of shape — that he's a clumsy, inept dancer. Pete, on the other hand, is an excellent dancer, and seems to be gaining favor in Minnie's eyes. Mickey's quick-witted response is to stuff a balloon in the back of his shorts, making him so buoyant that Minnie is impressed and begins to reconsider. But Pete soon exposes Mickey's ruse, leaving him in misery.

Along with the parrot from *Steamboat Willie* and the de facto Pete, *The Barn Dance* offers early traces of supporting characters to come. The dance band is led by an elderly goat wearing a sheriff's star, who would feature in several later cartoons and print products, sometimes known as Gideon Goat. Mickey's precocious carriage horse, too, held possibilities for future reuse — and was called out in at least one trade review as a standout character.[14] That said, not every character planned for *The Barn Dance* actually ended up in the picture. An early story treatment describes a hen and rooster "doing [a] very fast and exciting dance"[15] that is interrupted so the hen can lay an egg, a sequence that was dropped from this picture and later used in *Mickey's Follies* (1929) instead.

A background painting from the opening sequence in *The Barn Dance*, showing Mickey's carriage as he waits for Minnie. Note that the horse remains motionless in this scene, and so can be inked and painted directly on the background painting.

A background painting from the opening sequence of Oswald the Lucky Rabbit's *Neck 'n' Neck* (1928), showing the home of Oswald's girlfriend. Both gags and staging in *Neck 'n' Neck* directly anticipate the opening of *The Barn Dance*.

MICKEY
MOUSE
HERE TODAY!

PAT POWERS AND NATIONAL DISTRIBUTION (1929–1930)

Along with sound recording, Powers's interests included film distribution. His company distributed films by the "states' rights" system, subcontracting the exhibition rights for a particular state or territory to regional distributors. During Walt's stay in New York, Powers offered to distribute the Mickey Mouse series through this network. Ultimately Walt and Roy agreed, and by mid-December 1928, distributors were contacting the Powers office in New York to sign contracts.

The states'-rights market was a disorganized way of distributing motion pictures; regional distributors could acquire a film at any time, and theaters in their territories were likely to book films, especially short subjects, on a haphazard schedule. Because of this, Mickey Mouse did not have an overnight success. *Steamboat Willie* enjoyed a successful New York opening in November 1928, but word began to spread slowly, and delighted viewers in Chicago were just discovering it for themselves in June 1929.

In addition, the relationship between the Disney studio and the Powers company was complex and not always smooth. For a short time, Walt continued to make the cross-country

The Disney studio produced individual posters to advertise each Mickey Mouse cartoon separately, but also created generic stock posters like this one for theaters that were playing the Mickey series.

Early 1929 pencil drawings by Les Clark for two publicity poses used on early stock posters. The hat-tipping Mickey, later modified to remove his hat and the fifth digit on his left hand, would evolve into a famous marketing design. The mandolin-playing Mickey is a piecemeal copy of earlier artwork; his head pose is borrowed from a *When the Cat's Away* drawing, while his hands and mandolin come from *Gallopin' Gaucho* publicity art.

trip to record his soundtracks in New York, but this was clearly a clumsy working arrangement. Powers soon convinced him to lease a Powers Cinephone recording unit, and by late April 1929 the Disneys were recording their own soundtracks in California, experimenting with the new equipment and learning by trial and error. The studio was obliged to record both film soundtracks *and* phonograph-record versions of their films, for sound-on-film and sound-on-disc systems were both in use in movie theaters across the country. As the Disneys struggled to master the arbitrary demands of this technology, there were numerous missteps that led to friction with the New York office.

As Mickey's success increased, Walt began to suggest production innovations that were not always well received by Powers and his staff. Walt was now an independent producer who owned the rights to his character and his films, but some of his correspondence with Powers, and with Charles J. Giegerich of the Powers office, began to evoke his earlier

correspondence with other distributors who had likewise tried to keep the headstrong young producer in check.

Still, the Mickey Mouse series was an undeniable success—a success that seemed to increase with each passing month—and that was cause for celebration for *all* concerned. Step by step, the Powers forces extended Mickey's visibility across the United States and, beginning in February 1929, began to extend it overseas as well. Meanwhile, the Disney studio was building on those first four shorts with new Mouse pictures. The contract with Powers called for a total of 12 shorts to be delivered to the New York office at monthly intervals. The pressure of meeting that schedule, along with the added challenge of sound, took a toll on the films, resulting in a rushed, careless look to some of the animation. The tradeoff is a lively spontaneity that adds to the fun. Walt quickly took steps to ease the burden on Iwerks and the other animators by hiring additional artists, some

Walt and friend pose with Mickey for a publicity shot in 1931. The juxtaposition of real cat with cartoon mouse mirrors a gag that Walt had used in his silent *Alice's Wonderland*, produced eight years earlier in Kansas City.

A model sheet circa 1929 includes poses from *Mickey's Follies* and other period shorts.

This Mickey Mouse school tablet inaugurated what would become a Disney merchandising empire.

Mickey's international fame, as early as 1929, is reflected in this Japanese promotional flyer.

with experience at the East Coast studios. Ben Sharpsteen, Norm Ferguson, and other future luminaries made their Disney debuts during that hectic year.

Having established a strong musical precedent in the earliest pictures, the studio followed up with more musically oriented cartoons, continuing to exploit their method of tight synchronization between sound and picture—an effect that was still a refreshing novelty for audiences, and which, for the time being, no other cartoon studio had managed to duplicate. Pressed to deliver a new picture every month, Walt and his team produced stories that were simple in the extreme: usually just a string of gags, liberally spiced with music. As delighted audiences across the country and around the world began to discover Mickey Mouse for themselves in 1929, they found a character free of complexity or pretension. He was simply a friendly, lively, sometimes mischievous, sometimes resourceful, always cheerful cartoon mouse.

FILMS DISTRIBUTED BY PAT POWERS (1928–1929)

Because of the variable timing of Powers's states-rights distribution, there are no definitive release dates for the first fifteen Mickey Mouse pictures. The dates listed below are not release dates but shipping dates, when the Disney studio shipped the completed films to the Powers office in New York.

WALT DISNEY'S
MICKEY MOUSE
Synchronized Sound Cartoons
Recorded by Powers CINEPHONE System
パワース・シネフォーン式
本邦最初、隨一の發聲漫畫
ウォルト・ディスネー氏作畫
ミッキーマウス
（フイルム式 レコード式 両種あり）
愈々輸着
その他新作品 續々入荷
パワース・シネフオーン會社極東總代理店
イー・ケー・ダイヤー商會
營業主任 エス・エフ・リンドストロム
神戸市江戸町九四（江戸ビル四階）
電話三宮四八八四番

THE OPRY HOUSE

(March 20, 1929)

Based on a vaudeville story suggested by Ub Iwerks, Mickey's fifth cartoon was started in the autumn of 1928 while Walt was still in New York. As he had done with *The Barn Dance*, he offered comments and direction by mail as Iwerks started the animation in California. The finished film shows Mickey essaying many roles in a small-town "opry house": at the beginning he sweeps the sidewalk outside, and by the end of the picture he's appearing onstage as the featured act. This is another story with a heavy emphasis on music, and Mickey's piano solo devolves into a wild brawl between Mickey and the piano. *The Opry House* also adds a new item to Mickey's wardrobe: his gloves. He appears without them in the opening scenes, but by film's end they have become a permanent part of his appearance.

WHEN THE CAT'S AWAY

(ca. April 30, 1929)

This picture is a loose reworking of Walt's silent *Alice Rattled by Rats* (1925): When "Tom Cat" leaves his house to go hunting, Mickey, Minnie, and their fellow mice take over the house for a musical party. The mice are drawn here on the scale of real mice, a departure in the Mickey series. In the spring of 1929 the Disney studio leased a Powers Cinephone recording unit of its own and began to record its own soundtracks; *When the Cat's Away* was the first picture recorded under this new arrangement. As released, the film ends abruptly with Mickey and Minnie dancing. An early script called for a more extended finish: a pet parrot, tormented by the mice, called the cops, only for the mice to disappear quickly before the police arrived.

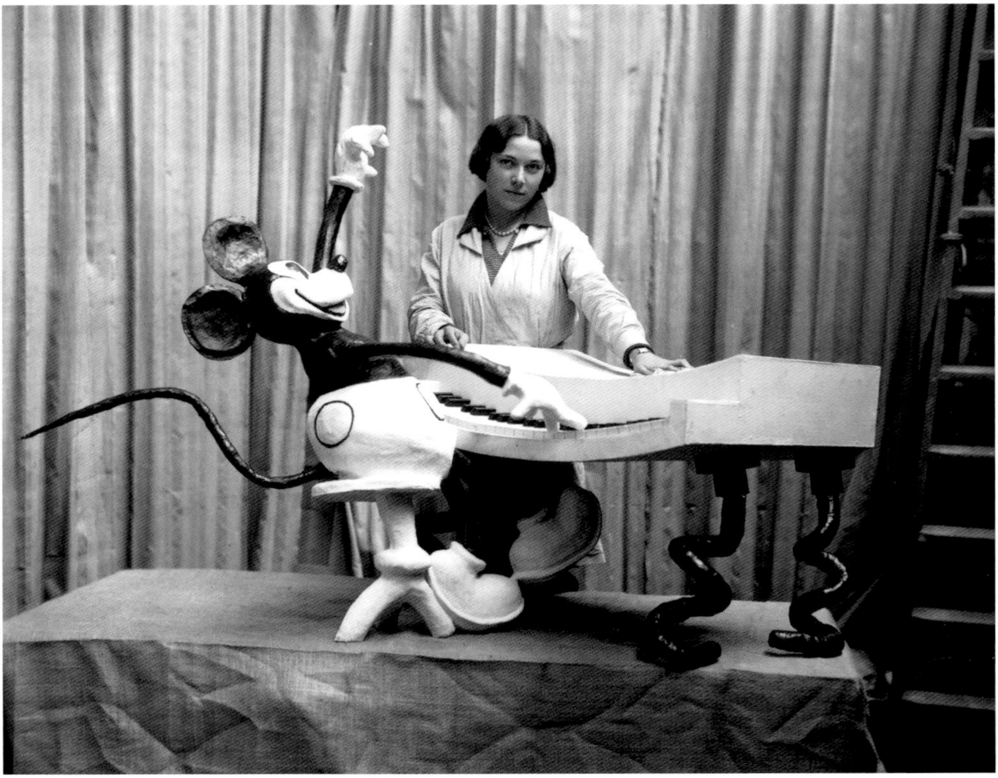

Mickey takes his place in Madame Tussauds wax museum in 1930, in a scene clearly inspired by *The Opry House* and *The Jazz Fool*.

A background painting for the opening scene in *The Opry House*. In the finished scene Mickey sweeps the boardwalk while foot and motor traffic passes. Production documents note "Minnie, the little girl mouse" on the *Yankee Doodle Girls* dance show poster.

Poster art for *When the Cat's Away*, reproducing the "gramophone" gag.

THE BARNYARD BATTLE
(ca. June 1, 1929)

Following the precedent of Julius the cat in *Alice's Little Parade* (1926) and Oswald the Lucky Rabbit in *Great Guns!* (1927), Mickey goes to war in *The Barnyard Battle*. "The Enemy" in this picture is an army of cats, all more or less identical and more or less interchangeable with Pete. Mickey's army is another assortment of interchangeable mouse-size mice. Even at the front, Mickey is never far from a piano, and when he runs out of machine-gun bullets he simply substitutes the piano keyboard and fires off a salvo of musical notes. Released in 1929, *The Barnyard Battle* faced a battle of its own the following year when it was banned in Germany because of the cat army's Germanic helmets.[16]

THE PLOWBOY
(ca. June 28, 1929)

Mickey, on a farm, flirts with Minnie between chores, but becomes a little too forward and is crowned with a milk bucket for his trouble, much to the amusement of Minnie's cow and Mickey's plow horse. The latter two characters have not yet evolved into the characters we know today as, respectively, Clarabelle Cow and Horace Horsecollar, but this film marks a further step in that direction. (As early as 1933, *The Plowboy* would be cited by the studio as Horace's debut.)[17] This picture also marks Minnie's first appearance wearing gloves, an accessory which, like Mickey, she will retain for life. Upon the film's release, the cow created censorship problems for Walt when some exhibitors objected to the milking gags, featuring her prominent udder.[18]

A background painting for *The Barnyard Battle*. In this setting Mickey defends himself from the enemy, first with machine-gun bullets, then with piano keys. The keyboard itself, which moves in the course of the scene, is not seen here because — like the machine gun, and Mickey himself — it will be animated separately on cels.

A poster for the French release of *The Plowboy*. Early publicity art like this, created outside the studio, is sometimes fascinating because it varies so widely from the style of authentic studio art. Here Mickey is more or less on-model, but the cow looks nothing like the proto-Clarabelle who appears in the film — and who is never harnessed for plowing!

Another *Barnyard Battle* background. Cat soldiers knocked cold by Mickey. In the finished scene more enemies land on top of them, and Mickey stands triumphantly atop the pile.

IMAGED BY HERITAGE AUCTIONS, HA.COM

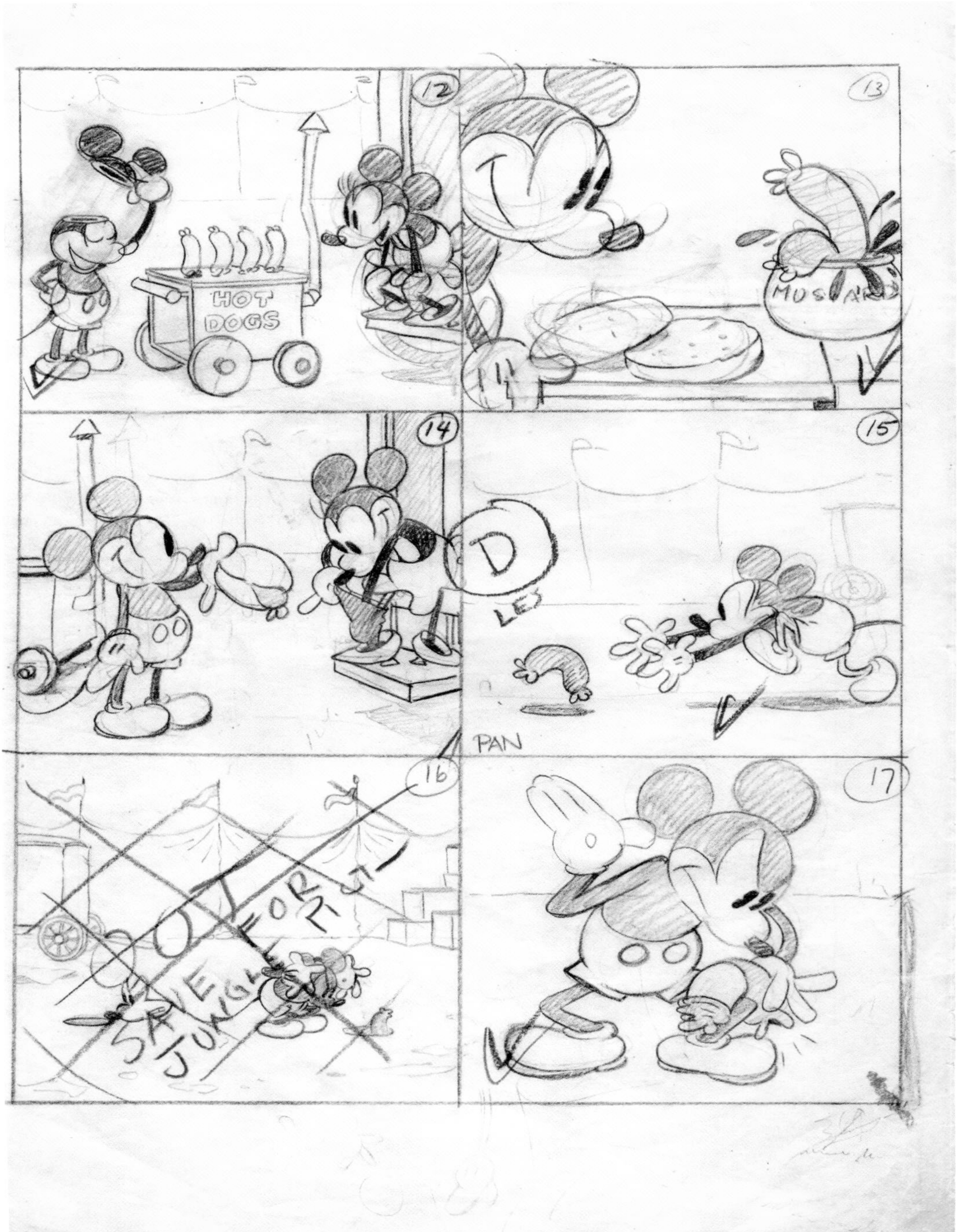
12
13
HOT DOGS
MUSTARD
14
15
D
PAN
16
17

THE KARNIVAL KID

(July 31, 1929)

From the beginning, Mickey's success had been linked to sound, primarily by way of his musical performances. In *The Karnival Kid* he takes the next step and actually speaks dialogue. Walt was much excited over this development; Pat Powers was less enthusiastic, fearful that an English-speaking Mouse would be less appealing to international audiences.[19] In this picture Mickey appears as a hot dog vendor who plies his trade at a carnival, romances Minnie, the Shimmy Dancer, and tangles with the carnival barker — a direct forerunner, in both looks and behavior, of the later comics character Kat Nipp. In the last sequence Mickey courts Minnie with a second-hand serenade, recruiting two cats to yowl "Sweet Adeline" outside her window.

MICKEY'S FOLLIES

(August 28, 1929)

Having spoken dialogue in the previous picture, Mickey *sings* in this one. His song is "Minnie's Yoo Hoo," a new number composed by Carl Stalling especially for this picture. Mickey's singing voice is supplied by an unknown studio hand; not until later did Walt become the exclusive voice of Mickey Mouse. The barnyard audience applauds the song wildly, and in real life "Minnie's Yoo Hoo" was published later in 1929, the Disney studio's first original song. It became the theme music of the Mickey Mouse series, played under the main titles of every Mouse picture for the next four years.

MICKEY'S CHOO CHOO

(September 26, 1929)

Mickey the locomotive engineer romps around the engine yard, shares lunch with his dog (the dachshund from *Plane Crazy*), pauses for a musical interlude with Minnie, sets off with her on a journey (giving her all his attention and letting the engine fend for itself), and heroically saves her from the runaway train when the engine gets out of control. Along the way this cartoon recycles some gags and basic situations from the Oswald short *Trolley Troubles* (and, in fact, the working title for this film was "Engine Troubles"). Following the precedent of the previous two pictures, Mickey sings and speaks dialogue, this time in a voice that sounds like Walt's.

Story sketch page for *The Karnival Kid*. Note that Walt vetoes one gag, preferring to save it for *Jungle Rhythm*. But, in fact, the gag — previously used in some of Walt's silent Alice and Oswald cartoons — did not appear in *Jungle Rhythm* either.

Publicity art for *The Karnival Kid*. In the film, of course, Mickey does not appear as a peanut vendor; but his wide-open mouth in this drawing suggests the importance Walt attached to his spoken dialogue.

Two background paintings from *Mickey's Choo Choo*. At left, the engine at rest in the railyard. When Mickey stops for lunch, he thoughtfully feeds the locomotive its "lunch" as well: a heaping serving of coal. Below, the scene of a showdown between the runaway train and an assortment of recalcitrant livestock.

Background paintings from *Mickey's Follies*, the film that introduced Mickey's theme song. The box in the center, above, is Mickey's piano; the keyboard doesn't appear here because it moves as Mickey plays it, and is animated on cels. The "gallery," right, is a clothesline with long johns and other laundry hanging from it; members of the audience cheer (or razz) the performers from this elevated vantage point.

hello folks!
COLUMBIA PICTURES presents
MICKEY MOUSE
in
HAUNTED HOUSE
Produced by WALT DISNEY
COLUMBIA PICTURES
Morgan Litho Co.
This Poster is the Property of Columbia Pictures Corporation, and it is leased, not sold
M 6210
Made in U. S. A.

THE JAZZ FOOL

(October 15, 1929)

Another musical performance, this time featuring Mickey as an itinerant musician who parades through town on a wagon, playing a steam calliope. His wagon is drawn by the precocious horse we've seen in other pictures, still evolving into Horace Horsecollar. On reaching the performance site, the horse divests himself of his harness and becomes a percussionist, playing drumbeats on a wagon wheel, his own head and feet, and a small cat who makes the mistake of sitting too close to him. Mickey's piano solo becomes aggressive and climaxes with another physical combat between himself and the piano.

JUNGLE RHYTHM

(November 9, 1929)

Mickey goes big-game hunting in the jungle—as earlier Disney characters had done, but with very different results. Julius the cat and Oswald the Lucky Rabbit had appeared in silent cartoons, and neither had Mickey's obsession with music. Here, threatened by fierce beasts, Mickey nervously begins to whistle a tune. Soon his melody becomes a full-fledged concert, and not only the beasts but the entire jungle population is swinging along with him. *Jungle Rhythm* brought Walt more trouble with state censor boards. Here a hula-dancing lion wriggled his torso, tossed his navel into the air, and caught and swallowed it; the censors were not amused.[20]

A Columbia Pictures stock poster for Mickey Mouse. Early in 1930 the Disney studio began to produce new Mickeys for Columbia release, but Columbia also reissued *The Haunted House* and other Powers releases.

The Jazz Fool: a background painting for a musical performance by Mickey and his horse, which holds their listeners spellbound (and motionless).

THE HAUNTED HOUSE
(December 2, 1929)

Venturing inside a haunted house was a favorite device, both for cartoon characters and for live-action comedians; here Mickey gets his turn. On a dark and stormy night, Mickey takes refuge inside the house and has encounters, both comic and genuinely spooky, with the malevolent spirits inside. Like other contemporary Mickeys, *The Haunted House* has a strong musical element: here a hooded skeleton sits Mickey down at an organ and orders him to play so that the skeletons can frolic and dance. By autumn 1929 Ub Iwerks was devoting most of his time to the Silly Symphonies, but this picture recycles one of his dancing scenes from *The Skeleton Dance*, nine months earlier, now adapted with new action by Ben Sharpsteen. Once again Walt ran afoul of the state censors; this time they objected to two gags involving, respectively, a chamber pot and an outhouse.[21]

WILD WAVES
(December 18, 1929)

Lifeguard Mickey rescues Minnie from drowning, then comforts the distraught girl by treating her to an impromptu musical performance. Oswald the Lucky Rabbit had earlier tried his hand as a lifeguard in *All Wet* (1927). Here Mickey repeats some of Oswald's gags, but most of this film's footage is reserved for the musical interlude. Carl Stalling later claimed to have recorded Mickey's voice for this picture.[22] Mickey actually has separate speaking and singing voices in *Wild Waves*; if Stalling did provide one of them, it was probably his speaking voice. Stalling also claimed to have provided the voice for the walrus who sings "Rocked in the Cradle of the Deep" (in nonsense syllables) in a raucous bass.

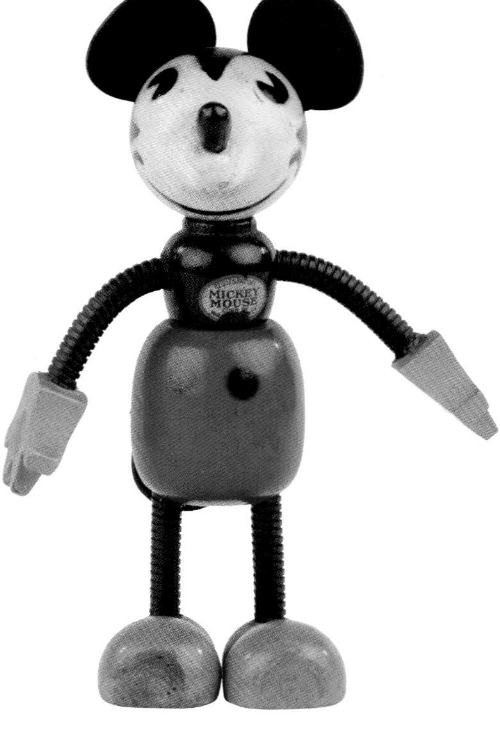

This "Fun-E-Flex" wooden figure with bendable limbs, manufactured and distributed by the George Borgfeldt company, was one of many Mickey Mouse toys marketed during the early 1930s.

An earlier Columbia stock poster, still crediting Ub Iwerks and Powers Cinephone (and with a title strip advertising *Wild Waves*, the last of the Powers releases).

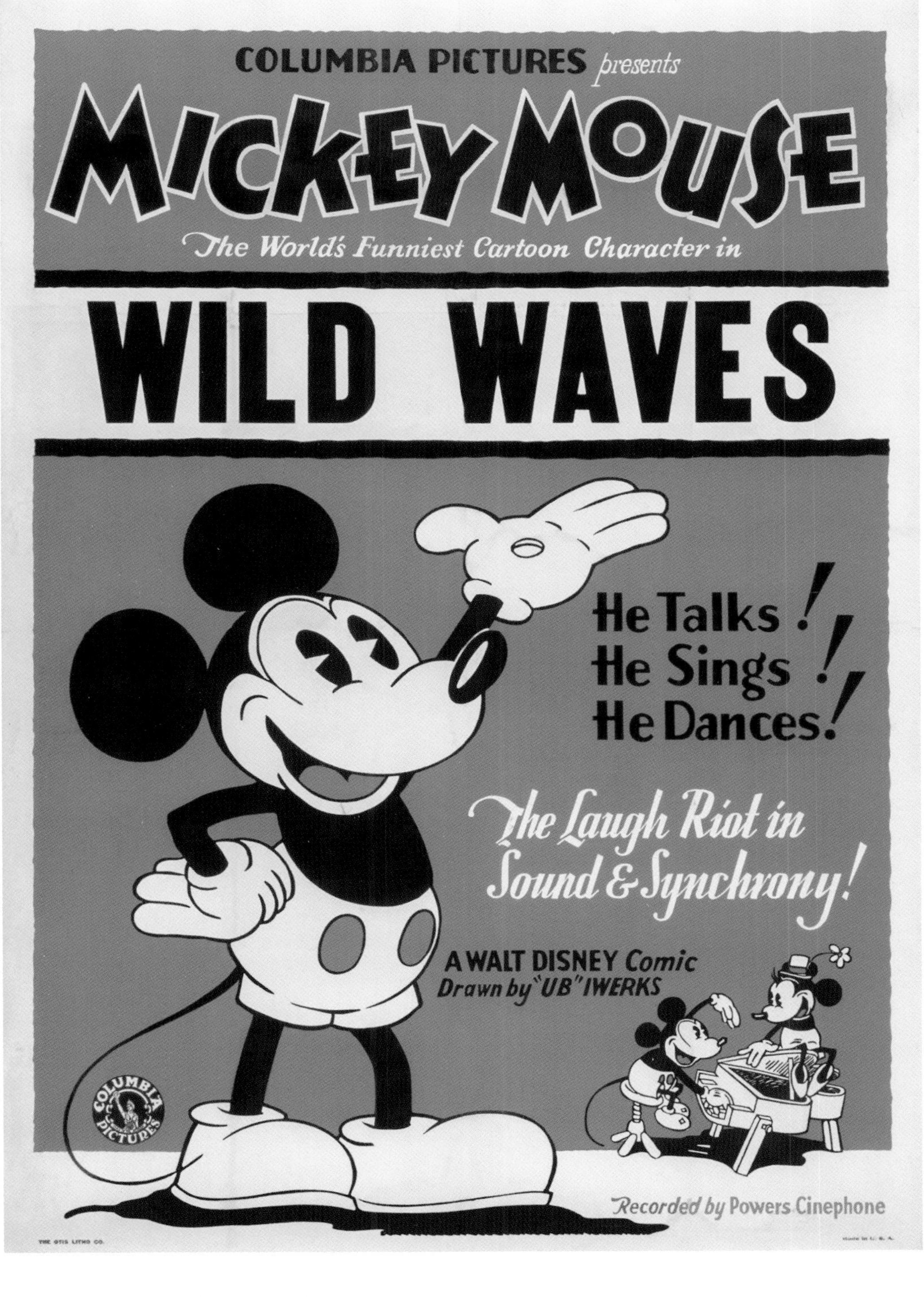

COLUMBIA PICTURES presents
MICKEY MOUSE
The World's Funniest Cartoon Character in
WILD WAVES
He Talks!
He Sings!
He Dances!
The Laugh Riot in Sound & Synchrony!
A WALT DISNEY Comic
Drawn by "UB" IWERKS
COLUMBIA PICTURES
Recorded by Powers Cinephone

IMPORTANT 1/4 inch is allowed on all seam-edges. All seams are indicated by broken lines; all cutting lines by continuous double lines. A narrow margin surrounds each pattern piece, making it easier to cut accurately. **Cut pattern and material together through the white center of the double line. The margin falls away as you cut through pattern and material.** Every mark is important for the construction, so before removing the pattern from the material, mark carefully with tracing wheel, tailor's chalk or thread markings.

United States Patents Nos. 1,387,723 and 1,527,518. Foreign Patents and Pending United States and Foreign Applications.

McCALL PRINTED PATTERN with TRANSFER

91 SIZE LARGE 10 Inches

YELLOW 35c

The Mickey and Minnie Mouse Dolls

EARLY MERCHANDISING

The success of the Mickey Mouse shorts brought out a strong entrepreneurial instinct in Walt. He remained primarily focused on production of the films, but in the meantime began to explore promotional opportunities that would help to spread Mickey and Minnie's fame. As early as mid-1929 he was writing to Charles Giegerich: "I should think that there would be a big market for Mickey dolls, toys and novelties for the coming season and it may not be a bad idea to feel out the possibilities along these lines as these things are also considered very good for publicity."[23] He followed up with detailed suggestions for promotional items. By year's end the song "Minnie's Yoo Hoo," from *Mickey's Follies*, had been published, and the studio was beginning to produce small novelties bearing Mickey's image. A line of school writing tablets was reportedly the first commercial product licensed; early marketing model sheets, drawn by Les Clark and Win Smith, provided a number of designs and poses that were used on promotional items.

From that modest beginning sprang an enterprise that would become an international marketing empire. Walt

Besides promoting the Charlotte Clark Mickey and Minnie dolls, Disney also licensed a McCall's sewing pattern so that enterprising individuals could make their own.

The classic Mickey and Minnie dolls produced by Charlotte Clark, here in designs dating from about 1931.

continued to pursue further opportunities to merchandise Mickey and Minnie, but one of the most notable early items came to *him* when Charlotte Clark, a local citizen, approached the studio early in 1930 with a stuffed Mickey doll she had designed and hand-sewn. Walt and Roy were delighted with this doll and hired Ms. Clark to produce more of the same, renting a small house where she and her helpers could work. But this "cottage industry" could never supply enough dolls to sustain a nationwide marketing campaign, and the Disneys also contracted with George Borgfeldt & Company, manufacturers and importers, to mass-produce Mickey and Minnie dolls along the lines of the Clark models. Borgfeldt had a reputation for quality toys, but while their products were sold for several years, they were never quite able to duplicate the quality of the Charlotte Clark Mickey and Minnie dolls to Walt's and Roy's satisfaction. A similar mass-producing effort by Dean's Rag Book Company, Ltd.,

in England was likewise unsatisfactory.[24] For about a year's time, conflict boiled between unauthorized English Mickey toys — produced before Disney fully established its character rights in Europe — and those approved by William Banks Levy, Disney's personal U.K. representative, who set up shop in June 1930.[25] To distinguish the Dean's Rag Book Mickey doll from unlicensed rivals, Dean designer Richard Evans Ellett uniquely gave it large teeth and whiskers — which successfully defended the doll from infringement in court, but ironically left it looking less like the screen Mickey than its competitors did.[26]

In England Mickey inspired a highly popular series of postcards, issued by the publisher Inter-Art in 1930, that subtly adapted Mickey and Minnie to British culture. A concurrent British toothbrush holder features a decidedly off-model Mickey, his striped pants likely inspired by the postcards.

Walt proudly poses in 1932 with what was already a sizable assortment of licensed Mickey merchandise.

MICKEY MOUSE CLUBS

In September 1929, another enterprising individual came to Walt with another idea that immediately captured his attention. An exhibitor named Harry Woodin had inaugurated Mickey Mouse Clubs for children at his theaters in Venice and Ocean Park, California, devoting Saturday matinee programs to Club meetings. The meetings featured activities for children and, of course, a movie program featuring the latest Mouse cartoon. At Woodin's invitation Walt and Carl Stalling attended one of these meetings, and Walt was delighted. In a letter to Giegerich he enthusiastically described the program and suggested that the Disney forces should adopt and expand on the Club idea: "I am sold 100 percent on the idea and would like to see us get after this and put it over in a national way immediately. It is just good enough that I believe if we neglected it that Universal would be liable to take it up and use it for their Oswalds."[27]

Woodin continued to promote his idea, and Walt continued to embrace it enthusiastically. A scant two weeks after his first letter, he sent Giegerich a second in which he reported that Woodin had offered to make a personal tour of the nation, establishing Mickey Mouse Clubs at theaters in key cities. Giegerich responded warmly to the idea of the Clubs but was quick to discourage the idea of Woodin's personal tour. He strongly preferred promotional schemes

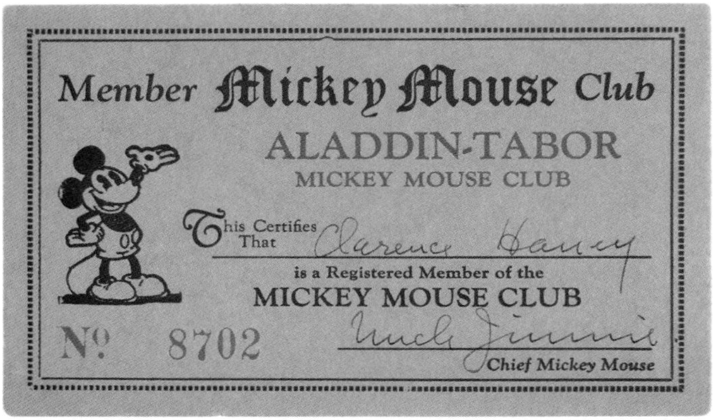
Member Mickey Mouse Club
ALADDIN-TABOR
MICKEY MOUSE CLUB
This Certifies That Clarence Haney
is a Registered Member of the
MICKEY MOUSE CLUB
No. 8702
Uncle Jimmie
Chief Mickey Mouse

Winners of "Mickey Mouse Week" prizes at Russell's Restaurant, Leicester Square, London, England, 1930. This contest was held by the *Sunday Pictorial* newspaper, for which Disney's comics team produced a unique series of Sunday strips.

These buttons, created for the Mickey Mouse Clubs, could be personalized with the name of the individual chapter. The iconic image of Mickey walking and waving had evolved from the early publicity pose seen on page 45.

Membership in one of the Mickey Mouse Clubs brought an official membership card and other benefits.

Following This new main title card appeared at the beginning of each Columbia Mickey Mouse short. Here Mickey and Minnie are seen holding a schoolchildren's slate, with attached sponge for erasures — a sight that 1930s audiences would immediately recognize — and with the individual film's title rendered in white in the center.

COLUMBIA
WALT

CTURES CORP.
ENTS
ISNEY'S
MOUSE
N

"Ray for Charlie and Doug!" — Mickey.
CHAPLIN CHOOSES MICKEY MOUSE
as a running mate for his Broadway engagement of "City Lights" beginning at the George M. Cohan Theatre February 6.
And FAIRBANKS teams up daily with MICKEY at the New York Criterion in "Reaching for the Moon."
A WALT DISNEY COMIC
COLUMBIA PICTURES
There's more proof that
COLUMBIA beats 'em all in shorts!

that involved little or no expense. But Walt continued to champion the Clubs and to argue, characteristically, against pinching pennies.

FILMS RELEASED THROUGH COLUMBIA PICTURES (1930-1932)

As we've seen, the Disney studio originally contracted with Powers to release twelve Mickey Mouse shorts, one per month, for the first year. In late 1929 Walt and Roy assumed that the Powers contract would be renewed, and continued to send new Mouse cartoons to the New York office on a regular schedule. In the meantime they had launched a second series of cartoons, the Silly Symphonies, and Powers had helped them to secure a distribution contract with Columbia Pictures for this new venture.

But trouble was brewing behind the scenes. Pat Powers had provided the Disney brothers the crucial assistance they needed in 1928 to bring their Mouse to market, but his motives were not strictly altruistic. Now, unbeknownst to the Disneys, he quietly approached Ub Iwerks and offered him the opportunity to head a cartoon studio of his own—the actual ownership remaining in Powers's hands—and made a similar offer to Carl Stalling to become the musical director of the new enterprise. In January 1930, almost exactly two years after losing Oswald the Rabbit, Walt lost two of the most valuable members of his team.

This time, however, Walt had taken precautions to secure full ownership of Mickey Mouse—and in January 1930, Mickey was perhaps his most valuable asset of all. After a long struggle, the Mouse was standing on the threshold of international success; and if Walt had not knuckled under to Mintz's

More proud advertising, playing up Mickey's prestigious association with Chaplin and Fairbanks, two of the principals behind United Artists. There's a certain irony here: by the time Columbia placed this ad in 1931, Disney had already negotiated a new distribution arrangement with United Artists, which would take effect the following year.

Columbia Pictures lost the Disney distribution contract in 1932 but still had a backlog of Mickey Mouse cartoons in circulation. This 1933 trade ad reflects Columbia's new promotional priorities: Mickey joins the parade of shorts stars but takes a back seat to current Columbia properties like Scrappy and Charles Mintz's version of Krazy Kat.

bluff in 1928, he certainly wasn't going to be defeated by this one. The Disneys severed their ties with Powers and renegotiated their contract with Columbia. The company would now distribute both Silly Symphonies *and* Mickey Mouse. Beginning with *Fiddling Around*, the cartoons proudly announced Mickey's new association from the screen with a handsome new main title card.

The new fully committed Columbia connection was a boon to the Disney studio. Columbia Pictures was not the most prestigious studio in Hollywood, but it was a definite step up from the haphazard world of states'-rights film distribution. Like the major studios, Columbia could provide a coordinated national release of each new cartoon. The agreement brought with it a certain irony: the Disney studio was once again indirectly linked with Winkler Pictures,

whose Krazy Kat cartoons were likewise distributed by Columbia. But it didn't matter. Mickey Mouse's popularity with audiences was just beginning to come into full flower, and now he had the support of a Hollywood studio with a well-organized distribution network to bring his latest pictures to the screens of the world.

Walt met this good fortune by upgrading the production values of the Mickey shorts. He had already started this initiative in late 1929 with the start of the second series: *Jungle Rhythm*, *The Haunted House*, and *Wild Waves*, all distributed under the original arrangement with Powers, displayed a new level of visual excellence and detail. Now, producing his films for Columbia release, Walt expanded in this direction. The 1930 Mickeys boasted a handsome look that went beyond the simplicity of the earliest efforts. The loss of Ub Iwerks was a

In 1930 it was a different story: Columbia proudly announced their new Disney affiliation with color ads in their 1930–31 exhibitors' book. Note that the featured images include pre-Columbia-era publicity drawings for *The Barn Dance*, *The Opry House*, and *Mickey's Choo Choo*, already released by Powers in 1929.

In December 1931 the *Los Angeles Times* published a special 50th-anniversary issue, featuring tributes from celebrities. Here Walt and Mickey take the opportunity to extend their thanks, not only to the *Times*, but to the national and international press at large, for their widespread coverage of Mickey's rise to fame.

serious blow to the studio, but Walt's prior diversification of the animation staff paid off during this crisis: Ben Sharpsteen, Les Clark, Norm Ferguson, and other artists were already well-schooled in animating Mickey. In addition, each of them brought his own unique style to the Mouse's appearance and movement.

Walt also supplemented the ranks of the animators by hiring a complement of new artists, including, again, some with extensive experience in East Coast cartoon studios. Some, such as Gilles "Frenchy" de Trémaudan and especially Dave Hand, would become key members of the Disney staff. Along with the animation, the background paintings were getting an upgrade of their own. No longer were the backgrounds simply delegated to any junior animator who wasn't busy at the moment; Carlos Manríquez, who had joined the staff in mid-1929, was joined in the spring of 1930 by Emil Flohri. Together this two-man background department gradually improved the look of Mickey's world.

The stories, too, were becoming more ambitious. Mickey's earlier pictures had been simple and improvisational; now Walt and his crew began to plot their stories with greater care, hiring Ted Sears in 1931 specifically to head a story department.[28] The strong musical orientation of the Powers shorts continued unabated at Columbia: Mickey remained ready to perform a musical number at the slightest provocation. And, as the films became more elaborate, Mickey himself continued to develop. Those glimmers of personality that had appeared in the Powers shorts were increasingly fleshed out into more of a full-fledged character. As 1929 gave way to 1930, Mickey's cheerful, hopeful underdog attitude exercised an irresistible appeal to movie audiences entering the dark days of the Great Depression. His native ingenuity remained in place, too, and made him

doubly appealing; whatever his troubles, Mickey usually responded with a can-do resourcefulness that helped him overcome any obstacle. Minnie, meanwhile, remained a stalwart co-star—often the classical damsel in distress, but just as often Mickey's equal-time partner in music and dance performances. Now and then she seemed to take a direct swipe at traditional stereotyping: while *Pioneer Days* sees her captured by the bad guys, Mickey is caught too upon coming to her rescue—after which *she* rescues *him*!

As Mickey's and Minnie's personalities became more firmly established, their voices on the soundtrack became consistent and recognizable. At first, assorted studio hands (and perhaps occasional outside talents, such as the aforementioned Count Cutelli) had simply taken turns supplying Mickey's voice, but in 1930 Walt himself was established in the role. Walt's breathless, cheerful, boyish falsetto proved to be the perfect expression of Mickey's emerging personality, and he and the Mouse soon became inseparable. With few

Mickey is contemplated by the immortals in this Karl Arnold drawing for the satirical German weekly, *Simplicissimus*, in January 1931.

MICKEY MOUSE MODEL Nº1

The first formalized Mickey animation model sheet, circa 1931, postdated several earlier sheets of marketing poses — but played the more important part of standardizing Mickey's appearance on screen. Under its influence, individual animators' Mickey designs became more consistent than before.

exceptions, Walt remained Mickey's exclusive voice talent for the better part of the next two decades.

This distinctive voice, in turn, helped further to define Mickey's character and suggested subtle new traits. Without losing his bold, adventurous side, Mickey's personality developed a facet of shyness, and he sometimes punctuated his dialogue with a nervous little laugh.

As Mickey's voice was established, so was Minnie's. Minnie, too, had spoken occasional dialogue from the beginning, and in a variety of voices supplied by anyone who happened to be available (starting with Walt himself in *Steamboat Willie*). In the spring of 1930, however, Marcellite Garner, a recent hire in the studio's Ink and Paint Department, took over the role and remained the voice of Minnie Mouse for more than a decade. Marcellite brought an added dimension to Minnie's personality: she could be by turns adoring, teasing, independent, and occasionally downright angry—and, as a bonus, she could sing.

(Note: here again, announced release dates for the Columbia releases are arbitrary and, in some cases, inconsistent. Dates listed below are delivery dates, when the Disney studio delivered the completed films to Columbia.)

Mickey embraces high culture in *Fiddling Around*, his first release for Columbia. The background painting of stage and curtains was later reused for the *Minnie's Yoo Hoo* sing-along film.

Publicity art for a United Artists reissue of *The Barnyard Concert*, ca. 1934. This image, originally drawn for a *Mickey & Minnie Mouse* coloring book in 1933, does not resemble any scene in the film, but it does suggest Rossini's *William Tell* Overture—which did figure prominently in the far more ambitious *The Band Concert*, a few years later.

FIDDLING AROUND
(March 6, 1930)

Mickey inaugurates his Columbia contract by giving a concert — not as a vaudeville performer, but as a classical violinist, complete with serious repertoire. This cartoon is an oddity, an exercise in minimalism that consists *entirely* of Mickey standing still (more or less), performing his half-serious concert. Of course this is an animated cartoon, and Mickey makes his bid for culture with tongue in cheek: preening his mane of long hair with haughty arrogance, and attacking Brahms's "Hungarian Rhapsody" with superhuman vigor. Many latter-day reference sources have identified this film by its working title, "Just Mickey," which was used in some pre-release Powers advertising. In fact, however, the final title — under which the film was copyrighted, distributed by Columbia, advertised, and exhibited — is *Fiddling Around*.

THE BARNYARD CONCERT
(April 5, 1930)

In another musical performance, slightly less "arty" than *Fiddling Around*, Mickey conducts a barnyard orchestra in Franz von Suppé's *Poet and Peasant* overture. Walt's story outline for this picture has survived, with suggestions for a series of situations — "The Cow Gag," "The Pig Gag," "The Bass Fiddle Gag," and so on — most of which do appear in some form in the picture. "The Fly Gag" showcases a nice example of cartoon pantomime: Mickey's frustration grows as one passage is repeatedly marred by a sour note from the porcine trumpet player. At length the pig meekly demonstrates to Mickey that he's only playing the music as written — whereupon they both discover that the "note" was actually a fly on the musical score!

"BARNYARD CONCERT"

The end of the climactic chase in *The Cactus Kid*. This cel setup conflates two separate parts of a scene into one image as Pete, undone by his own depredations, plunges over a cliff.

The original main title from *The Cactus Kid*. This cartoon, like many contemporary Mickeys, includes an extended musical performance, but a healthy share of footage is reserved for exciting Western action. In one scene Mickey directly parodies *The Virginian*, which had been released by Paramount in 1929.

Mickey finds an original way to rescue Minnie from a burning building in *The Fire Fighters*.

THE CACTUS KID

(May 10, 1930)

In Mickey's first Western since *The Gallopin' Gaucho*, he costars with Minnie as a fiery señorita, Pete as the villain, and the horse — by now officially christened Horace — as Mickey's trusty steed. Pete kidnaps Minnie from the cantina, but Mickey and Horace give chase and bring the villain to justice — recycling, along the way, a notable bit of animation from the Oswald cartoon *Sagebrush Sadie* (1928). The film's soundtrack is notable too, partly because it marks Marcellite Garner's first performance as the voice of Minnie Mouse,[29] and partly because the dialogue and sound effects are *prerecorded* for the first time in a Disney cartoon.[30] Here the animators match their action to an already-recorded soundtrack, allowing for even more elaborate synchronization than before.

THE FIRE FIGHTERS

(June 20, 1930)

Mickey appears here as the captain of a small-town fire department, leading his crew as they respond to a nocturnal alarm. Even in such a dangerous occupation, Mickey lives in a musical world. An early outline for this picture depicted him making music at the firehouse before the alarm rings; and although that sequence does not appear in the finished film, the firemen do perform a whistling chorus of "There'll Be a Hot Time in the Old Town Tonight" en route to the fire. The closing scenes feature Mickey's unorthodox heroics, rescuing Minnie from a burning upper window by means of a pair of overalls suspended from a clothesline.

THE SHINDIG
(July 11, 1930)

Mickey, Minnie, and their friends attend a barn dance. Mickey dances with an enormous pig in a scene, animated by Norm Ferguson, that will reappear two years later in *The Whoopee Party*; Wilfred Jackson animates Mickey's harmonica solo *and* plays the harmonica on the soundtrack. Clarabelle Cow, responding to censors' earlier complaints about her exposed udder, wears a skirt here — but even this concession is made with tongue in cheek. Clarabelle makes an elaborate show of donning the skirt, and then only after we see her lying skirtless in the barn — while reading *Three Weeks*, Elinor Glyn's scandalous best seller of 1907. Once again, the censors were not amused.[31]

THE CHAIN GANG
(August 18, 1930)

Today, in light of Mickey's harmless latter-day image, it may seem jarring to see him in prison — and making his escape. In 1930 it was a different story: Mickey was following the jailbreak-movie tradition of numerous live-action comedians (including Walt's own "Alice"). *The Chain Gang* is celebrated today as the debut appearance of Mickey's dog, Pluto — which it is, in a very loose sense. After the breakout two bloodhounds are dispatched to track down the escapees, and one of their scenes, animated by Norm Ferguson, proved so memorable that it did lead to further development of a dog character. In addition, that same piece of animation was reused for Pluto in no fewer than *four* later cartoons!

The British release of *The Shindig* gives the film new main-title art — and, incidentally, a new title.

Disney publicity art, 1930–32 vintage. Note that a creative copywriter has assigned new names to the cow (Catherine) and the horse (Horatio), and moreover has recast Clarabelle, in the bottom drawing, as a horse named Hortense! Unfazed by the censors' complaints over her exposed udder, Clarabelle makes an impishly exaggerated show of modesty.

They're World Favorites of Screen

Here is the group of funmakers which have become world favorites, and yet are only products of Artist Walt Disney's versatile imagination. Top left—Mickey Mouse, himself; top right—his sweetie, Minnie Mouse; center—Catherine Cow; lower left—Horatio Horse and the apple of his eye, Hortense; lower right—Pluto, the Pup, a very, very funny fellow.

THE GORILLA MYSTERY
(September 22, 1930)

This short is a spoof of contemporary popular culture: the 1925 Broadway play *The Gorilla*, which had already been adapted as a successful film and was, in autumn 1930, in the works as a sound remake. Here the gorilla escapes, makes his way to Minnie's house, and captures her. A horrified Mickey hears her screams over the phone and races cross-country to her house, and the rest of the reel depicts his search of the dark house and eventual confrontation with the gorilla. Through a combination of bravery and dumb luck, he and Minnie manage to subdue and tie up the gorilla at the iris-out. Some later studio documentation retroactively identifies this gorilla as the same beast, eventually called Beppo, who would appear in *Mickey's Mechanical Man* and *The Pet Store* (both 1933).

One scene in *The Gorilla Mystery* utilizes both of these background paintings. At left, Mickey takes refuge in an outbuilding, then realizes that eight pairs of eyes are watching him in the dark. He switches on his flashlight — and, at right, finds himself in a hen-house, confronting the chickens. Mickey remains motionless in this second part of the scene, so Tom Palmer's animation drawing of him is inked and painted directly on the background.

THE PICNIC
(October 9, 1930)

Mickey and Minnie enjoy a picnic in the country, accompanied by Minnie's dog. The big news in this short is the dog, another evolutionary ancestor of Pluto, here called "Rover." Building on Norm Ferguson's groundbreaking bloodhound animation in *The Chain Gang*, this dog contributes most of the comedy content in *The Picnic*, and once again Ferguson animates his best scenes. His huge, floppy presence is played for laughs: Minnie asks to bring "my little Rover" to the picnic, Mickey agrees, and then is astonished when a dog fully his own size comes bounding up to him. Tied to the back of Mickey's little roadster, Rover trots obediently along behind the car—but when a couple of rabbits distract him he takes off in pursuit, easily dragging the car behind him.

PIONEER DAYS
(November 20, 1930)

This picture tells the epic tale of wagon trains moving west, with Mickey and Minnie among the hardy pioneers. In what was becoming a regular practice, this cartoon is both a spoof of a popular genre and an exciting adventure in its own right. *Pioneer Days* circulates today in two different versions, one missing an elaborate ending sequence that appears in the other edition. The shorter version is not simply an incomplete print, but an authentic studio version with a standard iris-out inserted at the end of *its* final scene. The two versions display other variations as well, including alternative background paintings in some scenes.

Another token of international success: a French title card for *Pioneer Days*, derived from the Powers-era American title card design.

A technique sometimes used by animators — "flopping" characters from one side of the frame to the other, to form a mirror image of the action — is used here in a background for *The Birthday Party*. Viewers, their eyes drawn to the dancing figures in the center, rarely notice the duplication.

THE BIRTHDAY PARTY

(January 2, 1931)

Today's Disney fan recognizes November 18, 1928, *Steamboat Willie*'s opening date at the Colony Theatre, as Mickey's "birthday." During the 1930s the Disney studio was casual about pinpointing a specific date, but did produce this short to celebrate Mickey's second birthday. Appearing in theaters early in 1931, *The Birthday Party* actually was *produced* in November 1930. Minnie and friends throw the birthday boy a surprise party that features music: Mickey receives a piano as a gift, all the guests dance, and Mickey winds up the proceedings riding a runaway xylophone like a bucking bronco.

TRAFFIC TROUBLES
(March 7, 1931)

As a taxi driver on city streets, Mickey endures rude drivers, rough and muddy streets, a tough traffic cop, and a large passenger who outweighs the taxi itself, his cheerful attitude remaining more or less intact all the while. Minnie, late for her music lesson, hails his taxi, and the short proceeds with a series of gags culminating in a wild chase through the countryside. One gag—showing Mickey's ruse to avoid a ticket for parking next to a fireplug—was eliminated from the final cut of the film, but did appear in newspapers in the comic strip adaptation. In 1931 *Traffic Troubles* inaugurated a regular booking in which every new Mickey Mouse played New York's prestigious Roxy Theater.[32]

Walt poses proudly at the studio with a specially decorated Baby Austin and performer Toots Novelle, who was costumed as Mickey for these promotional appearances—and, eventually, for the "Mickey Mouse Idea" stage show (see Chapter 2).

Mickey, as a taxi driver, tries to cope with an undersized cab and an oversized passenger in this cel setup from *Traffic Troubles*.

THE CASTAWAY

(March 27, 1931)

The Castaway marks the directorial debut of Wilfred Jackson, an erstwhile animator who would ultimately become one of the top Disney directors. As Jackson himself recalled it in later interviews, this significant development came about almost by accident: Walt, pressed to keep up with Columbia's release schedule, asked him to assemble a picture with a heavy quota of reused animation from earlier films.[33] The resulting tale of Mickey washed ashore on a tropical island duly balances new animation with recycled stock scenes. The closing gag, in which Mickey outwits a lion and an alligator at the same time, had originally been planned for *Jungle Rhythm*, and in the interim had also appeared in the *Mickey Mouse* newspaper comic strip. *The Castaway* also marks another significant debut: an original musical score by Frank Churchill, who would go on to a legendary career of his own.[34]

IMAGED BY HERITAGE AUCTIONS, HA.COM

THE MOOSE HUNT
(April 30, 1931)

Mickey goes moose hunting with his dog, identified for the first time as "Pluto" (a timely topical reference in 1931).[35] Not that Pluto's character is fully established yet: in the film's most famous scene he winks at the camera and speaks dialogue! Elsewhere his behavior is more doglike, and includes another reprise of Norm Ferguson's bloodhound animation from *The Chain Gang*. In turn, two pieces of animation in *this* picture, by Ferguson and Dave Hand, will themselves turn up again in later cartoons.

THE DELIVERY BOY
(June 6, 1931)

Mickey never actually delivers anything in this picture, but his wagonload of musical instruments provides the wherewithal for another rousing musical party. Surprising Minnie at her washing, he diverts her into a rousing song-and-dance number that cannot be dampened by either a hornets' nest or a dynamite explosion. The proceedings include a charming piece of Mickey-Minnie personality animation by Tom Palmer, and an extended Charleston sequence animated by Dick Lundy, who was already established as the studio's dance specialist. Lundy's drawings were later reproduced in storybooks to create a "flip-book" scene of Mickey's and Minnie's dance.

A *Delivery Boy* story sketch: Wienie the dachshund is uniquely equipped to play the accordion.

Script page for *The Delivery Boy*, depicting scenes in the climactic musicale. Disney scripts at this date combined detailed written descriptions of action and technical instructions with story sketches, a precursor of bona fide storyboards. In the finished film, the rabbit in the trio is replaced with a goat, as suggested in the sketch.

26 This is a L.S. probably covering the trio, which is the first 40 feet of the music. Horizontal pan, camera travels along and stops at various set-ups disclosed in the pan. Includes a rabbit jumping up and down on a base drum, which is lying on a pig. This makes pig play a cornet. Hen pecking up and down on the keys.

Calf blowing on a trombone with the slide of the trombone hooked over the handle of a grindstone. Duck running on the stone to make it revolve.

Little rabbits' head sticking up out of the ground playing on a clarinet, with worm dancing on the keys for the fingering.

Raccoon in tree nearby playing a flute.

Squirrel playing a saxophone, either with bycycle pump or the old farm pump.

Base violin with two squirrels playing see-saw with the bow and another on the strings.

1

Bathroom scene, sink at left. Arrangement of room indicates that seat is at right but out of scene. Open with Mickey stirring lather in mug and swaying to rhythm of "Ding Dong Daddy". He turns and kisses Minnie's picture at end of first phrase. On second phrase he lathers his face, turns and kisses photo again, leaving lot of lather on photo. Look of surprise on his face when he sees lather, turns around and shaves lather off picture. Business of throwing lather off stage and watching it. Expression as he hears off-stage splash. He turns and at measure 13 hits various bathroom articles, getting last two beats by reaching out to right. Action indicating he banged seat up and down twice. Action is repeated in measure 15 and 16. Chorus begins. Mickey sings first two lines of "D.D.D." during which he strops razor to rhythm. Next phrase he shaves to rhythm, sand paper sound for shaving effect. Business of throwing lather and watching it splash off stage. Repeat business of playing with fixtures and seat. He throws razor against wall and it sticks there. He picks up soap and starts to wash hands, soap slips out of his hands and goes off stage. He shrugs shoulders, turns and pulls out lights and exits to left.

FOOTAGE-66-12

MICKEY STEPS OUT
(July 10, 1931)

Mickey, accompanied by Pluto, goes calling on Minnie. This simple visit becomes the occasion for a musical interlude and a riot of slapstick gags. Pluto's new name is confirmed in writing in this cartoon, lettered on the front of his doghouse — to which Mickey ties the hapless pooch in an effort to keep him from tagging along. (It doesn't matter; Pluto tags along anyway and simply drags the doghouse with him.) Highlights include Dave Hand's animation of Minnie's pet canary, swinging on a perch and whistling to her piano accompaniment — a technical challenge which Hand still remembered with pride decades later.[36]

BLUE RHYTHM
(August 7, 1931)

Most of this musical short consists of a performance of W. C. Handy's classic "St. Louis Blues." The song was enjoying a renewed vogue in the early 1930s, thanks largely to a landmark 1925 recording by Bessie Smith. Here, after a short piano introduction by Mickey, Minnie strolls onstage and belts out the song in her best Bessie Smith imitation. The number is then taken up by Mickey's jazz orchestra, including Horace Horsecollar, Clarabelle Cow, and Pluto, the latter more humanized than in any other appearance — wearing gloves and playing the trombone.

Script page from *Mickey Steps Out*. Mickey in his bathroom spruces up for a date. Note that the artists place the toilet offscreen, where no censor can object to it — but then plant some teasing gags, making its presence unmistakable.

Mickey's piano introduction is enhanced by dramatic lighting in this story sketch for the opening scene in *Blue Rhythm*.

FISHIN' AROUND
(September 1, 1931)

Having tried moose hunting earlier in the year, Mickey and Pluto go on a fishing trip. Mickey disregards the "No Fishing" sign, runs afoul of a local sheriff, and escapes from him in the closing scenes. Once again the picture includes animation recycled from earlier cartoons. Little by little the studio was assembling a virtual stock library of these reusable scenes, which saved time and helped considerably in meeting Columbia's release deadlines. Norm Ferguson's animation of the sniffing Pluto in *The Chain Gang* was a key piece of that library — but *Fishin' Around* was the only cartoon in which Pluto went sniffing underwater!

THE BARNYARD BROADCAST
(September 30, 1931)

Radio was a vital force in American popular culture by 1931, an enormously powerful medium in which Mickey Mouse himself had already begun to establish a presence. Here he acknowledges the medium onscreen with a program of live music, broadcast from his barn "studio" to the farm animals outside, all avid radio fans. Movie audiences in 1931 would have recognized the joking references to the chimes which were already NBC's familiar signature, the attempt to maintain silence inside the studio, the inevitable flubs and missed cues of live broadcasting. An invasion by a family of yowling cats, and Mickey's attempts to eject them, provide the short with its expected quota of slapstick.

Fishin' Around inspired an unusual line of promotional merchandise: tableware decorated with designs based on scenes in the film, some of those scenes also selected for the storybook *Mickey Mouse Movie Stories* (see Chapter 4). On the side of this cup, Mickey "catches" himself.

Story sketches for *Fishin' Around*. Above, Mickey "catches" Pluto just in time to be caught himself; at right he is taunted by the fish.

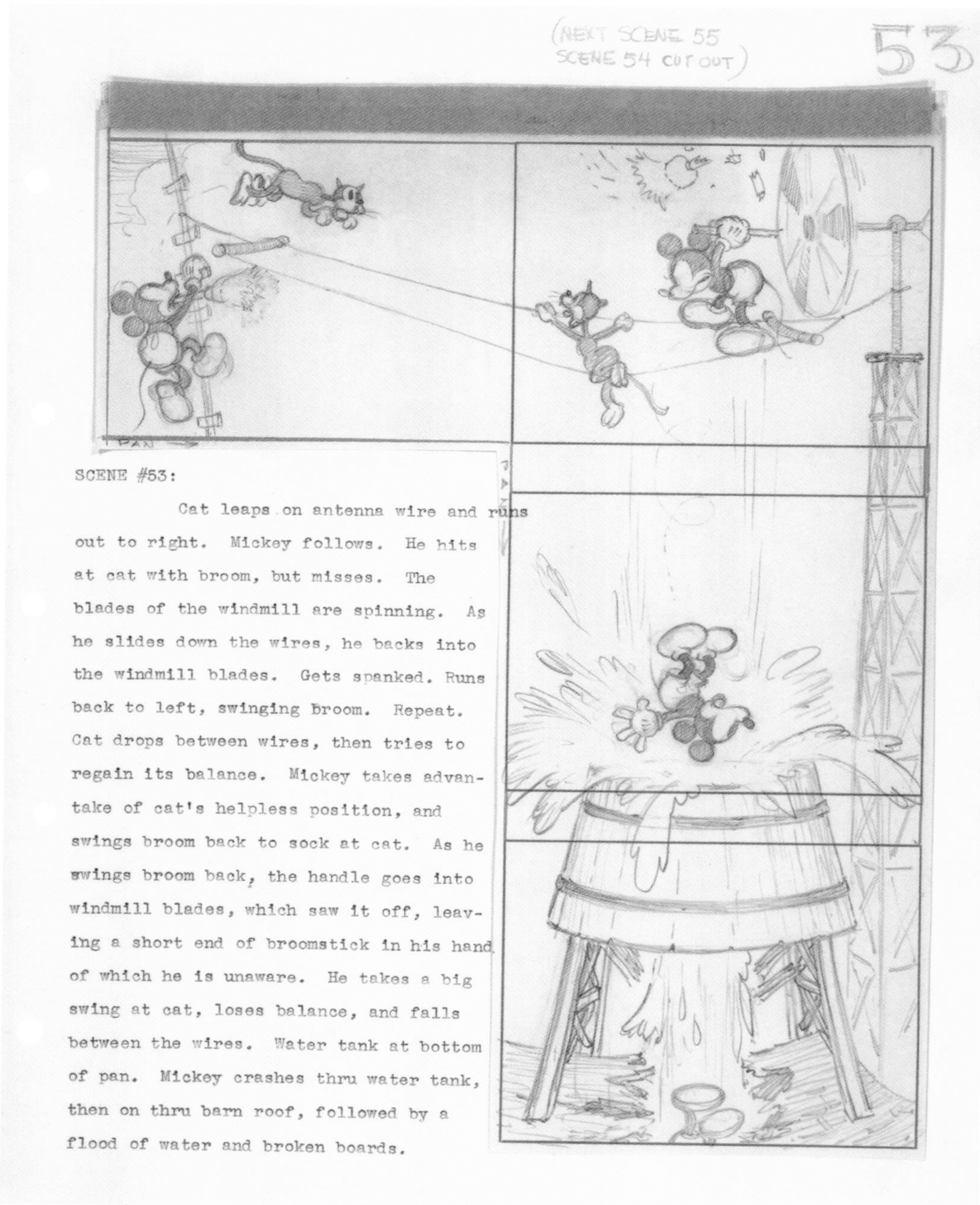

SCENE #53:

Cat leaps on antenna wire and runs out to right. Mickey follows. He hits at cat with broom, but misses. The blades of the windmill are spinning. As he slides down the wires, he backs into the windmill blades. Gets spanked. Runs back to left, swinging broom. Repeat. Cat drops between wires, then tries to regain its balance. Mickey takes advantake of cat's helpless position, and swings broom back to sock at cat. As he swings broom back, the handle goes into windmill blades, which saw it off, leaving a short end of broomstick in his hand of which he is unaware. He takes a big swing at cat, loses balance, and falls between the wires. Water tank at bottom of pan. Mickey crashes thru water tank, then on thru barn roof, followed by a flood of water and broken boards.

A script page for *The Barnyard Broadcast*. Mickey chases the cats outside again and the chase continues on the roof, leading to a wet, messy ending.

A background painting providing an overview of Mickey's barnyard environs, with his makeshift radio station at the center.

Story sketches for *The Barnyard Broadcast*. Mickey (backed by his horseshoe "chimes") makes an announcement; Minnie plays a solo.

THE BEACH PARTY
(October 28, 1931)

Mickey and Minnie, Horace Horsecollar and Clarabelle Cow, and Pluto enjoy a picnic at the beach—enjoy it, that is, until Pluto ventures into the water and tangles with an octopus. The climactic scenes depict the rest of the gang's battle with the creature. In between we see several gems of character animation, including Pluto's encounter with a crab—the first of numerous such scenes in his career, animated, like many of the others, by Norm Ferguson. By this time the studio was catching up with Columbia's release schedule and could afford the luxury of occasional changes in mid-production; here the entire ending sequence was reworked from its original version—which had shown the octopus rallying an *army* of octopi to chase away the picnickers.

MICKEY CUTS UP
(November 25, 1931)

The title is a pun; Mickey is mowing grass and performing other yard work, all while playfully showing off. This leads to a musical sequence featuring Mickey and Minnie, and a chase featuring Pluto and a cat. This may be the first Mickey Mouse short to formally adopt the system in which "crews" of junior animators, supervised respectively by Dave Hand and by Ben Sharpsteen, were assigned large blocks of scenes. Here Hand's crew animated Pluto and the birds listening to Mickey's and Minnie's musical performance, the cat's attack, and the start of the chase; the bulk of the chase itself was animated by Sharpsteen's crew.

MICKEY'S ORPHANS
(December 5, 1931)

A special holiday-themed short, released in time to appear in theaters for Christmas 1931. The opening scenes are richly atmospheric: snow falls; Minnie, in her snug little home, plays "Silent Night" on a pump organ; Mickey decorates the tree; Pluto snoozes by the fire. A mysterious figure leaves a basket on the doorstep, containing a litter of kittens. Mickey and Minnie bring the little tykes inside and Mickey decides to play Santa for them, and at this point *Mickey's Orphans* abandons any semblance of warm sentiment. Santa's bag seems to contain a large proportion of hammers, saws, hatchets, and popguns, and the kittens run wild, destroying furniture and driving Mickey and Minnie to distraction—though they try to take it all in stride.

A story sketch for *Mickey's Orphans* depicts Mickey, Minnie, and a gaggle of the title characters.

Mickey, Minnie, and their pals enjoy a seaside picnic in *The Beach Party*. The battle with the octopus is preceded by extended gags in this picnic sequence, including Clarabelle's getting the olive bottle stuck in her throat, and Horace's uncouth methods of eating corn on the cob and watermelon.

18

SCENE #18:

This is a fast pan of dog and horse running. Mickey passes them up. They reach the lunch spread-out, and all dive into the middle of the picnic. They land seated, and all begin eating.

THE DUCK HUNT
(January 21, 1932)

Once again Mickey and Pluto go hunting, and once again they are mocked and humiliated by their intended prey. The ducks openly taunt Mickey and Pluto and, in the end, turn the tables by victimizing *them*. One engaging sequence, in which Pluto swims in the pond with a decoy mounted on his head, was later echoed in the *Mickey Mouse* Sunday comic strip. Pluto is animated by several hands in this picture but, as before, Norm Ferguson is his leading exponent.

THE GROCERY BOY
(February 8, 1932)

Mickey, as a grocer's assistant, delivers an order of groceries to Minnie's house, then stays to help her cook a meal—his good intentions undercut when Pluto steals a turkey from the oven and runs wild through the house, wreaking slapstick destruction. The highlight of the short is perhaps the opening sequence, featuring charming personality animation of Mickey and Minnie by Rudy Zamora, Ben Sharpsteen, and especially Tom Palmer. Here again, the climactic episode of the film was adapted for the comic strip.

THE MAD DOG
(February 27, 1932)

One of the oddities of Mickey's early years, this short offers a change of pace from his customary musical and romantic high jinks. Mickey gives Pluto a bath; Pluto swallows the soap and is soon foaming at the mouth, and runs down the street while bystanders flee in terror from the "mad dog." The misunderstanding turns deadly when Peg Leg Pete, as a sadistic dogcatcher, corners Pluto in a vacant lot and prepares to shoot him. In the end, Pluto and Mickey narrowly escape. The musical score for the opening scenes is based on a promotional song, "The Wedding Party of Mickey Mouse."

Mickey and Pluto set out with high hopes in *The Duck Hunt*. Before the film's end they will be mocked, borne aloft and dragged across a rooftop and through a chimney, and generally manhandled by their intended prey. Years later, the Warner Bros. cartoon department will build a virtual franchise on this simple story idea.

The original poster for *The Mad Dog*, depicting Pluto's bath in the opening sequence, which sets the rest of the story in motion.

WALT DISNEY'S
MICKEY MOUSE
in
COLUMBIA PICTURES
THE MAD DOG
A COLUMBIA PICTURE
This advertising is the property of Columbia Pictures Corporation and is leased, not sold. The Exhibitor must not trade, sell, give away or sublease it, and it should be returned within 10 days after showing of the picture.

The poster for *Barnyard Olympics*, featuring a scene that appears nowhere in the film (and, in fact, suggests a gag in *The Barn Dance* four years earlier, in which Mickey improved his dancing with a balloon that made him lighter on his feet).

Below and opposite above Story sketches for *Barnyard Olympics*. Note the sketch below; the camera move suggested here is carried out in the finished film.

Reconstructed cel setup from *Barnyard Olympics*. Wienie the dachshund's long, pliable shape, which he occasionally used to advantage, becomes a liability during the bicycle race.

51
PERSPECTIVE PAN

Scene 51

A story sketch for the historic debut of the character that will eventually become known as Goofy. While billed as Dippy Dawg in publicity for *Mickey's Revue*, he was already known, within the studio, as "the Goof."

The poster for *Mickey's Revue* portrays Mickey with a variation on the homemade one-man-band contraption that he plays in the film.

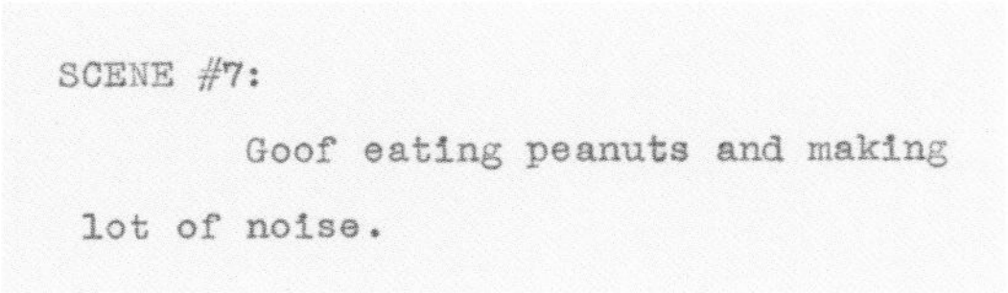

SCENE #7:

Goof eating peanuts and making lot of noise.

BARNYARD OLYMPICS
(April 13, 1932)

In 1932 the Olympic Games were held in Los Angeles, and some movie studios took advantage of that proximity to work the Olympics into the stories of their current features. In this short Mickey and his supporting players get Olympic fever, staging games of their own in what must be a very large barnyard. The main event is a cross-country race, Mickey and Pete (no peg leg this time) prominent among the contestants, and Pete takes every opportunity to sabotage Mickey—or otherwise outshine him. (In a sequence storyboarded but later removed, Pete even showed off his tattoos!) Needless to say, Mickey not only survives but prevails at the finish line.

MICKEY'S REVUE
(May 12, 1932)

Another "performance" short with a variety of musical acts, something we haven't seen since the autumn of 1931. *Mickey's Revue* is remembered today for introducing a major supporting character. The yokel in the audience who guffaws obnoxiously at every act, to the vast annoyance of other spectators, is a newcomer who was known at the time as Dippy Dawg, and would later evolve into the character we know today as Goofy. In this debut performance, his chief characteristic is that witless laugh, provided by Pinto Colvig (the laugh can actually be *heard* on the soundtrack of *Barnyard Olympics*, but this is the first time we *see* the giggling simpleton who goes with it).

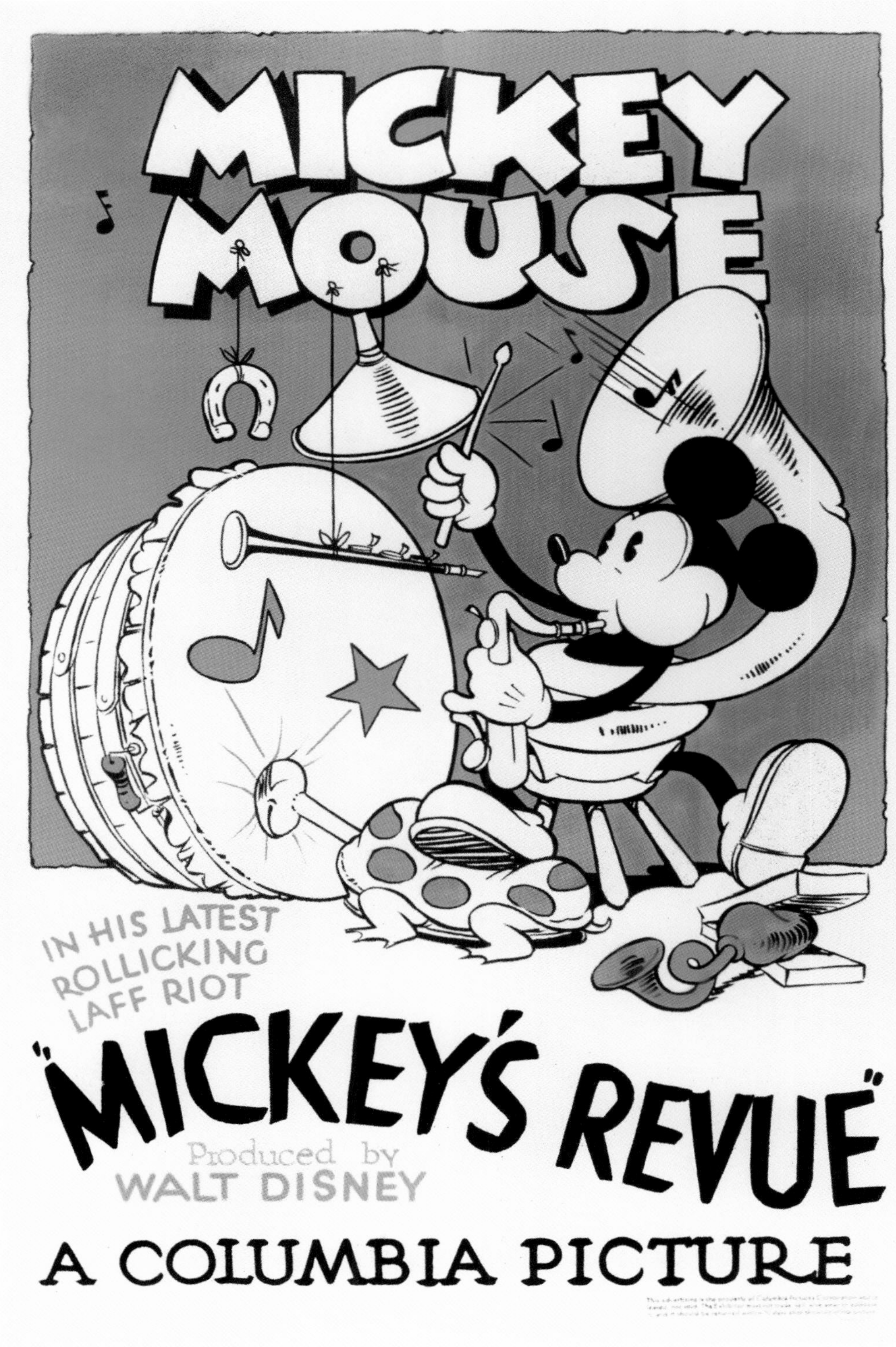
MICKEY MOUSE
IN HIS LATEST ROLLICKING LAFF RIOT
"MICKEY'S REVUE"
Produced by
WALT DISNEY
A COLUMBIA PICTURE

MICKEY MOUSE
IN
"THE MUSICAL FARMER"
Produced by WALT DISNEY
A COLUMBIA Picture
Copyrighted by Columbia Pictures Corp., New York, N. Y., 1932
This advertising is the property of Columbia Pictures Corporation and is leased, not sold. The Exhibitor must not trade, sell, give away or sublease it, and it should be returned within 10 days after showing of the picture.

MUSICAL FARMER
(June 8, 1932)

Mickey, Minnie, and Pluto are back on the farm, performing their everyday chores — but, as the title suggests, music soon proves too much of a distraction and the chores are forgotten altogether. The second half of the film revisits a droll conceit that Walt had introduced in his silent *Alice's Egg Plant* (1925): the idea of a henhouse as an "egg plant," i.e., a factory where hens produce eggs as if working on an assembly line. Here one hen, humiliated by her inability to lay a single egg, is vindicated when, at last, she produces an *enormous* egg.

MICKEY IN ARABIA
(July 11, 1932)

Mickey's final Columbia release is an adventure story, the kind of vehicle in which he would soon appear more frequently onscreen and in the comics. It was not without precedent — this picture is a loose remake of Oswald's *Harem Scarem* (1927), and also suggests Mickey's own *Gallopin' Gaucho*. Here he and Minnie are tourists in Arabia, and Pete, as an evil sheik, kidnaps Minnie. Mickey pursues them on his camel, which has been sampling beer and is now thoroughly inebriated. The camel is one of the highlights of the picture, his tipsy, weaving movements animated variously by Tom Palmer and by Ben Sharpsteen's crew of junior artists.

The poster for *Musical Farmer* (here with *The* tacked onto the title), featuring a minor gag from the first part of the film.

A background painting showing the entrance to the city in *Mickey in Arabia*. The actual gates do not appear here because they are animated on cels.

Painted metal figures were another popular type of Mickey toy, and came in a variety of poses. This German example dates from about 1932.

Swedish poster for the German film *Die vom Rummelplatz* (1930), in which Anny Ondra (who had starred in Hitchcock's first sound film, *Blackmail*) performs in costume as Mickey, enacting a comic piano solo likely inspired by *The Opry House*.

Following Where Mickey led, his early 1930s animated rivals followed. Just as Mickey appeared on ad signs outside theaters, the Mickey-like character "Foxy" (see page 116) tried to entice moviegoers with a Mickey-like ad sign for his *One More Time* (1931).

THE INTERNATIONAL MOUSE

Almost from the beginning, Mickey's appeal crossed national boundaries. As early as 1929, the Powers group negotiated overseas distribution contracts that brought the cartoons to movie audiences in Great Britain and Europe, Brazil, and South Africa. In 1930, first the films' local distributors, then George Borgfeldt and William Banks Levy, began to license foreign merchandise. As Mickey's fame increased, his territory expanded accordingly. By 1931 he could claim fans on several continents. In Germany, despite the censorship of *The Barnyard Battle*, audiences took Mickey to their hearts as passionately as anywhere else; Mickey's popularity was reflected on the screen in Fritz Lang's *M* (1931), in which a Mickey shop display is seen, and in *Die vom Rummelplatz* (Germany, 1930; dir. Carl Lamač), in which actress Anny Ondra performs a costumed Mickey pantomime sketch visibly inspired by *The Opry House* and *The Jazz Fool*. In England, Mickey was added to the gallery of personages in Tussauds Wax Museum, and the London Film Society screened his pictures alongside the works of Eisenstein and René Clair. The Eisenstein connection (his *Battleship Potemkin* was screened with *The Barn Dance* in 1929) was perhaps especially notable. The great Soviet director visited the Disney studio in 1930 and was gifted with the original art from an early Mickey comic strip, and became a passionate and vocal Disney admirer, writing at length on Walt's contributions to cinema.

By this time there was no mistaking the fact that Mickey Mouse was an international phenomenon. As he continued his conquests at home and abroad, the Hollywood filmmaking community began to accord him a level of prestige unprecedented for a cartoon character. Walt was a lifelong movie fan, and we can only imagine his excitement when Douglas Fairbanks, one of the most successful movie stars in the world—whom Mickey had emulated from afar in *The Gallopin' Gaucho*—invited Mickey to make a cameo

Anny Ondra
FLICKAN MED
MUSSE PIGG-
HUMÖRET
Siegfried
Arno
Margarete
Kupfer
Vidor
Schwanecke
VARIETÉNS
SKÄLMUNGE
Regi: Karl Lamac
J. OLSÉNS LITOGR. ANST. STHLM

CONSTANCE
BENNETT
Constance
Bennett
BOUGHT
Ben Lyon
Richard Bennett
Dorothy Peterson

VITAPHONE
ETT IN "BOUGHT"
E OF HER CAREER
"BOUGHT"
OM THE FAMOUS "JACKDAWS STRUT"
ORTABLE INSIDE
UGHT" WITH BEN LYON
RIGERATION
"MERRIE" MELODIES
"ONE MORE TIME"

Ideas
FANCHON & MARCO'S
MICKEY MOUSE
IDEA
MICKEY MOUSE
YooHoo!
IT'S ME
MICKEY
MOUSE!
I'M HERE
ON THE
STAGE
NOW!
A NEW
EUROPEAN
BEAUTY
SENSATION
IN A DARING
ROMANTIC
DRAMA.
FOX

appearance in *his* latest feature. The film, an anomaly in Fairbanks's career, was titled *Around the World in Eighty Minutes with Douglas Fairbanks* and was essentially an extemporaneous eight-reel travelogue.[37] It included a visit to Siam (now Thailand), where Fairbanks commented on the grace and distinctive arm movements of a group of native dancers. On cue, Mickey stepped onto the screen and, in a special scene animated by Dick Lundy, performed a dance scene of his own — first imitating the Thai dancers, then introducing some uniquely American moves. In later years Mickey would appear in further feature-length films, but in 1931 he made his entrance into the feature arena in the company of royalty.

The Mickey Mouse Clubs continued to flourish. Walt and Roy hired Harry Woodin to manage the Clubs, and Roy's secretary, Lucille Benedict, became Woodin's assistant. Together they created a handbook for theater managers who hosted local Clubs, and the studio produced a regular newsletter as well as an array of paraphernalia — membership cards, buttons, and other novelties — for the young members. "Minnie's Yoo Hoo," the theme song of the Mickey films, became the theme song for the Mickey Mouse Clubs as well, and the studio produced a special trailer for the host theater to show at Club matinees.

Meanwhile, if imitation is the sincerest form of flattery, Mickey was being extravagantly flattered by rival cartoon studios, almost all of whom included *very* Mickey-like characters in their pictures. Despite the fact that Walt had copyrighted and trademarked his Mouse, some of these producers indulged in surprisingly blatant plagiarism. At the Leon Schlesinger studio, producing Looney

More Mickey-centric promotion at the movies. Here, in early 1931, the prestigious Loew's State Theatre simultaneously promotes Mickey cartoons *and* Fanchon and Marco's "Mickey Mouse Idea" stage show (see Chapter 2).

In another British postcard, Mickey takes a teasing swipe at the movie giants who are now his peers.

"Minnie's Yoo Hoo!"
MICKEY MOUSE
THEME SONG
As sung by—
WALT DISNEY'S
WORLD FAMOUS
CARTOON CHARACTER
MICKEY MOUSE
Villa Morét Inc.
MUSIC PUBLISHERS
KRESS BUILDING
SAN FRANCISCO
"THE VOICE OF THE WEST"

"MINNIE'S YOO HOO"

(Special sing-along trailer, 1930)

This short (four-minute) reel was created expressly to lead young Club members in singing Mickey's theme song at meetings. The trailer was cannily produced from existing art: Mickey sings the song in Ben Sharpsteen's animation from *Mickey's Follies*, standing before a stage backdrop from *Fiddling Around*. Much footage is consumed by title cards with printed song lyrics, and Sharpsteen evidently delegated to junior artists the few remaining scenes: a raucous "yoo-hoo!" at the end of the chorus, and Mickey's direct addresses to the audience before each verse. Curiously, while the *animation* of Mickey singing the song comes from *Mickey's Follies*, his voice track is newly recorded. The first round approximates Mickey's usual falsetto, but the second round is in an uncharacteristic, German-accented baritone.

Disney studio records also suggest that another trailer was produced for the Mickey Mouse Clubs, combining new Mickey and Minnie footage with live action of Lawrence "Noodles" Fagan, a period vaudeville comedian. While copies of the film have not surfaced at this writing, numerous animation drawings showing Mickey posing excitedly and waving a megaphone may possibly have been created for it.

"Minnie's Yoo Hoo" was the studio's first original published song and became the theme song of the Mickey Mouse film series until mid-1933. Above, Carl Stalling at the piano leads a studio group (including Walt, second from left) in a chorus; a prototype of the song sheet sits on the piano. Opposite, the published song-sheet cover, penciled by Les Clark and inked by Win Smith.

A 1931 promotional stunt in the *Mickey Mouse* comic strip (see Chapter 2) invited readers to send a self-addressed envelope; the studio was promptly swamped with a deluge of letters. Here Walt and Mickey pose with some of them.

Tunes and Merrie Melodies for Warner Bros., former Disney staffer Rudolf Ising introduced a character called Foxy, a "fox" whose ears were round, like Mickey's, and whose behavior was likewise suspiciously familiar. In time, Walt personally asked Ising to stop using the character.[38] Some producers skipped even the pretense of creating an original character, and simply inserted Mickey-like mice into cartoons nominally starring their own characters. *Spooks* (1930), Universal's cartoon burlesque of *The Phantom of the Opera*, ostensibly featured Oswald but was punctuated by frequent appearances by a faux-Mickey mouse. In *Hold Anything* (1930), Warners' early character Bosko supervises a construction crew of identical mice—identical to each other and to Mickey, more or less, apart from their tiny size. Some of their scenes were recycled two years later in *It's Got Me Again*.

For Walt and Roy, the last straw was the outright thievery of the Van Beuren studio. In 1929 and 1930, after an unsuccessful bid to distribute the Disney pictures, Van Beuren produced several cartoons with a mouse couple who were simply crude, unmistakable copies of Mickey and Minnie—not as supporting players at the periphery, but featured as the starring characters. The Disneys brought a lawsuit against Van Beuren in the spring of 1931, charging that "Mickey's alleged double is doing all sorts of things Mickey wouldn't think of doing and has brought down a flood of irate letters and complaints."[39] Van Beuren countered that they were the current producers of the Aesop's Fables cartoons, which had nominally featured Milton and Mary (or Rita) Mouse throughout the 1920s, and suggested that any plagiarism was actually on Disney's side![40] But Milton and his girlfriend had spent most of their screen life as unclothed, only partly humanized rodents. The Disney case pointed out that Van Beuren's new redesign, blatantly mimicking (however amateurishly) the designs, costumes, and actions of Mickey and Minnie, was a clear infringement. The court upheld Disney's claim, issuing an injunction that prevented Van Beuren from producing any further cartoons with their impostor mice. Ironically, while Disney's complaint against Van Beuren included a callout of the faux Mickey's improper behavior, fallout from *The Shindig* brought the censors down on Disney at about the same time. Walt and his artists may have inserted the sensitive gags in *The Shindig* in a spirit of harmless mischief, but the move backfired when censors viewed those gags and were less than amused. Their complaints caused further troublesome delays, and were highlighted in a number of film journals in late 1930 and early 1931.[41] Later in the year, Walt commented ironically on the experience to some interviewers: "You just can't please everybody."[42] Now the Disney pictures became noticeably more circumspect: *Traffic Troubles* marked the last time Mickey used an unwilling animal as a prop, and *Musical Farmer* showed a cow's udder only in a milking scene. Later cartoons showed the animals udderless as a rule.

The Hall Brothers Company, later renamed Hallmark, produced Disney greeting cards starting in 1932. This birthday card, among Hall Brothers' earliest designs, is modeled loosely on a Les Clark publicity drawing from 1929.

Following **Hyperion studio staff holding Mickey Mouse dolls. Standing left to right: Cecil Surrey, Wilfred Jackson, Tom Palmer, Jack King, George Lane, Walt Disney, Les Clark, Burt Gillett, Dave Hand, Ben Sharpsteen, Emil Flohri, Bert Lewis. Seated from left to right: Gilles "Frenchy" de Trémaudan, Jack Cutting, Merle Gilson, Dick Lundy, Chuck Couch, Johnny Cannon, Norm Ferguson, Tom McKimson, Floyd Gottfredson.**

WALT DISNEY STUDIO

'EAR, 'EAR!
AH! IF I HAD A PENNY, I WOULD GET SOME CHOCOLATE
PULL
THIS EAR SHOULD FIT THAT SLOT
PULL
AH! A PERFECT FIT
PULL
OW!
ZIP!
REJECTED COINS
PULL

CHAPTER TWO

Mickey Comes to the Comics

For generations, comic strips and books have been among the Disney company's most important storytelling forms. Before the onset of the television age, the medium functioned as many fans' most readily available source of Mickey Mouse entertainment—and brought Mickey himself immeasurable growth as a nuanced character.

But every success has to start somewhere. In 1956, Walt rather casually recounted the launch of the Mickey Mouse newspaper strip enterprise:

> *[In 1929 we were looking for] ways to exploit characters like the Mouse. The most obvious was a comic strip. . . . As I was producing the first one, a letter came to me from King Features [Syndicate] wanting to know if I would be interested in doing a comic strip featuring Mickey Mouse. Naturally I accepted their offer.*[1]

As later recalled by Ub Iwerks, Walt's interest in comics predated Mickey by many years.[2] His youth at Chicago's McKinley High School found him writing and drawing for the school magazine, the *Voice*, producing gag panels reflective of the era's popular newspaper comics.[3] Carey Orr's *Kernel Cootie*, a domestic strip featuring a squabbling couple, was a major influence on Walt; not surprisingly, Walt's first effort at a self-drawn newspaper comic moved in the same direction.[4] Surviving examples of his "Mr. George's Wife,"

A one-page gag and a single-panel cartoon from British *Mickey Mouse Annual* 1 (1930); story and art by Wilfred Haughton. The earliest European Disney comics featured metamorphosis gags reminiscent of Mickey's very first animated appearances: here, his ears can become coins.

KING SIGNS YOUNG STRIP ARTIST

Photograph shows Walt Disney, whose "Mickey Mouse" has been a hit with the talkies, and is now to appear in strip form, signing on the dotted line designated by Ward Greene, executive editor of King Features Syndicate, which is distributing the feature. Disney started his career when he was 17. He is now 28.

an unsold daily strip from about 1920, show rather clichéd gags starring an unlucky middle-aged husband.

It is perhaps not surprising that "Mr. George's Wife" failed to click with a syndicate. But as we have seen, Walt Disney drove himself to turn failure into success, and moving beyond clichés was part of that drive. In the years that followed, Disney's silent cartoons filled up with anti-clichés: creative young heroes who always stood out, bursting with unique, inventive solutions to problems. That Mickey should win Walt his long-sought comic strip success, where "Mr. George" had failed, must have seemed to Walt like a tempting possibility.

This brief human-interest article announced Disney's move into comics. King Features executive editor Ward Greene is better known among Disney fans for his later role in developing *Lady and the Tramp* (1955): Greene's "A Fable for Grownups: Happy Dan, the Cynical Dog" (often misremembered as "...Whistling Dog"), a story in the February 1945 issue of *Cosmopolitan*, inspired the Tramp character. Later, Greene wrote both the official novelization of Disney's *Lady* film and the early months of King Features' spinoff comic strip, *Scamp*.

While Walt later recalled having created the Mickey comic strip before King Features requested it, the historical record reveals otherwise. Walt was indeed thinking about comics in mid-1929, but no actual work had yet begun at the time. Surviving correspondence shows that Charles J. Giegerich of the Powers office suggested getting a move on:

I cannot say what success we would have in placing a comic page with the newspaper syndicates, but it certainly would be good publicity. If you will send me a couple of sample pages, I will take it up with the syndicates. . . .[5]

"Mr. George's Wife," an unsold comics concept dating from about 1920, was Walt's first effort at a newspaper strip. Still learning the art of fiction, Walt created in Mr. George less a unique character than a sitcom cliché: the resigned doormat.

But as of June, Walt's team had not yet produced those samples, and finding time to make them proved difficult. Into this impasse walked Joseph Connolly, president of King Features Syndicate. His July 24, 1929, letter to "U. B. Iwerk, Esq." [*sic*] began:

I think your mouse animation is one of the funniest features I have ever seen in the movies. Please consider producing one in comic strip form for newspapers. If you can find time to do one, I shall be very interested in seeing some specimens.[6]

GEE !! - BUT ID LIKE TO FLY, AND BECOME A GREAT AVIATOR LIKE COL. LINDBERGH !!
HOW TO FLY
WELL! WELL !! IF IT ISN'T MICKEY MOUSE !! IM GLAD TO MEET YOU MICKEY, AND SURELY GLAD TO KNOW YOU HAVE BECOME SUCH A GREAT AVIATOR!

WAIT TILL LINDY SEES MY AIRSHIP-HE'LL BE SO JEALOUS-HE'LL RESIGN FROM THE ARMY !!!
WELL WELL! WEINNIE, YOU'RE JUST THE GUY I'VE BEEN LOOKING FOR-YOU AND I ARE GOING TO HAVE A LOT OF FUN IN JUST A MINUTE !!!

Original syndicate proofs for the first week of the *Mickey Mouse* daily strip, written by Walt Disney, penciled by Ub Iwerks, and inked by Win Smith. "Lost on a Desert Island," the strip's first serial, opens with a sequence based on *Plane Crazy*: Mickey launches a homemade "aeroplane" with help from his dachshund friend, now named Wienie.

It didn't take long for Walt to decide to write the Mickey strip himself, while Iwerks handled the art. But the pair had other tasks weighing on them due to heavy cartoon production. August and September found Walt caught unawares by lack of time, while Giegerich grumbled about the samples' absence.[7] On October 19, Walt admitted to Connolly:

> *The artist that we have had working on [the strip] has made up quite a few specimens but we have not as yet been able to satisfy ourselves with the results.*[8]

But one month later—on November 18, exactly one year after Mickey's screen debut in *Steamboat Willie*—a set of studio-approved samples were finally sent to King Features.

It is hard to determine what finally brought the strip into focus; no rejected preliminary "specimens" seem to survive to tell us. But the first published Mickey daily strips were based directly on preexisting cartoons, an obvious story source.

Joining writer Walt and pencil artist Iwerks for the launch was inker Win Smith, then an in-house studio publicity artist. Smith's bulbous character designs and heavily shaded art style had previously been in evidence on several of the first Mickey marketing model sheets: pages of fully inked character callout drawings that were used as clip art sources for film promotions and merchandise. One extra-large page of poses, penciled by Les Clark and inked by Smith in about December 1929, was initially designed for King Features strip ads. A telegram from King outlined the plan:

> NEW YORK MIRROR WISHES TO BEGIN PUBLICITY ON MICKEY MOUSE NEXT WEEK AND START STRIP WEEK THEREAFTER STOP . . . PROSPECTS EXCELLENT THAT MICKEY WILL BE BIG COMIC HIT OF NINETEEN THIRTY.[9]

The *Mickey Mouse* daily strip was promoted in the *Mirror* with a big King Features launch pack. But only one other

An early 1930 introductory comic, drawn by Win Smith, was designed for newspapers picking up the *Mickey Mouse* daily strip midstream. Pete's alias of "Terrible Tom" may represent an effort to differentiate him from the bear-Pete who had been Oswald's enemy.

"Lost on a Desert Island" found writer Walt still learning the ropes of serial storytelling. A sequence with Mickey playing first surrogate sibling, then babysitter to two vulture chicks finishes with Mickey seemingly *walking* home to his farm, even though he'd flown over water to reach the desert island.

paper, California's *Oakland Post-Enquirer*, actually ran the daily from its January 13 start. In practice, the comic Mickey proved slow to pick up steam.

Inspection of the strip's early promotion and its first ongoing story, "Lost on a Desert Island,"[10] suggests what the problem may have been. An increasing number of comic strips at the time were delivering thrilling adventure tales. Yet the *Mickey Mouse* launch ads spoke not of thrills, but of laughs: "a whole trunk full of laughs." And while the ads did introduce a crafty-looking villain — "Terrible Tom," the prototypical Pete — whose presence suggested dramatic story lines, the "Desert Island" story line neither included Pete nor proved very dramatic. Moments of fear for Mickey are often cast as end-of-strip cliff-hangers, and his prankish outwitting of hostile jungle animals as triumphs; but Mickey can also spend days at a time calmly babysitting vulture chicks, and one day pulling an aching tooth — a moment of discontinuity that doesn't even require our hero to be on a desert island.

Another discontinuity struck "Lost on a Desert Island" behind the scenes. Three weeks into the story — beginning with the February 3 daily — Ub Iwerks was gone, and inker Smith began pencilling as well.

Cover to *Albums Mickey* 2 (1932), a French comic album reprinting the second half of "Mickey Mouse in Death Valley." Published by comics licensee Hachette, still a major Disney partner today, this album was reprinted into the 1950s; later editions sported a redesigned cover, showing a streamlined postwar Mickey wielding the miner's pick.

This special strip starring Mickey and Pluto was drawn by Gottfredson and Taliaferro for the November 21, 1931 issue of *Film Weekly*; but its gag appears to have been adapted from *Bobby Bumps and the Hypnotic Eye* (1919), a Bray Studios animated cartoon directed by Earl Hurd — who would himself later become a Disney story man.

ENTER FLOYD GOTTFREDSON

By this time, the strip had also acquired a new and game-changing creative head. When Utah-born projectionist and magazine cartoonist Floyd Gottfredson applied for a Disney job in late 1929, his stated goal had been to draw a Mickey Mouse comic strip. But Gottfredson was instead put to work as an in-betweener on such cartoons as *Cannibal Capers* (1930). Then, suddenly, everything changed.

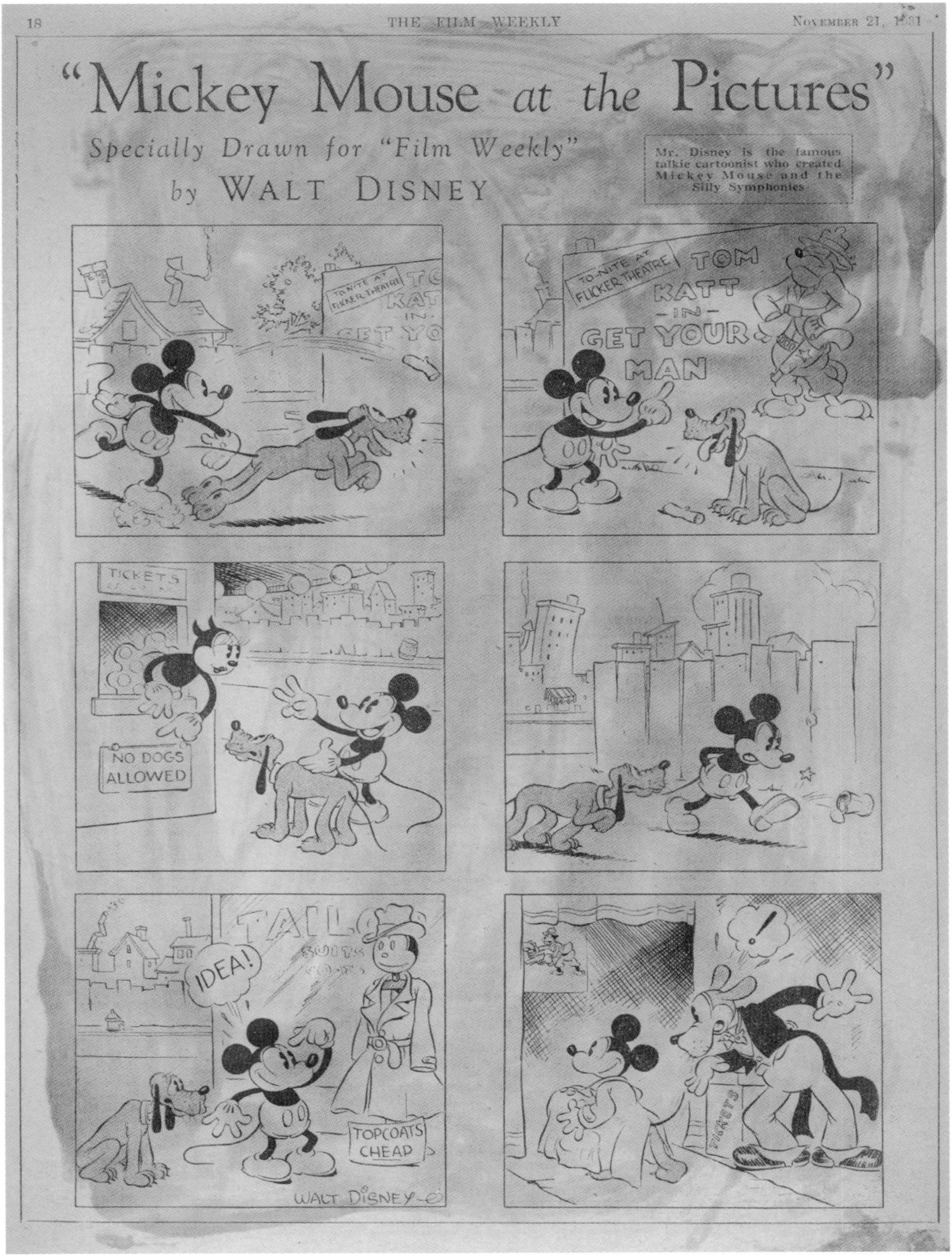
18 THE FILM WEEKLY November 21, 1931
"Mickey Mouse at the Pictures"
Specially Drawn for "Film Weekly"
by WALT DISNEY
Mr. Disney is the famous talkie cartoonist who created Mickey Mouse and the Silly Symphonies
TO-NITE AT FLICKER THEATRE
TOM KATT -IN- GET YOUR MAN
TICKETS
NO DOGS ALLOWED
IDEA!
TOPCOATS CHEAP
TICKETS
WALT DISNEY

COME ON, MINNIE!! THEY CAN'T BLUFF US— JUST HOLD ON TO MY HAND, AND DON'T MAKE ANY NOISE!!!
I'D LIKE TO SEE ANYBODY TRY TO SEPARATE US!!!
CREAK
©By Walter E. Disney, Great Britain rights reserved

THATS NICE, MICKEY. KEEP ON BEING NICE TO HER. SHE'S STARTING TO WEAKEN!!
DON'T YOU SEE, MRS. COW— THIS IS A MAP TO A GOLD MINE IN DEATH VALLEY AND WE'RE BEING CHASED BY A CROOKED LAWYER AND HIS HENCHMAN— IF THEY CATCH US THEY'LL TAKE THE MAP AND STEAL OUR GOLD MINE!!
DO YOU UNDERSTAND NOW?— DO YOU SEE WHAT IT MEANS TO US FOR YOU TO GET OFF THE TRACK?
By Walter E. Disney, Great Britain rights reserved.

One “Mickey Mouse in Death Valley” strip drawn by Win Smith, another by Floyd Gottfredson; midway through the story, Smith left the studio and Gottfredson took over. Gottfredson later wondered why Smith — who got along badly with Walt — had not departed sooner: Smith “was sort of a strange character anyway. He had a big brass spittoon in the corner of his [office].”[1]

When not busy inking the *Mickey Mouse* strip in late 1930, Hardie Gramatky — a part-time staffer who would eventually become a full-time animator — handled the bulk of illustrative duties for Saalfield's *Mickey Mouse Coloring Book* (1931), to which Gottfredson himself also contributed. Pictured here: a Gramatky-drawn interior page.

> *Walt... had been trying to get Win [Smith] to take over the writing [on the strip] as well as the drawing.... I guess they had a big blowup in his office, because Win came storming out to my desk and he said, "I guess you got a new job."*[11]

Gottfredson was at first assigned to draw the *Mickey Mouse* daily on a temporary basis, but there was no permanently unseating him; in June, he took over the writing duties as well. A future Mouse master was steering "Death Valley" toward the finish line.

Contrasting Walt's strip-Mickey with Floyd's reveals the progress of fleshing the character out for comics, improving Mickey's internal consistency in the process. Some Walt-written strips had shown a go-getter hero full of real bravado, while others portrayed a mouse too timid to accomplish his goals. On February 18, Mickey ponders human nature: "When they get all through fighting — they won't

know who *started* the trouble!" But on April 24, Mickey's easy capture by Pete recasts the philosopher as a foolhardy, impulsive naïf.

To some degree, the nebulous nature of the early comics Mickey matched that of many early comedy stars: little was out of character as long as it felt funny at the moment. Gottfredson would help the Mouse past this unsettled state. By the latter half of "Death Valley," Mickey is less likely to flee unless he has a plan in mind; less likely to be beaten without refocusing and rebounding. Gottfredson casts Mickey less as a coward, a fool, or a pushover than simply an earnest youth caught, now and then, at an awkward moment: a characterization that, in its depth, looks ahead to much later Mickey animation.

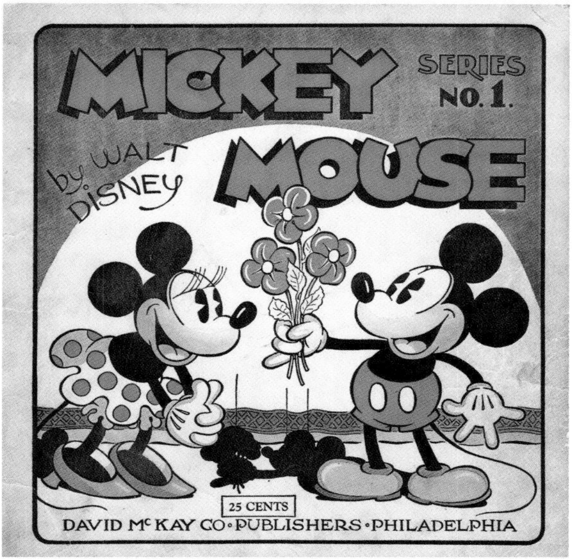

IMAGED BY HERITAGE AUCTIONS, HA.COM

As "Death Valley" continues, Mickey and Minnie are framed as desperados; Minnie is captured and jailed, and Mickey chased over a waterfall before finally reaching Uncle Mortimer's gold mine—and finding it empty. In the end, the mysterious Fox reveals that he is actually Uncle Mortimer, who faked his own death and set up the mine as a ruse to expose Sylvester's criminality. It is a tidy conclusion to a complex plotline, but leaves a few loose ends; in the process of exposing Sylvester, for instance, Uncle Mortimer comes off as having unwittingly—but repeatedly—put Minnie in preventable danger.

This is not, of course, to diminish the overall accomplishments of "Death Valley" and the subsequent works of Gottfredson's team.

The first American collected edition of *Mickey* daily strips was *Mickey Mouse Series* No. 1 (1931), published by David McKay. Under this original Gottfredson cover appeared a truncated version of his "Mr. Slicker and the Egg Robbers" serial.

DIDN'T PEOPLE DRESS FUNNY IN THE OLD DAYS, MR. SLICKER? HERE IS MY GRANDPA, MARSHAL MOUSE—AND THAT'S GRANDMOTHER, MATILDA MOUSE—THIS GROUP DOWN HERE IS UNCLE MILTON MOUSE AND HIS FAMILY!
WALT DISNEY

I KNOW MINNIE LIKES ME —BUT THAT SLICKER WITH HIS CITY WAYS! GOSH! I'M AFRAID SHE MIGHT FALL FOR HIM!
WHAT SHALL I PLAY NEXT, MR. SLICKER?
PLAY TH SAME SC AGAIN- IT WAS BEAUTIFU

In two strips from "Mr. Slicker and the Egg Robbers" (1930), the eponymous Slicker seems to have won Minnie's heart; soon he has framed Mickey for a bank robbery, too. But Mickey, now a fugitive on the run, puts the brakes on Slicker's swindle by befriending Bozo Butch — the hard-boiled leader of Slicker's gang — and convincing him that Slicker is swindling the gang as well. Minnie, meanwhile, rallies to Mickey's side, having become disillusioned with Slicker's "city ways" on her own.

FIRST BRITISH COMICS

Mickey and Bozo Butch on stage in a "Mickey Mouse Idea" performance. While billed only as "Bozo" in early ads, Butch was called by his full name in other literature about the show; and his costume and attitude made clear who audiences were seeing.

Mickey is feted at Loew's State Theatre in Los Angeles—the launching point of all Fanchon and Marco "Idea" shows—with a Disney company car in attendance.

We have already noted how Mickey's overseas debut led to the appearance of merchandise, too, in foreign markets; and how, before Disney fully established its character rights in Europe, those markets were awkwardly divided among authorized products, products sublicensed by the films' local distributors, and products handled from June 1930 onward by William Banks Levy, Disney's U.K. representative.

The first British Mickey Mouse print spin-off appeared several months prior to Levy's start on the job. Created by cartoonist Ernest "Ern" Shaw and titled *The Adventures of Mickey Mouse*, it was a crude, seemingly unlicensed weekly newspaper feature that began in the *Gloucester Journal* on February 1, 1930. Primitive, off-model, and legally nebulous as it was, however, Shaw's series indicated a ready British audience for Mickey print products—and King Features' studio-approved *Mickey Mouse* daily, which launched on March 17.

MICKEY MOUSE" IDEA
LOS-VIC INCE AND BAND
Marco STAGE IDEAS
ARRELL-ELISSA LANDI
I.P.M. 35¢
LOEWS STATE Theatre NOW
in a Fanchon & Marco Idea
WALT DISNEY PRODUCTIONS LTD
MICKEY MOUSE
CARTOONS

The story "High Society" (1931) finds Mickey and Butch as local celebrities, getting Mickey's photo taken for the tie-in fan card shown here. In-story, Mickey's and Butch's popularity reflects Mickey's recent prizefighting win against Creamo Catnera; in real life, their fame also reflected the still-running "Mickey Mouse Idea" stage show. Butch, in Gottfredson's art, even adopts the thick, striped sweater that he was first given to wear in the show (and which, in more recent comics, he continues to wear today).

The next chapter in Mickey's British comics career began, oddly enough, in Germany. Much like the United Kingdom, Germany witnessed conflict between rival Mickey merchandisers before Disney worked out its local conflicts of interest. Some German Mickey products were licensed by George Borgfeldt; some were licensed by Levy; some were unlicensed but still, at this early stage, technically legal; and some were licensed by Britain's Ideal Films, which had entered into its own Mickey contracts with several German toy makers.

One such firm, Tipp & Co., manufactured a crude Mickey motorcycle toy under Ideal's auspices. Later in the year, perhaps due to compromises among Ideal's, Borgfeldt's, and Levy's licensees, the export firm Eisenmann & Co. began marketing this motorcycle in new territories—with significantly improved character designs. Levy demanded "a *competent* artist to draw Mickey Mouse"[12]; relatively speaking, he had found one.

MICKEY MOUSE ANNUAL

Since 1926, London-born cartoonist Wilfred Haughton had been working with local publisher Odhams Press and

with toy manufacturer W. H. Cornelius, who introduced him to Levy. The new artwork on the bike toy was Haughton's, and along with it Eisenmann exported a raft of additional Haughton-illustrated Mickey items, including the Johann Distler firm's legendary Mickey and Minnie "organ grinder" tin toy. The mice had five-fingered hands and toothy grins, but they were nevertheless more Disney-friendly than their predecessors. They were also a hit, leading Haughton to his next assignment. Odhams' first *Mickey Mouse Annual*—a collection of original comics, to be printed by sister publisher Dean & Son for Christmas 1930—needed an artist to handle half of its 128 interior pages. Haughton excitedly took the job and began turning out Mickey comics full of slapstick, veddy-British music hall humor.

Future *Mickey Mouse Annual* star talent Wilfred Haughton shared drawing duties on the first volume with another, less accomplished artist; that other artist's "Cheese It" draws on reference material by Les Clark and Win Smith, but imitates it crudely. By contrast, the cover of *Mickey Mouse Annual* 2 (1931) finds the more professional Haughton developing rapidly. While his Mickey still mimics a 1929 character design, the appealingly stylized art looks ahead to great achievements.

Was Haughton himself responsible for his stories' wild style? Likely so; he is thought to have insisted on writing all material he drew. Nevertheless, Haughton was promoted to drawing the entirety of the interior material for *Mickey Mouse Annual* 2 (1931), and with that same volume, the cover as well. From the present vantage point, it's not hard to see why; Haughton's artwork was improving by leaps and bounds, becoming fully professional and "Disney" in a way his collaborator on *Annual* 1 could never have been.

FIRST ITALIAN COMICS

Just as the King Features Mickey strip took a few months to find itself—and find an audience—in the United States, so it went in Italy. Lorenzo Gigli, editor of the *Gazzetta del Popolo* newspaper in 1930, was the first in the country to obtain a Disney license.[13] Gigli went on to publish "Lost on a Desert Island," but ran the strips on an infrequent weekly basis—and quite out of order, leading to reader disinterest. Gigli dropped Mickey from the *Gazzetta* when the serial was over; conventional wisdom held that the Mickey strip was too American in some way. Maybe Mickey comics needed to be rebooted as a more conventionally Italian product.

From April 16 to August 13, 1931, the newspaper *Il Popolo di Roma* ("The People of Rome") tried to make this happen. *Il Popolo* launched its own exclusive weekly Mickey comic strip: an original series created by Guglielmo Guastaveglia, a well-known local gag cartoonist, and subcontracted for Disney by King Features, as indicated by an "exclusively for Italy" notice beneath each strip.[14]

Guastaveglia had earlier been a writer and editor at various popular humor journals, and his first Mickey pages reflected this past experience. Settings were typically Italian in design.

UNSRE ACHTE MICKY-MAUS-REIHE

As British and Italian Disney licensees began making their own Mickey Mouse comics, other countries' publishers occasionally gave it a shot as well. On February 14, 1931, Germany's *Kölnische Illustrierte Zeitung*, the local publisher of King Features' *Mickey* daily, wanted a Gottfredson strip to tie into the German holiday of Fasching — a Mardi Gras-like carnival — but no such strip existed. *Zeitung* cartoonist Frank Behmak took the opportunity to produce this one-off original Mickey story, using recent dailies as a guide to drawing Mickey and Butch.

Cover art by Michele Rubino for *Albi d'oro* 4 (1937), an Italian comic album reprinting "Mickey Mouse, Boxing Champion" (1931). In Gottfredson's story, Mickey accidentally pummels Ruffhouse Rat, Minnie's boxer cousin, and ends up hired as his coach. Ruffhouse bears the proud title of "heavy-lightweight champion," but he is a hopeless athlete; upon learning that his mystery opponent is the barbarous Creamo Catnera (his name a takeoff on real-life boxer Primo Carnera), Ruffhouse panics and skips town. Mickey is forced to fight Catnera instead — until Butch breaks jail and manages to fix the fight in Mickey's favor.

Rhyming narration—an Italian tradition—usually replaced voice balloon dialogue. Gags showed Mickey outwitting a black cat resembling Felix the Cat, another King-licensed property.

Three weeks in, either King Features or Italian Disney representative Guglielmo Emanuel eliminated the faux Felix, then evidently supplied Guastaveglia with Gottfredson photostats for future reference use.[15] Details of Guastaveglia's later Mickey strips—a character pose here, a borrowed gag there—reveal that the artist carefully studied these American dailies, none yet published in Italy at the time. Then he combined their flavor with his own.

The results seem to have been a success. *Il Popolo* gave Mickey a short run similar to the *Gazzetta*—but devoted far more space to him, suggesting a much greater level of satisfaction. Mickey's peers were now Gottfredson-style dogs and pigs; his new enemy was Kat Nipp. And their ensuing high jinks actually did Gottfredson one better. Guastaveglia's later stories began to feature escalating gags and fairly complicated setups: the kind that Gottfredson, in 1931, could not have put across in a four-panel daily strip.

In his peculiarly traditional, rhyming, Rome-centric way, Guglielmo Guastaveglia directly anticipated longer-form American Mickey comics to come.

The 1930 Disney studio Christmas card features an original Mickey design drawn by Floyd Gottfredson — as of this writing, the earliest Gottfredson image scholars know to have been printed in full color.

CHAPTER THREE

Mickey Mouse the Movie Star

UNITED ARTISTS

In 1930 the Columbia Pictures distribution contract had seemed a godsend to the Disney studio, but all too soon it proved a mixed blessing. Columbia did afford Mickey and the Silly Symphonies nationwide and international visibility, but the company seemed to take a casual approach to its short-subject bookings, rather than offering the Disney shorts a favored showcase. When Disney was late for a delivery date, Columbia simply substituted one of Mintz's Krazy Kat shorts instead. In addition, Roy Disney felt the rental returns from Columbia were sometimes suspiciously low.

Meanwhile, Mickey's rapidly growing popularity was elevating Walt's and Roy's status in Hollywood. They were beginning to form a relationship with United Artists (UA), a company that enjoyed considerably more prestige in the industry than Columbia Pictures. Formed in 1919, UA was not a *studio*—that is, a production entity like Paramount or Universal—but strictly a *distributor*, formed to release the films of Charlie Chaplin, Douglas Fairbanks, D. W. Griffith, and Mary Pickford, four of the biggest names in the movies at the time, each of whom maintained his or her own production company. As the events of the 1920s unfolded, the company added other producers to its roster and began to enjoy a fabulous history of its own. By the early 1930s, UA was well established as a boutique company

In a sign of Walt's and Mickey's rising status in Hollywood, they began to enjoy the attention that comes with celebrity. Here Walt sits for a 1933 *Vanity Fair* portrait, flanked by papier-mâché advertising figures of Mickey and Minnie manufactured by the Old King Cole company. Photograph by Edward Steichen.

Variants of this giant close-up, introduced with the start of the United Artists releases, became the standard opening for Mickey cartoons for the rest of his screen life. When first seen in 1932, the sunbeams behind Mickey's head rotated; the pictured version, used from late 1933 to 1935, was one of the first to show nonmoving sunbeams. In between came a version, not seen here, with a different, more thick-lined drawing of Mickey's head.

During the 1920s, illustrator Louis Biedermann launched a unique annual specialty: a calendar, produced for King Features Syndicate, that pictured all the star characters of King Features comic strips in elaborately detailed crowd scenes. Mickey Mouse, having joined the King Features lineup in 1930, promptly took his place (somewhat off-model) in Biedermann's 1931 calendar.

representing the upper strata of the film industry.

Now, in what must have been a heady development for Walt, the UA principals began to express their admiration for his work. As early as 1930, company cofounder Mary Pickford identified Mickey Mouse as her "favorite movie hero."[1] Chaplin selected Disney shorts to accompany both the New York and London openings of his film *City Lights* in 1931. And Mickey was invited to make a cameo appearance with Fairbanks, another UA giant, in his film *Around the World in Eighty Minutes* (1931).

Clearly, an alliance with UA would mark a great step up for the Disney studio. Walt and Roy wasted no time pursuing this connection, and signed a distribution contract with UA in December 1930. But, of course, the new arrangement could not take effect until the terms of the Columbia contract were completed—an obligation that was not satisfied until more than a year later. In the spring of 1932, as the final Columbia Mickey shorts were appearing in theaters, Walt was laying the groundwork for the new series. Without stinting any effort on the Columbia titles, he was nevertheless determined to strive for an even higher level of quality in Mickey's prominent new showcase. His story outline for the first short was headed with the words THE FIRST UNITED ARTISTS MICKEY MOUSE (WHICH IS A VERY GOOD REASON WHY IT MUST BE A GOOD PICTURE).[2]

The UA release did mark a turning point in Disney fortunes. The new association was a mutual source of pride; UA proudly announced its acquisition of the Disney contract with large trade ads. The Disney studio, for its part, prepared a striking new main-title card for the films. A few months into the series, Walt even inserted an in-joke as a nod to his new business associates: in 1932's *The Wayward Canary*, Minnie's home was decorated with signed portraits of Douglas

Fairbanks and Mary Pickford. Other contemporary-Hollywood references would find their way into Mickey's adventures during the UA years, in *The Pet Store* and, especially, *Mickey's Gala Premier*, acknowledging the character's increasing status in the movie community.

The UA series also inaugurated a new convention: each picture opened with a huge, screen-filling, smiling close-up of Mickey himself. In the first few shorts, this headshot was given a dramatic presentation, moving in closer and closer to the camera until it exploded! The explosion was retired after just a few films, and the design of the Mickey close-up reworked several times in succeeding years, but the convention remained in place. Throughout Mickey's movie life, that giant portrait, radiating joy, continued to open each picture with the exhilarating announcement that the audience was about to witness Mickey's latest adventure.

The Wornova Manufacturing Co. produced popular Disney character costumes in the mid-1930s. The studio of photographer William L. Koehne created this pleasing scene of numerous Wornova Mickeys and Minnies teasing a "feline" bad guy.

As Walt had urged, the studio established a new level of production gloss for the UA release. Within a few months the Silly Symphonies began to appear in full Technicolor, a dazzling development that excited audiences and critics and sent shock waves through the animation industry. Mickey, too, would later make the transition to Technicolor, but beginning with *Mickey's Nightmare* in the summer of 1932, he would appear in 31 black-and-white shorts for UA over a period of three years. Perhaps overshadowed by the color Silly Symphonies, these films are sometimes overlooked today.

But animation aficionados recognize this period as the beginning of Mickey's true golden age. Indeed, these 31 black-and-white films constitute a remarkable body of work in their own right, a high point in the art of the animated short. If Mickey had been seen for the previous three years as a scrappy underdog, a delightful newcomer on the horizon, he now cemented his position as the star of the cartoon universe—with a growing sense of the gravitas that stardom might bring. The rough edges of his earliest films had radiated a charm of their own, but by now those rough edges had been polished away, replaced by a fresh new level of production value. The new Mickey films sparkled with handsome layouts and backgrounds, smoother and more sophisticated camerawork, more carefully developed stories and gags. Disney soundtracks jettisoned the inferior Powers Cinephone sound process, once the studio satisfied its commitment to *that* contract late in 1932, and replaced it with the state-of-the-art RCA system. Pictorially, the new films boasted a refined standard of inking and painting,

Mickey's golden age saw him feted in popular song around the world (see pages 218–223). English comics artist Wilfred Haughton drew and signed the cover art on this British song sheet for Pola and Vienna's "The Wedding of Mister Mickey Mouse."

Mickey's popularity in other lands is reflected on the covers of magazines: the Belgian *Piccolo* and Spanish-language *Cinelandia*.

with an enhanced range of gray tones that simulated subtle lighting effects.

Most importantly, Mickey himself arguably looked better than ever. A scant two years had elapsed since Ub Iwerks departed the studio in 1930, but in that two years the studio had developed a whole team of Mickey specialists, artists with a special affinity for the character. Some of these artists would remain with the studio for the long term and would help to define Mickey's character on the screen: Les Clark, Johnny Cannon, Gilles "Frenchy" de Trémaudan, Marvin Woodward. When Mickey or Minnie broke into a dance, as they still did on frequent occasions, Dick Lundy, the studio's resident dance specialist, could be counted on to capture their rhythmic moves. One artist, Fred Moore, started at the studio as a raw beginner in 1930, but soon showed an instinctive gift for animation. His talent flowered suddenly and noticeably in 1933, the enormous natural appeal of his drawings perfectly suited to Mickey. In time, Moore would establish himself as perhaps the leading Mickey Mouse animator of them all.

Along with his appearance, Mickey's personality also crystallized definitively during the UA years. On one hand he was still the rugged little adventurer, tackling perilous exploits in *The Klondike Kid* and *Shanghaied*—and, perhaps most notably, *The Mail Pilot*, which was coordinated with a contemporaneous serial of the same name in the *Mickey Mouse* comic strip. On the other hand, Mickey's shy, friendly, romantic side also came fully into focus during these years in films like *Puppy Love*, which made increasing demands on his acting abilities (and those of his animators). Other memorable entries, *Giantland* and *Gulliver Mickey*, stretched the boundaries of graphic invention in animation, and

CINELANDIA
15 ¢ O A
Noviembre, 1932
En esta edición: La biografía de MICKEY MOUSE
PUBLICADA EN HOLLYWOOD

brought Mickey into a new world of imaginative fantasy. And from time to time, Mickey continued to appear in burlesques of popular movie genres, now more witty and elaborate than ever: horror films in *The Mad Doctor*, Westerns in *Two-Gun Mickey*.

It's a purely subjective judgment, but one might go so far as to declare that 1933 was, in some ways, the peak year of Mickey's entire screen career. It was the year in which he definitively broke free of the limitations of his earliest films and reached for the stars, tackling an unprecedented range of stories, genres, and acting challenges. Not yet hampered by expectations of acceptable behavior, his popularity not yet challenged by a rising generation of supporting characters, Mickey Mouse appeared in a nearly unbroken string of classics in 1933—still in his ascendancy, his preeminence unquestioned in the world of cartoons. Nothing, it seemed, was beyond his reach.

Succeeding years would, of course, add facets of their own to the star's legend. And, by any standard, his 31 black-and-white shorts for UA represent an indelible landmark in animation history.

Mickey generally did not appear in the Silly Symphonies, but the UA title cards for the series capitalized on his popularity anyway. This rare first-release title card for *Bugs in Love* was long believed lost; for years, home video releases featured a modern re-creation.

The Einson-Freeman Co. manufactured a famous Mickey and Minnie paper mask design in 1933. The Mickey Mouse Clubs famously used the masks in promotion; here, hundreds of moviegoers wear them for a posed shot.

THE UNITED ARTISTS BLACK-AND-WHITE SHORTS (1932-1935)

Beginning with the United Artists contract, release dates for Mickey's films are far more reliable than those in preceding years. The actual opening dates of the cartoons sometimes varied widely from the formal releases, but the dates listed below, and throughout the rest of this book, are the official release dates announced by the distributors.

Joseph M. Schenck
presents
WALT DISNEY'S
MICKEY
MOUSE
MICKEY'S
NIGHTMARE
UNITED ARTISTS PICTURE

The original poster for Mickey's first release under the UA banner.

In a story sketch for the opening sequence in *Mickey's Nightmare*, the nightmare begins as a sweet dream.

MICKEY'S NIGHTMARE
(August 13, 1932)

Mickey's first UA release is a remake of *Poor Papa*, the first Oswald the Lucky Rabbit cartoon — which had initially been rejected by its distributor! Mickey, like Oswald, is faced with the demands of fatherhood when his home is overrun by dozens of babies. The scenes of the babies' wholesale destruction play almost like a continuation of *Mickey's Orphans*, with tiny mice in place of the tiny kittens. But *Mickey's Nightmare* is faithful to Walt's request for a higher standard of quality, with beautiful character animation and atmospheric candlelight and shadow effects in the opening scenes. And it concludes with a happy ending: it was all a dream.

WALT DISNEY'S
MICKEY MOUSE
in
"TRADER MICKEY"
UNITED ARTISTS PICTURE

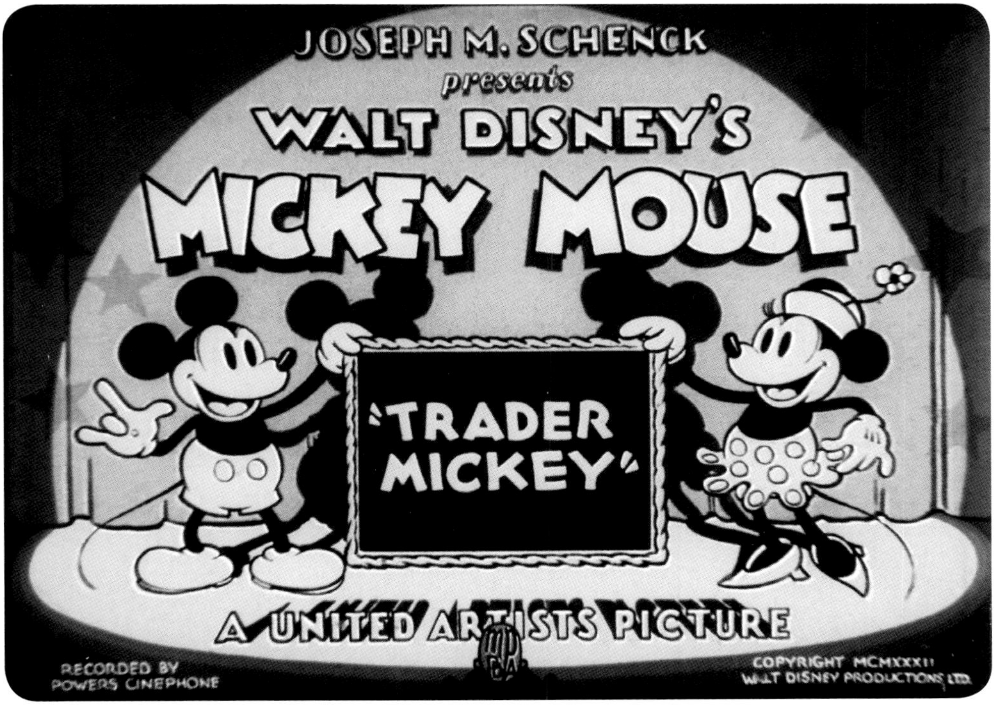

The poster for *Trader Mickey* suggests a parody of a scene in MGM's *Trader Horn*. This scene did not actually appear in the cartoon.

A new distributor, a new main title card. The association between Mickey and United Artists, a source of mutual pride, is celebrated in this handsome title design. Note that the credited sound-recording process is still Powers Cinephone, an association that will be upgraded before the end of 1932.

TRADER MICKEY
(August 20, 1932)

As the title suggests, this cartoon is a spoof of *Trader Horn* (dir. W. S. Van Dyke), MGM's hit feature of the previous year, depicting an American trader's adventures in Africa. Here it's Mickey and Pluto who float down an African river on a raft, menaced by hippos and crocodiles. Captured by cannibals, our heroes are momentarily dismayed; but when the natives unload Mickey's cargo of musical instruments, he turns the occasion into another musical party. The cannibal king—voiced with Pinto Colvig's goofy guffaw, even as the studio prepared a return appearance by Dippy Dawg—is particularly taken with the power of music, and by film's end he and Mickey have become pals.

The poster for *Touchdown Mickey* features a dramatic moment of action. Art by Tom Wood.

Another musical celebration: Mickey and Minnie strike a peppy pose in the poster for *The Whoopee Party*.

THE WHOOPEE PARTY
(September 17, 1932)

With its high energy and irresistible musical gags, *The Whoopee Party* is the apotheosis of Mickey's musical shorts, the one invariably singled out for comment.[3] Guests at this party include Dippy Dawg and Clarabelle Cow, played off each other in a prank war. Mickey's dance with the large lady pig, animated by Norm Ferguson for *The Shindig*, reappears here; in the interim she had been christened Patricia Pig (sometimes Pigg) in comics and merchandise. Like *Pioneer Days*, this delightful short has circulated in two different versions. This time the differences are relatively slight and include alternative camera setups and other discrepancies.

TOUCHDOWN MICKEY
(October 15, 1932)

Mickey takes to the gridiron in a cartoon released to theaters in time for the 1932 football season. Here "Mickey's Manglers" are pitted against the "Alley Cats," a gang of hulking, Pete-like cats who try to dominate the field through sheer brawn. Virtually all of Mickey's "stock company" is on hand in this picture. Minnie, Clarabelle, and Horace cheer Mickey on from the stands (as do hot dogs on a vendor's grill); Pluto is the water boy; lesser-known regulars—Wienie the dachshund, huge Percy Pig—turn up as members of Mickey's team. Dippy Dawg returns as a radio announcer, a role that requires him to supplement his manic giggle with a modicum of dialogue.

JOSEPH M. SCHENCK
presents
WALT DISNEY'S
MICKEY MOUSE
IN
"The WHOOPEE PARTY"
UNITED ARTISTS PICTURE

The original poster for *The Wayward Canary*. Four years after Mickey's debut, music was still a key ingredient in his films and remained a feature of advertising art. This poster depicts a scene in the film in which Mickey and Minnie perform an original Bert Lewis composition titled "Disney One-Step."

The hero and heroine about to be menaced by "Terrible Pierre" in the poster for *The Klondike Kid*.

THE WAYWARD CANARY
(November 12, 1932)

Mickey surprises Minnie with the gift of a pet canary—a gift that seems like a good idea, at first. *The Wayward Canary* qualifies as a partial remake of *Mickey Steps Out*: a pleasant musical interlude with the singing canary, followed by a slapstick chase. This canary is a mother with a brood of youngsters, and as they fly through the house, destruction follows. The fledglings overturn an ink bottle and start to splatter ink on everything in sight, including signed portraits of Douglas Fairbanks and Mary Pickford, two of the principals behind United Artists.

THE KLONDIKE KID
(November 12, 1932)

Another adventure story, with Mickey in the far North playing piano in a saloon. We never see him prospecting for gold, but he rescues Minnie twice—first from a snowstorm, then from capture by Peg Leg Pete. (Cast as a French-Canadian villain in this picture, Pete adopts a pseudo-French accent and is known as "Terrible Pierre.") The atmospheric opening scenes benefit from recycled effects animation from earlier films. Animators include a newcomer named Art Babbitt, here making his Disney debut with extended scenes during the chase.

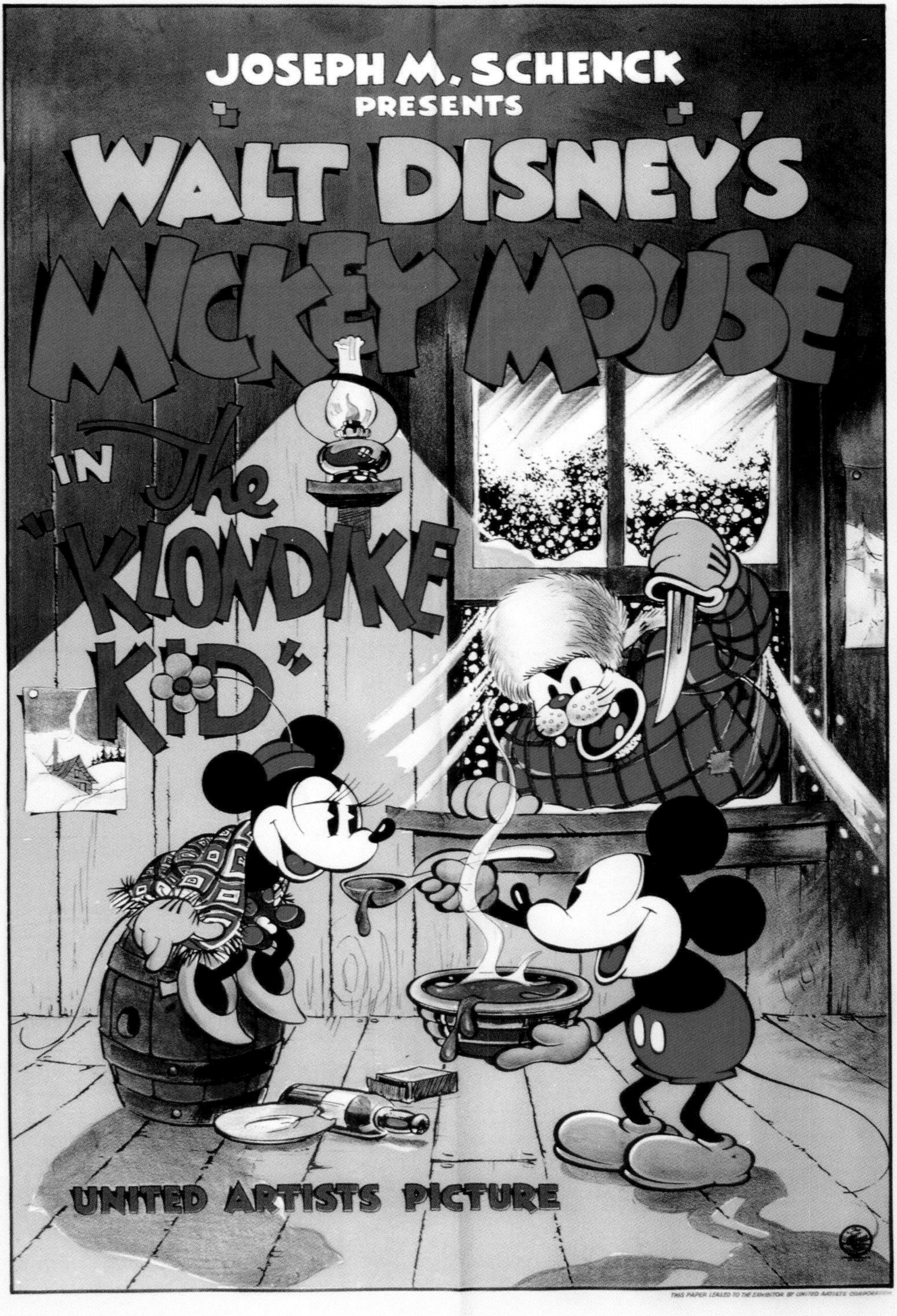
JOSEPH M. SCHENCK
PRESENTS
WALT DISNEY'S
MICKEY MOUSE
IN The
"KLONDIKE
KID"
UNITED ARTISTS PICTURE
THIS PAPER LEASED TO THE EXHIBITOR BY UNITED ARTISTS CORPORATION

Joseph M. Schenck
presents
WALT DISNEY'S
MICKEY MOUSE
in
"MICKEY'S GOOD DEED"
UNITED ARTISTS PICTURE
THIS PAPER LEASED TO THE EXHIBITOR BY UNITED ARTISTS CORPORATION

A poster design suggesting the holiday atmosphere of *Mickey's Good Deed*. The Yuletide flavor extended into the film's opening titles, during which sleigh bells underscore the "Minnie's Yoo Hoo" theme song.

A background painting depicting the restaurant where Mickey and Pluto can't afford to eat. (Pluto licks the ham through the window anyway.) The Disney artists were continuing to effect subtle refinements to the visuals in their films; note the charming effect of light from the window on the snow outside.

MICKEY'S GOOD DEED
(December 17, 1932)

This second holiday-themed short is a film of bitter-sweet charm and a strikingly Depression-oriented story. Mickey's "good deed," as a poor street musician, is to sell his pal Pluto as a Christmas gift for a rich man's son, and use the money to play Santa to a family of poor youngsters. The ending, in which he is reunited with Pluto after all, packs a surprising emotional punch. This film and another holiday cartoon, *Santa's Workshop*, marked the Disney studio's first use of the superior RCA Photophone recording system for their soundtracks. With their multiyear contract having drawn to a close, Walt could finally put Pat Powers's Cinephone—and all of Powers's attendant mischief—behind him.

A background painting for *Building a Building*. In the finished scene this structure is filled with busy workers who instantly abandon their posts at the sound of the lunch whistle.

The poster for the film. *Building a Building* was nominated for an Academy Award for the 1932–33 season but lost to *Three Little Pigs*.

BUILDING A BUILDING

(January 7, 1933)

Another Disney luminary, Dave Hand, steps into the director's role for the first time with this close remake of the 1928 Oswald short *The Sky Scrapper*. *Building a Building* reprises numerous elements of the Oswald short: slapstick gags on a construction site, the arrival of the hero's girlfriend selling box lunches, and a battle with the burly foreman. With the addition of sound, it also offers Minnie's song, "Who'll Buy a Box Lunch?"—a charming original tune by Frank Churchill. This short was started in summer 1932, then temporarily suspended while the animators worked to finish *Mickey's Good Deed* in time for Christmas. *Building a Building* was then completed and released early in 1933.

Joseph M. Schenck
presents
WALT DISNEY'S
MICKEY MOUSE
in
"BUILDING
a BUILDING"
MICKEY MOUSE
UNITED ARTISTS PICTURE
THIS PAPER LEASED TO THE EXHIBITOR BY UNITED ARTISTS CORPORATION

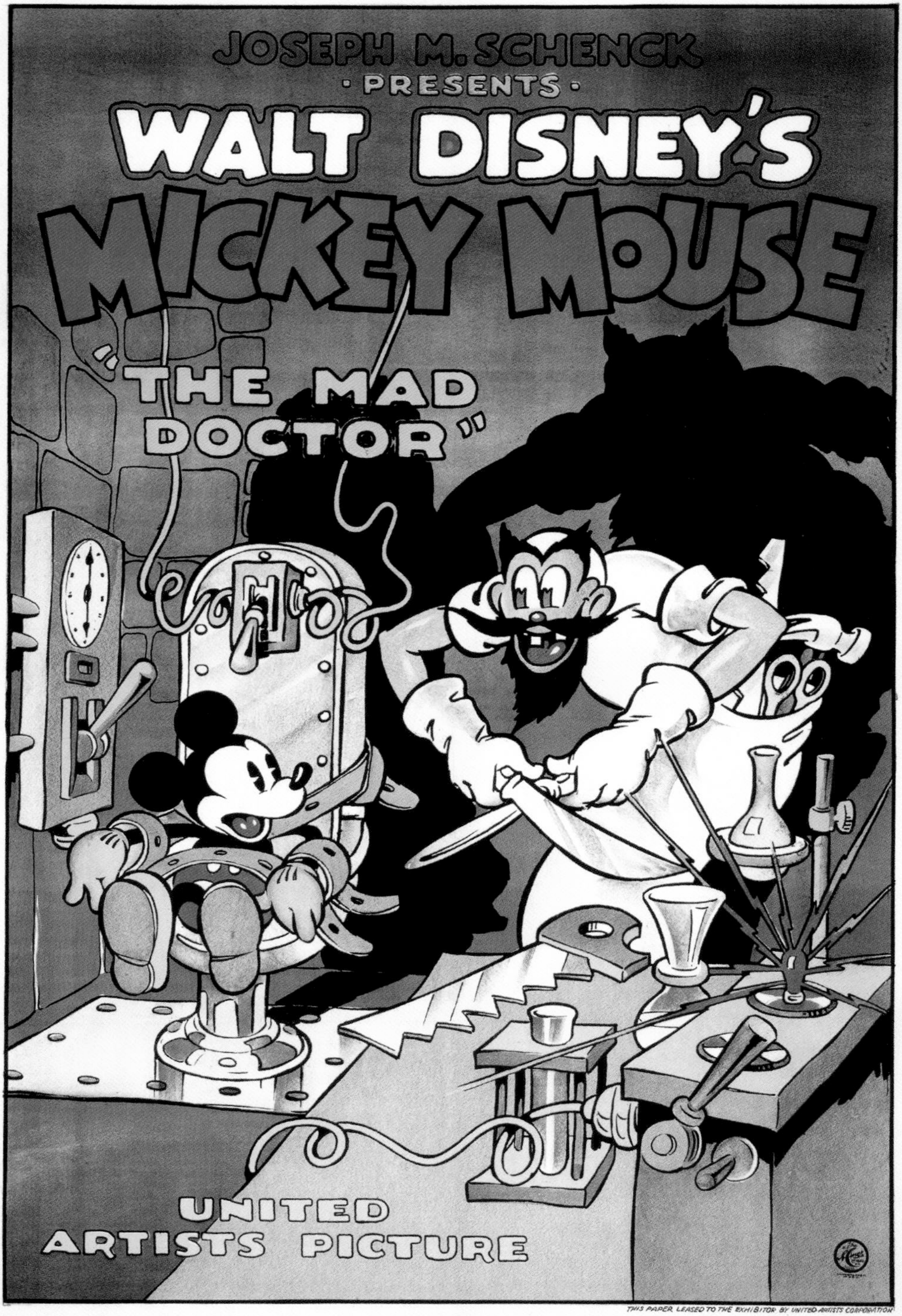
JOSEPH M. SCHENCK
· PRESENTS ·
WALT DISNEY'S
MICKEY MOUSE
"THE MAD DOCTOR"
UNITED
ARTISTS PICTURE
THIS PAPER LEASED TO THE EXHIBITOR BY UNITED ARTISTS CORPORATION

Tom Wood's creepy poster art for *The Mad Doctor*. Like the cartoon itself, the poster lampoons such contemporary horror films as *Doctor X* (1932; dir. Michael Curtiz) but packs some genuine shudders of its own.

The poster for *Mickey's Pal Pluto*. Pluto is perplexed as the intruders take over his territory. Not seen here are Pluto's good and evil selves who counsel him in the course of the film.

THE MAD DOCTOR
(January 21, 1933)

Surpassing earlier horror-film spoofs, *The Mad Doctor* sets a new standard for fabulously horrific visuals. On a dark and stormy night, Mickey dreams that a mysterious figure kidnaps Pluto and takes him to a forbidding castle, Mickey in pursuit — running a gauntlet of menacing shadows, bats, and malevolent living skeletons. The film's gruesome imagery owes much to its settings, painted by Mique Nelson.[4] For the Silly Symphony *Egyptian Melodies*, Dave Hand had animated an impressive scene in which the camera seemed to move down a hallway and turn a corner; here that scene makes a partial reappearance.

MICKEY'S PAL PLUTO
(February 18, 1933)

Like *Mickey's Good Deed*, this short is both entertaining and quietly touching. Pluto helps Mickey and Minnie rescue an abandoned litter of kittens, then watches as the kittens take over his bed, his food dish, and Mickey's and Minnie's affections. He's counseled by the good and evil sides of his nature, pictured as a little Pluto with wings and a halo, and another with horns and a pitchfork. Burt Gillett is not one of the more celebrated Disney directors today, but it's worth noting that his handling of this story — with Pluto at first misunderstood and unfairly punished, but ultimately vindicated — is doubly effective through subtle understatement.

A scene from *Mickey's Mellerdrammer*: Minnie makes up her face for her role in the play. This scene, animated by Les Clark, was one of the many that were altered in the film's December 1932–February 1933 makeover; here the artists added an overlay of the dressing-room door, and started the scene with a camera move toward the door and into the interior.

Mickey as a wandering minstrel and Minnie as a princess in distress in the poster for *Ye Olden Days*. Disney's earlier Oswald cartoon, *Oh, What a Knight* (1928), had likewise cast Oswald as a traveling minstrel; here, the addition of sound allowed the audience to hear Mickey's song in the opening scene.

MICKEY'S MELLERDRAMMER
(March 18, 1933)

Mickey and his friends mount a stage production of a rip-roaring melodrama, attended by an enthusiastic audience. The actors are plagued by a series of slapstick mishaps, and the audience becomes a little *too* enthusiastic, finally bringing down the house in a chaotic finish. (One member of the audience, a dignified-looking hen in a picture hat, seems to be an early version of the character we'll come to know as Clara Cluck.) The film was near completion in December 1932 when the decision was made to revise it in its entirety, cutting some scenes, adding new ones, and reworking practically every existing scene with new animation, camera moves, or timing. The extra effort was justified; it resulted in an unusually strong, well-crafted cartoon.

YE OLDEN DAYS
(April 8, 1933)

A loose remake of two earlier Disney silents, this period story presents Mickey as a minstrel in medieval times who rescues Minnie from an arranged marriage. Characteristically, Walt seizes the opportunity to "plus" the earlier stories with fresh sight gags, as well as another original song and some droll dialogue. Mickey's rival, whom he battles in the climactic duel, is not some hulking bruiser but the Goof, here identified onscreen as "Dippy Dawg" for the only time in his career. Later in 1933 a scene from this picture was borrowed as an insert in the Fox feature *My Lips Betray* (1933; dir. John G. Blystone, Henry King).[5]

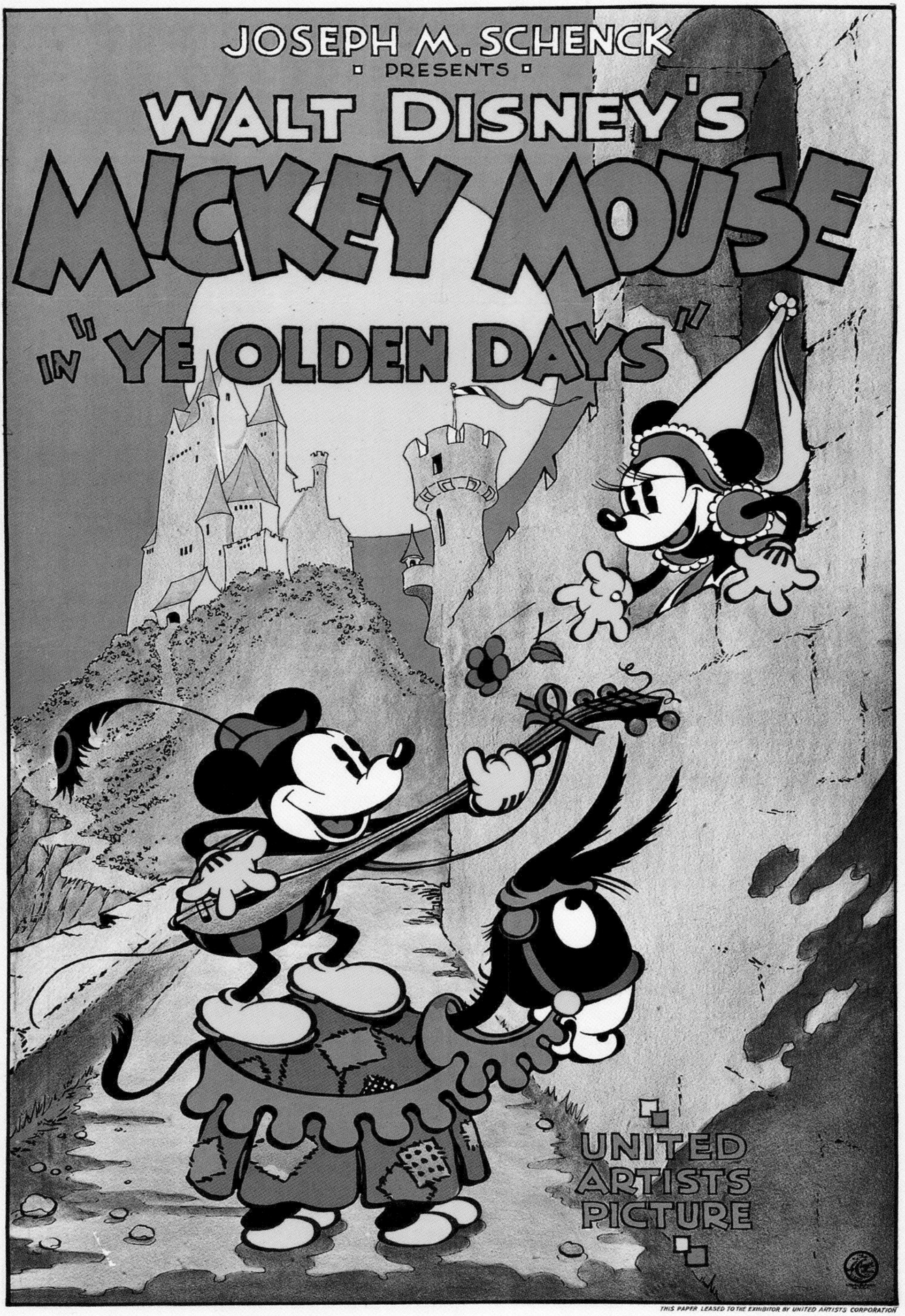
JOSEPH M. SCHENCK
PRESENTS
WALT DISNEY'S
MICKEY MOUSE
IN "YE OLDEN DAYS"
UNITED
ARTISTS
PICTURE
THIS PAPER LEASED TO THE EXHIBITOR BY UNITED ARTISTS CORPORATION

Mickey menaced by Pete in poster art for *The Mail Pilot*. Note the striking design of Pete's "bat plane." Four years later, in the *Mickey Mouse* comic strip, Pete turned up with a similarly wicked-looking plane in the "Island in the Sky" continuity (see Chapter 5).

Tom Wood's poster art for *Mickey's Mechanical Man*. No such peaceful moment actually occurs onscreen in the climactic boxing match.

Following Mickey is honored with a glamorous Hollywood premiere at Grauman's Chinese Theatre in the opening sequence of *Mickey's Gala Premier*.

THE MAIL PILOT
(May 13, 1933)

This is possibly the archetype of all Mickey's adventure stories. Mickey flies the mail to a distant destination, against the odds—the odds including Pete, the mail bandit, who attacks Mickey along the way. Mickey not only brings the mail through safely but, after an adventure balancing exciting action and clever sight gags, captures Pete and turns him over to the authorities. Two home-video releases of this cartoon have featured a special bonus for animation fans: a surviving pencil test of master animator Les Clark's scenes (assisted by junior artists Archie Robin and Joe D'Igalo).

MICKEY'S MECHANICAL MAN
(June 17, 1933)

Mickey builds a mechanical man and enters him in a boxing match against "the Kongo Killer," a trained boxing gorilla—in essence, a repeat performance by *The Gorilla Mystery*'s eponymous bad guy. This robot has a peculiar trait: the sound of Minnie's auto horn drives him berserk, throwing punches at any image of the Kongo Killer until he destroys himself and everything around him. Notable touches in this short include Mickey's unique method of training the robot: coaching him from the piano with a little training song composed by Leigh Harline—remembered today as one of the top Disney composers, here making his Mickey Mouse debut.

JOSEPH M. SCHENCK
PRESENTS
WALT DISNEY'S
MICKEY MOUSE
IN "MICKEY'S MECHANICAL MAN"
UNITED
ARTISTS PICTURE

GRAUMA
MICKEY

CHINE

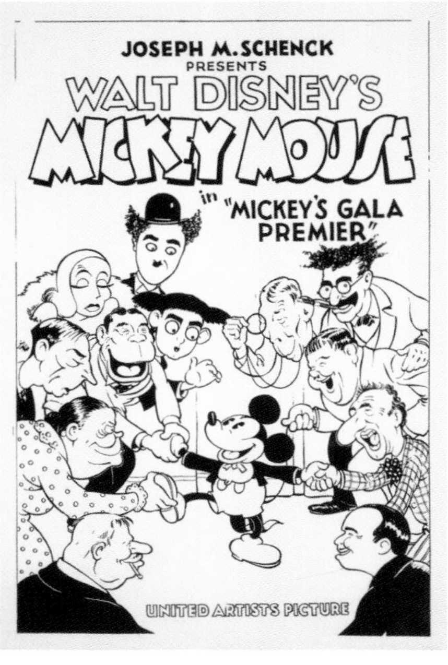

In *Mickey's Gala Premier*, Mickey the movie fan is actually bowled over by Garbo's attentions — and vastly disappointed when Pluto awakens him and he learns it was all a dream.

The highlight of *Mickey's Gala Premier* was a succession of brilliant movie-star caricatures, designed by Joe Grant, who had been brought to the studio specifically for this film. Grant also created special publicity drawings to promote the picture, as can be seen in the poster art.

Mickey and Minnie perform the number from *Puppy Love* as a duet. For sharp-eyed members of the audience, the song sheet on the music rack gives Frank Churchill a rare screen credit.

MICKEY'S GALA PREMIER
(July 1, 1933)

The cream of Hollywood society, in the form of movie-star caricatures, turns out to see the fabulous premiere of Mickey's latest cartoon in this cult favorite. This was the picture that brought Joe Grant to the Disney studio; his drawings of movie stars in the *Los Angeles Record* had caught Walt's eye, and Walt asked him to design celebrity caricatures for *Mickey's Gala Premier*.[6] The cartoon-within-the-film, "Galloping Romance," is a musicale-cum-Western, a sort of pastiche of *The Birthday Party* and *The Cactus Kid*. Its titles are musically underscored with "Minnie's Yoo Hoo," the series' stock theme for the previous four years, but *Mickey's Gala Premier* itself opens with original main-title music. By the end of 1933, every new Mickey Mouse short will do the same.

PUPPY LOVE
(September 2, 1933)

Love is in the air as Mickey and Pluto call on Minnie and her pet Pekingese, Fifi. (This is Fifi's screen debut, although, as "Flapper," she had made one previous appearance in the comics.) Mickey and Minnie, and simultaneously the two dogs, enjoy a romantic interval, fall out over a misunderstanding and quarrel, then reunite for a happy ending. This charming short may have had a special significance for Walt, for the emotional interactions of its characters made fresh demands on the animators—and they rose to the challenge. In particular, this film marked a turning point for Fred Moore, establishing him as one of the very top tier of Mouse artists.

THE STEEPLECHASE
(September 30, 1933)

This slapstick romp casts Mickey as a jockey, hired to ride Thunderbolt, a prize horse. Thunderbolt finds a jug of gin hidden in his stall, gulps it down, and soon is in no condition to race. Resourceful as ever, Mickey stuffs two stablehands into a horse costume and rides the preposterously ungainly "horse" through a gauntlet of hurdles, water, and a hornets' nest to an unlikely victory. Under the working title of "Shuffling Hoofs" [*sic*], *The Steeplechase* began development as a musical, but there are no songs in the finished film. The abundance of crowd scenes and fast action is spread over a large contingent of animators, much of the chase being assigned to Ben Sharpsteen's crew of junior artists.

THE PET STORE
(October 28, 1933)

Mickey takes a job as an assistant in a pet store. Minnie drops in to see him, prompting a succession of gags involving animals and props. One of the "pets" is "Beppo, the Movie Monk" — the gorilla we've seen in earlier cartoons, here cast as a movie fan. Beppo is given to perusing fan magazines and mimicking the pictures, and his discovery of *King Kong* (1933; dir. Merian C. Cooper, Ernest B. Schoedsack) inspires him to kidnap Minnie and go on a rampage in the store. *The Pet Store* was the first short to offer an onscreen hint of the impending association between Disney and RKO Radio, the studio that had produced *Kong*.

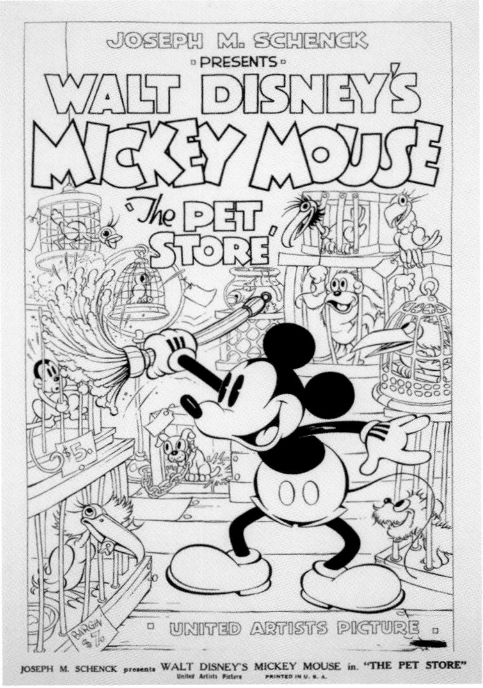

Mickey astride his less-than-convincing "horse" in publicity art for *The Steeplechase*. This cartoon had an indirect influence on the *Mickey Mouse* comic strip in more ways than one; it inspired the creation of another horse character, Tanglefoot, who appeared in more than one horse-racing story.

Tom Wood's poster art for *The Pet Store* depicts Mickey in a moment of calm before the wild climactic sequence.

The poster art for *Giantland* suggests a far friendlier relationship between Mickey and the giant than the one we actually see onscreen.

GIANTLAND
(November 25, 1933)

As the Mickey Mouse cartoons embraced an increasingly ambitious scope, Mickey began to make occasional appearances in extravagant fantasy stories. *Giantland* was the most extravagant yet: a loose retelling of "Jack and the Beanstalk" with Mickey in the role of Jack. Mickey tells the story to the mischievous baby mice from *Mickey's Nightmare*, here recast as slightly older neighborhood kids. Among *Giantland*'s animation challenges is the giant himself, fantastic and cartoony but beginning to embody some convincing human traits, and animated principally by Dick Huemer and Ham Luske. The Mickey specialists, too — Les Clark, Johnny Cannon, Fred Moore, and Gilles "Frenchy" de Trémaudan — were strategically deployed in this picture.

JOSEPH M. SCHENCK
Presents
WALT DISNEY'S
MICKEY MOUSE
in
'SHANGHAIED'
UNITED ARTISTS PICTURE

SHANGHAIED

(January 13, 1934)

Mickey and Minnie are not so much "shanghaied" (forcibly recruited) as kidnapped and held prisoner aboard Peg Leg Pete's ship in this adventure story. By reel's end, of course, Mickey has singlehandedly defeated Pete and his entire crew in a series of amusing sight gags. The picture ends with Mickey and Minnie in control of the ship, a subdued Pete and his crew in tow. In an unusual piece of casting, Norm Ferguson animated the entire sequence in Pete's cabin, up to and including part of the duel—working with two assistants, but also, himself, assisting two recently promoted animators with *their* scenes.

CAMPING OUT

(February 17, 1934)

Based on a story outline that ultimately furnished enough material for two cartoons *and* a comics continuity, the finished version of *Camping Out* pictures Mickey, Minnie, Clarabelle, and Horace enjoying a camping trip until they run afoul of an army of mosquitoes. This film would prove to be one of Horace Horsecollar's last extended performances. The musical score is jointly credited to Frank Churchill and Bert Lewis. Churchill's infectiously cheerful instrumental tune, "Oh, Boy, Ain't Nature Grand," was composed even before story development began; the balance of the score is Lewis's work.

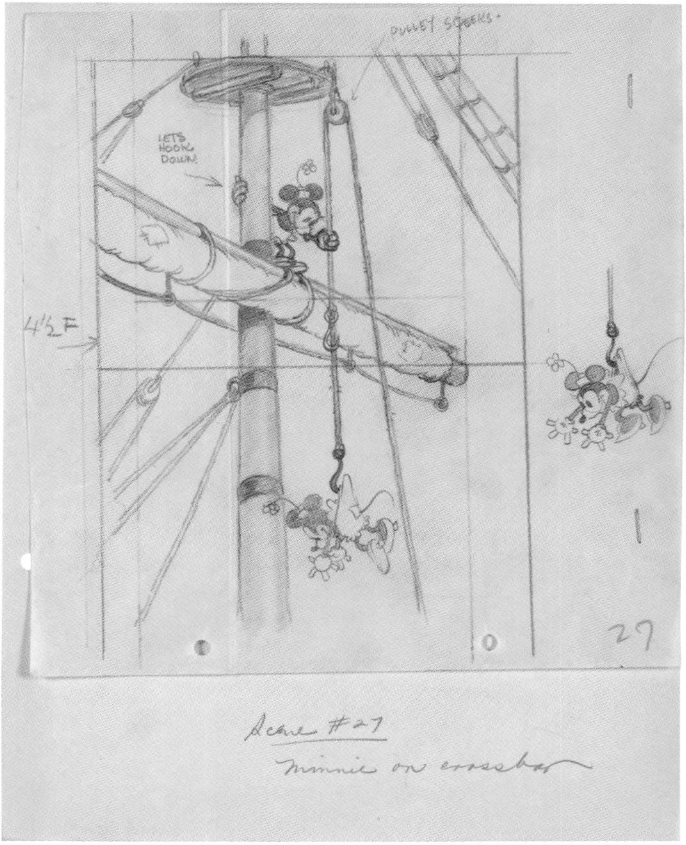

The poster art for *Shanghaied* transplants the action from the sequence in Pete's cabin to the main deck of the ship.

A story sketch for the scene in which Mickey hoists Minnie up to the yardarm for safety. The sketches suggest Minnie's successive poses in the course of the scene and indicate the staging of the scene as the camera "travels" up in a vertical pan.

The introductory sequence in *Camping Out*: Clarabelle prepares a cake while Mickey, Minnie, and Horace perform a catchy Frank Churchill melody. This opening scene, and much of the other action in the film, was animated by the under-appreciated Ed Love, a reliable Disney animator throughout most of the 1930s.

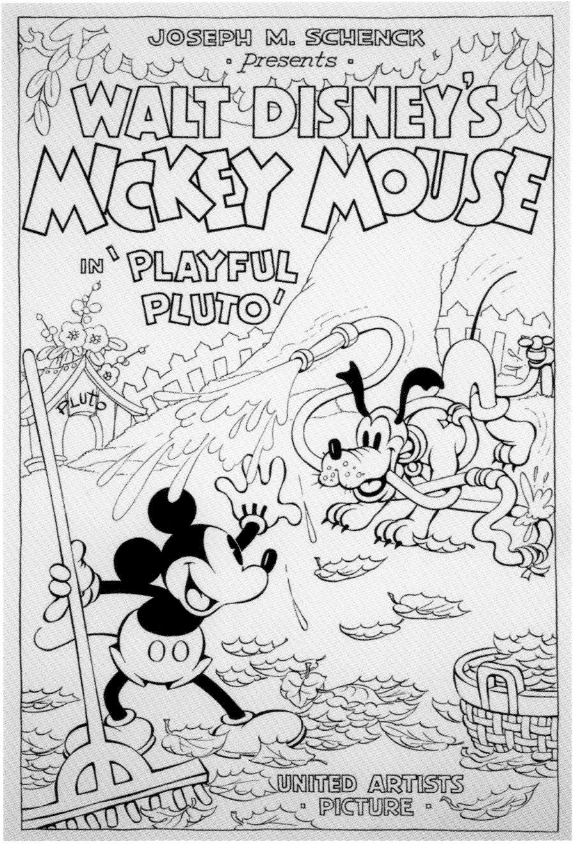

Tom Wood's poster art for *Playful Pluto* depicts the film's opening sequence: Mickey endeavors to rake leaves while Pluto romps with the garden hose.

Mickey easily pulls loose from the Lilliputians' bonds in the film and in this *Gulliver Mickey* poster art. Jack Kinney, who animated on this cartoon, recalled that the differences in scale were the animator's responsibility: "At that time we had no way of shooting anything except a five field . . . In those days, if they were little tiny characters, we had to *draw* them little tiny. If they were large we had to make extremely large faces, heads, bodies."[1]

PLAYFUL PLUTO
(March 3, 1934)

Mickey attempts to clean up his yard, with Pluto's less-than-helpful help. This is one of the legendary Disney cartoons, its place in history assured by the landmark Flypaper Sequence: Pluto accidentally gets a sheet of flypaper stuck to his nose, then goes through an extended struggle, brilliantly animated by Norm Ferguson, to get himself unstuck. So pervasive is the fame of this sequence that it has obscured other good sequences in the same cartoon, including Mickey's attempt to rake leaves in the face of a little whirlwind that blows them away — a sequence that is almost always forgotten today, but was reused as the basis of *The Little Whirlwind* seven years later.

GULLIVER MICKEY
(May 19, 1934)

Mickey tells the little mice another fantastic tale of his adventures, this time based on *Gulliver's Travels*. When he lands in Lilliput, the tiny natives are alarmed at his intrusion and launch a military attack. Mickey, unharmed by their assault, maintains his friendly, sympathetic attitude toward them, and even takes on an aggressive giant spider that threatens the little community. *Giantland* had posed one kind of graphic challenge; *Gulliver Mickey* reverses the scale, with Mickey as the "giant" in a world of miniature buildings, animals, and people.

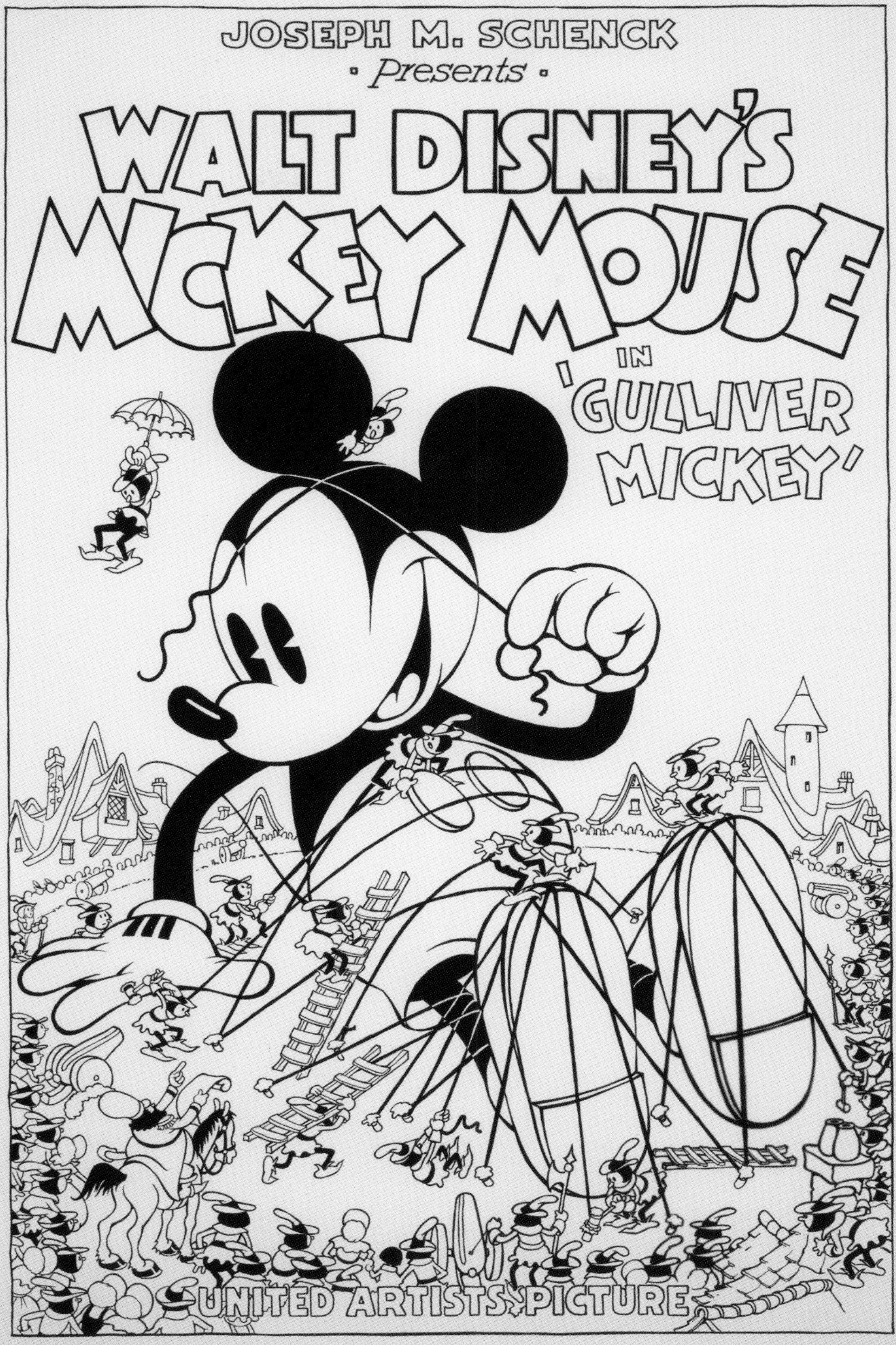

JOSEPH M. SCHENCK
Presents
WALT DISNEY'S
MICKEY MOUSE
IN
'GULLIVER MICKEY'
UNITED ARTISTS PICTURE

Mickey, Minnie, and the nephews in a relatively peaceful moment in poster art for *Mickey's Steam-Roller*.

The opening scene in *Orphans' Benefit* shows the orphans marched into the theater in regimented order — the first and last time we will see them behaving themselves.

IMAGED BY HERITAGE AUCTIONS, HA.COM

MICKEY'S STEAM-ROLLER
(June 16, 1934)

Mickey the workingman is seen driving a steamroller. Nursemaid Minnie brings Morty and Ferdie to watch him at work, and Mickey gives his nephews a ride, towing their baby buggy behind the "choo-choo." But then he turns his attention to romancing Minnie, distracted just long enough for the nephews to commandeer the steamroller for a joyride. Before he can stop them, the engine runs wild and causes wholesale destruction. After it demolishes a hotel, the cartoon originally ended with Mickey and Minnie frantically searching the wreckage, finding the nephews, and scolding them before forgiving them. This dramatic finish was cut during production, replaced with the shorter, simpler ending we see in the finished film.

ORPHANS' BENEFIT
(August 11, 1934)

This musical "performance" short finds Mickey staging a free show for the little mice, here settling into a long-term group role as mischievous orphans. The Goof, who had merely been glimpsed as an extra in *Mickey's Revue*, is by now a full-fledged member of the troupe, and the film also introduces Clara Cluck, "the Barnyard Nightingale"—considerably developed from the dignified matron glimpsed in *Mickey's Mellerdrammer*. Most significantly, the show also features an appearance by Donald Duck, who had made his official debut earlier in the year in *The Wise Little Hen*. Quickly recognizing that Donald's weakness is his temper, the orphans goad him into the first of his classic tantrums, animated by Dick Lundy.

MICKEY PLAYS PAPA
(September 29, 1934)

A mysterious figure leaves a baby in a basket on Mickey's doorstep in the dead of night, thrusting him into unexpected parenthood. This isn't the first time this has happened to Mickey, but here the emphasis is, first, on spooky atmospherics as Mickey and Pluto hear frightening sounds in the night; and, second, on Mickey's earnest efforts to accommodate the child. This is material that calls for animation of depth and subtlety, and Marvin Woodward, Johnny Cannon, and Fred Moore deliver. So does Bob Wickersham, an animation veteran who had recently joined the Disney staff.

THE DOGNAPPER
(November 17, 1934)

Peg Leg Pete kidnaps Minnie's pet dog Fifi (last seen in *Puppy Love*) and officers Mickey Mouse and Donald Duck set out to bring him to justice. The chase leads to Pete's hideout in an abandoned sawmill, where he fights a slapstick battle with Mickey and Donald. Michael Barrier has pointed out that Dick Lundy, who had animated the Duck's memorable tantrum in *Orphans' Benefit*, was specially tapped to contribute a single scene to this picture.[7] But Donald shows a new facet of his personality in *The Dognapper*—not an idle loafer, not an irritable hothead, but simply an inept, bungling sidekick who constantly gets in Mickey's way as he tries to get the best of Pete.

A story sketch for the opening sequence of *Mickey Plays Papa*. The finished scene closely follows the staging and atmospherics suggested here, with only negligible differences: the two extra books are missing, and Mickey wears a nightshirt with an open collar.

Pete, playing the title role in *The Dognapper*, takes Fifi to his hideout in an abandoned sawmill in this cel setup. This scene was animated by Clyde "Gerry" Geronimi, later a prominent Disney director.

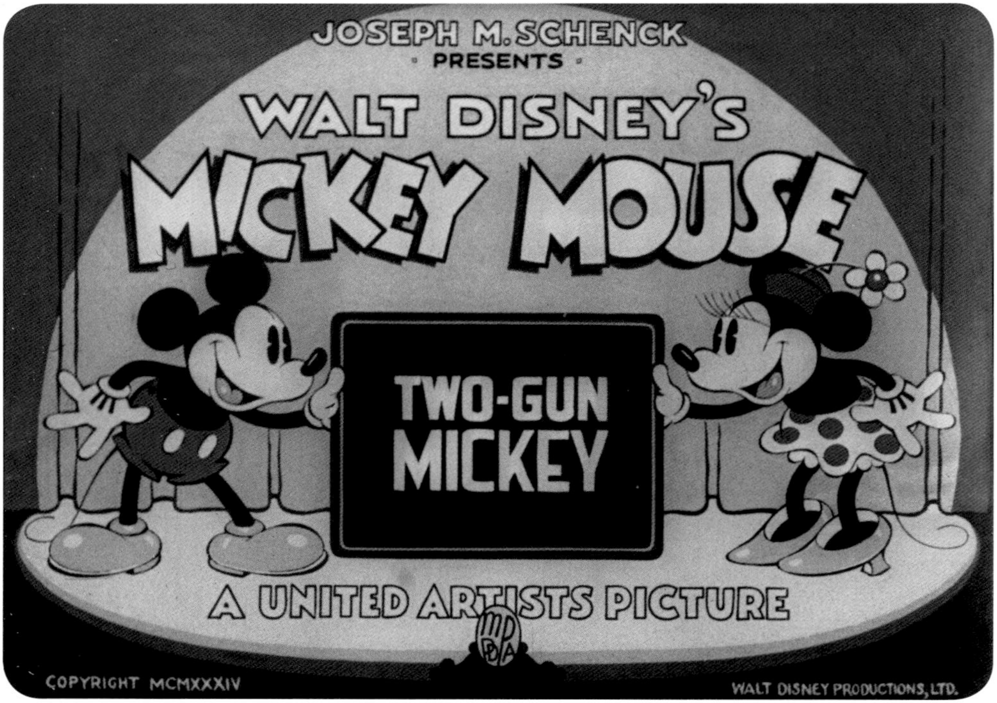

TWO-GUN MICKEY
(December 15, 1934)

Mickey stars in another action adventure, and a Western to boot. This picture marks another directorial debut: Ben Sharpsteen, after years as a supervising animator, here becomes a full-fledged director. His "cast" includes Eric Larson, who will go on to become one of Disney's "Nine Old Men." Minnie Mouse shows her acting range: here she's no helpless damsel but a plucky Western gal who turns up her nose at Mickey's initial overtures: "On your way, cowboy; I can take care of myself!" Peg Leg Pete, too, is reliably on hand as the bad guy but has a guise and an accent for every occasion: "Hmm, soch a beeg bondle for soch a leetle lady!"

By the time of *Two-Gun Mickey*, the original United Artists main title card (see page 159) had been replaced by this updated design. Ongoing refinements to the appearances of Mickey and Minnie, within the cartoons themselves, were now reflected in the opening titles.

Mickey ready for action in the poster art for *Two-Gun Mickey*.

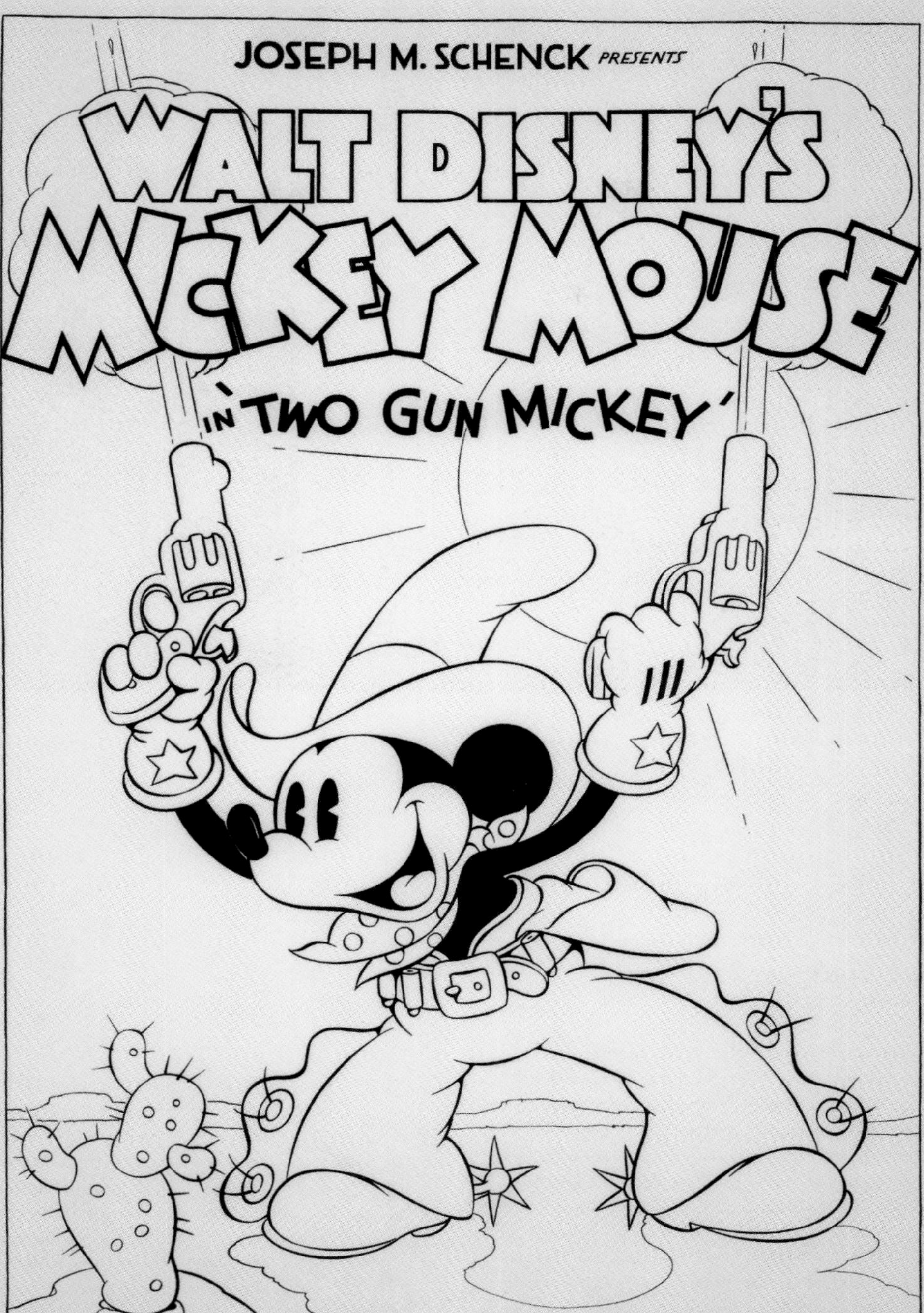
JOSEPH M. SCHENCK PRESENTS
WALT DISNEY'S
MICKEY MOUSE
IN 'TWO GUN MICKEY'
UNITED ARTISTS PICTURE

MICKEY'S MAN FRIDAY
(January 19, 1935)

Having essayed the role of Gulliver, Mickey takes on another literary character: Robinson Crusoe. Here he lands on a cannibal island and rescues one little cannibal from his fellows, after which Mickey and "Friday" are obliged to defend themselves from the rest of the tribe. The contrivances they construct are less engines of destruction than slapstick props, with an emphasis on ingenious sight gags: a yanked rope squeezes an auto-horn bulb, sounding an alarm; a pelican on a leash opens its bill, dropping coconuts on the attackers below.

MICKEY'S SERVICE STATION
(March 16, 1935)

Mickey the workingman is back in this short, managing a service station, and trying to locate and remove a squeak in gangster Pete's car. This film inaugurates a formula that would serve the studio well for years: the Mickey-Donald-Goofy trio cartoon. After an introductory setup, the action splits up into three threads, each character pursuing a separate series of gags — each animated independently by a separate artist or group of artists — then reunites them for an exciting climax or wrap-up gag at film's end. It's an ingeniously efficient use of animation talent, and produces a satisfyingly entertaining cartoon.

Mickey navigates his homemade raft toward the island in publicity art loosely based on the opening scene in *Mickey's Man Friday*. Only Mickey could make a shipwreck look like so much fun.

A *Mickey's Service Station* story sketch: efforts to fix Pete's car get wildly out of hand.

Cel setup from *Mickey's Kangaroo*. Mickey and the kangaroo, animated by Fred Moore, on their way to Mickey's makeshift gym.

MICKEY'S KANGAROO
(April 13, 1935)

Mickey receives a crate containing one parent and one baby kangaroo. While he takes on the adult in a one-sided boxing match, Pluto scrutinizes the youngster. This was another idea that would become a useful premise in Disney cartoons: Pluto's encounter with a strange new creature. This cartoon tries a device suggested by MGM's film version of *Strange Interlude* (1932; dir. Robert Z. Leonard): as Pluto looks into the camera, his thoughts are spoken directly to the audience in a voice-over.[8] It's an interesting experiment, but it was not repeated in subsequent films.

Walt, Roy, and Mickey pose proudly with the special Academy Award for Mickey's creation in 1932.

An historic occasion: Mickey Mouse appears onscreen in Technicolor for the first time in *Parade of the Award Nominees.*

INCREASING WORLD FAME

A few months into Disney's UA release, Mickey's rising status in Hollywood was confirmed when the filmmaking community accorded him its ultimate accolade: an Academy Award. The Oscars were only a year older than Mickey himself—the 1932 ceremony was only the fifth in the Academy's history—and had been framed in terms of the highest possible distinction, honoring not only artistry in filmmaking, but the prestige of Hollywood's most respected artists and studios. Producers of animated cartoons were hardly to be considered in such distinguished company.

In November 1932 the Academy broke that precedent, twice, for Walt Disney. The 5th Academy Awards were the first to include the categories Short Subject (Comedy) and Short Subject (Novelty)—and if *cartoon* short subjects were to be recognized at all, the Disney studio was, by now, clearly the class of the field. The Academy chose *Flowers and Trees*, Disney's breakthrough Technicolor debut, as the best cartoon of the year, and also conferred on Walt a Special Award for the creation of Mickey Mouse.

That Academy ceremony on November 18 was a doubly notable one for the Disney studio as, for the entertainment of the guests, Walt produced a special short film. Here Mickey made his Technicolor debut—in a film that was never meant to be seen by the public.

IMAGED BY HERITAGE AUCTIONS, HA.COM

PARADE OF THE AWARD NOMINEES
(Special reel for Academy Awards banquet, 1932)

Cementing Walt's and Mickey's new standing in Hollywood, Mickey and Minnie lead a parade of caricatured acting nominees in this special short—widely circulated among today's Disney fans, but originally created for an exclusive private showing at the 1931–32 Academy Awards ceremony. Moreover, the reel was produced in Technicolor. Here, more than two years before *The Band Concert*, we see Mickey in a colorful band uniform, complete with *green* shorts. Walt and Roy had an ulterior motive in producing this special reel: Roy had managed to convince United Artists to release the Silly Symphonies in Technicolor, but the company had balked at the extra cost of adding color to the Mickeys. Now that the color Symphonies were meeting with fabulous success, might not this delightful short, screened for such a distinguished audience, bring the UA executives to reconsider?

The attempt was unsuccessful. Al Lichtman, of United Artists, wrote to Roy: "I saw the print of the *Parade of the Nominees* [sic], and Mickey certainly looks grand in color. I think it would [be] just marvelous to have Mickey in color and I have given a lot of thought about it for next season. To be frank, though, conditions will have to improve to enable us to afford it . . ."[9] The company stood firm, and for the time being Mickey's theatrical shorts continued in black and white.

MICKEY MOUSE
MERCHANDISE
PUBLISHED BY KAY KAMEN, Inc. NEW YORK, U.S.A.
Sole Representative
WALT DISNEY ENTERPRISES

KAY KAMEN AND A NEW LEVEL OF MERCHANDISING

In the meantime, Mickey marketing was not only continuing—it was rapidly escalating. Roy and Walt may have been dissatisfied with the merchandising efforts of George Borgfeldt and William Levy, but a dynamic new representative entered their lives in the summer of 1932, just about the time the first UA releases were appearing in theaters. The new arrival was Herman "Kay" Kamen, who had already earned a reputation for his energetic marketing efforts and who now courted Walt and Roy with the same aggressive energy he had shown in other pursuits. Impressed with his methods, the Disneys contracted him. In short order, licensed Mickey Mouse products, already plentiful in the marketplace, began to proliferate. By the autumn of 1932 UA was tying in with Kamen's licensees to promote Mickey toys, handkerchiefs, clothing, costumes, china, and other items. As time passed and the old Borgfeldt contracts expired, Kamen's presence in the marketplace became more expansive and vigorous. Retailers were sent detailed annual catalogs of new Disney merchandise; interoffice communications from Kamen himself were not memos but "Mickey Mouse Hustle-Grams."

Of all the by-products of Mickey's movie career, the most important was the newspaper comic strip. Other products, such as storybooks, will receive more detailed attention in a later chapter. For now, two additional Mickey items are too important *not* to receive special mention here. One was the Mickey Mouse watch. Reportedly conceived by Kamen himself, the Mickey timepieces—both wristwatches and pocket watches—were copyrighted and patented by Disney and manufactured, under an exclusive license, by the Ingersoll-Waterbury Company. Ingersoll introduced the watches as a novelty in the summer of 1933

The success of the Mickey merchandising campaigns owed much to the enthusiastic salesmanship of Kay Kamen. Here, the 1934 (opposite) and 1935 (below) covers of his annual merchandise catalog.

Following The catalog pages reproduced here give some idea of the staggering range of Mickey Mouse merchandise that flooded into the marketplace with the advent of Kay Kamen's marketing strategies. Seen here (pages 198–207) are pages from Kamen's U.S. catalog for 1935, featuring popular items, such as the Lionel trains and Ingersoll watches, alongside more obscure items. These merchandising efforts were not confined to the United States; samples from the 1935 U.K. catalog follow, on pages 208–213.

MICKEY MOUSE ALUMINUM TOY

ATING SETS, COOKIE CUTTERS, ETC.

HERE you see only a few of the high grade aluminum-ware articles in our Mickey Mouse line. Intriguing eating sets, percolator sets, cooking sets, individual pieces—toys that are actually cooking utensils. Note the deep dish, cup and napkin set—there's nothing cuter on the market today. Also, note the cookie and biscuit cutters on the left hand page. It is, incidentally, the very best cutter made, and you can imagine the excitement it will cause in every household where youngsters' meals are served. To add to this line, we are now designing aluminum molds for ice cream, desserts and salads, which will be available in the near future. Like the balance of this great line, these molds will retail at popular prices, assuring tremendous volume.

Write for full particulars

ALUMINUM SPECIALTY CO.

Licensee

General Office: Manitowoc, Wis.

DISTRICT OFFICES:

New York: 200 5th Avenue
St. Louis: 2400 N. 10th Street
Chicago: 1400 Merchandise Mart
San Francisco: 712-716 Mission Street

M I C K E Y   M O U S E   E N T E R

TH YEAR WITH BORGFELDT'S
SINCE 1928, Mickey Mouse and Geo. Borgfeldt Corp. have been "clicking" in every important American market. The magnetic appeal of Mickey Mouse has produced rapid turnover and steady profits for retailers handling our line.
Write for full particulars
GEO. BORGFELDT CORPORATION
Licensee
44-60 East 23rd Street, New York, N. Y.

INGERSOLL . . . MICKEY MOUS
PRESTO! HERE'S YOUR
Ingersoll
MICKEY MOUSE WATCH
Specia
Ten thousand retail stores are featuring this large, illuminated action display in their windows —attracting crowds every minute of the day. Cash in by displaying your Mickey Mouse watches prominently.
MICKEY MOUSE
INGERSOLL MICKEY MOUSE
$2.95

. . MORE POPULAR THAN EVER

As this illustrated display shows Mickey—The Magician—pulling watches out of thin air, so Ingersoll-Mickey Mouse wrist and pocket watches maintain their miraculous sales volume, in season or out. Pocket watches with fob retailing at $1.50—Wrist watches with ornamental bracelet or strap at $2.95—Alarm clocks at $1.50—have taught and are teaching millions of youngsters the correct reading of time. Stock up and maintain your stocks!

Write for full particulars

INGERSOLL-WATERBURY COMPANY
Licensee
Waterbury, Connecticut

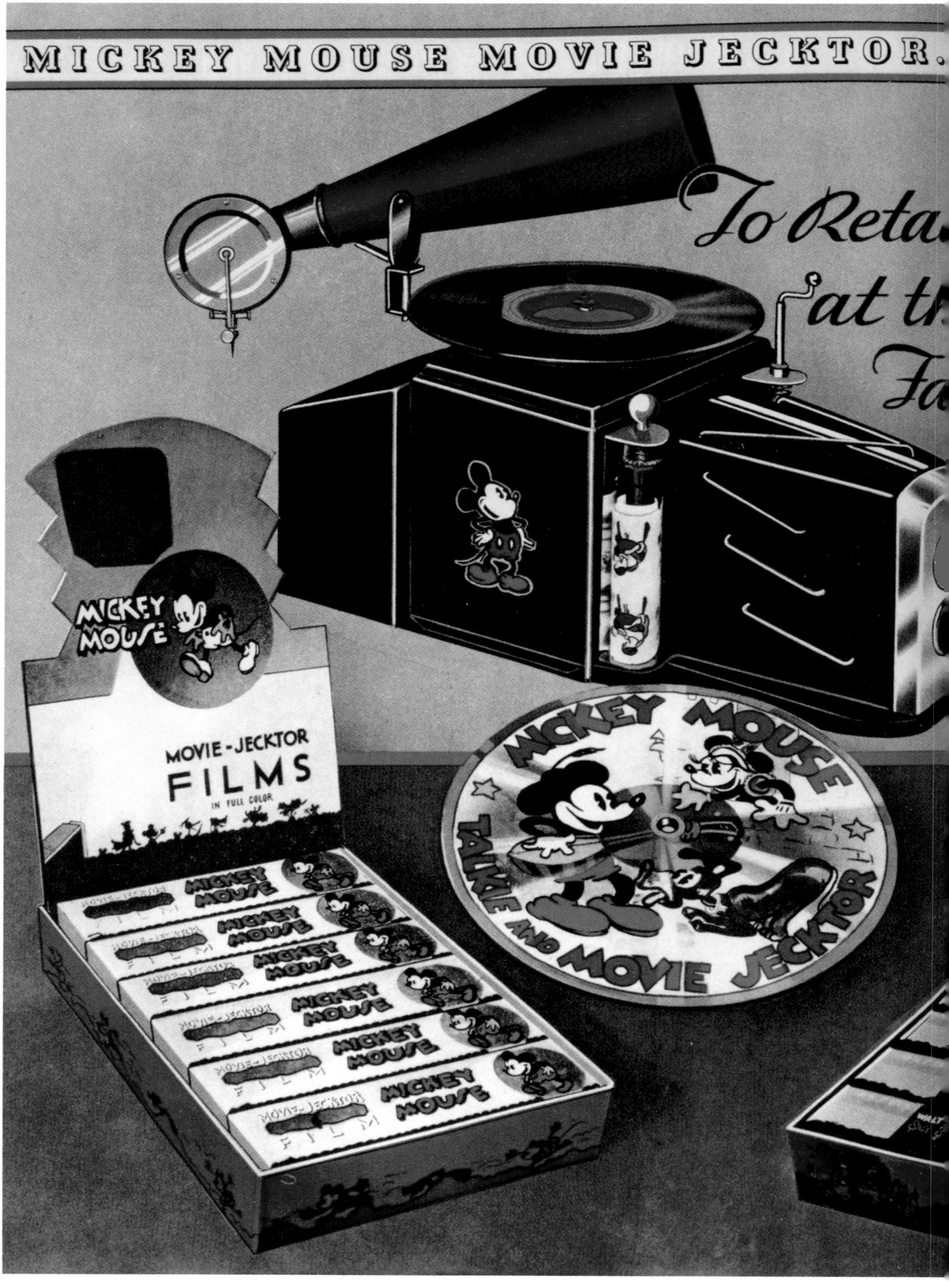

MICKEY MOUSE MOVIE JECKTOR.
To Reta
at th
Fa
MICKEY MOUSE
MOVIE-JECKTOR
FILMS
IN FULL COLOR
MICKEY MOUSE TALKIE AND MOVIE JECKTOR

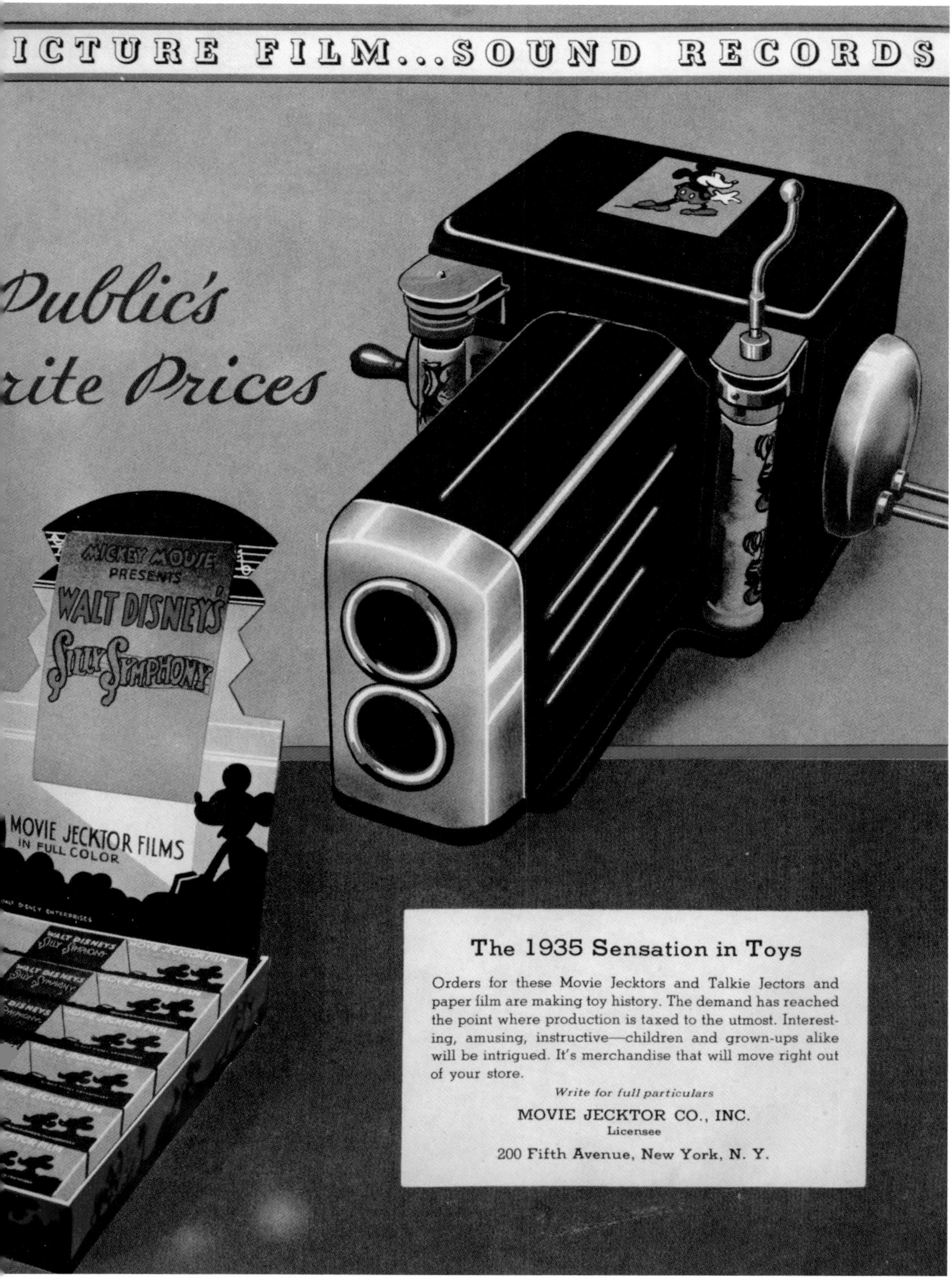
ICTURE FILM...SOUND RECORDS
Public's
rite Prices
MICKEY MOUSE PRESENTS
WALT DISNEY'S
SILLY SYMPHONY
MOVIE JECKTOR FILMS
IN FULL COLOR
The 1935 Sensation in Toys
Orders for these Movie Jecktors and Talkie Jectors and paper film are making toy history. The demand has reached the point where production is taxed to the utmost. Interesting, amusing, instructive—children and grown-ups alike will be intrigued. It's merchandise that will move right out of your store.
Write for full particulars
MOVIE JECKTOR CO., INC.
Licensee
200 Fifth Avenue, New York, N. Y.

LIONEL PRESENTS MICKEY MOU

MICKEY MOUSE and his tribe of movie stars are in the circus now. The whole Walt Disney family is on this decorated circus train that's hauled by the wind-up Commodore Vanderbilt and stoked by Master Mickey Mouse himself. And what a stoker he is! As the train whizzes around the track, his shovel goes up and down and bingo--right toward the firebox. And look at the tent that comes with the train. A set-up, made of heavy cardboard, 20 inches long, 14 inches high to the top of the flagpole. Outside is a moulded Mickey Mouse barker. Inside is an arena of fun and a flying trapeze. There are regulation circus tickets, a commissary auto, gas station and other cardboard accessories. Band car, dining car and animal car are made of steel, gilded and lithographed in many colors. Train measures 32 inches. 10 sections of track supplied form an oval 27 by 35 inches.

No. 1536 Retail price, complete, $2.00

Write for full particulars

THE LIONEL CORPORATION
Licensee
15-17-19 East 26th Street, New York, N. Y.
Chicago Office: 58 East Washington Street

Mickey Mouse starred in the fastest

CIRCUS TRAIN WITH BIG TENT

ving performance of his career

PICK UP YOUR ORDER PAD AT ONCE AND WRITE YOURSELF A TICKET FOR THE RINGSIDE

BIRN BROTHERS LTD.

67-70 BUNHILL ROW, LONDON, E.C. 1

FOR the third year in succession Ingersoll Ltd. have renewed their licence with Walt Disney-Mickey Mouse Ltd. This confidence is reflected in the response of the buying public to Mickey Mouse watches and clocks. There are over 9,500,000 children in Great Britain, each one a potential customer for Ingersoll Mickey Mouse watches • Every child wants a watch and every child loves Mickey Mouse. This then is the strongest combination of sales promotion that it is possible to create. Display Ingersoll Mickey Mouse Watches and Clocks in your windows and bring the children with their parents to your store.

INGERSOLL LTD.

223-227 ST. JOHN STREET, LONDON, E.C.1

A. WELLS & CO. LTD.

PROGRESS WORKS, WALTHAMSTOW, LONDON, E.17

New City Showrooms (1936) 23 White Street, Moorfields, London, E.C.2

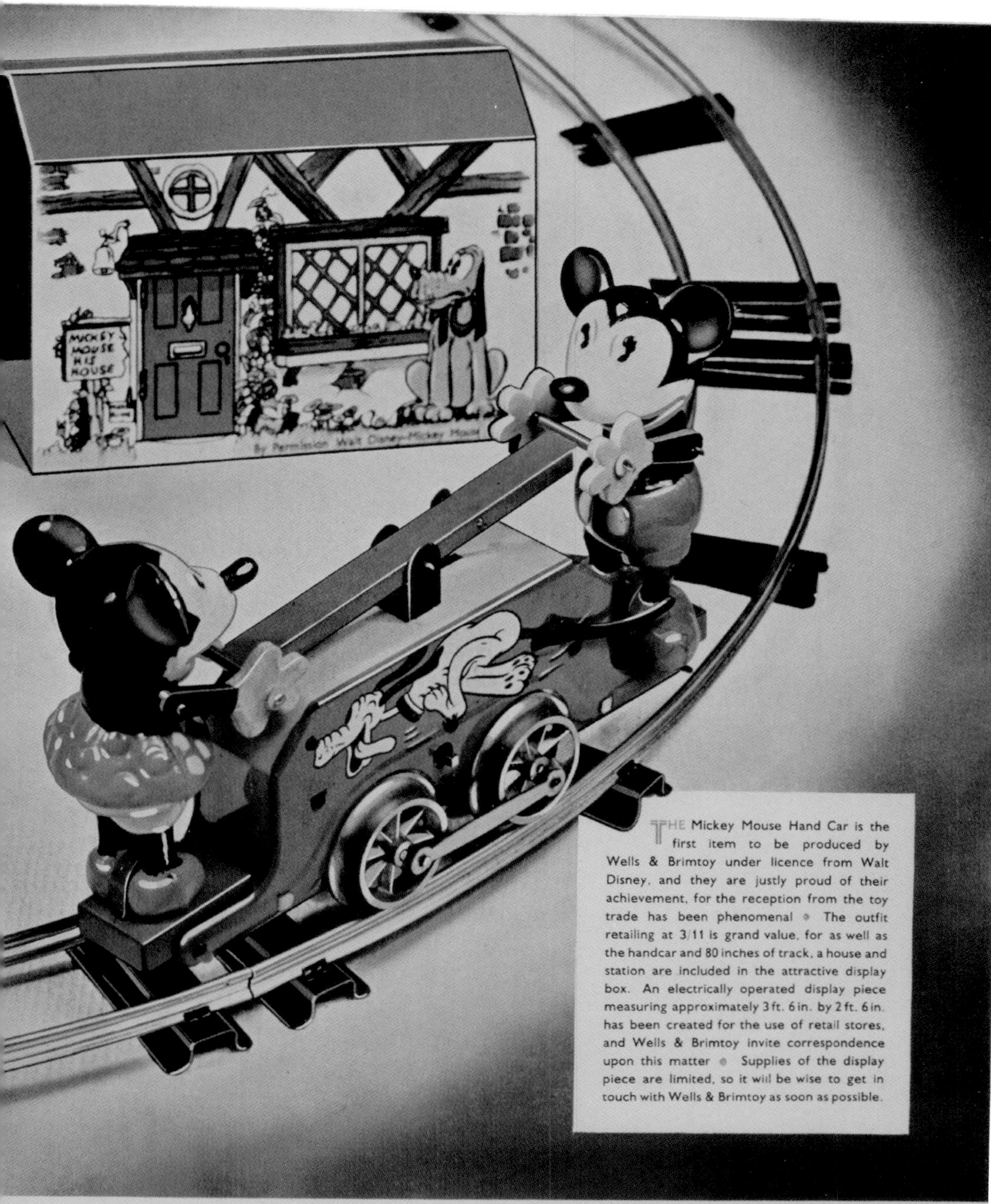

THE Mickey Mouse Hand Car is the first item to be produced by Wells & Brimtoy under licence from Walt Disney, and they are justly proud of their achievement, for the reception from the toy trade has been phenomenal • The outfit retailing at 3/11 is grand value, for as well as the handcar and 80 inches of track, a house and station are included in the attractive display box. An electrically operated display piece measuring approximately 3 ft. 6 in. by 2 ft. 6 in. has been created for the use of retail stores, and Wells & Brimtoy invite correspondence upon this matter • Supplies of the display piece are limited, so it will be wise to get in touch with Wells & Brimtoy as soon as possible.

A. WELLS & CO. LTD.

PROGRESS WORKS, WALTHAMSTOW, LONDON, E.17

New City Showrooms (1936) 23 White Street, Moorfields, London, E.C.2

QUALITY, price and advertising created and have maintained the terrific demand for Sharp's Mickey Mouse Toffee • Messrs. Sharp have consistently advertised their Toffee in the national press and are reaping the reward of their initiative. During the past twelve months the tonnage of Sharp's Mickey Mouse Toffee would have been sufficient to provide every boy and girl in England with two pieces of toffee per day every day for the whole year. Are you getting your share of this regular business?

E. SHARP & SONS, LTD.

KREEMY WORKS, MAIDSTONE

IMAGED BY HERITAGE AUCTIONS, HA.COM

A wave of Mickey merchandising exploded in the mid-1930s, featuring the Mouse's smiling countenance on a variety of goods, including food products. Sometimes the advertising benefits worked in both directions: the Post Toasties ad at left was featured on the back cover of *Mickey Mouse Magazine* in 1935.

and quickly scored a success for which they were not prepared; within two years, the watches had already sold in the millions.

Another notable Mickey connection during these years was with the Lionel Corporation, makers of toy trains. Disney contracted with Lionel in July 1934, at a time when the toy company was in receivership. The following Christmas season Lionel introduced a new railroad toy: a windup handcar with Mickey and Minnie Mouse at the controls, priced at one dollar. The handcars sold so well, and in turn provided such a strong promotional push for Lionel's *other* products, that by January 1935 the company was back on the road to financial recovery. The press seized on the story, reporting delightedly that "Mickey and Minnie Mouse . . . pulled the Lionel Corporation, Irvington toy manufacturers, back into the black."[10] This would become one of Mickey's most widely circulated success stories during the Depression years, and Lionel would follow up with additional toys featuring Mickey, as well as other Disney characters.

The renowned Mickey Mouse watch in two of its configurations. The watch in the upper photo is the first English Mickey Mouse pocket watch, produced in 1934. It came with a leather strap and an enameled fob which, like the watches themselves, depicted Mickey Mouse in color. The lower photo shows the original wristwatch, issued in 1933 with a chrome-plated metal link band, seen here in its original box.

The Mickey Mouse Clubs, already successful during the Powers and Columbia years, reached new heights of popularity during Mickey's tenure at UA. By mid-1932 they claimed one million members nationwide, and one journalist observed that their membership "approximates that of the Boy Scouts of America and the Girl Scouts, combined."[11] By now, in fact, the Clubs had expanded their purview to include some of the same goals as the Scout programs, instilling principles of good citizenship in their young members. When a representative of the Birmingham chap-

The Famous LIONEL
MICKEY MOUSE
HAND CAR
LIONEL CIT
MICKEY MOUSE HAND CAR
Their arms pump up and down, their bodies bend back and forth as the wind-up handcar rushes around its 27-inch circle of track.
Mickey Mouse and Minnie Mouse are five inches high. The handcar is nearly eight inches long, equipped with a clock-work motor, bell and brake. It is enameled in rich, brilliant color. Eight sections of regular Lionel mechanical track are included.
SOLD AT ALL STORES
for $1.00
(Slightly higher in Far West)
NOW Two LIONEL Craft
THE BOATS THAT STEER THEMSELVES
No. 43 or No. 44
$3.50
44
LIONEL
ELECTRIC TRAINS, MECHANICAL TRAINS MODEL RAILROAD ACCESSORIES, SPRING-MOTOR SPEED BOATS AND SPECIALITIES
The boat that has been winning races everywhere, No. 43 (above). It will do anything on water a boy wants it to do. Patented rudder can be set three ways—(1) for the boat to streak out in a straight line, swing round and come back—(2) zoom continuously in circles—(3) make a bee-line straight out for two or three hundred feet. Your Lionel dealer is displaying this boat now. Ask him to show it to you. No. 43, complete with cradle, $3.50.
No. 44—The new Lionel Speedster! And what a rakish racing boat this is!—look at it! Exactly 17½ inches of heavy steel, beautifully enameled in brilliant colors, adorned with a mahogany deck, trimmed with brass and manned by two operators. As in No. 43, the rudder can be set three ways. Your Lionel dealer will have his supply of these boats soon. Ask him to save one for you. No. 44, complete with cradle, $3.50.
THE LIONEL CORPORATION
15 East 26th Street, New York, N. Y.

Trade advertising for "the famous" (as the ad notes) Mickey-Minnie hand car that helped the Lionel Corporation recover from its financial woes.

In the mid-1930s new and relatively more refined Mickey merchandise — licensed and overseen by Kay Kamen — rapidly replaced the earlier, cruder products that had been managed and manufactured by George Borgfeldt. The latter are exemplified here by Borgfeldt's charming but primitive box designs for acrobat- and motorcycle-themed toys.

ter offered a membership to Eleanor Roosevelt, she reportedly answered: "Aren't you going to invite the president too? He is crazy about Mickey Mouse."[12] The President and First Lady were duly appointed Chief Mickey and Chief Minnie of the Birmingham Club. Nor were the clubs confined to the United States alone; large and enthusiastic new Mickey Mouse Clubs sprang up in Shanghai, Dublin, Edinburgh, and other cities around the world. In India, a new chapter announced that it had already recruited 800 members and added: "Dogs are eligible for membership as well, and are known as 'Mousers.'"[13]

From the Disney studio's standpoint, the Mickey Mouse Clubs peaked in 1933 — the year in which the town of Worcester, Massachusetts, first hosted its "Mickey Mouse Days" celebration, an officially sanctioned city carnival built almost entirely around Mickey Mouse Club activities and marketing tie-ins. Yet 1933 was also the year in which Disney ended its formal connection with the clubs. They had been seen as an invaluable promotional tool in 1929, but within four years the organization had grown so huge and unmanageable that it taxed the studio's resources, necessarily focused on the production of films. In addition, the promotional advantage granted to the Club-sponsoring theater in any

One recording of "Mickey Mouse and Minnie's in Town" was this Frank Luther side, one of a set of special Disney picture discs issued by Victor in 1934. Floyd Gottfredson's comics team provided the label art.

Ann Ronell, the songwriter who contributed additional lyrics to the published version of "Who's Afraid of the Big Bad Wolf?," also penned this original song. Lyrics included: "Clarabelle the Cow makes a moo and how / When she hears his footfall; / Horace champs in his stall: / 'Mickey's Mouster of them all.'"

given city was apt to create ill will among competing theaters in the same city. The Disney studio withdrew its official support from the clubs in 1933, but some of the individual clubs continued to thrive for years, and sometimes decades, afterward.

MICKEY IN THE WORLD OF POPULAR MUSIC

"Minnie's Yoo Hoo" was only the beginning. By late 1929, Mickey had already become such a well-known figure that songwriters and popular musicians outside the studio began to celebrate him in song. The earliest such Mickey Mouse song originated in Europe: Harry Carlton's "Mickey Mouse" in Great Britain, published before the end of 1929 and translated into German, French, and other languages during 1930. While the song was authorized by Ideal Films — Disney's first distributor in the United Kingdom — and recorded by no small number of talents, this veddy-British number seems never to have made it Stateside:

All the fishes wagged their tails —
On the top of all the sails —
Smiling like the Prince of Wales — was —
Mickey! Mickey! Mouse!

The Bibo and Lang *Mickey Mouse Book*, published in 1930, included Henry Cohen and Irving Bibo's original song "Mickey Mouse (You Cute Little Feller)," which had an interesting history of its own. The book's second printing, in December 1930, featured a completely rewritten song in place of the original! The title, and Bibo's composer credit, remained intact. The Disney studio helped to cross-promote the song: the soundtracks of *The Birthday Party* and *Traffic Troubles*, both released in 1931, incorporated the chorus of the original song in their

MICKEY MOUSE AND MINNIE'S
IN TOWN
BY
ANN
RONELL
Irving Berlin, Inc.
MUSIC PUBLISHERS
1607 Broadway New York
MADE IN U.S.A.
© BY SPECIAL PERMISSION WALT DISNEY ENT.

The Whitman Publishing Company, which published a variety of Mickey storybooks, also produced Disney playing cards. The full color artwork pictured here, with Minnie given top billing, was mass-produced in two-color form as the box for a bridge deck; other games were also available.

music scores. The following year, when Bibo and Lang published a new song, "The Wedding Party of Mickey Mouse," the studio again featured the song instrumentally in the score for *The Mad Dog*.

This kind of cross-promotional cooperation came naturally, since the Disney studio was invested in the Bibo and Lang publications: the *Mickey Mouse Book* was sent to theaters hosting the Mickey Mouse Clubs and distributed to the young attendees. But other Mickey-centric popular songs were soon forthcoming from outside the studio, and Walt cooperated with those efforts too, licensing the use of Mickey's name and supplying studio art for the covers of song sheets. One of the most notable examples was Irving Caesar's "What! No Mickey Mouse? (What Kind of a Party Is This?)," published in 1932:

Your dogs bow-wow, your cats me-ow,
I know that you can milk a cow,
But Mickey makes me laugh, and how?
And I want Mickey now;
So, where's that tricky mouse?

The N. N. Hill Brass Co. manufactured this Mickey toy telephone in the mid-1930s. The image on the stem is a pose from Floyd Gottfredson's and Al Taliaferro's 1931 marketing model sheet.

For the Disney studio, the turning point was the surprising smash success of "Who's Afraid of the Big Bad Wolf?" from *Three Little Pigs* in 1933. This was the studio's first bona fide hit song, and led to a regular song-publishing arrangement with Irving Berlin, Inc. Many of the newly published songs were, like "Who's Afraid," taken from the scores of Silly Symphonies, but name songwriters also penned original songs featuring Mickey. Ann Ronell, who had contributed new lyrics to the published version of "Who's Afraid," also composed the jaunty "Mickey Mouse and Minnie's in Town." A few years later, "Mickey Mouse's Birthday Party" observed the title occasion in song. Like Carlton's "Mickey Mouse" before them, some of these songs were also issued on records by pop-

Mickey

ular singers and dance bands, and here again the Disney studio offered its cooperation, contributing label art to some of these releases. The trend continued concurrently in Europe, with British songs most often staying in Britain: the very subject matter of "Mickey's Son and Daughter," published in 1935, seems to suggest why Walt might have preferred the tune not reach Mickey's American fans. And soon Mickey's success led to yet another musical milestone: soundtrack recordings, a novel concept in 1936. Thanks to an agreement between Disney and RCA (whose sound system was used to record the Disney soundtracks), a series of 78 rpm records made original Disney cartoon sounds available to the public. The records were issued in America on the Bluebird label and, in Britain, on British HMV. Leigh Harline's score for *Mickey's Grand Opera*, and Frank Churchill's for *Orphans' Benefit*, became two of the earliest soundtrack records in history.

Oswald the Lucky Rabbit, created by Walt Disney in 1927, was still going strong in 1935. His cartoons continued to be distributed by Universal Pictures, and when the studio's founder, film pioneer Carl Laemmle, celebrated Universal's 20th anniversary, Walt sent Laemmle this cartoon tribute.

Atop a background from *Mickey's Good Deed* are various early 1930s merchandise items, including Borgfeldt Fun-E-Flex jointed wooden figures, an Emerson box radio with full-color design, and two German items: a jointed Mickey doll on skis made by Ferdinand Riffeser for export to England, and a Mickey wind-up drummer from the firm Distler, here in a variant sold in South America and continental Europe by the exporter Eisenmann & Co. Another variant was sold in North America by Borgfeldt.

Following Atop a background from *Mickey's Orphans* the merchandise parade continues. The items include the first American Mickey wooden figure, designed by Burt Gillett and manufactured by Borgfeldt; another Ferdinand Riffeser jointed doll; an Ingersoll electric clock; a Japanese-made celluloid rocking horse; a cup holder from the British firm Crown Devon; American and British home-movie releases; and the second printing of the first Mickey Mouse *Big Little Book* (see pages 259, 272).

MICKEY MOUSE STRATOSPHERE
HOLLYWOOD FILM ENTERPRISES
Hollywood, California
MICKEY MOUSE
CINE ART
FILMS
MICKEY MOUSE
Ciné "Kodagraph"
Largeur 8%
MARQUE DÉPOSÉE
FABRIQUÉ EN FRANCE
"KODAK"
CINE ART
MICKEY MOUSE
FILMS
"Ciné" Kodagraph"
Film "KODAK" de Sécurité
MICKEY CHAUFFEUR DE TAXI
MICKEY MOUSE

Mickey Mo

Walt Disney's
TECHNICOLOR FEATURE TRIUMPH
FANTASIA
Distributed by RKO Radio Pictures, Inc.

CHAPTER FOUR

Technicolor Extravaganzas

By the mid-1930s, Mickey Mouse had reached a watershed in his career. The raw simplicity of the early Mouse had exercised an irresistible appeal to audiences and had made him a beloved figure around the world. Now his popularity remained undiminished, and, in fact, continued to grow steadily—but Mickey himself became increasingly refined, conceived and drawn with ever-greater sophistication. Much of this new polish was due to Fred Moore, who had enjoyed an overnight success of his own within the studio. Walt Disney, quick to notice Moore's instinctive knack for appealing animation and its salutary effect on Mickey's cartoons, had seized on that native ability and placed Moore in a position of influence. Only a few years earlier, Moore had been a novice; now the other Mickey animators looked to him for guidance. He wore his new supervisory mantle lightly, explaining his subtle refinements to the "old" Mickey body: "It is good to compare your drawing to the old Mickey just for height."[1]

This new graphic sophistication came at a price. Mickey's visual development was paralleled by a corresponding refinement of his personality, emphasizing his kindly, cheerful, and modest traits. Ted Sears, of the story department, outlined his ideas of optimal story material for Mickey: "His comedy depends entirely upon the situation he is placed in . . . Mickey is most amusing when in a serious predicament trying to accomplish some purpose under difficulties or against time."[2] In other words, the mischievous early Mickey was gradually being

Fantasia represented a groundbreaking advance in many ways, but in advertising it the Disney marketing forces were careful to include the reassuring presence of Mickey's familiar face.

The conversion of the Mickey Mouse series to Technicolor was recognized in the animation industry as an event, and was proudly touted by United Artists in special trade ads.

Another United Artists trade ad. The distribution practices of some major studios required the exhibitor to book *all* of a studio's program in order to get any part of it. United Artists, because of its loose-knit association of production companies, made no such demands.

Fred Moore's refinement of Mickey and Minnie in the mid-1930s included several pages of instructional model sheets. The ineffable appeal of Moore's drawings is highlighted in this example, his instinctive design principles broken down into technical guidelines.

phased out in favor of Mickey the earnest, responsible citizen. All well and good, but as Donald Duck and other colorful characters—dynamic characters with arresting, and perhaps less courteous, personalities—began to assume more and more screen time in the Disney cartoons, Mickey, the nice guy, was increasingly in danger of being overshadowed. "Donald Duck... is just plain 100 per cent tough," wrote United Artists representative Rob Lawson in 1934. "His voice is tough. His attitude is tough. Even when he is totally surrounded and lusciously covered with sweet custard pies, his mood is pugnacious."[3] What straight man could compete?

In the mid-1930s, however, Mickey was still the center of the Disney universe, and Walt was continuing to embellish his cartoons. We've seen that he had tried to convert the Mickey series to Technicolor as early as 1932, but that United Artists had balked at the increased cost. Now, with Disney's exclusive Technicolor contract approaching the end of its term, Walt reiterated his appeal, portraying the change to color as a practical necessity. His color Silly Symphonies had created such a sensation in the movie world that other animation studios were anxiously awaiting the lapse of that exclusive contract, and the opportunity to produce three-strip Technicolor cartoons of their own. Walt was not about to let Mickey Mouse be left behind, and this time United Artists agreed. Mickey's first color film was in story development by mid-1934.

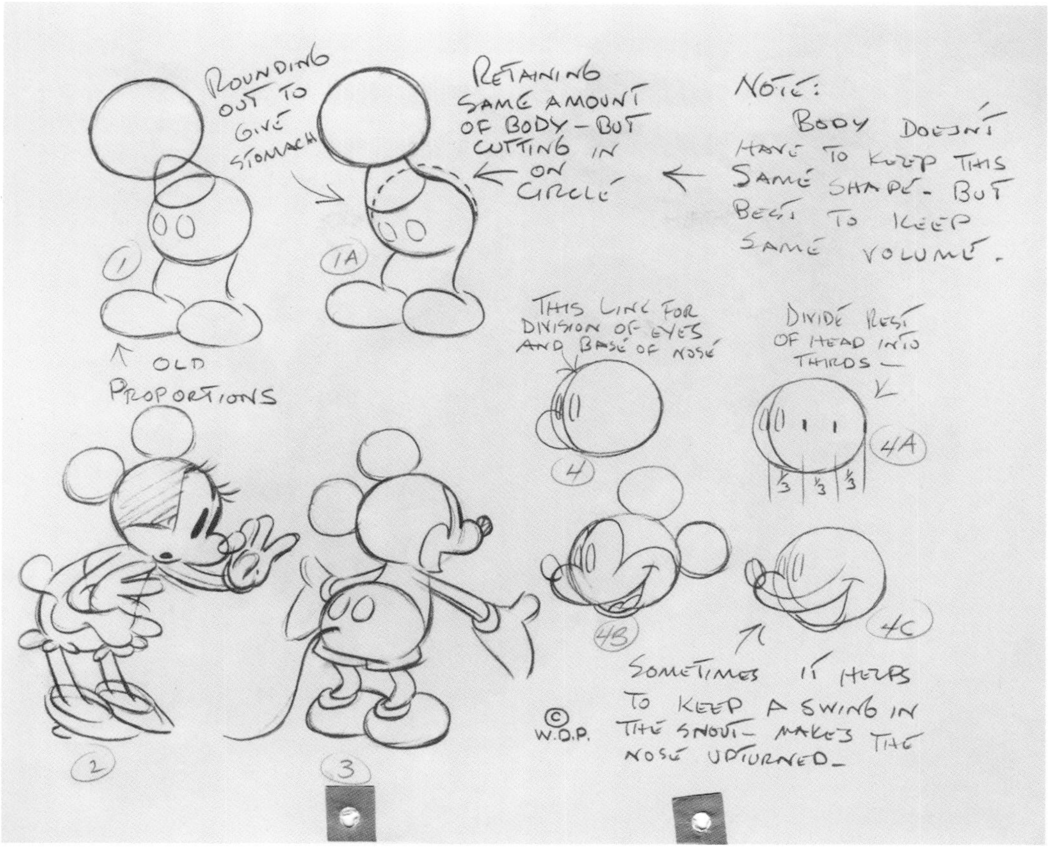

THE UNITED ARTISTS TECHNICOLOR SHORTS (1935-1937)

THE BAND CONCERT

(February 23, 1935)

For Mickey's public debut in Technicolor, Walt and the studio spared no effort. Story development began as early as the spring of 1934. The original story outline was roughly similar to the finished film, but suggested a number of scenes and gags that were later cut: musicians on the bandstand tuning up, Mickey's arrival in a chauffeured Model T, some gags for Mickey's mischievous nephews, isolated vignettes of small-town atmosphere. The finished film dispenses with all this and, in turn, replaces the planned "baby tornado" — which had been pictured demolishing a hothouse and then daintily picking the flowers — with a full-size *monster* of a tornado that roars through the park in a spectacular show of natural force.

This is more than mere showiness; the tornado scenes underline the overall musical brilliance underpinning *The Band Concert*. The originally planned gag, the musicians so absorbed in their work that they fail to notice the tornado, is enhanced here: our sense is that the band, playing the storm section from the "William Tell" Overture, has conjured up a real storm. As the musicians are hurled through the air, furiously playing, they and nature itself are united in a joint comic expression of Rossini's music. Earlier, when Donald Duck undercuts their performance of the famous trumpet theme by playing "Turkey in the Straw" on his piccolo, his comic audacity is compounded by our delight when the two melodies dovetail perfectly. Wilfred Jackson, the director with a sensitivity to musical gags, joins forces with Leigh Harline, the cartoon composer with a classical background; small wonder that Toscanini reportedly expressed his admiration for *The Band Concert*.[4]

Visually, of course, the film is a treat. The musicians greet their Technicolor debuts in an array of colorful uniforms, Mickey himself sporting a bright red coat several sizes too large. Some of the best animation talent in the studio was reserved for this picture; Les Clark's opening close-up of Mickey at the conductor's stand remains one of the most famous images of the Mouse. Ugo D'Orsi proves himself as an effects animator with his powerful scenes of the approaching tornado. Gerry Geronimi's animation of Goofy and Clarabelle's musical flirtation is a relatively minor scene, but because of *The Band Concert*'s prominence as a milestone film, it was seen frequently in later years and was burned into fan memory. Eventually it led to the part-time dissolution of Clarabelle's pairing with Horace — and her involvement, instead, with Goofy in many of Mickey's modern-day TV cartoons.

The band takes a bow after its first number in this completed cel setup. Ferdinand Horvath, an all-around artist best remembered today for his Disney concept art, was the animator of this and other opening scenes in the film *The Band Concert*.

IMAGED BY HERITAGE AUCTIONS, HA.COM

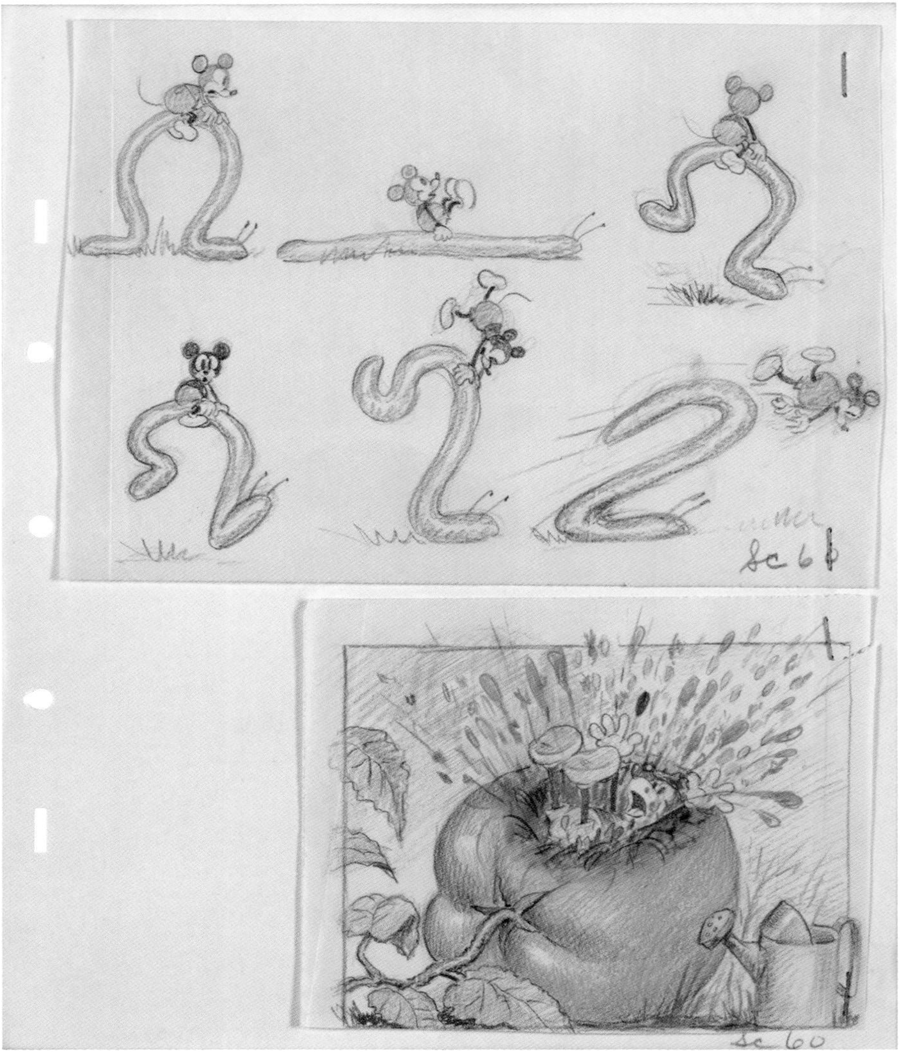

Experimental story sketches for *Mickey's Garden*, picturing Mickey's nightmare adventures when reduced to tiny size. His efforts to ride a snake lead to a clever visual effect; and, at bottom, he takes a fall into what is now an enormous tomato. Both these ideas were used in the film.

The boarding house in flames in the opening sequence in *Mickey's Fire Brigade*. Crowd scenes like this, with many simultaneous lines of action, were among the most intricate and difficult assignments for an animator. Milt Schaffer animated this one in the film, and executed it so well that he was promptly assigned *more* crowd scenes in subsequent Disney pictures.

MICKEY'S GARDEN
(July 13, 1935)

Mickey goes after the bugs in his garden with insecticide, accidentally gets a dose of it himself, and is plunged into a chemical-induced dream in which the plants and pests in the garden grow to monstrous proportions. The plants and weeds become a jungle, while the insects — looming monsters who guzzle the intended poison — go on an intoxicated rampage, and pursue Mickey and Pluto for revenge. Mickey's second Technicolor outing hasn't the sense of an "event" that we get from *The Band Concert*, but it packs a visual wallop of its own, filling the screen with the most phantasmagorical imagery of any Disney cartoon to date.

MICKEY'S FIRE BRIGADE
(August 3, 1935)

The second Mickey-Donald-Goofy picture, and the first in color, reprises Mickey's role as a fire chief. The three-man fire brigade is summoned to a burning boarding house, where our heroes ineptly battle the blaze and then "rescue" a reluctant occupant, Clarabelle Cow, from an upper floor. The cast of animators includes two unexpected names: Vladimir "Bill" Tytla and Grim Natwick — both new additions to the Disney staff in 1934, and both destined for legendary careers in animation. Cy Young, an up-and-coming effects animator, added an imaginative main-title sequence: as the title card announces *Mickey's Fire Brigade*, it's consumed by flames and burns away, revealing the opening scene.

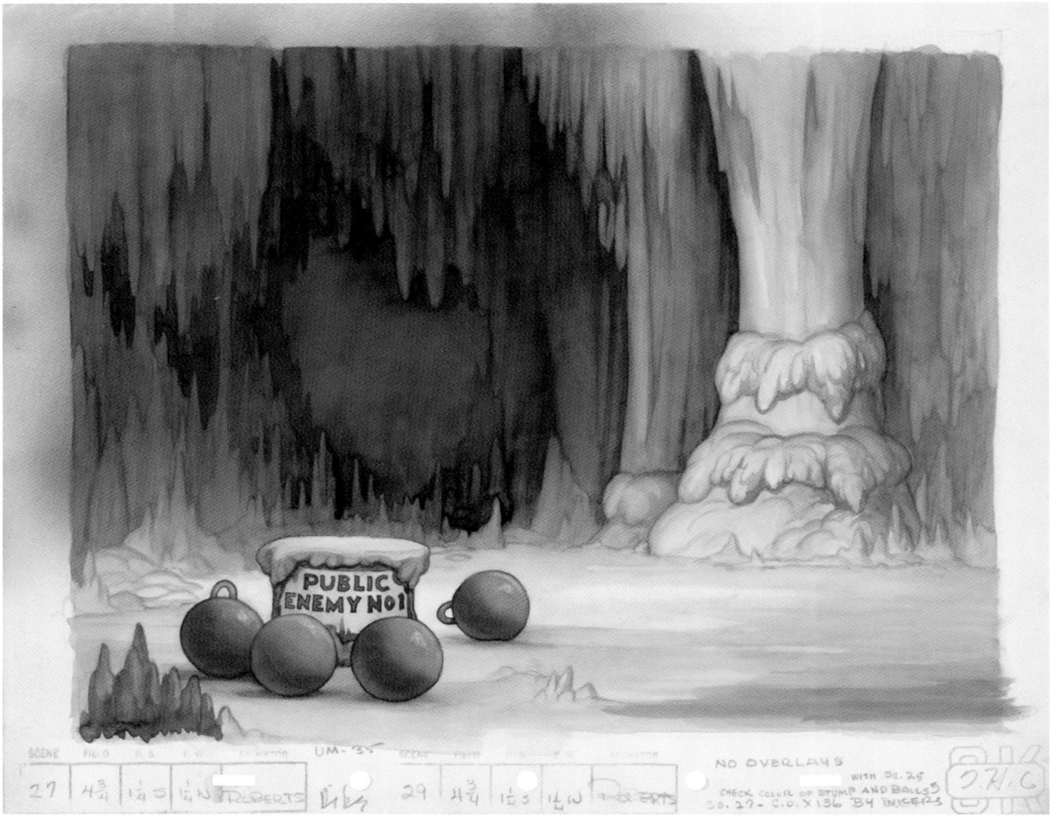

PLUTO'S JUDGEMENT DAY
(August 31, 1935)

This gem, one of the all-time classic Disney shorts, is nominally a Mickey Mouse picture but focuses primarily on Pluto—a situation that would occur more frequently in later years. Caught chasing a kitten and warned by Mickey that he'll have much to answer for on his judgment day, Pluto endures a horrific nightmare in which an all-cat court condemns him to a fiery doom. Joe Grant and Bill Cottrell, the story team responsible for some of the best Silly Symphonies of 1935, also concocted this sophisticated fantasy.

A background painting for the fearsome cavern "courtroom" where Pluto is put on trial for his life in *Pluto's Judgement Day*. The iron balls are attached to Pluto's legs by chains, which rattle and vibrate as he shivers in fright, and are therefore animated on cels.

Story sketches for Pluto's nightmare in *Pluto's Judgement Day*. Right, a taunting demon cat lures Pluto into the cats' underworld lair; below, Pluto faces "justice" in a courtroom where his conviction is guaranteed. The spectacular entrance to the cats' domain was designed by Joe Grant; the trial itself was filled with witty, sophisticated touches likewise contributed by Grant and by Bill Cottrell.

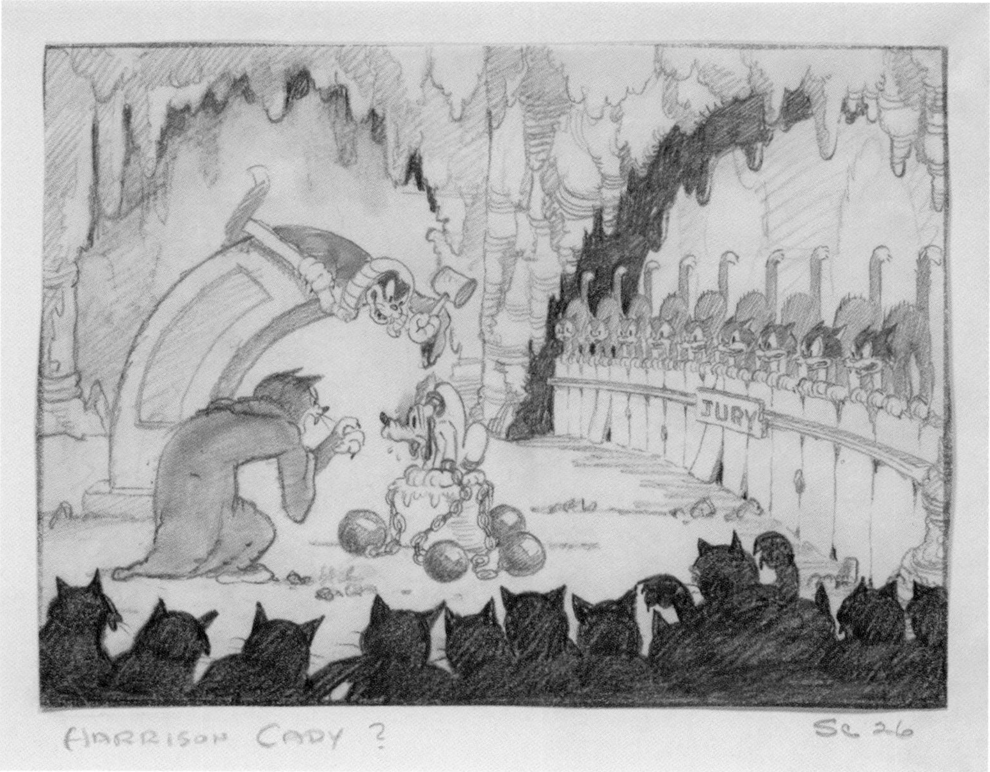

ON ICE
(September 28, 1935)

Mickey and his friends converge on a frozen river for a skating party. The principle of the Mickey-Donald-Goofy pictures — giving each character a separate story thread of gags, animated by a separate artist or artists — is expanded here to include Pluto, and incidentally Minnie, who shares Mickey's scenes. Mickey tries to teach her to skate, then shows off his own skating prowess, until he becomes a little too cocky and winds up embarrassing himself. Goofy, animated by Art Babbitt, has two "firsts" in the short: his first appearance with the big chin and sleepy eyes of his mature character design, and his first entrance singing "The World Owes Me a Living" — a song that had been introduced, in the same Pinto Colvig voice, by the Grasshopper in *Grasshopper and the Ants*, and subsequently became an unofficial theme song for Goofy.

MICKEY'S POLO TEAM
(January 4, 1936)

Hollywood-centric comedy returns with a vengeance in this picture. The game of polo was a popular diversion in the movie community during the 1930s, and Walt famously took it up himself. Inevitably, his studio produced a polo cartoon, with a team made up of Mickey and his pals matched against a team of movie-star caricatures. Members of the celebrity team were shuffled and replaced during story development — as were members of Mickey's team. Initially cast as an off-the-field supporting player in this picture, Donald Duck became a star character during 1935, and was given a place on Mickey's team, and a considerable share of footage, in the finished film.

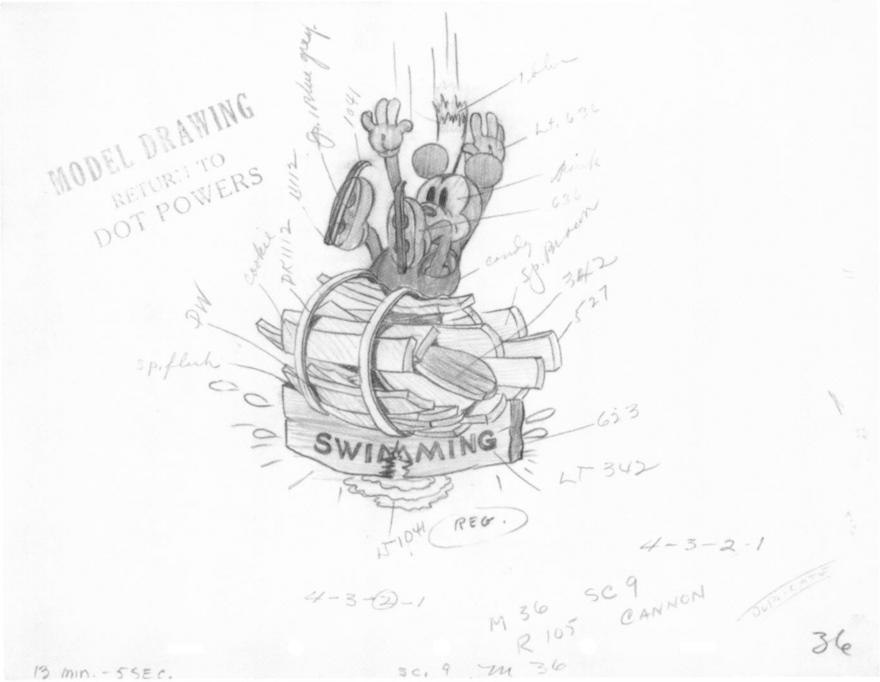

A story sketch for *Mickey's Polo Team*, showing the entrance of the Movie Stars team, with horses (or, in Harpo's case, an ostrich) that resemble their riders. At the time this sketch was prepared, the writers intended that Will Rogers would appear as a member of the team. After the real Rogers's tragic death in August 1935, the artists decided a caricature would be in poor taste, removed him from the cartoon and replaced him with Charlie Chaplin. Another pre-release change to *Polo Team* came late in production: a sequence of Mae West in the crowd, flirting with the Grasshopper from the Silly Symphony *Grasshopper and the Ants* (1934), was fully animated by Grim Natwick before being dropped.

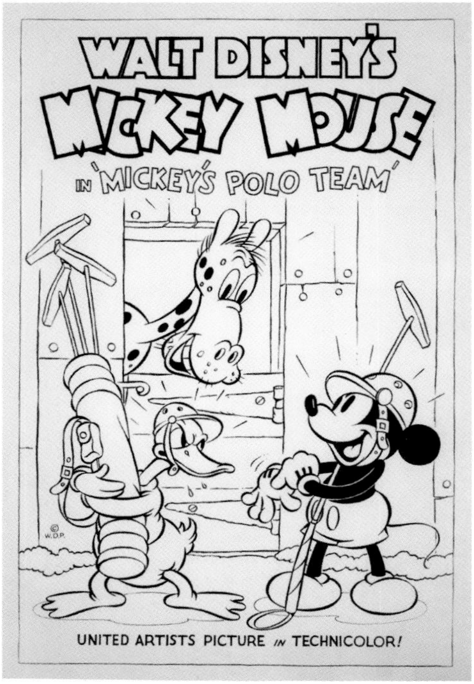

Opposite In Johnny Cannon's animation of the finished scene of *On Ice*, Mickey pays the price for showing off. His moment of impact with both the barrel *and* the "NO SWIMMING" sign provides the perfect opportunity to single out a clean-up drawing as a color model, assigning color values to all the disparate elements of the scene. The Ink & Paint department used these models as a guide when painting the cels.

Right The poster art for *Mickey's Polo Team* has practically nothing to do with the action in the film. Instead it bears a strong resemblance to the cover of the storybook *Mickey Mouse and His Horse Tanglefoot*, published the same year.

ORPHANS' PICNIC
(February 15, 1936)

The mischievous orphan mice, having previously harassed Donald Duck in *Orphans' Benefit*, get a second shot at him when Mickey and Donald treat them to a picnic in the country. The original story outline depicted the orphans indulging in wildly destructive pranks, directed at Mickey. In the finished film their actions are more benign, Donald is their principal target, and the accent is on personality animation as Donald loses his temper by degrees. Donald's character design would develop into its final form in the course of 1936; we can see the beginnings of that evolution in this picture.

MICKEY'S GRAND OPERA
(March 7, 1936)

This little gem is a combination of two story ideas: an opera performance and Pluto's discovery of a magician's magic hat backstage at the theater. Both these ideas originated in a single 1935 story outline, "Mickey's Vaudeville Show," which would ultimately furnish story material for *Magician Mickey* as well as this short.[5] The opera sequence is based on the delightful premise of casting Donald Duck and Clara Cluck as opera singers, attacking (and *attacking* is the word) the Quartet from *Rigoletto*. The two story threads are united when a crowd of rabbits and pigeons, escaping from the hat, spill onto the stage during the performance. With so much going on, Mickey's footage, animated largely by Norm Ferguson and Frenchy de Trémaudan, is once again reduced.

A story sketch for the opening scene in *Orphans' Picnic*. As the sketch suggests, the scene begins with a close-up of the banner; then the camera pulls back to a longer view, revealing Donald perched on the cab of the truck as he leads the orphans in song.

The sign outside the theater, advertising the prestigious program to be presented. In the film *Mickey's Grand Opera,* sweeping searchlights and the sound of bustling traffic heighten the sense of anticipation.

In this poster art for *Mickey's Grand Opera*, Mickey, the orchestra, Donald, and Clara tackle *Rigoletto* — as they do in the film — with far more gusto than expertise.

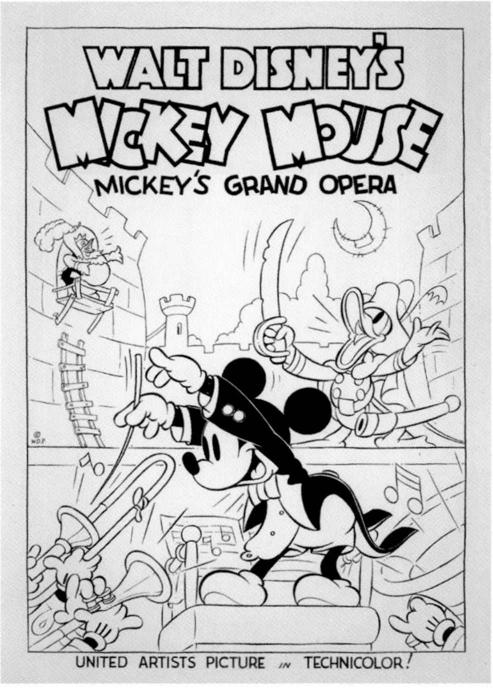

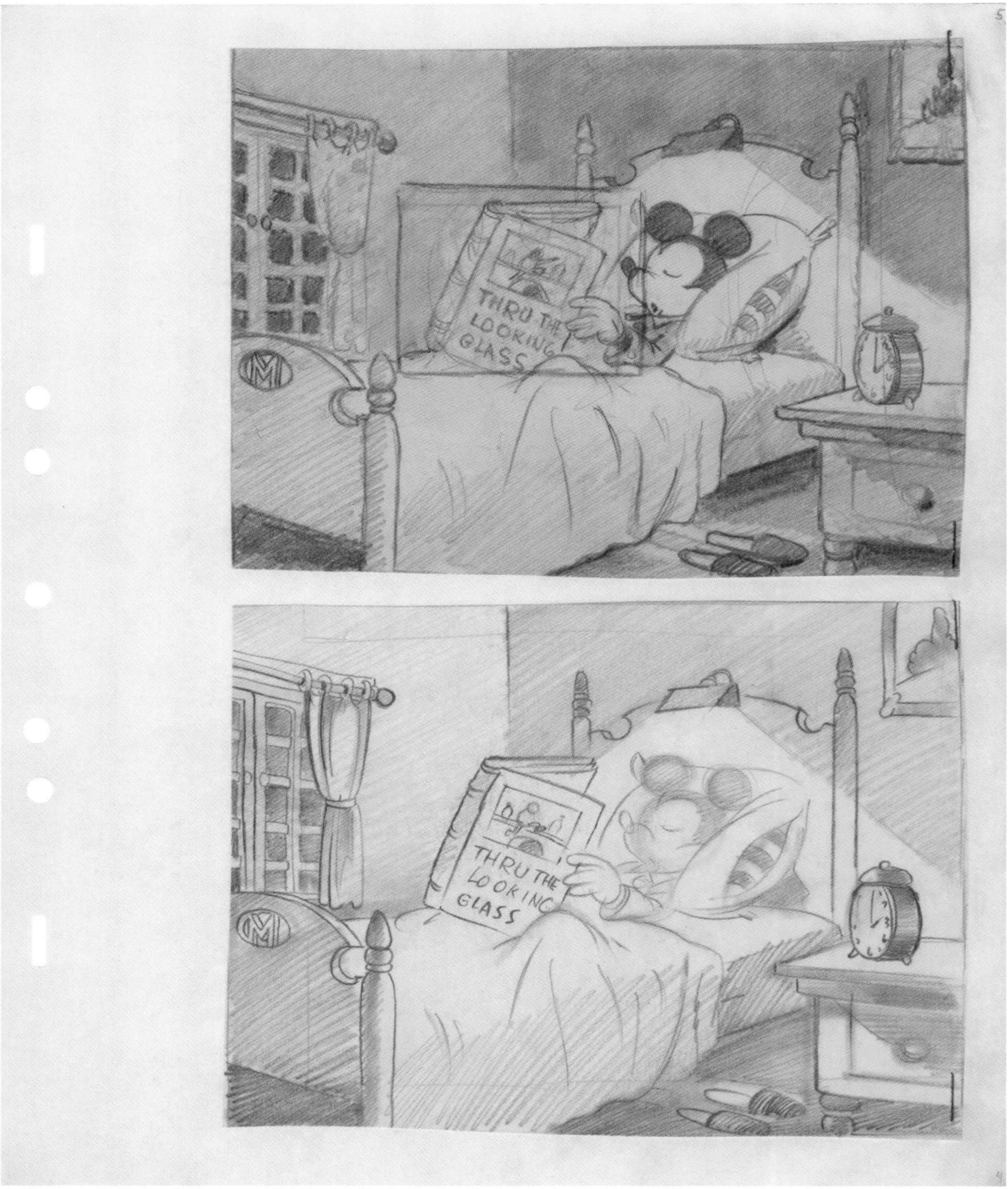

Story sketches for the opening scene in *Thru the Mirror*, as Mickey, after reading Lewis Carroll, dreams his way into a fantastic adventure of his own. These sketches suggest the tight opening close-up of the book cover, as well as the changes in lighting as Mickey's dream self rises from his sleeping body to begin his adventure.

Also like Alice, Mickey mingles with royalty in the form of humanized playing cards. Mickey's adventure includes a dance with the Queen of Hearts. After this sketch was prepared, Joe Grant and Bill Cottrell introduced a new twist: in the film, the Queen of Hearts is no anonymous stock figure but a caricature of Greta Garbo. Mickey's dance with her leads him into a duel with the jealous King of Hearts — Charles Laughton, who had recently starred in *The Private Life of Henry VIII*.

THRU THE MIRROR

(May 30, 1936)

Mickey returns to the literary classics, this time in color. This *very* free adaptation of Lewis Carroll is better than most, precisely because it avoids slavish imitation. Mickey, in his dream, passes through the mirror into an alternate world ruled by verbal and visual illogic. A highlight of the film is Mickey's dance number à la Fred Astaire, animated by dance specialist Dick Lundy. Mickey's distinctive musical theme for this sequence is Frank Churchill's "Seagull Shore," composed two years earlier for *Shanghaied*.

MOVING DAY

(June 20, 1936)

Mickey and Donald are evicted from their house for nonpayment of rent, their furniture repossessed by Sheriff Pete, doubtless a familiar situation to Depression-era audiences. Goofy, the iceman, arrives in his truck and agrees to help them move, rounding out the trio for a vintage Mickey-Donald-Goofy picture. Classic set pieces of action were developed for Donald and, especially, Goofy in this picture. As a result, Mickey is again reduced to the role of straight man, if not minor character; a planned sequence in which he wrestled with a folding ironing board was dropped. His remaining scenes are animated primarily by Paul Allen and Marvin Woodward.

MICKEY'S RIVAL

(June 20, 1936)

Mickey and Minnie's romantic picnic in the country is marred by the unexpected appearance of Minnie's "old time admirer,"[6] whose name is Mortimer! The interloper is an obnoxious show-off with an endless supply of practical jokes, and to make matters worse, Minnie still finds him amusing. This refreshingly off-beat cartoon introduces, in effect, several new characters: Mortimer; Mickey's beautifully anthropomorphized car; and the large, angry bull from a neighboring pasture, which Mortimer accidentally unleashes on the picnickers (after which Mortimer himself quickly disappears!). The planned ending pictured Mickey playing one of Mortimer's gags on Minnie with a trick extending glove; in the final version he simply shakes Minnie's hand.

Goofy loads the piano onto his truck in this *Moving Day* story sketch. In the film Art Babbitt develops this sequence into a tour de force of character animation: the piano develops a will of its own and rebels against Goofy, refusing to stay put.

Mortimer intrudes on Mickey's and Minnie's picnic in two *Mickey's Rival* story sketches. At right, he gives Mickey a demonstration of his obnoxious personality; above, he eagerly helps himself to the food at the picnic (while a note at the bottom of the sketch suggests that he has already disposed of much of it). Here, Mickey looks happier with the situation than he ever does in the film.

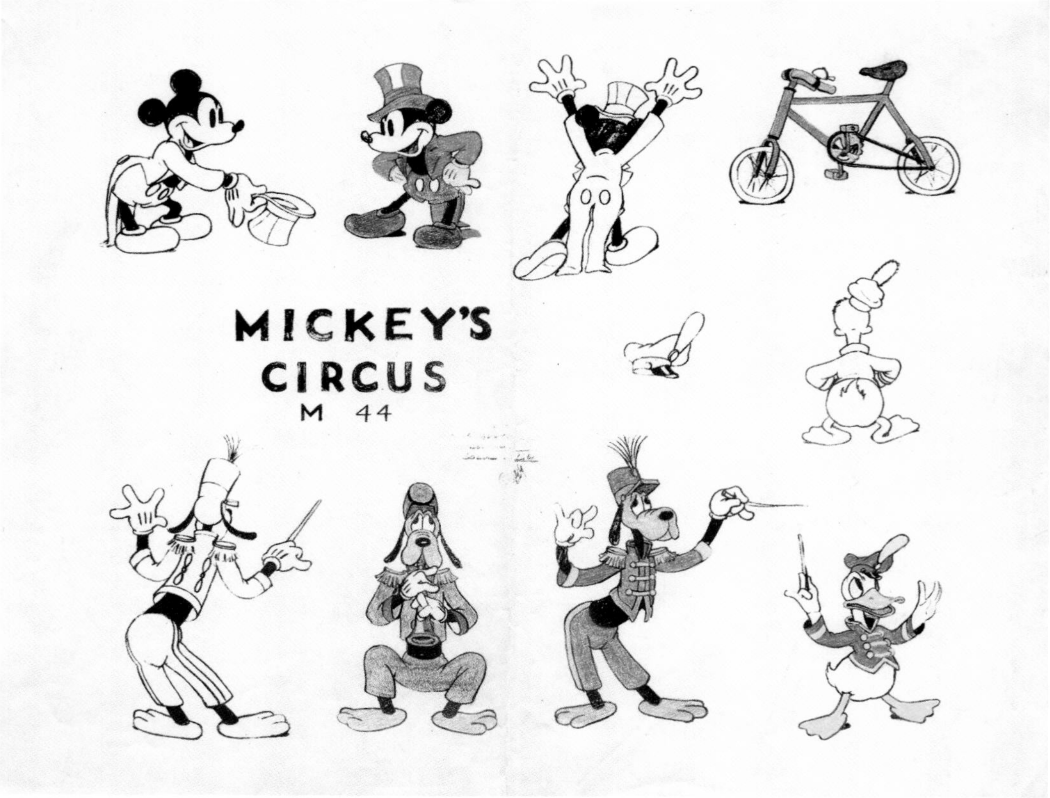

Experimental sketches for costumes and props in *Mickey's Circus*. Since Mickey and Donald both wear special costumes in this cartoon, not only the appearance but also the *colors* of the costumes must be predetermined. In the film, the bandleader, like Mickey, is splendidly attired in red.

ALPINE CLIMBERS
(July 25, 1936)

This is a group picture that varies the pattern: here it's Mickey, Donald, and Pluto who are climbing a mountain, each finding separate adventures. Donald soon has an altercation with both a baby mountain goat and its far more formidable father. Pluto makes a new friend: a large, mournful-looking St. Bernard, designed by Joe Grant. Mickey is not overshadowed in this picture, thanks to a deliberate effort by the writers; he tries to collect eggs from an eagle's nest and soon finds himself under attack by the adult eagle and *its* brood of baby eaglets.

MICKEY'S CIRCUS
(August 1, 1936)

Having treated the mob of orphans to a vaudeville show and a picnic, Mickey now hosts them at a circus, with himself as ringmaster and Donald Duck's trained-seal act as the principal attraction. And, once again, the orphans respond to this kindness with maniacal misbehavior. The climactic scenes find both Mickey and Donald stranded high in the air on a tightrope—which the orphans slather with oil, then connect to a high-voltage wire! Another of Donald's bêtes noir, the smallest and youngest seal, particularly appealed to Walt; he suggested gags for the character and later sought to revive him in other films.[7]

The poster for *Alpine Climbers*, featuring the film's three principals. Note that it's Pluto who rounds out the trio this time, and that he is pictured carrying a keg under his own chin. This idea had been suggested in the original story outline, but in the finished cartoon the keg is carried by a new St. Bernard character. Pluto's encounter with this newcomer, and his efforts to befriend him, make up a major sequence in the picture. Disney comics artist Al Taliaferro would later adapt the new character, eventually named Bolivar, for use as Donald Duck's dog in the comics — a role in which he continues today.

IMAGED BY HERITAGE AUCTIONS, HA.COM

A background painting for *Mickey's Elephant*. Some cartoons portrayed Mickey building a doghouse for Pluto; here he constructs a home for Bobo, so highly customized that it includes an extension for Bobo's trunk! This structure, built with such care, is demolished before the end of the cartoon.

Story sketch for *Mickey's Elephant*.

MICKEY'S ELEPHANT

(October 10, 1936)

In 1934 the *Mickey Mouse* comic strip had introduced a baby elephant named Bobo, and in this cartoon Bobo comes to the screen. The original story outline for this film suggested that the comedy would arise from the little elephant's interactions with Mickey, Donald, and Pluto. In the finished cartoon, Donald never appears at all and Mickey is once again reduced to the role of straight man. The bulk of the footage is another exercise in personality animation, focusing on Pluto (and his devilish alter ego) as he becomes jealous of Bobo.

THE WORM TURNS

(January 2, 1937)

This quirky little story idea was introduced in 1935 and percolated in the story department for months before being produced in its finished form. Mickey develops a "Courage Builder" chemical that gives any creature the courage to stand up to its traditional oppressor: a fly thrashes a spider, and a mouse tosses a cat out a window. The reversals continue up the chain of persecution as the cat, threatened by Pluto, gets a dose of Mickey's chemical and chases Pluto out of the neighborhood. Pluto, in turn, cornered by Pete the dogcatcher, becomes a raging beast and frightens Pete out of his wits and over a cliff.

Publicity art for *The Worm Turns*. Mickey's potion in the film is a "courage builder" that makes any creature brave enough to stand up to its enemies. This drawing suggests an entirely different idea: a "Super Tonic" which Mickey uses to create an enormous bone, much to Pluto's delight.

IMAGED BY HERITAGE AUCTIONS, HA.COM

The poster for *Magician Mickey*. This particular gag is not seen in the film, but it conveys the sense of the proceedings: Donald tries to get the better of Mickey, but succeeds only in outsmarting himself.

Story sketches for *Magician Mickey*. The reworked story pictured Donald as a member of the audience, obnoxiously heckling Mickey. This approach was more in keeping with their characters: Mickey remains unflappable, keeps smiling, and comes out on top, while Donald's mischief inevitably backfires on him and sends him into another hysterical tantrum.

MAGICIAN MICKEY

(February 6, 1937)

Another offshoot of the story outline that had produced *Mickey's Grand Opera*, this story originally cast Mickey as a magician and Donald as his onstage assistant, deliberately undercutting his magic tricks. In the finished version Mickey's magical powers are genuine, and Donald is a member of the audience, heckling the magician mercilessly. This picture offers a useful summary of the characters' relationship: Mickey is a nice guy, Donald is anything but. As the picture continues, however, Mickey cleverly finds ways of causing the Duck's spiteful pranks to backfire on him. In the end, Mickey prevails but remains sympathetic, while Donald explodes in a paroxysm of fury.

Poster art for *Moose Hunters*, picturing a far gentler moose than those we see in the film. This docile creature, allowing himself to be led by a string, seems primarily to have designs on Mickey's hat.

MOOSE HUNTERS
(February 20, 1937)

In 1931 Mickey had starred with Pluto in *The Moose Hunt*; nearly six years later, he hunts again, this time with Donald Duck and Goofy—and with the same degree of success. Here Donald and Goofy, in a ridiculous disguise, impersonate a female moose in order to lure a bull within range. Inevitably the plan misfires, and the three hunters are unmasked and barely escape with their own lives. In an interesting departure, the backgrounds for this picture were painted, not with watercolors, but with poster paints, in an effort to create flat areas of color consistent with the look of the painted characters on the cels.[8]

MICKEY'S AMATEURS
(April 17, 1937)

Mickey hosts an amateur show in his final release for United Artists. Remarkably, the story team responsible for the short—Pinto Colvig, Ed Penner, and Walt Disney's childhood pal Walt Pfeiffer—became the directors as well. The result was an extremely offbeat cartoon, with wild, free-wheeling gags and animation that suggest other studios as much as Disney. Al Eugster, who animated Donald Duck, recalled the experience with pleasure: "I felt I had more freedom during my assignment on this film."[9] Again Mickey, animated by Marvin Woodward, is reduced to a straight man at the center of the wild action.

Story sketch depicting Goofy's one-man-band contraption in *Mickey's Amateurs*. The device in the film is bigger and more complicated than this sketch suggests, and Goofy's wild performance of "There'll Be a Hot Time in the Old Town Tonight," animated over a period of weeks that ran far over schedule, is a highlight of the film.

Publicity art by Tom Wood for *Mickey's Amateurs*. Amateur talent contests were a staple of radio in the 1930s. In this cartoon Mickey burlesqued the conventions of the genre, including the ringing of a gong to cut short a subpar performance.

One of the first major storybooks to feature Mickey was this handsome edition, published in 1931 with cover art by Roy Nelson. Shown here is the scarce British edition lacking the note "Book 1."

STORYBOOKS

Although Mickey Mouse's appeal covered a wide demographic spectrum, children were considered an important part of his audience from the beginning. When the studio began to explore the possibilities for Mickey merchandising, storybooks for children were an early and popular item.

Published in November 1930 by Bibo and Lang, *Mickey Mouse Book* is recognized today as the first Mickey storybook. Along with the song "Mickey Mouse (You Cute Little Feller)" and a cutout card game, this independent publication featured "The Story of Mickey Mouse," purportedly written by Bobette Bibo, the copublisher's 11-year-old daughter. This version of Mickey's backstory depicted him as the mischievous "mouse number thirteen," forcibly ejected from Mouse Fairyland for "playing tricks and cutting capers." Falling through the air, the mouse landed in California. There he met Walt Disney, who was so amused by his lively antics that he renamed the rodent Mickey and cast him in a series of comedy films. The story ended with an account of Mickey and Minnie's celebrity lifestyle, driving around in a little green roadster and attending glamorous movie premieres.

Coinciding with *Mickey Mouse Book* was the first international Disney publication, Dean and Son's British *Mickey Mouse Annual* No. 1—which, following the usual pattern of British children's annuals, was technically considered the annual for 1931, but went on sale for Christmas 1930.[10] The chunky, 132-page hardback, like many of its British successors, was much closer to a first-run comic book than a storybook, and as such has already been discussed earlier in this volume.

These twin debuts soon led to bigger things. *Mickey Mouse Book* was copyrighted in Walt's name, but it had been conceived and produced outside the studio, with art provided by New York–based freelancer Albert Barbelle.[11] *Mickey Mouse Annual*, too, was drawn by local freelance artists rather than Disney's own. By the end of 1930 the David McKay Company, a high-profile American publisher of children's books, had contracted for something far more substantial: Mickey Mouse storybooks created, or at least illustrated, within the studio. The first McKay book, *The Adventures of Mickey Mouse, Book 1*, was published in 1931. Handsomely illustrated in color, in part by Mickey comic-strip inker Roy Nelson,[12] it told a story in which Mickey—pictured behaving at times like a real mouse, as in *When the Cat's Away*—lived in a nest underneath a barn. The villain, "Claws, the Cat," attempted to catch him, but Mickey handily outwitted her efforts, then invited Minnie and all his other friends to a barn dance at which he played all the instruments. Mickey's friends in this story included approximations of Horace and Clarabelle called "Henry" and "Carolyn," strongly suggesting that the manuscript was still written, or finalized, outside the studio. Whether created in-studio or out, however, this same 1931 manuscript included a notable coincidence: a passing reference to a character called "Donald Duck"!

McKay soon supplemented this original storybook with other books that drew directly on the Disney films and comic strips. *Mickey Mouse Movie Stories* was a book of nearly 200 pages that retold the stories of 11 Mickey films, couched alternately in prose and in verse. The book was copiously illustrated with scene stills from the original

The first *Big Little Book* featuring Mickey, simply titled *Mickey Mouse*, appeared in several different forms. The first edition featured awkward cover art, replaced for the second edition with the jaunty cover seen above. At bottom: in England the "Big Little Book" was rebranded as a "Great Big Midget Book," its cover art reworked by British artist Wilfred Haughton.

cartoons *and* augmented with animation drawings from *The Delivery Boy*, on the lower page corners, by which the reader could flip the pages and watch Minnie and Mickey dancing the Charleston. McKay soon produced more economical editions, *Mickey Mouse Story Book* and *Mickey Mouse Stories: Book II* (both circa 1934, although dated 1931), each of which featured four of the stories from the original book and retained the flip-book drawings. As if *that* were not enough, the publisher also produced *Mickey Mouse Series No. 1*, a compilation of reproduced 1930–31 installments from the *Mickey Mouse* newspaper comic strip.

By the end of 1931, then, McKay had inaugurated three separate Mickey publishing franchises: one book designed, written, and produced as a traditional storybook, and two other formats derived directly from Disney films and comic strips. All of these books sold well, and McKay continued to produce new entries in each of these categories. *The Adventures of Mickey Mouse, Book 2*, published in 1932, told a considerably more ambitious story than its predecessor, a tale loosely based on a contemporary continuity in the comic strip: Mickey, Minnie, and Pluto outwitted Peg Leg Pete and his gang as they tried to steal a buried treasure belonging to Captain Churchmouse's widow. A second volume of *Mickey Mouse Movie Stories* maintained the high standard of the first; it retold the stories of 12 more theatrical Mickey cartoons, generously illustrated with full-page scene stills. *Mickey Mouse*, the series of comic-strip reprints, ultimately produced *four* volumes—one of them composed of full-color 1932 Sunday comics.

By 1932, foreign Mickey book production was also expanding by leaps and bounds. In France, publisher Opera Mundi was the local licensor of King Features comic strips, Disney included. After running the first Mickey strip

Mickey "pops up" in Tom Wood's cover art for *The Pop-up Mickey Mouse*, the background retaining the circus theme.

IMAGED BY HERITAGE AUCTIONS, HA.COM

serials in the newspaper *Le Petit Parisien*, Opera Mundi owner Paul Winkler teamed up with fellow publisher Hachette to reprint the serials in color albums — in essence, a classier version of the McKay strip reprint format. In a bow to French comics tradition, these *Albums Mickey* replaced the strips' dialogue with descriptive prose by Hachette editor Magdeleine du Genestoux.

Then du Genestoux moved on to something new: a Mickey-based young adult novel. *Mickey et Minnie* (1932), an extended prose version of the first two Mickey strip serials, joined Hachette's prestigious *Bibliothèque Rose* book series. Working with du Genestoux was artist Félix Lorioux, a regular Hachette contributor. World-famous for illustrating such children's books as *Fables de La Fontaine* (1929), Lorioux is said to have met Walt — as a post-World War I ambulance driver in France — more than a decade earlier.[13] Now Lorioux reinterpreted the comic strips' imagery in a wild avant-garde style, creating an irresistible combination with Genestoux's breathless prose (translated here):

> *"Stop! One move forward and they'll be walking slowly behind you!"*
>
> *In his haste, Mickey had not drawn his gun. He had reached into a basket behind him and drawn an umbrella.*

The Pop-up Mickey Mouse brought another eye-catching twist to the world of Mickey Mouse storybooks. The book included three pop-ups; this first one, drawn by Tom Wood, was inserted at the frontispiece. After this introductory image, with Mickey and Minnie about to enter the circus, the story proceeded with a circus setting. Floyd Gottfredson and Al Taliaferro drew the book's standard-format illustrations.

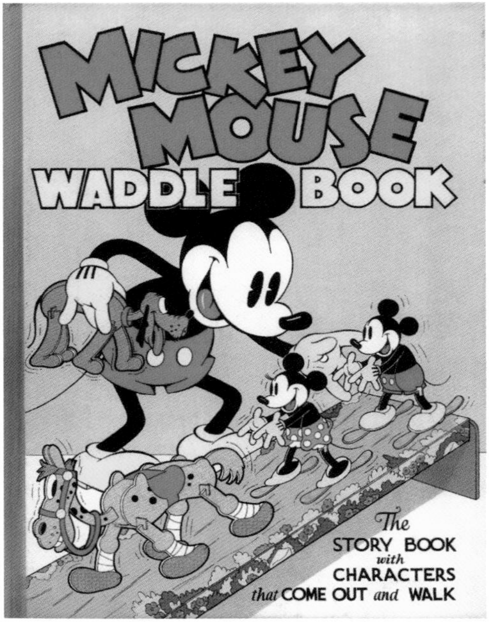

Further blurring the distinction between storybooks and toys, *Mickey Mouse Waddle Book* told a story of Mickey's efforts to train Tanglefoot as a racehorse, *and* included detachable pieces that could be assembled as three-dimensional figures and made to "waddle" down a ramp, illustrating the story.

The "waddle" figures, perforated, printed on both sides of the page, and designed to be punched out and folded as three-dimensional figures. In addition to the Mickey and Tanglefoot pages seen here, the book also included separate pages with the Minnie and Pluto figures. These were further supplemented by a ramp, also ready for assembly.

It popped open in Pete's direction with a harmless rustling sound.

Mickey's bold mistake roused Pete to side-splitting laughter. The thug held his belly and guffawed like an ape. "Some joke, Mouse! I might be in a stormy mood, but an umbrella won't protect yuh."

"A magician musta transformed my gun," muttered Mickey. "That always happened to Don Quixote, too." Then, seeing Pete about to stomp him with both feet, Mickey turned and fled. He had to escape this villain—Minnie must be found![14]

A North American brand of Mickey novelizations was launched in 1933, when Sam Lowe, of the Whitman Publishing Company, contacted Walt with a sample of Whitman's new product line for children: the Big Little Books. These fat little books, measuring a few inches square and running hundreds of pages, were based—like the Hachette albums—on

Walt helps to promote the *Waddle Book*, posing with the book and the assembled figures and ramp.

MICKEY MOUSE
MERCHANDISE
1936-37
Published by
KAY KAMEN LTD
EXCLUSIVE REPRESENTATIVE
WALT DISNEY ENTERPRISES
ROCKEFELLER CENTER
1270 SIXTH AVENUE
NEW YORK U S A

recycled comic strips with added text, but featured an ingenious new format. The first Big Little Book, *The Adventures of Dick Tracy*, published in 1932, had established the form: an illustration from the *Dick Tracy* strip on one page, with text, paraphrasing the story, on the facing page. Most of the succeeding Big Little Books had been based on "adventure" strips such as *Tarzan*, *Flash Gordon*, and *Tailspin Tommy*. Now, Lowe wrote, "We wonder if it is possible to get the right to 'Mickey Mouse' in a book of this kind, which is different than anything already published."[15]

Because they could be produced so cheaply, the Big Little Books could be marketed for a 10-cent cover price, affordable for many children even in the Depression years. Moreover, many of Floyd Gottfredson's adventure-story continuities for the *Mickey Mouse* strip were made to order for adaptation to the Big Little format. The Disneys happily agreed to Lowe's proposition, and *Mickey Mouse*, the first Disney Big Little Book, was published later in 1933. Repurposing the 1931

Kay Kamen's merchandise catalog for the 1936–37 season, now with a full-color cover. Note that Mickey has discarded the *old* catalogs, and that Donald Duck is now prominently featured by his side.

Above and following A look inside Kay Kamen's 1936–37 catalogs for the U.S. (black and white) and the U.K. (color) featuring assorted Mickey Mouse merchandise. The high quality standard of the licensed product was reflected in these lavishly designed and printed volumes.

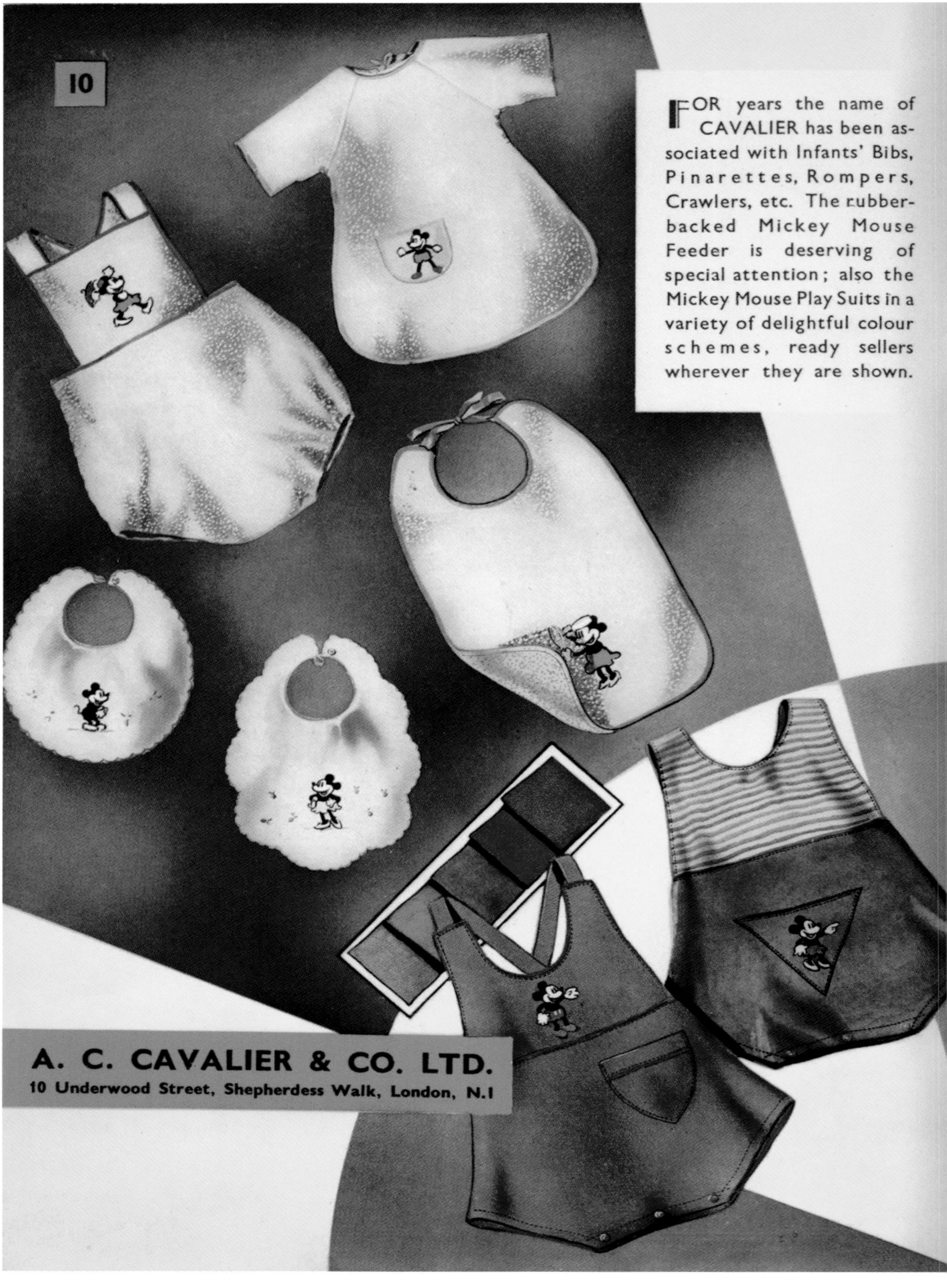

FOR years the name of CAVALIER has been associated with Infants' Bibs, Pinarettes, Rompers, Crawlers, etc. The rubber-backed Mickey Mouse Feeder is deserving of special attention; also the Mickey Mouse Play Suits in a variety of delightful colour schemes, ready sellers wherever they are shown.

A. C. CAVALIER & CO. LTD.

10 Underwood Street, Shepherdess Walk, London, N.1

THE use of aluminium jelly moulds is becoming increasingly popular every year. Mickey Mouse Jelly and Jellette Moulds are an 'all the year round' line, for not only are they welcomed everywhere in the summer season, but also there is a constant demand for 'out of the ordinary' jelly moulds for use during the winter months when dances and parties are at their height.
MICKEY MOUSE
JELLY MOULD
MICKEY MOUSE
Jellette
MOULDS FOR
JELLIES & CAKES
SELLMAN & HILL LTD.
Church Lane, Wolverhampton

MICKEY MOUSE box covering papers by Sanderson—designs can be adapted to include your own name or trade mark—sample sheets of stock always available for experimental purposes.

The back cover of this book is Sanderson's Flock paper. Special Mickey Mouse and Three Little Pigs designs are obtainable in Sanderson Fabrics.

ARTHUR SANDERSON & SONS, LTD.

51/52 Berners Street, London, W.1

19
DONALD DUCK torpedoes, Pluto rousers, Mickey's nightmare and dozens more. All of the old favourites and many new ones. Every Mickey Mouse firework has been specially designed in the Walt Disney studios. Children from 6—60 will want Mickey Mouse fireworks in the coming season and they will ask for them.
SEPH WELLS & SONS LTD.
rt Firework Factory, Honor Oak Park, London, S.E.23
PLUTO

ADDIS of Hertford are continuing their excellent range of Mickey Mouse toothbrushes and also they are producing a novel Mickey Mouse nailbrush which is available in six brilliant colours. The manufacture of all these brushes follows the same strict supervision in every stage of production that is accorded to all Addis merchandise.

The Oldest Firm of Toothbrush Manufacturers in the World. Established 1780.

ADDIS
Brushworks, Hertford

MICKEY MOUSE balloons in all shapes, sizes and colours. This popular line enjoyed an enthusiastic reception and will continue to please everywhere by its ready acceptance by children of all ages and by social secretaries of clubs for their carnival nights.

EWIS KNIGHT LTD.

Bunhill Row, London, E.C.I

"HIS MASTER'S VOICE"
BEST sellers for Christmas and all the year. Exclusive "His Master's Voice" records of the actual sound of Mickey Mouse and Silly Symphony films. Price 1/6 each. Stores holding the "His Master's Voice" dealership should feature the special Mickey Mouse Albums in their Christmas Bazaars.
THE GRAMOPHONE CO. LTD
98-108 Clerkenwell Road, London, E.C.1

HERE is a selection from the furniture included in Messrs. W. Hands & Sons' list. Each article bears a cheerful picture of Mickey Mouse or his companions, and is so designed that it combines beauty with utility. Parents throughout the land will find this furniture irresistible.
W. HANDS & SONS, LTD.
High Wycombe
Every piece of Mickey Mouse nursery furniture lends itself admirably to window display.

MICKEY MOUSE Toy Lantern Outfits, with *full colour* slides, provide a source of endless fascination to children by bringing Walt Disney's Silly Symphonies into the home. Each outfit contains full descriptive story. The lantern is fitted with a powerful lens, an electric battery and a spare lamp bulb. In addition, an all-mains model is available, complete with lamp and connections.

ENSIGN LIMITED

Ensign House, 88-89, High Holborn, W.C.I

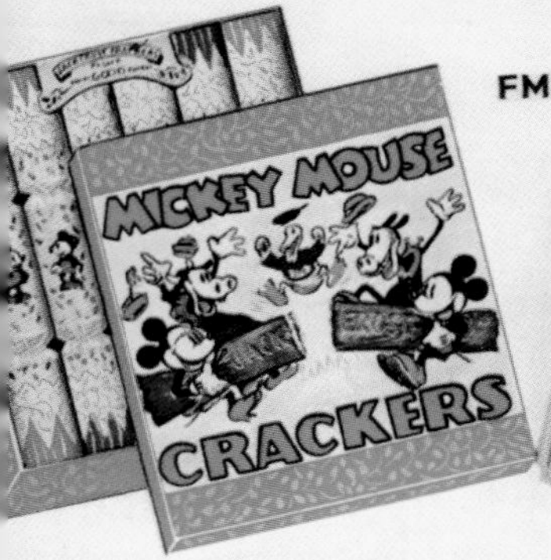

THESE illustrations show some of the famous Mickey Mouse Christmas Cracker novelties produced by Jack Frost Ltd.

Works:
183-185 CENTRAL STREET
LONDON, E.C.1

JACK FROST LTD.
4 Golden Lane, London, E.C.1

40
PRICE'S MICKEY MOUSE
NIGHT LIGHTS
8 HOURS
1D each
TO BURN WITHOUT WATER
PRICE'S
MICKEY MOUSE
NIGHT LIGHTS
TO BURN WITHOUT WATER
PRICE'S MICKEY MOUSE NIGHT LIGHTS
PRICE'S
MICKEY MOUSE
NIGHT LIGHTS
TO BURN IN A SAUCER WITHOUT WATER
PRICE'S Mickey Mouse Night Lights introduce the familiar product in a bright new form. Each Mickey Mouse Night Light is individually packed in a carton bearing amusing silhouettes of the Disney characters. Marketed in brilliantly coloured display cartons containing 36 lights; also in 10-light cartons.
PRICE'S PATENT CANDLE CO. LT
Battersea, S.W.II

NOW bath time's better fun for kiddies thanks to Fields. Beautiful models of Mickey, Minnie, Donald and Pluto in finest Toilet Soap are now available, packed singly in gaily decorated window boxes, specially designed to give maximum display value. This line is a "winner" and the retail price is attractive, only 6d. per model.

J. C. & J. FIELD LTD.

LONDON, S.E.I

Established 1642, in the Reign of Charles I

"Ransom Plot" continuity from the comic strip, *Mickey Mouse* was a great success and led to many more Disney Big Little Books, appearing well into the 1940s (and then again, with new titles, in the 1960s–80s). As the series continued, new variations were introduced: Better Little Books and, in one instance, a Big Big Book. The story of Mickey's horse Tanglefoot prompted an intriguing departure: the narrative was divided into six "Wee Little Books," packaged together in a slipcase. The *Mickey* comic strip and, later, comic books provided an endless source of material for these books, but in two cases they were based on original material: *Mickey Mouse and Minnie at Macy's* celebrated Mickey's appearance in the Macy's Thanksgiving Day parade in 1934, and a sequel, *Mickey and Minnie Mouse March to Macy's*, appeared the following year. While most Big Little Books took pains to make the comics' adventure stories seem equally believable in prose, the first Macy story included the uniquely bizarre idea that the Macy's Mickey character balloon was actually Mickey himself, inflated to giant size and disoriented by the experience!

Another innovation was launched in 1933: pop-up books, with three-dimensional set pieces that unfolded into view when the pages were opened. Published by Blue Ribbon Books, these colorful concoctions provided a natural showcase for Disney characters and stories. *The Pop-up Mickey Mouse*, featuring original illustrations by Floyd Gottfredson and Al Taliaferro, led the way with a story of Mickey and Minnie helping stranded circus animals to return to their natural habitats. *The Pop-up Minnie Mouse* followed, with Minnie and Mickey rescuing the newly hatched "Moby

Soundtrack recordings of both Mickey Mouse and Silly Symphony cartoons were released on the Bluebird label in the U.S. and on British HMV in the U.K. The British records could be purchased separately, but were also available as a set in this colorful album.

A "bookplate," available with the HMV album, for personalizing the records as a gift.

Duck" from a hungry hawk named Clutch. These books were successful enough to warrant further Disney pop-ups, including an even more elaborate production: *Mickey Mouse in King Arthur's Court*. With a story constructed very loosely from the film *Ye Olden Days* and the traditional tales of King Arthur, this lavish storybook related Mickey's adventures in medieval times, and ended with his marriage to Princess Minnie. The rival prince played by "Dippy Dawg" (the early Goofy) in *Ye Olden Days* became a redesigned monkey character, "Prince Addlepate," in the Blue Ribbon version of the story.

The success of the pop-up Disney books, featuring Silly Symphony characters as well as Mickey and Minnie, encouraged Blue Ribbon to design further "mechanical" novelty books. In 1934 the company published *Mickey Mouse in Ye Olden Days*, an economical and much smaller (about the size of a Big Little Book) edition of *Mickey Mouse in King Arthur's Court*, with a highly condensed version of the original text and one little pop-up of its own. *The Mickey Mouse Waddle Book* included heavy board pages with characters that could be punched out and assembled, and came packaged with a ramp that could also be assembled, and down which the characters would "waddle" with the help of gravity and a gentle push. While elaborate and only intermittently functional, *The Mickey Mouse Waddle Book* was still successful enough to be reprinted in foreign markets—a privilege few other Blue Ribbon Waddle Books earned.

In due time the path also began to run the other way: foreign Mickey storybooks began crossing the pond to North America, and then moving from one European country to another. While the Dean and Son *Mickey Mouse Annual* volumes were reprinted by the Canadian publisher Musson, they never saw a United States reprint. But substantial inroads were

Arranged on a background painting from *Mickey's Grand Opera*, this Mickey merchandise grouping includes Mickey and Minnie stuffed toys based on the McCall's sewing pattern (see Chapter 1); the famous 1936 Marks Brothers Co. Mickey Mouse Piano "With Dancing Figures"; two mid-1930s bisque figurines; a 1937 Ingersoll watch design with packaging; several varieties of 1931 George Borgfeldt wooden jointed and "Fun-E-Flex" figures; a mid-1930s jointed doll; an elephant mahout toy; a boxed whirligig wind-up; a Marks Brothers Co. Mickey and Minnie megaphone; a small-size Dean's Rag Book stuffed Mickey from 1930; and two more mid-1930s Mickey and Minnie figures.

Following Posed before a background painting for *Traffic Troubles*, another assortment of Mickey merchandise. Items pictured here include a George Borgfeldt Mickey and Pluto celluloid figure; a Mickey-Minnie railroad handcar, produced as a British counterpart to the American Lionel handcar; a Borgfeldt jointed wooden toy with a December 16, 1930 patent on its label; an early (and possibly unlicensed) wire figure; and two more celluloid figures — an "umbrella whirligig" and a tricycle toy — made in Japan for mid-1930s American distribution.

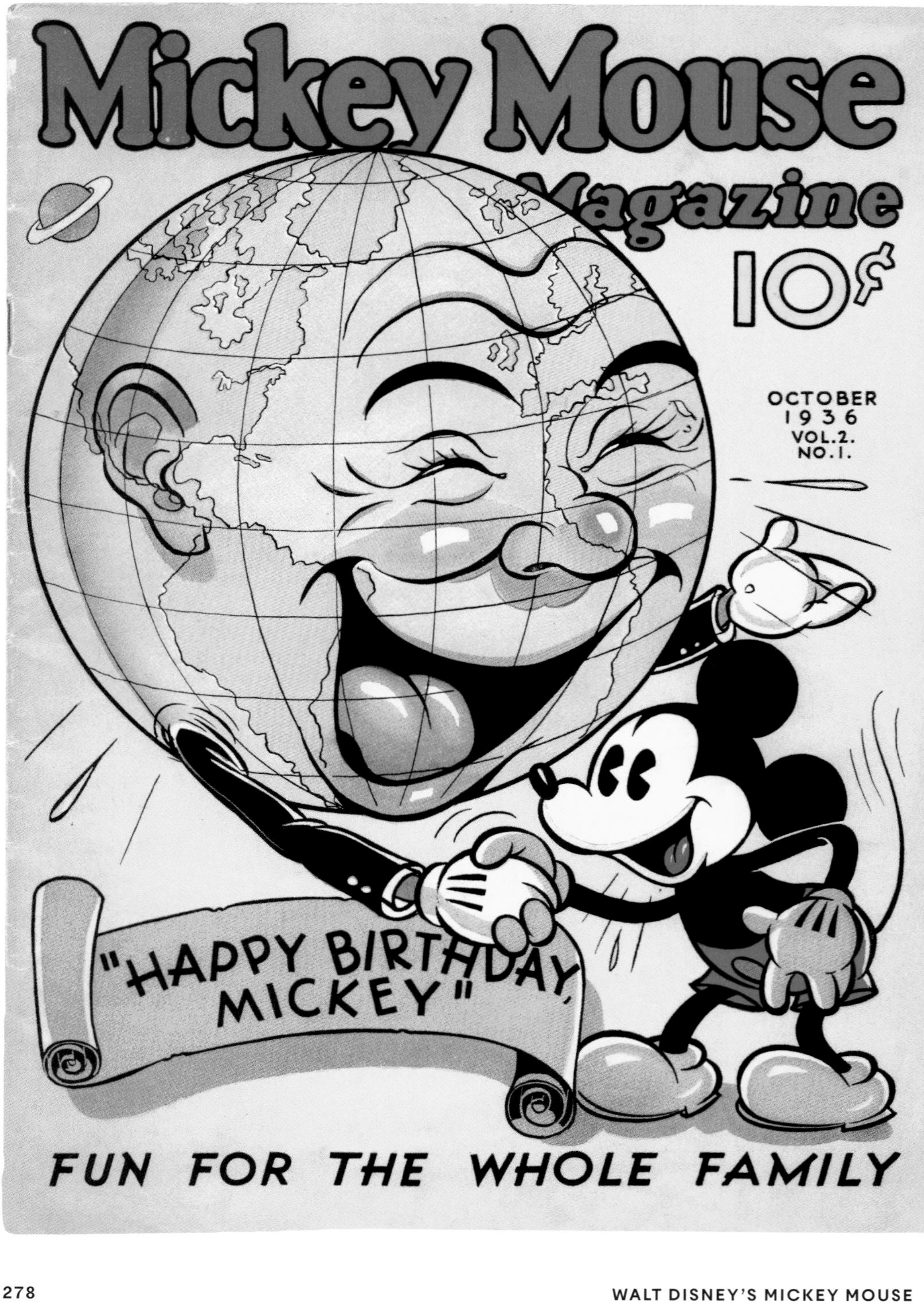
Mickey Mouse
Magazine
10¢
OCTOBER
1936
VOL.2.
NO.1.
"HAPPY BIRTHDAY,
MICKEY"
FUN FOR THE WHOLE FAMILY

made by the more elaborate Mickey storybooks that two more British licensees, Collins Clear-Type Press and Birn Brothers Ltd., began to publish mid-decade. Featuring masterful art by an apparent shared pool of artists, multichapter volumes such as Birn's *A Trip with Mickey Mouse* (circa 1935)—featuring an original story of Mickey, Minnie, Horace, and Clarabelle traveling around the British Isles—and Collins's *Don Mickey* (1937), with Mickey and Donald as an ersatz Quixote and Sancho Panza, were every bit the equal of their American chapter-book equivalents. The books began to be recognized abroad: *Don Mickey* was reprinted in Spain, Sweden, and Italy (in two editions, one a "digest" with the localized Big Little Book brand). Then, when the same creative team moved on to books that were expansions of screen cartoons, such as Collins's *Mickey Mouse in Pigmy Land* (1935, i.e., *Gulliver Mickey*) and *The Mickey Mouse Fire Brigade* (1936), best-selling reprints in the United States began. Not every attempt to expand a cartoon to novel length could be called a *critical* success—*Fire Brigade* tried humanizing the flames, naming one Archibald!—but the effort did constitute a major international milestone.

By this time the publication of Mickey Mouse and other Disney storybooks, illustrated and largely produced by the studio, had blossomed into a side industry of its own. It continued to proliferate throughout the 1930s and into succeeding decades. Big Little Books and Hachette albums were localized and reprinted in numerous countries, sometimes leading to local spin-offs in the same format. Selected Mickey cartoons (such as *Brave Little Tailor*) received special promotional storybooks of their own; other story ideas, rejected for production, were issued as storybooks *instead* of films. A growing number of books included games and puzzles alongside, or in place of, stories. In time McKay and Whitman were joined by other

By the autumn of 1936, United Artists was prepared to launch a full-scale promotional campaign in honor of Mickey's eighth birthday. Of course the Disney studio lent its wholehearted support to the campaign. Here, on the cover of *Mickey Mouse Magazine*, the whole world (literally) congratulates Mickey on his birthday.

In promoting the special theatrical programs, United Artists pulled out all the stops. Advertising for the shows was not restricted to trade ads, targeted at exhibitors, but also included ads in the popular press, taking the promotional push to the general public. In addition, along with the posters for individual cartoons, UA also issued the special poster seen below to theaters showing the programs.

Dear Pal:
Instead of you sending me birthday greetings this year. I'm turning things around a little and sending my own greetings to you. Be sure and attend my Eighth Birthday Party at your nearest theatre during the week of September 25th to October 1st inclusive! And thanks for all your kind words.

Love and Kisses xxxxx
Mickey Mouse

©W. D. P

Disney-licensed publishers: D. C. Heath produced a line of school readers, while Grosset & Dunlap and Random House published high-end deluxe editions featuring Mickey and other characters. In the early 1940s Simon & Schuster launched the Little Golden Books for children; within a few years Mickey and his friends were prominently featured. All in all, the making of Mickey Mouse storybooks was established as an active field that has continued, in one form or another, to this day.

MICKEY'S BIRTHDAY

The idea of celebrating a cartoon character's "birthday" may seem only a whimsical notion, but Mickey Mouse was no ordinary character. As early as 1930, Columbia Pictures, Disney's distributor, was touting Mickey's second anniversary as a promotional event. November 18, 1928, the opening day of *Steamboat Willie* at the Colony Theatre, is recognized today as

A full week at the end of September was designated for the festivities in honor of Mickey's 8th birthday. This card was sent to the members of the Mickey Mouse Clubs, inviting them to special theatrical showings of Mickey's cartoons.

In 1936 birthday promotional art, Donald Duck marks the occasion by teasing Mickey over his "baby pictures."

A posed group shot of popular characters in the Disney stock company, 1939.

Mickey's "birthdate," but in 1930, Columbia and the Disney studio were not fussy about pinpointing a specific date. It was enough to observe that the event had occurred during the autumn months, and "for practical purposes, the exact day may be assumed to be some Saturday about the middle of the latter part" of October.[16] Columbia encouraged exhibitors to observe the occasion by booking all-Mickey cartoon programs, *sometime* during the early days of the school year. The Disney studio supported the campaign with promotional art,[17] and produced a special cartoon, *The Birthday Party*—but, as we've seen, this film was not completed and released until the following January. In 1931 Columbia repeated their promotional effort for Mickey's third birthday.

By the time his *fourth* birthday rolled around in 1932, Mickey had the combined promotional forces of Kay Kamen and United Artists behind him. Together they mounted a considerably more enthusiastic campaign in his honor:

J. Edgar Hoover, founding director of the FBI, wears an Einson-Freeman Co. Mickey Mouse mask at a New Year's Eve party in the elegant Stork Club at the end of 1937.

a 48-page campaign book mailed to exhibitors in America and abroad, detailing the dozens of Disney licensees whose products could be tied in with special showings of Mickey's cartoons. The birthday celebration was extended to a full week; the hundreds of Mickey Mouse Clubs across the nation held special parties for Mickey, and the occasion was marked by national radio broadcasts. In New York, United Artists hosted a "mousewarming" at the first-run Rivoli Theatre; in Los Angeles, children attended a free party at Grauman's Chinese, while older celebrants were invited to a celebration at the Cocoanut Grove.

The resulting hoopla was a promotional bonanza for the Disney studio, participating licensees, and exhibitors, and celebrations of Mickey's birthday became an annual event. Local exhibitors and merchants happily pitched in. "More than 450 reels of Mickey Mouse and Silly Symphony cartoons have been booked into local theatres," wrote a Chicago correspondent in 1935, "for the celebration of Mickey's seventh anniversary."[18] The commemorations didn't end there; a song, "Mickey Mouse's Birthday Party," was published by Irving Berlin, Inc., and promoted in connection with the 1936 campaign. Roy Disney was enormously pleased with these developments and made every effort to cooperate with the promotions. "This 'birthday week' makes a very nice annual event," he wrote to Walt, "and acts like a 'sale' with respect to our pictures."[19]

For the first few years, Mickey's birthday was a moveable feast; a variety of September and October dates were put forward from year to year as the official day. In 1935, the year of Mickey's "lucky seventh" birthday, United Artists settled more or less arbitrarily on the 28th of September, and for years afterward that date was unquestioningly accepted as Mickey's actual birthday. In 1936, one journalist took it literally and wrote an account describing *Steamboat Willie*'s 1928 opening on the same bill with Paul Fejos' *Lonesome*—the feature that had been shown at the Colony in late September 1928 (and a far more distinguished film than Bert Glennon's *Gang War*, which actually *had* been shown with Mickey's debut in November).[20] Not until 1978, as Mickey approached the 50-year mark, did The Walt Disney Company formally establish November 18, once and for all, as Mickey's official "birthday."

THE "COMEBACK"

Even as these annual celebrations were demonstrating Mickey's unflagging popularity with the public at large, Donald Duck and other colorful new characters were continuing to crowd him to the sidelines. Walt was not unaware

Colorful cover art for the British storybook *A Trip with Mickey Mouse*, ca. 1935. This lavishly illustrated book told the tale of Mickey, Minnie, Horace, Clarabelle, and Morty and Ferdie touring the U.K. The gang's adventures include an encounter with "The Man from the Isle of Man," as well as boastful Horace's bungling attempt to help Mickey kiss the Blarney Stone.

Original art by Hank Porter for the November 6, 1937 issue of *Collier's* magazine portrays Mickey, Donald, and Goofy at the Detroit Auto Show.

of this development. The success of his newer characters must surely have pleased him, but Walt was not about to abandon his Mouse. Being personally invested in the character, he felt a certain loyalty to him (not to mention commercial considerations). He had already taken steps to find special story material—distinctive vehicles, like *Thru the Mirror*, in which Mickey's personality could be displayed to better advantage than in slapstick cartoon shorts.

Late in the 1930s, Walt reached a turning point. He determined to redouble his efforts on Mickey's behalf, reinvigorating his career with exceptional, prestigious productions. By the summer of 1937 the first of these special pictures, *Brave Little Tailor*, was under way. Walt made no secret of his plans, and interviewers, informed of this new initiative, actually described it as Mickey's "comeback." "Mickey, who made his first hit ten years ago, is still the No. 1 star," reported one journalist in 1938. "Disney says so. But Mickey was almost crowded out as the Disney family grew. It's strictly on his creator's orders that he's making a comeback this year."[21]

The comeback involved more than an injection of prestigious story material: in 1938, Mickey got a makeover. Fred Moore's position as the studio's leading Mickey animator had solidified since his 1935 analysis and model sheet; by now he was the studio's Mickey guru, the guiding artist to whom the other Mickey animators turned for advice. In 1938, with Walt's blessing, he created a fresh redesign of the character. The most radical change was evident at first glance: Moore redesigned Mickey's eyes.

IMAGED BY HERITAGE AUCTIONS, HA.COM

Perhaps this change was inevitable. Mickey had been born in 1928 out of a graphic tradition that was common at Disney and other cartoon studios in the 1920s: characters

designed along lines of strict black-and-white simplicity, with black dots for eyes set in the middle of a masklike face. By 1938, 10 years later, that design principle was no longer current—and, with a certain irony, it had been made obsolete by the Disney studio itself. With the shift to Technicolor production and other visual refinements during the 1930s, the Disney studio had led the way in establishing a style that might be called "cartoon realism." Among other things, this involved eyes that functioned like human eyes, with clearly defined pupils set within the white of an eyeball. By the late 1930s, Mickey and Minnie (and Morty and Ferdie) were the only Disney characters who did *not* have the "new" eyes. There was much more to the new style, of course, and in 1937 *The Worm Turns* had offered the jarring spectacle of seeing Mickey Mouse side by side with a "real" mouse. Now Moore effected a compromise, one that made Mickey a kind of hybrid: retain-

Mickey's appearances in the Macy's Thanksgiving Day Parade in New York were not isolated phenomena. Here he is escorted along the route of the Boston parade in 1938.

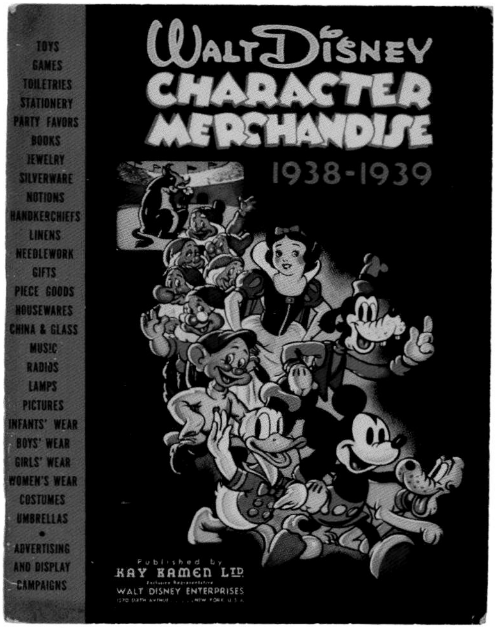

Kay Kamen's 1938–1939 catalog features much merchandise for Disney's feature film *Snow White and the Seven Dwarfs*, whose stars join Mickey, Donald, Goofy, and Pluto on the cover illustration. It remains an invaluable source of reference for collectors.

From the beginning, the popularity of animated cartoons has inspired the public's curiosity about how cartoons are made. This 1933 *Modern Mechanix* cover seems to promise a technical account of motion-picture cartoon camera work. Actually, the story inside was primarily about newspaper comic strips, and scarcely touched on Mickey at all.

ing his distinctive ears and other features of the 1920s tradition that made him recognizably Mickey, but now outfitted with eyes with pupils.

To the animators, this was a marked improvement. Frank Thomas and Ollie Johnston wrote that the original design had worked against subtleties of expression. "It was cute and made a great design, but it created an almost impossible job for the animator who was trying to draw a look in any direction other than straight out in front." Mickey's redesign "[opened] up new acting possibilities. He could now look innocent or embarrassed out of the top of his eyes — or he could glance to the side without the expression falling apart."[22]

The redesign involved other elements, too, and younger members of the animation staff attended classes to learn the fine points of animating the new Mickey. "Mickey's head in relation to his body is larger than it used to be," Riley Thomson told one group. "I know that Walt always stresses the fact that Fred Moore's Mickeys have a backbone, and that it gives him a perky look."[23] The studio made plans to introduce Mickey's new look to the screen in another "prestige" vehicle, *The Sorcerer's Apprentice*, and in the meantime Floyd Gottfredson launched it without fanfare in the newspaper comic strip on December 2, 1938. As time went on, the artists continued to tinker with Mickey's appearance. For a time during 1940 they experimented with the design of his ears, giving him three-dimensional ears that turned in perspective, but this and other ideas were soon dropped.

MODERN MECHANIX AND INVENTIONS
NOV.
NOW 15¢
IN CANADA 20¢
SEE PAGE 32
NRA
HOW COMIC CARTOONS MAKE FORTUNES
World Celebrates The Airplane's 30th Birthday

THE EARLY RKO RADIO SHORTS (1937-1940)

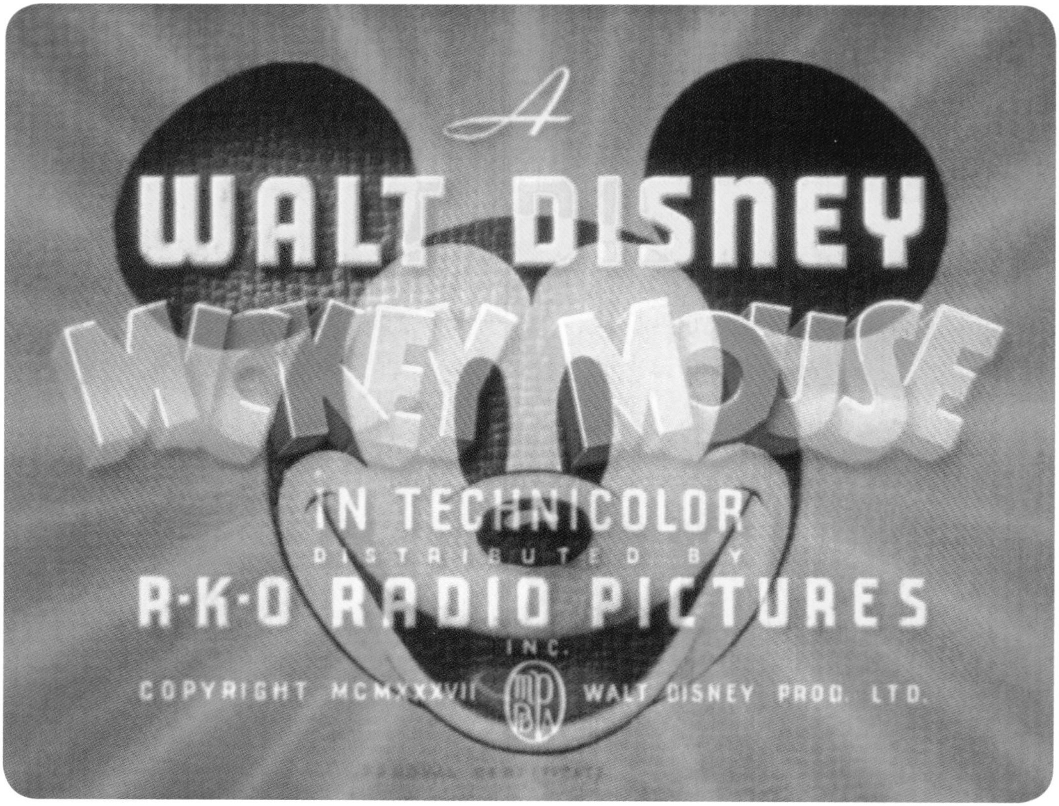

Mickey's iconic introductory close-up continued to evolve after the early version shown on page 148. The first color version in 1935 put rigid, chemtrail-like beams of light behind Mickey's head; with the move to RKO, the final version was introduced, showing more natural-looking sunbeams. Here we see this final version midway through a cross-dissolve to the standard-issue RKO Mickey title card.

During development of *Hawaiian Holiday*, numerous story ideas were considered and discarded, including this one involving Mickey, Minnie, and Pluto rushing to rescue surfer Goofy from trouble. In the finished film, all three characters remained ashore. "Please do not overlook Mickey and Minnie gags," the original story outline admonished, but once again both Mickey and Minnie were relegated to short opening and closing appearances in the finished film.

HAWAIIAN HOLIDAY
(September 24, 1937)

The five major characters in the Disney stock company — Mickey, Minnie, Donald, Pluto, and Goofy — celebrate their new distribution arrangement with a Hawaiian vacation. The setting is simply a hook for set-pieces of character animation, especially involving Goofy and Pluto. Jimmie (later known as Shamus) Culhane, already an animation veteran, made his mark at the Disney studio with his loose, spontaneous animation of Pluto's encounter with a crab.[24] The opening scenes featured Mickey's Hawaiian guitar solo and Minnie's accompanying hula, animated by the reliable Frenchy de Trémaudan.

CLOCK CLEANERS
(October 15, 1937)

The original outline for this picture had Mickey, Donald, and Goofy operating a little clock-repair business, advertising that they would clean any clock for a dollar. City official Pete accepted their offer, and then revealed that the timepiece in question was a colossal clock housed in a tower, high above the city streets![25] The finished film discards this opening business and Pete himself, and opens with the trio already on the job, following their separate adventures as they clean the inside and the outside of this behemoth. The climactic passage is a thrill-comedy sequence reminiscent of Harold Lloyd and other live-action comedians.

A story sketch from the opening sequence of *Clock Cleaners*, depicting Mickey's action as he cleans the face of the massive tower clock.

LONESOME GHOSTS
(December 24, 1937)

Mickey, Donald, and Goofy, proprietors of the Ajax Ghost Exterminating Company, are hired to rid a house of ghosts — hired, that is, by the ghosts themselves, who are bored and looking for diversion. This is another cartoon whose plot was completely reworked in story development; originally the house's ghostly presence was to have been an elaborate hoax engineered by Pete, as a fugitive gangster, to scare witnesses away from his hideout. The finished film offers more sequences of character animation (including a substantial role for Mickey himself), as well as a rich complement of effects animation, establishing the spooky atmosphere and uncanny goings-on as our heroes investigate the old house.

Atmospheric sketch for *Lonesome Ghosts* introducing the three bored spirits, inside the house, who initiate the film's action. This visual concept was *not* duplicated in the finished film. Boasting a rich assortment of effects animation and plagued by numerous false starts, the film ultimately went far over schedule and over budget. It would be one of the last Disney shorts directed by Burt Gillett.

A story sketch for the opening sequence in *Boat Builders*. Mickey, Donald, and Goofy happily peruse the manufacturer's pictures and look forward to the completed *Queen Minnie*.

BOAT BUILDERS
(February 25, 1938)

Mickey, Donald, and Goofy build a boat from a prefabricated kit. This, and other shorts animated in 1937, obliged their directors to work around the animators reserved for *Snow White*. Mickey's most extended action in this picture is an escalating tug-of-war with Donald, animated by Frenchy de Trémaudan: Mickey at the ship's wheel, Donald at the rudder, each inadvertently yanking the other back and forth. Early development had called for an appearance by Minnie at the opening, but in the finished film she appears only at the end, christening the boat before its disastrous launch. Glimpsed in the crowd: Horace Horsecollar, Clarabelle Cow, and the nephews, Morty and Ferdie (making their last animated appearance for more than a decade).

MICKEY'S TRAILER
(May 6, 1938)

Mobile-home trailers were enjoying a wave of popularity in the late 1930s, and in this short Mickey, Donald, and Goofy hit the road in a trailer of their own. *Mickey's Trailer* brims with ingenious space-saving gags: the touch of a button activates a series of sliding panels and compartments to turn a bedroom into a bathroom, complete with tub (which "unzips" for use, already filled with water!), then converts *that* into a dining room. The only faulty component is the operator. Goofy, driving the car, abandons his post, leading to another thrill-comedy sequence as the disconnected trailer careens backward down a mountain highway.

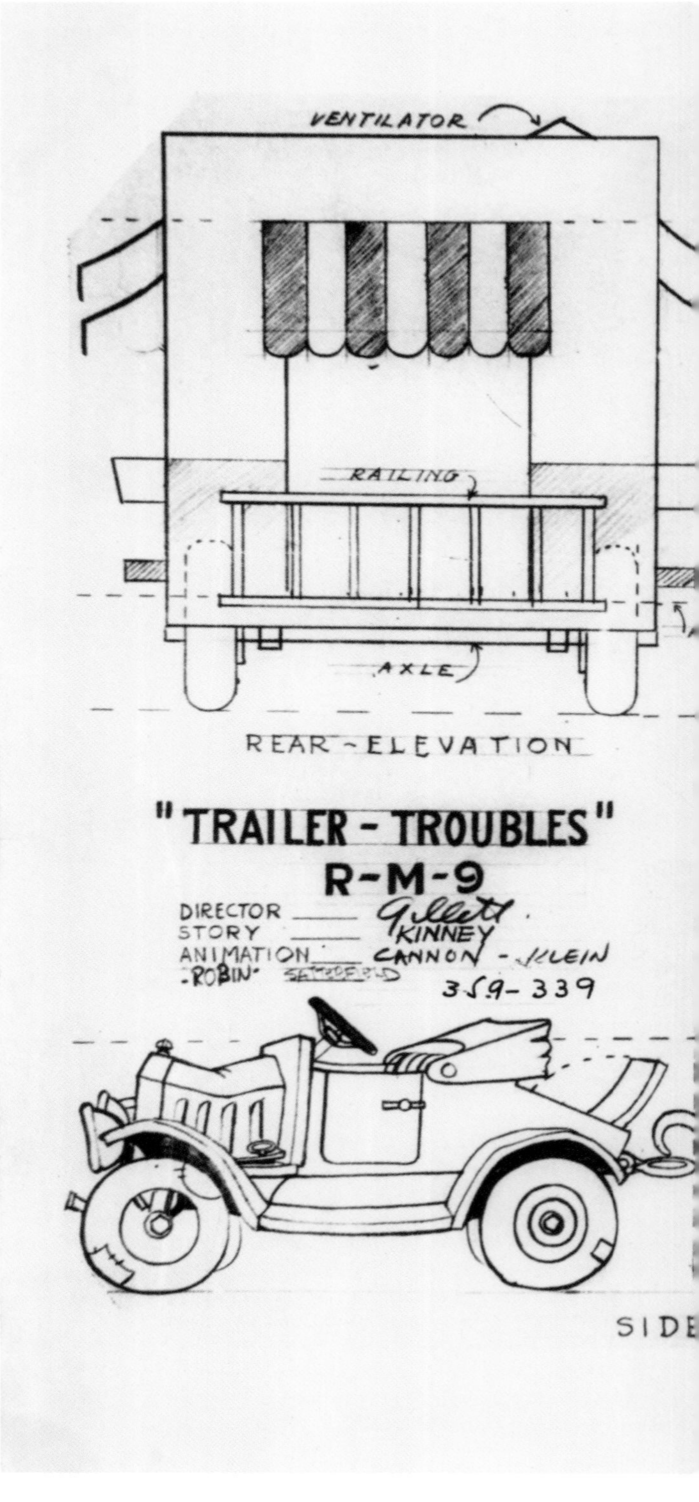

A model sheet for the trailer itself in *Mickey's Trailer* (here with a working title), establishing comparative sizes with mechanical-drawing exactness. This film was partially inspired by engineer/inventor William Stout, who visited the studio to give Walt a demonstration of a mobile home trailer he had designed.

COMPARATIVE SIZES
LIBRARY OF THE WALT DISNEY STUDIO
©
WALT DISNEY PRODUCTIONS LTD.
ELEVATION

Story sketches for Mickey's one major sequence in *The Whalers*: Mickey tries to empty a bucket by tossing the water overboard, but the wind blows the water back into the bucket. Originally conceived as a Peg Leg Pete gag for the unmade *Navy Mickey*, this was developed here into an extended Mickey sequence, animated by Marvin Woodward, in which our hero tries repeatedly to empty the bucket but is constantly outwitted by the water.

THE WHALERS
(August 19, 1938)

Mickey, Donald, and Goofy are the crew of a whaling ship in one of two shorts directed by veteran animator, and future legendary Disney writer, Dick Huemer. His crew of animators included a fellow veteran, Preston Blair, newly arrived at the studio. "I'd been an established animator on the outside," Blair recalled, "and people like Ben Sharpsteen and others were not very friendly with outside animators. So I had to sort of dispel the prejudice against being an outsider."[26] Blair proved himself with a short climactic passage showing Mickey, on deck, trying to head off an impending collision with a charging whale.

MICKEY'S PARROT
(September 9, 1938)

A talking parrot falls off the back of a truck on a rainy night and takes refuge in Mickey's house. Originally planned as another Pluto-meets-strange-creature story, this short was reworked to give Mickey more of a central role. Walt was immensely pleased: "You can have these two characters — Mickey and the dog — scared stiff. That's a swell Mickey type of story."[27] Mickey also benefits from unusually beautiful animation. In this and other shorts of mid- to late 1938, the Mouse was perhaps more perfectly drawn and animated than at any other time in his life.

Publicity art for *Mickey's Parrot*. Publicity drawings like these were sometimes created months in advance of a film's completion and release, and bore only a vague resemblance to the actual scenes in the film. Here one drawing is an approximation of Pluto's encounter with the parrot as seen onscreen, but the others are simply generic poses.

BRAVE LITTLE TAILOR
(September 23, 1938)

Brave Little Tailor was the first of the special productions that Walt initiated at this time for Mickey Mouse's "comeback." Like the concurrently produced feature *Snow White and the Seven Dwarfs*, it was based on a traditional tale that had been immortalized by the Brothers Grimm in the 19th century. The story had been proposed as a Silly Symphony as early as 1934 and had been shelved and revived repeatedly. After Walt designated it as a Mickey short—placing Mickey in a period story, and confronting him with a giant for the first time since *Giantland* in 1933—story development continued at a meticulous pace as all studio departments focused special care and attention on the project. Comic strip artist Al Taliaferro contributed an early, definitive sketch of the giant to a story outline—and added not only Mickey, for size comparison, but Mickey's mule from *Ye Olden Days*, revealing the importance of earlier "costume" pictures as an influence on this new initiative.

The end result is exactly what Walt hoped it would be: a short with all the production values of a feature. The lavish settings, the colorful crowd scenes, the richly imagined and staged visuals, the lovingly crafted musical score and effects animation, all add up to a film with an unusual feeling of luxury, even for the Disney studio. As one trade reviewer commented: "Will rank as one of the finest Disneys ever produced."[28]

At the heart of it all is the character animation, a craft that the Disney studio had honed to an all-time peak by 1937–38. For this one-reel short the traditional tale was simplified and became simply the story of a tailor who, through a misunderstanding, is dispatched to kill a giant. Mickey, of course, is cast as the tailor, and the animation crew reads like a who's who of top Mickey animators. Fred Moore, specifically, was an obvious choice and was initially given a large assignment of Mickey scenes. Soon after production started, however, Moore was moved into a supervisory capacity—animating some of Mickey's action himself, but otherwise overseeing the work of other artists. Many of his original scenes were reassigned to an emerging younger talent, Frank Thomas; other animators in the cast included Les Clark, Ollie Johnston, Ray Patterson, and Riley Thomson. The result is a miniature masterwork in which Mickey is, even more than in *Mickey's Parrot*, as beautifully drawn and animated as he would ever be.

Bill Tytla, an artist recognized for his animation of large, powerful characters, was assigned the giant. Called back East because of a death in the family, Tytla was absent from the studio for a month, and production of *Brave Little Tailor* was delayed. But his animation is worth the wait; the giant in the film is another triumph of the animator's art—overpowering in his titanic scale, but also humorous in his dull-witted, mindlessly malevolent personality.

Inevitably, all this quality came at a price. *Brave Little Tailor* in the end became a *very* expensive short. But Walt was so happy with the results onscreen that he continued to champion the film, even in story conferences on other cartoons: "Walt again mentioned that he wished he could produce more Mickey pictures as good as *Brave Little Tailor*."[29] When the studio announced that six of its shorts for the 1938–39 season would be released as "specials," *Brave Little Tailor* was the one Mickey Mouse on the list.[30]

A scene from the closing sequence, demonstrating the wealth of visual detail in *Brave Little Tailor*, unusually lavish even for Disney. The giant, animated by Bill Tytla, having been captured and subdued, the townspeople put him to work supplying a power source.

After working as an assistant to master animator Fred Moore, the young Frank Thomas was promoted to the position of full animator and quickly proved himself a major talent in his own right.

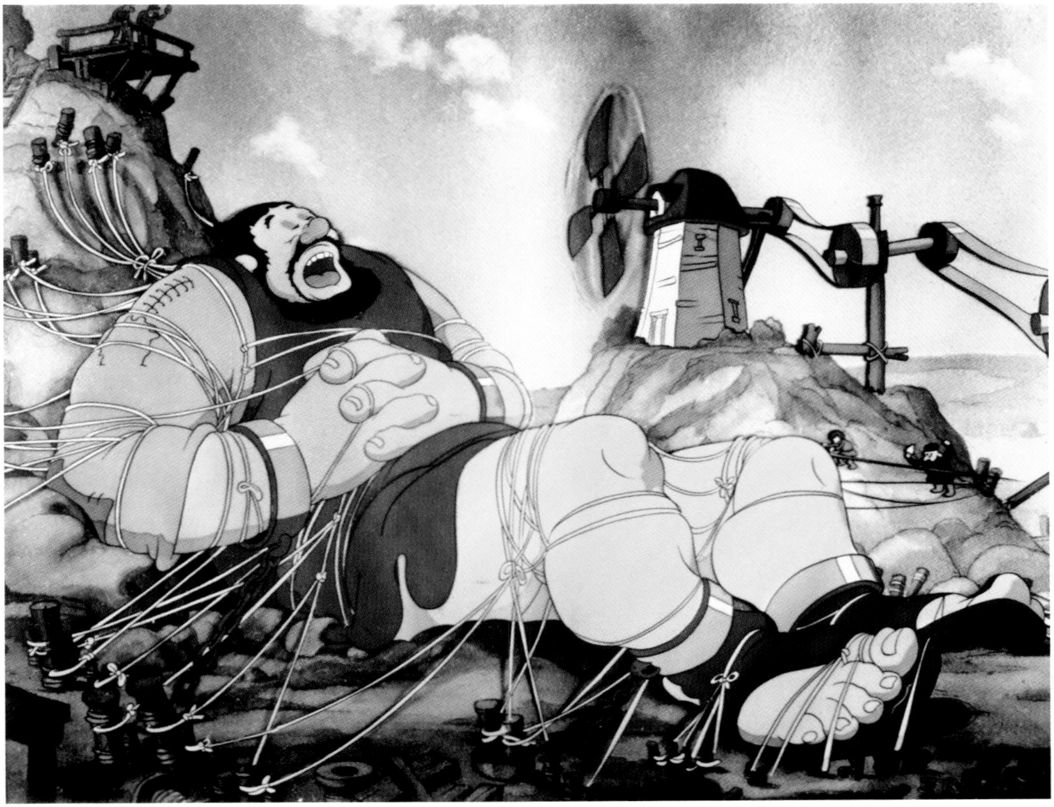

ART PROPS
RM14 Sc.29
79

WALT DISNEY'S
SOCIETY DOG SHOW
A
MICKEY
MOUSE
NO.
13
FLEA
POWDE
©
W.D.P
R.K.O. RADIO PICTURE IN TECHNICOLOR

SOCIETY DOG SHOW

(February 3, 1939)

Mickey, the poor kid from the wrong side of the tracks, enters Pluto in the high-society event of the title. The two bumpkins are out of their element, but Pluto doesn't care; he encounters Fifi the Pekingese (last seen in *Mickey's Polo Team*), flirts with her, and ultimately becomes a hero when he rescues her from a fire. *Society Dog Show* marks the last appearance of Mickey's original design, introduced in 1928 and refined during the intervening decade. As if to observe the occasion, a full complement of top Mickey animators contributed to this picture.

THE POINTER

(July 21, 1939)

The Sorcerer's Apprentice had been planned as a special showcase that would introduce Mickey's new design to the world — but by mid-1938 it was being delayed, pending completion of the other segments in *Fantasia*. In the meantime, apart from some advertising films which we'll consider presently, the "new Mickey" makes his debut in this short, trying, with great difficulty, to train Pluto as a hunting dog (and running afoul of a ferocious giant bear). A stellar crew of animators is on hand for the event, and their work is further enhanced by a layer of production gloss: rich color modeling and effects animation.

The poster for *Society Dog Show*. Here again Mickey applies perfume to Pluto, who is having none of it.

Story sketch by Earl Hurd for *The Pointer*. Story development of *The Pointer* began in spring 1938; note that Mickey is drawn in this sketch with his traditional button eyes.

In the *Pluto's Dream House* poster, Pluto happily looks forward to his new home.

The poster for *Tugboat Mickey*. Donald Duck and Goofy, who appear alongside Mickey in the film, are missing from the poster art; but the pelican that bedevils Mickey in an early sequence can be seen at upper left.

TUGBOAT MICKEY
(April 26, 1940)

The last of the Mickey-Donald-Goofy shorts is the third with a nautical theme: here the trio are operators of a tugboat for hire. When they hear a radio call for help from a ship in distress, they make an effort to hurry to the rescue but are hampered by their own ineptitude. In the end the boat runs wild in the harbor and explodes; and as our heroes flounder in the water, they discover that the distress call was only dialogue in a radio play.

PLUTO'S DREAM HOUSE
(August 30, 1940)

Mickey undertakes the building of a new doghouse for Pluto, consulting a plan that depicts an elegant moderne structure — unmistakably suggesting the Disney studio's own stylish new quarters in Burbank, into which the staff moved during production of *Tugboat Mickey* and this short. He gets unexpected help from a magic lamp that he finds by accident. The lamp takes over and builds a *spectacular* doghouse, then follows up by giving Pluto a bath, considerably enlivened by a welter of jumbled dialogue from a radio in the next room, which the lamp mistakes for instructions.

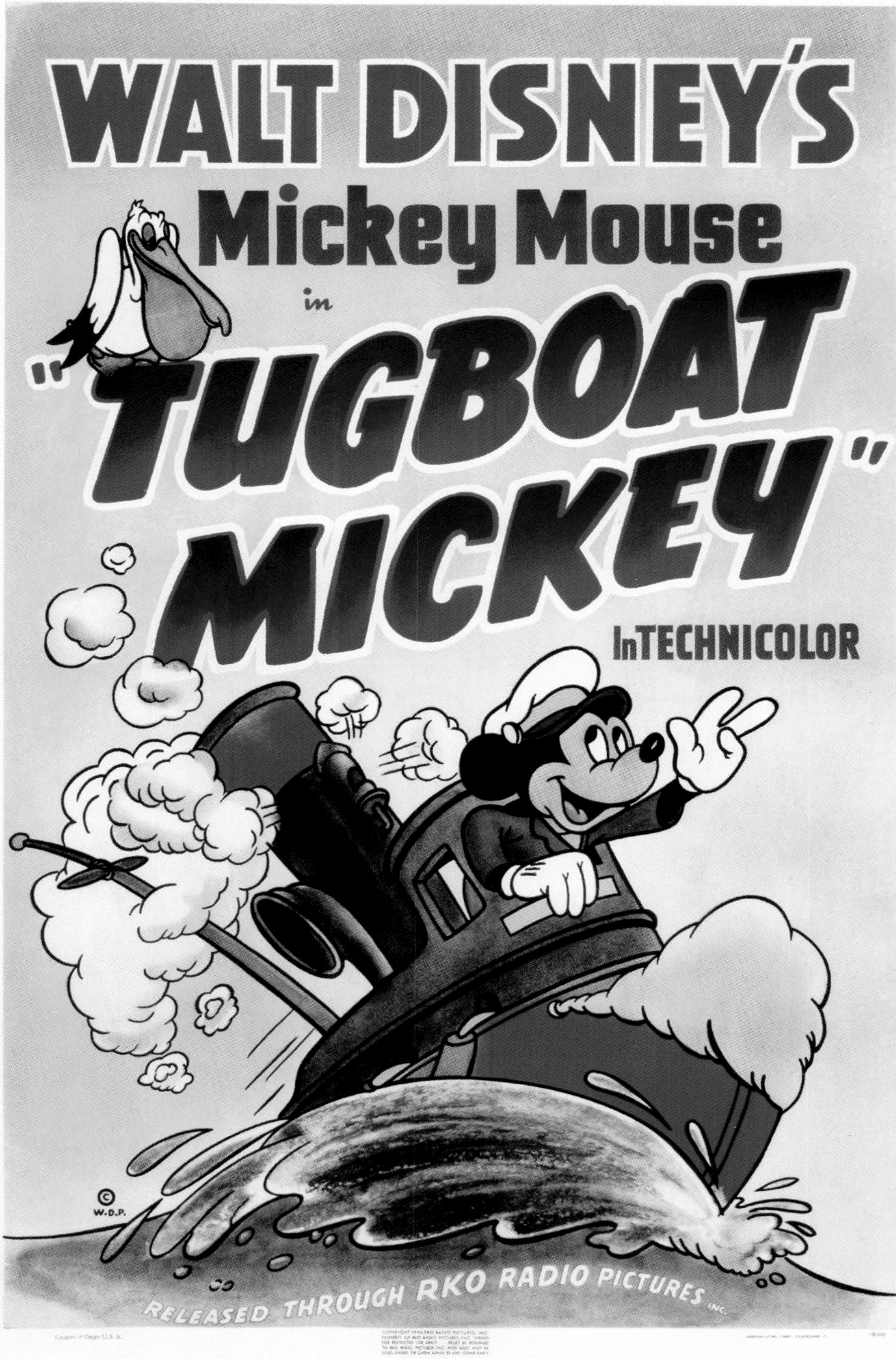
WALT DISNEY'S
Mickey Mouse
in
"TUGBOAT MICKEY"
In TECHNICOLOR
© W.D.P.
RELEASED THROUGH RKO RADIO PICTURES INC.
Country of Origin U.S.A.

WALT DISNEY'S
Mickey Mouse in
MR. MOUSE TAKES A TRIP
TICKET
5
M. M.
© W·D·P·
In Technicolor
RELEASED THROUGH RKO RADIO
Sacramento
Stockton
Jose
Pasadena
Glendale
Los Angeles
San Bernardino
Riverside
Country of Origin U.S.A.
4010/1567

The poster for *Mr. Mouse Takes a Trip*. Pete, the railroad conductor, makes the point unmistakable: dogs are not welcome aboard the train — though Pete notes that "I used to have a little *cat* once."

A Fred Moore model sheet, breaking down the details of his 1938 Mickey Mouse redesign. The new appearance of Mickey's eyes is supplemented by other refinements of body construction, but the inherent appeal of Moore's drawings cannot be reduced to a formula.

MR. MOUSE TAKES A TRIP
(November 1, 1940)

Mickey travels by train (leaving from the Burbank depot) and tries to take Pluto with him, despite the railroad's rule against dogs, and in the face of intimidation by the train's bullying conductor — none other than Pete. By the time Pete finally succeeds in throwing Mickey and Pluto off the train at reel's end, they've already arrived at their destination anyway. This short has become a cult favorite in the age of home video, when many Disney fans have enjoyed a live-action film clip of Walt Disney and Billy Bletcher recording, respectively, Mickey's and Pete's dialogue for *Mr. Mouse*.

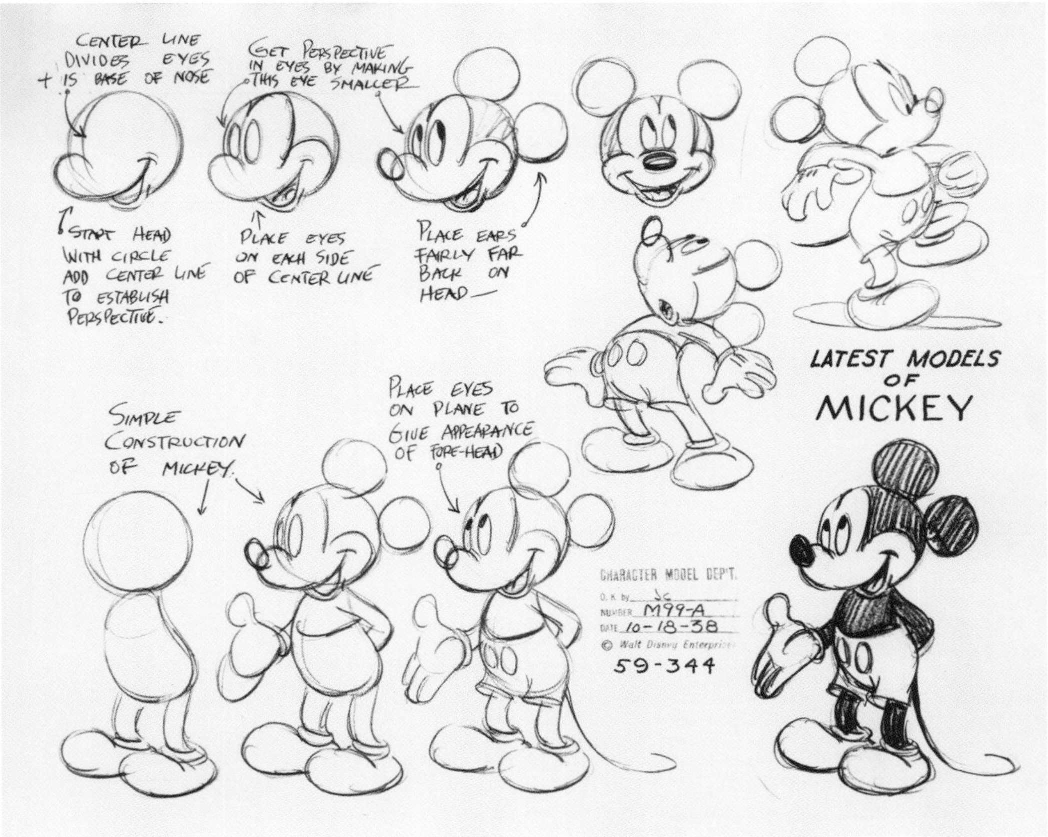

A model sheet for *Mickey's Surprise Party* (originally labeled with the film's working title). By this time the Disney artists were already well aware of the comparative sizes of Mickey, Minnie, Pluto, and Fifi — but such thorough preparation is characteristic of the special care that was expended on this little commercial production.

Story development for *Mickey's Surprise Party* started in the summer of 1938. Note that this story sketch, like that for *The Pointer*, portrays Mickey (and, this time, Minnie) with the traditional eye design of the earlier 1930s.

SPECIAL PRODUCTIONS

In addition to all these Mickey shorts, a full slate of shorts featuring *other* Disney characters, and an increasingly ambitious program of feature production, the studio also produced two minor "specials" during 1939 that have often been overlooked. Both were advertising shorts featuring Mickey Mouse.

THE STANDARD PARADE FOR 1939

(Standard Oil sales conventions, March 1939)

Late in 1938 the Disney studio contracted with Standard Oil to take part in Standard's upcoming advertising campaign. Disney characters extolled Standard Oil in newspaper ads, banners, billboards, and this very short (less than two minutes) film, shown in theaters hosting Standard's sales conventions. Here, in animation reworked from the 1932 *Parade of the Award Nominees*, Mickey leads a parade of other Disney characters carrying banners and signs. This time Mickey and Minnie are both drawn according to the new character design, featuring eyes with pupils — and, since this short was delivered to Standard's sales conventions in March 1939, it anticipated by several months the first theatrical shorts with the new design. One wonders how many of the convention attendees realized they were witnessing an historic moment in animation history.

MICKEY'S SURPRISE PARTY

(New York World's Fair, opening April 30, 1939)

Unlike *The Standard Parade*, this Nabisco-sponsored short was produced from scratch. It was also designed for a very different venue: while the Standard Oil short was exhibited briefly and privately at sales conventions, *Mickey's Surprise Party* was shown to a collective audience of millions in a special theatrical setting at the 1939 New York World's Fair. Perhaps for that reason, an unusual amount of care was lavished on this advertising reel. Mickey and Pluto call on Minnie and Fifi, but Minnie's effort to surprise Mickey with cookies "like your mother used to make" is spoiled when the cookies are burned. Minnie is utterly distraught, although Mickey explains that his mother used to *burn* the cookies. He saves the day with a quick shopping trip to purchase a full supply of Nabisco products — including Milk-Bones for Pluto and Fifi. A crew of distinguished animators worked for months on this little opus, producing a far more exquisitely crafted film than one might have expected in a commercial production. Like *The Standard Parade*, this short was seen by audiences months before the new Mickey's official debut in *The Pointer*.

FANTASIA
See it! In Multiplane
TECHNICOLOR
WALT DISNEY'S
FANTASIA
MUSICAL SCORE CONDUCTED BY STOKOWSKI IN THRILLING FANTASOUND
CANNOT BE SHOWN IN ANY OTHER THEATRE IN OR AROUND NEW YORK
ADVANCE TICKET SALE HERE
FANTASIA BOX OFFICE
WINES & LIQUORS
LEE WATER BLOC HATS

THE SORCERER'S APPRENTICE

(November 13, 1940 as part of the feature *Fantasia*)

In the spring of 1937, while story development of *Brave Little Tailor* was still in progress, Walt was already thinking about Mickey's next "comeback" film. Characteristically, he aimed even higher for the second outing. The vehicle he chose was Paul Dukas's 1897 musical tone poem *The Sorcerer's Apprentice*, based on the Goethe poem *Der Zauberlehrling*. The poem and the symphonic composition both depicted a wizard's lazy assistant who enchants a broom and commands it to execute his own water-carrying chores, then finds himself inundated with water when he can't figure out how to *stop* the broom. The Silly Symphonies had built their musical scores on thematic material from classical music ever since 1929, at first comically; then, as the studio's technique became more sophisticated, with increasing fidelity and depth. Now Walt envisioned a film that would be a sort of *über*-Silly Symphony, with Mickey in the lead.

Goethe's poem was written in 1797. It was based on a narrative tradition that extended back to the second century, and therefore, like the Grimms' stories, could claim deep multicultural roots — and, in fact, enjoyed a thematic relationship to *Frankenstein* and other tales of mortals who unleash forces they cannot control. Dukas composed his symphonic poem a full century later in 1897, closely following the contours of Goethe's text.

It's not clear exactly when the Disney story department first began to consider "The Sorcerer's Apprentice." The story had been filmed before, once as a 1930 one-reel short designed by William Cameron Menzies. There exists in the Walt Disney Archives a tentative story outline for a Silly Symphony based on the tale, submitted in the mid-1930s by animator Chester Cobb. His outline suggests a 1935 vintage Silly Symphony, along the lines of *The Golden Touch*, conveying a clear moral but with plenty of opportunities for laughs — and *without* Mickey or any of the other standard characters. He also proposes the use of Dukas's music in the score. Cobb's submission brought a response from Ted Sears, the head of the story department, who advised him that the writers had considered this story before but had decided against it, for a variety of reasons: unsympathetic characters, the writers' disappointment in earlier film versions, and the fact that "water in a cartoon has become very mild as a menace." Sears closed with sympathetic words: "Hope these depressing remarks won't discourage you — they were brought up at a couple of discussions, and there's no reason why they can't be overridden by a good story suggestion."[31]

Walt's interest in the story in early 1937, specifically as a Mickey vehicle, gave the story department a fresh motivation to consider it more carefully.

November 1940: more than three years after the beginning of story development on *The Sorcerer's Apprentice*, Walt's inspiration comes into full flower with the premiere of *Fantasia* at the Broadway Theater in New York.

During story development, the writers experimented with various approaches to the Sorcerer's display of magical pyrotechnics in the opening scenes. In this sketch he conjures something resembling a towering, multi-blossomed orchid.

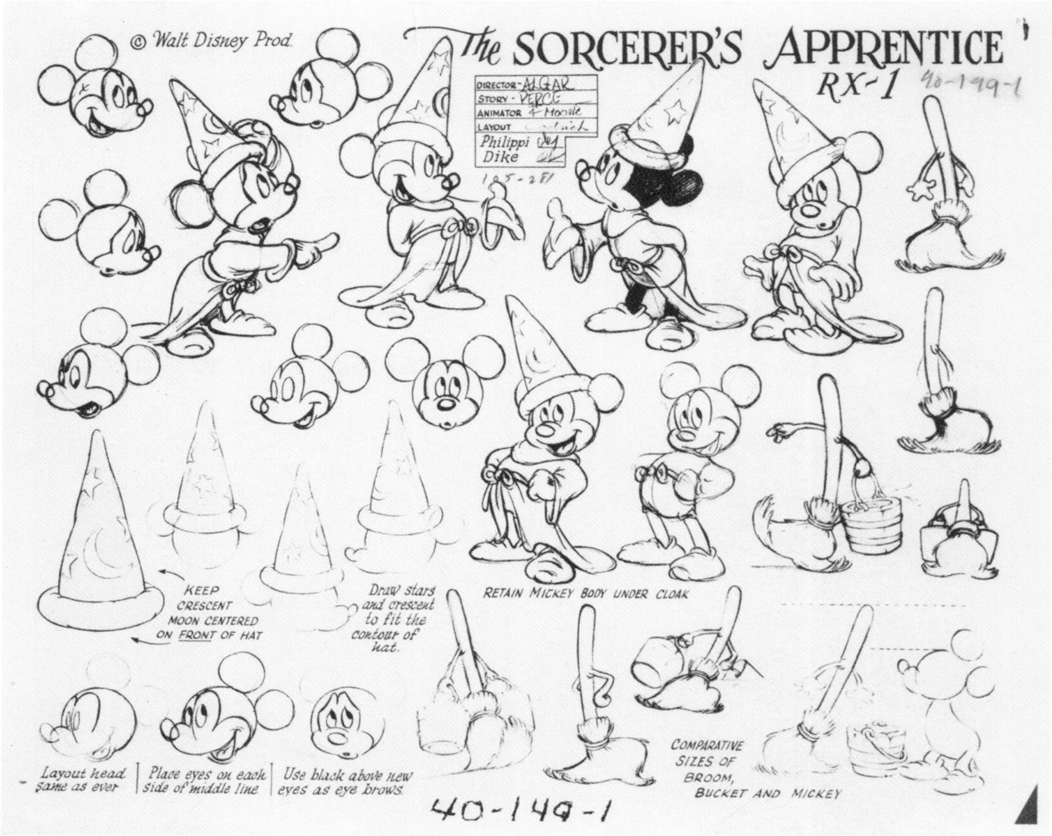

Another Fred Moore model sheet, this time designed specifically for *The Sorcerer's Apprentice* and delineating, not only Mickey's design, but that of his costume and of the broom. At Walt's request, Mickey wears a too-large robe, giving him the appearance of a child trying on adult clothing.

The style B poster for *Fantasia*'s original showings, like the style A poster (see page 226), features Mickey prominently among the sights in the film.

In July the studio secured the rights to Dukas's music and set to work on an adaptation. The project was already well advanced by the time of Walt's famous meeting with Leopold Stokowski, but the addition of the celebrity conductor to the nascent *Sorcerer's Apprentice* film gave it a perception of seriousness that outweighed Walt's original notion. Far from scorning the movies as some cultural icons did, Stokowski had embraced Hollywood and had appeared in some films as himself, most recently Universal's *One Hundred Men and a Girl* (1937; dir. Henry Koster). He enthusiastically supported Walt's idea and lent his name to the project. By late 1937 the trade press was reporting that Stokowski had "made an agreement with Walt Disney to co-star with Mickey."[32] *The Sorcerer's Apprentice* would still be a one-reel Mickey Mouse short, but it would be unlike any one-reeler ever seen before.

Meanwhile, the studio was at work on story development. The early decision to synchronize the

Walt Disney's
TECHNICOLOR FEATURE TRIUMPH
FANTASIA
Distributed by RKO Radio Pictures, Inc.

Several color sketches, depicting the cosmic forces that Mickey naively tries to control. Summoning planets and comets from opposite ends of the universe, he maneuvers them into a monumental collision just for the fun of it. The finished scenes in the film followed these sketches closely and offered a tour de force by the studio's effects animators.

This remarkable story sketch is *not* followed in the film. The pose here suggests nothing of Mickey's carefree aspirations in the finished version of *The Sorcerer's Apprentice*; if anything, it recalls the anguished, clutching reach of Chernobog toward the heavens in another "Concert Feature" segment, *Night on Bald Mountain*. In more ways than one, *The Sorcerer's Apprentice* was the gateway to the entire panoply of visual invention in the film that would become *Fantasia*.

entire film to a faithful performance of Dukas's music — rather than simply borrowing excerpts from it, as in many of the Silly Symphonies — meant that the pace and overall arc of the story were predetermined, precluding extensive adaptation of the plot. But the artists could shape the picture in other ways. As they were concurrently doing with *Pinocchio*, the Disney writers and concept artists made their version of *The Sorcerer's Apprentice* darker and more nightmarish than the original. The setting was literally dark: a castle interior filled with brooding shadows, few details visible, a period vaguely suggesting medieval times. "The things with which the Sorcerer works should not be too modern. They should be large, old, battered copper retorts and transparent receptacles. Earthenware and copper would be good. If glass receptacles are used, they should be in containers that look very old."[33] Goethe's version of the Sorcerer had been relatively benign; the Disney version reverted to older traditions in which the Sorcerer vented his anger at his hapless assistant. Goethe's apprentice seizes an axe and chops the broom in two, then is dismayed when both halves come to life and continue to carry water. Mickey, in a frenzy of panic, chops the broom into tiny splinters, then is horrified to find an *army* of brooms relentlessly flooding his quarters with a deluge of water.

Some even darker imagery was suggested during story development. An early continuity suggested "a shot of a skeleton leaning up against the wall. Water has risen up to the rib cage of the skeleton, and we see Mickey coming up inside this weird prison"[34] — recycling a gag that had appeared in *The Mad Doctor* (1933), but presumably to more ghastly effect. Within two weeks this idea had been embellished: "Water is rising all the time, forcing Mickey's head higher and higher into the skeleton... When Mickey sticks his hand in the skeleton's mouth, the teeth clamp down and bite his fingers, causing Mickey to react and go under the water again, taking the entire skeleton down with him." For good measure, this outline added, "Two rats are sitting on top of the skull, which was floating on the water, and a third one is trying to clamber up beside them for a place of security."[35] All these morbid details were eliminated from the finished film.

Other changes were made for other reasons. Early treatments of the story pictured an opening sequence in which the Sorcerer mixed chemicals

in a complicated network of tubes and retorts, finally distilling them into a mixture with which he conjured a miniature celestial display of swirling stars and comets in midair. Moving slowly backward as he conducted this spectacle, the Sorcerer tripped over the water buckets, carelessly left in the way by Mickey, and fell, causing his miniature galaxy to spin riotously out of control and collapse on the floor. The Sorcerer then magically commanded a broom to sweep up "the pile of celestial junk on the floor."[36] This opening would have given the film a symmetrical structure by "planting," in advance, both the broom and Mickey's dream of conducting the stars and planets.

In the film these ideas are sacrificed for a simpler opening: the Sorcerer conjures a huge, ghostly bat, transforms it into a beautiful shimmering butterfly, then retires for the evening — a continuity that forms a better fit with Dukas's music. Story adaptation here follows the trend established in *Snow White* and *Pinocchio*: to simplify, to tighten, to eliminate unnecessary detail. One effect of the change is not to underestimate the audience's intelligence: when Mickey brings the broom to life, the action makes perfect sense without any advance preparation. And when he conducts the celestial display in his dream, it's a compelling sequence not because it relates to an earlier scene, but because it expresses Mickey's soaring, unbounded spirit — an appealing vision, and quite likely one of Walt's reasons for producing the film in the first place.

Stokowski arrived in Los Angeles early in January 1938 to conduct the orchestra for the soundtrack. Walt made sure the press was aware of his arrival, and the event was duly covered in nationwide syndicated news items.

The Sorcerer's Apprentice providentially provided an outlet for Walt's *and* Stokowski's ambitions. Stokowski was enthused by the potential of the movies as a showcase for serious music, and for *One Hundred Men and a Girl* he had used his clout to secure an innovative multichannel RCA recording system for the musical sequences. "At various points among the group of musicians, 28 microphones were placed," a trade article reported, "each microphone being so spotted as to catch a particular choir of instruments. The volume of sound from each microphone was controlled as it was transmitted to a sound track, eight different tracks being used."[37] Of course, once Stokowski had mixed those separate tracks to his taste, Universal released the feature with a standard monaural soundtrack. But now Stokowski campaigned for a similar recording arrangement for *The Sorcerer's Apprentice*, and it's not difficult to imagine the next logical step, from multichannel recording to multichannel playback — the experience that a later generation would call stereophonic sound. And it's not difficult to imagine Walt's enthusiasm when such an idea was proposed to him. The idea of Fantasound was born.

Arrangements had been made to conduct this ambitious recording session at the Selznick Interna-

A story sketch charting the successive positions in Mickey's path as he leads the broom to the well and back, carrying the buckets of water.

More story sketches, depicting Mickey's futile effort to stop the broom.

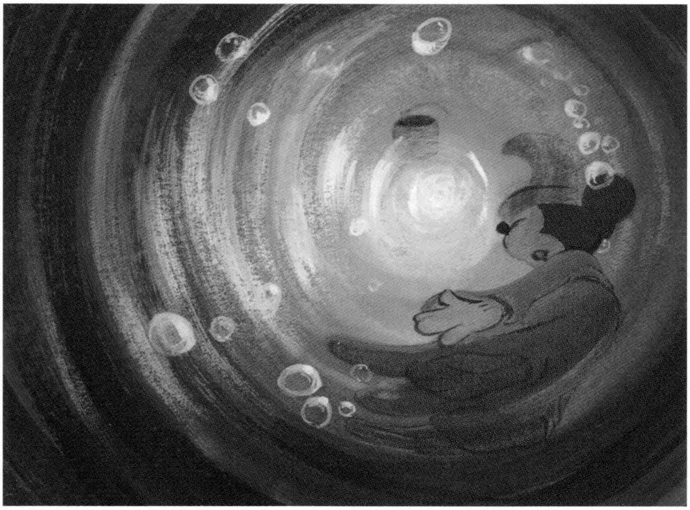

Desperate to stop the torrent of water, Mickey tries to consult the Sorcerer's book in an effort to find the proper incantation — but soon finds himself clinging to the book simply as a raft. The shadows on the wall behind him, suggesting the relentless march of the water-bearing brooms, were translated into more abstract terms in the film.

Another *Sorcerer's Apprentice* story sketch conveying a nightmarish image: Mickey trapped in the whirlpool, the bucket already swept far out of his reach.

tional Pictures studio in Culver City, California, and the session was set for the wee hours of January 10, 1938, beginning at midnight. Bill Garity, the Disney studio's resident technical wizard, was in charge of the recording. Garity, for one, was profoundly disappointed in Stokowski and in the musical results of that night's work. "My positive conclusion," he wrote in his private journal, "is that all we are getting for this very expensive work is Stokowski's name on the main title, and that the musical results, which may be spectacular and satisfactory to the average audience, do not even approximate the perfection which we had expected would result from this effort and expense."[38]

Meanwhile, work was getting underway on the animation. As a one-reel short subject, *The Sorcerer's Apprentice* was rapidly escalating to heroic proportions, and Walt determined that this exceptional film would be the deluxe showcase in which to unveil Mickey's new design. Special new Mickey model sheets were prepared, detailing the fine points of Mickey's eyes and other design features — as well as his costume, a robe several sizes too large for him. This look had originated with Mickey's conductor uniform in *The Band Concert*, and Walt evinced a special liking for it. (At a *Boat Builders* story conference he had commented: "They all ought to be dogged up in sailor uniforms. Mickey looks cute in a big coat."[39]) Director Jim Algar began to hand out the scenes to the animators in late January 1938.

Considering the role that Fred Moore had played in refining Mickey's graphic design, one might have expected that he would be assigned to animate the bulk of the Mouse's scenes in this picture. Instead, as on *Brave Little Tailor*, Moore was moved to a supervisory position from which he directed the work of the *other* animators. Artists like Riley Thomson and Marvin Woodward, assigned to animate Mickey scenes, were instructed: "When the first key poses have been drawn, please refer them to Fred Moore for possible suggestions. Fred Moore is assisting all animators on this picture in an attempt to make the Mickeys conform to a cute style."[40] Apart from Moore, Mickey's animators in this picture covered a range of seasoned veterans (Woodward, Les Clark, Bob Wickersham) as well as relative newcomers (Ollie Johnston, Preston Blair, and Thomson, who was rising rapidly through the animators' ranks and would soon become a prolific director of Mickey's cartoons).

At the time animation started, a portion of Mickey's action was assigned to Grim Natwick. Natwick had only recently finished his legendary assignment on *Snow White*, the Disney animation for which he is best remembered today, but during his time at the Disney studio he had also worked on *Alpine Climbers* and other Mickeys. For *The Sorcerer's Apprentice*, he was initially assigned a block of early scenes in which Mickey tried on the Sorcerer's hat and issued his magical commands to the broom. But Natwick left the Disney studio in the spring of 1938, and was soon back at the Fleischer studio, working on *Gulliver's Travels*. At that point his scenes were taken over by Riley Thomson, Les Clark, and, in one case, Fred Moore.

Together, this ensemble of artists created what is regarded by many as one of Mickey's all-time definitive performances. In this picture we see multiple facets of his personality: the small boy, the hapless clown, the irrepressible dreamer. Director Algar issued his scenes to the animators with meticulous attention to detail: "In regard to Mickey himself, guard against getting him too tall and skinny — too much the 12-year-old. For this picture we see him more the small-boy proportions — about those of a 6-year-old... Remember that everything in this particular picture is larger than Mickey — the props, broom, Sorcerer, castle, and even the elements and predicaments themselves."[41] When Mickey decides to appropriate the Sorcerer's hat: "Display a sly expression on his face, but do not try to convey through any 'Pluto expression' on the eyes that he is thinking about what to do. He already knows what he is going to do."[42]

Preston Blair was assigned a sequence of scenes depicting Mickey awaking from his dream, discovering the rising floodwaters, and sloshing through them to stop the broom in its course. He later wrote that he had been supplied with live-action reference footage to help him with these scenes: "an athlete from University of California, Los Angeles, had been hired to jump pell-mell over a bunch of barrels and boxes in a floundering action... I remember that the fellow had quite long hair, or hair that bounced all over the place. I studied the film for hours, made a lot of thumbnail sketches of the sequence, and studied the crazy timing... Using this hair as a guide I transposed all the data into Mickey's robe, that flops around as he grabs for his hat and flounders and falls."[43]

From the beginning, it was understood that animation of the Sorcerer could be assigned to only one artist: Bill Tytla. Far from the benign demeanor of Goethe's original Sorcerer, this one moves slowly and deliberately but projects an air of imposing authority, commanding his apprentice's respect. The character is never identified by name onscreen, but studio wags christened him Yen Sid — "Disney" spelled backward — and, in fact, he confronts Mickey in the closing scenes with the ferocious raised eyebrow typical of Walt in one of his critical moods. Yet Tytla's artistry endows the Sorcerer with just the subtlest touch of Walt's sense of humor as well: as the crestfallen Mickey tiptoes past him to return to his chores, a corner of the Sorcerer's mouth turns up ever so slightly — before he whacks Mickey with the broom and sends him flying.

Along with character animation, *The Sorcerer's Apprentice* represented a field day for the studio's effects animators. The picture brims with effects work, in particular the colossal quantities of water. It was produced concurrently with *Pinocchio*, which likewise features a literal ocean of water, and some of the same artists worked on both films, refining their techniques as they went. Streams of water, reflections on surging waves, splashes rendered on washoff relief cels, and other techniques — sometimes more than one of these combined together in a single scene — appear throughout the climactic scenes in *Sorcerer*. In many instances the effects artists worked closely with the character animators. Ed Love, who animated the army of brooms marching relentlessly with their buckets of water, recalled: "I did all that stuff, [but] I didn't do any water. And as they were walking, there was water splashing all over. Well, they just had an effects man go through and put water in every bucket!"[44] In other scenes at the height of Mickey's dream, the effects animators take over the screen altogether. In one scene (scene 38.2), comet fragments animated by George Rowley fall into a sea animated by Ugo D'Orsi. D'Orsi was one of the busiest effects animators on the picture, animating not only water effects, but also other images such as the ghostly giant bat and butterfly in the opening scenes.

Brave Little Tailor had been a very expensive short, but with all the extravagant production value being lavished on *The Sorcerer's Apprentice*, it was setting a new standard for expense. Before long it was clear that this sumptuous production could never be released as an ordinary short subject. By late March 1938, Walt and Stokowski had begun to hatch the idea of absorbing *The Sorcerer's Apprentice* into the "Concert Feature" that would eventually become *Fantasia*. And with this prestigious vehicle, Mickey would soon reach a new career milestone: playing a starring role in a feature-length film.

One of Joe Grant's early sketches for character design of the Sorcerer. The finished design of the character differed considerably from this one, but incorporated some of Grant's ideas.

An evocative story sketch for the entrance of the Sorcerer and his discovery of the chaos Mickey has wrought. Both the visual details and the camera move will be altered in the finished film, but the ominous *sense* of the Sorcerer's entrance is well suggested here.

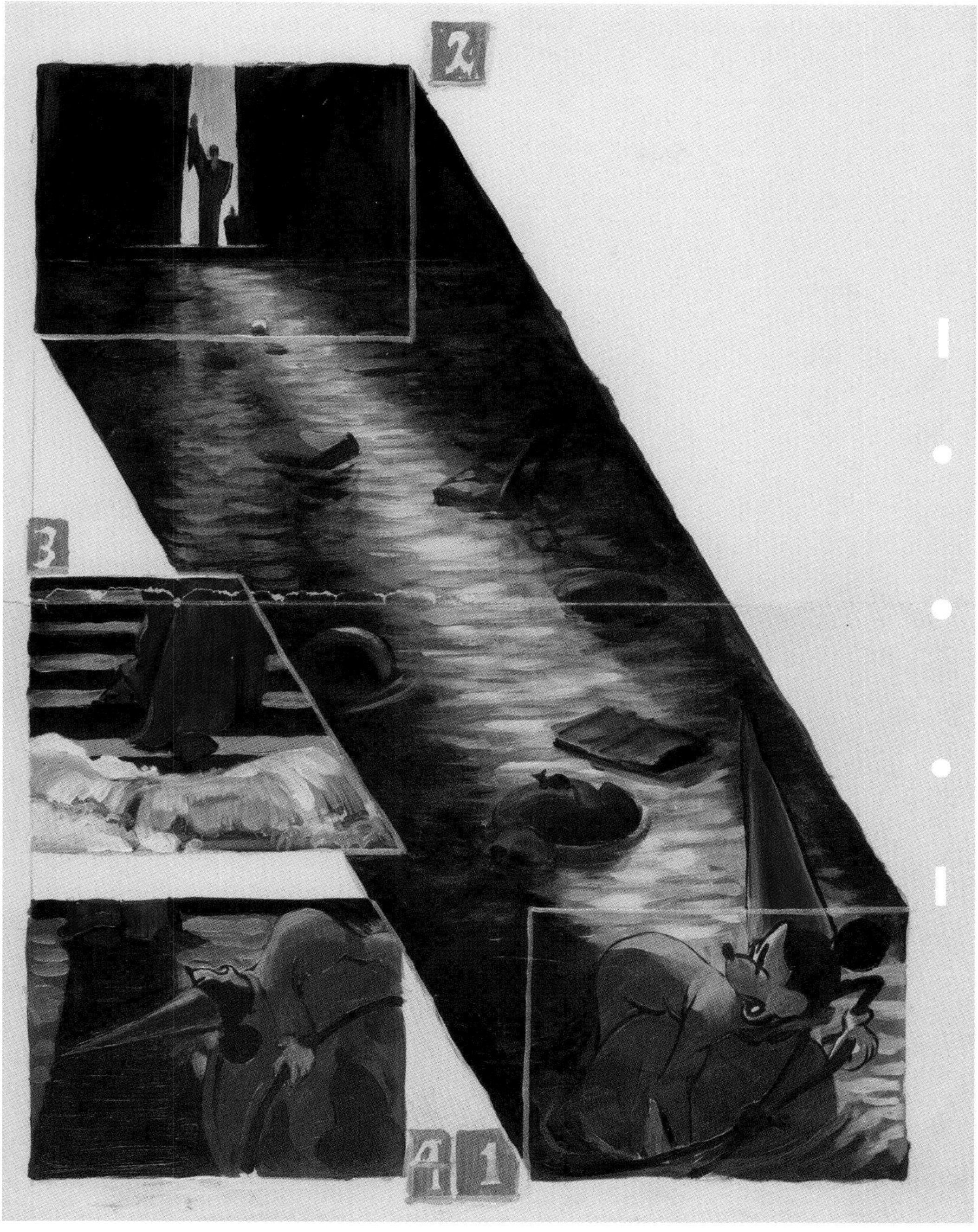
2
3
4 1

MICKEY MOUSE
MAGAZINE
25¢
30¢ in Canada
SUMMER QUARTERLY
A Fun-Book for Boys and Girls to Read to Grown-ups

CHAPTER FIVE

The Comics Adventurer

Well before feature-length stardom on screen, of course, Mickey Mouse achieved a different kind of extended-length notoriety—the deserved fame he had acquired, by the mid-1930s, as the star of increasingly powerful long-form comics. The promise of Floyd Gottfredson's daily newspaper strip, already the source of a stage show and a book series by the end of 1931, bloomed in 1932 into a series of arguably unparalleled epic tales, as comics historian Bill Blackbeard would later recall: "[Gottfredson's Mickey Mouse] was a death-defying, tough, steel-gutted Mickey Mouse... who held the kids of 1933 rapt with his adventures on pirate dirigibles, cannibal islands and bullet-tattered fighter planes..."[1]

These were the extended Mickey strip stories that ruled the comics world of the 1930s—and effectively created a new comics genre. At the time of Mickey's creation there were already adventure comics starring animals: sentient animals like Otto Messmer's Felix the Cat, who could talk to and travel with people—but who also meowed on the fence and often walked on all fours. There were adventure comics starring humans: funny humans like the Gumps, who could look like chinless, gawky figures even while enduring serious trials of love and loss. But there were no adventure comics starring *funny animals*: animals who were animal enough to have some animal instinct, but who otherwise lived human lives in humanlike worlds. Possessed of a mouse's curiosity and daring, but otherwise a boy on rip-roaring quests, Floyd

The giant-sized *Mickey Mouse Magazine* 1 (1935) was really just the first newsstand edition of this venerable title, previously sold at theaters and given away by dairies in a smaller-size digest form. Nevertheless, the title's newsstand debut marked an important moment in Disney history: for the first time, readers in Mickey's home country had the regular opportunity to read Mickey stories in an ongoing publication dedicated to them. As years passed, more and more of those stories would be told in comics form.

Walt sits for a studio publicity portrait, circa 1932. Beneath him on his desk are two Floyd Gottfredson ad drawings created for the launch of the *Mickey Mouse* Sunday strip.

Gottfredson's Mickey was blazing a uniquely new trail in comics every day.

While Mickey Mouse had made a successful jump to comics in 1930, the tone of his animated shorts arguably did not. The earliest *Mickey* daily strips tried to mimic cartoon sight gags; but the daily strip, limited to four or five panels per installment, could only carry slapstick so far—and, as we have seen, was only mildly successful until it moved away from a slapstick focus. Under Gottfredson's guiding hand, the daily evolved into an adventure serial, and rarely looked back at its cartoony origins.

But there was soon to be another comics canvas, where extended visual gags and animation-style situations had more breathing room to develop naturally. Launched in January 1932, this canvas was the *Mickey Mouse* Sunday color strip: proof, by its very existence, that Disney comics were achieving a loyal, growing audience. Gottfredson swiftly turned the Sunday into a product that preserved the daily's winning portrayal of an alternately adventurous and playful Mickey—while simultaneously using the lengthier, Sunday-only space to pioneer several unique storytelling techniques.

One technique involved more sophisticated pacing. Short daily strips had limited space per day to advance their plot points, whereas the new Sunday strip had room, by comparison, to let the action stop and start. The effect was filmic at its core; many a cartoon had used lulls to build up to a dramatic climax. But the effect also made for good comics storytelling, a kind that had been spatially impossible before 1932.

Two more Sunday-only techniques were the escalation plot and

IMAGED BY HERITAGE AUCTIONS, HA.COM

the final twist. Prefigured, again, by similar structures in animation, the Sunday edition had room to show an activity that got increasingly silly, frustrating, or dangerous as it went on; a hard concept to convey in four panels, but easy to express in twelve. The escalation worked even better with a final twist: after spending most of a Sunday strip on some sort of diligent effort, Mickey might find his fortunes reversed at the last moment. Gottfredson taught Sunday readers to expect the unexpected—and where the Sunday led, the daily soared to new heights.

Gottfredson's "Lair of Wolf Barker" (1933) Sunday serial inspired another burgeoning talent: future comics master Carl Barks found gainful employment at Disney in 1935 by submitting this and another original Mickey publicity drawing, both based on the "Wolf Barker" story.

Registered U. S. Patent Office

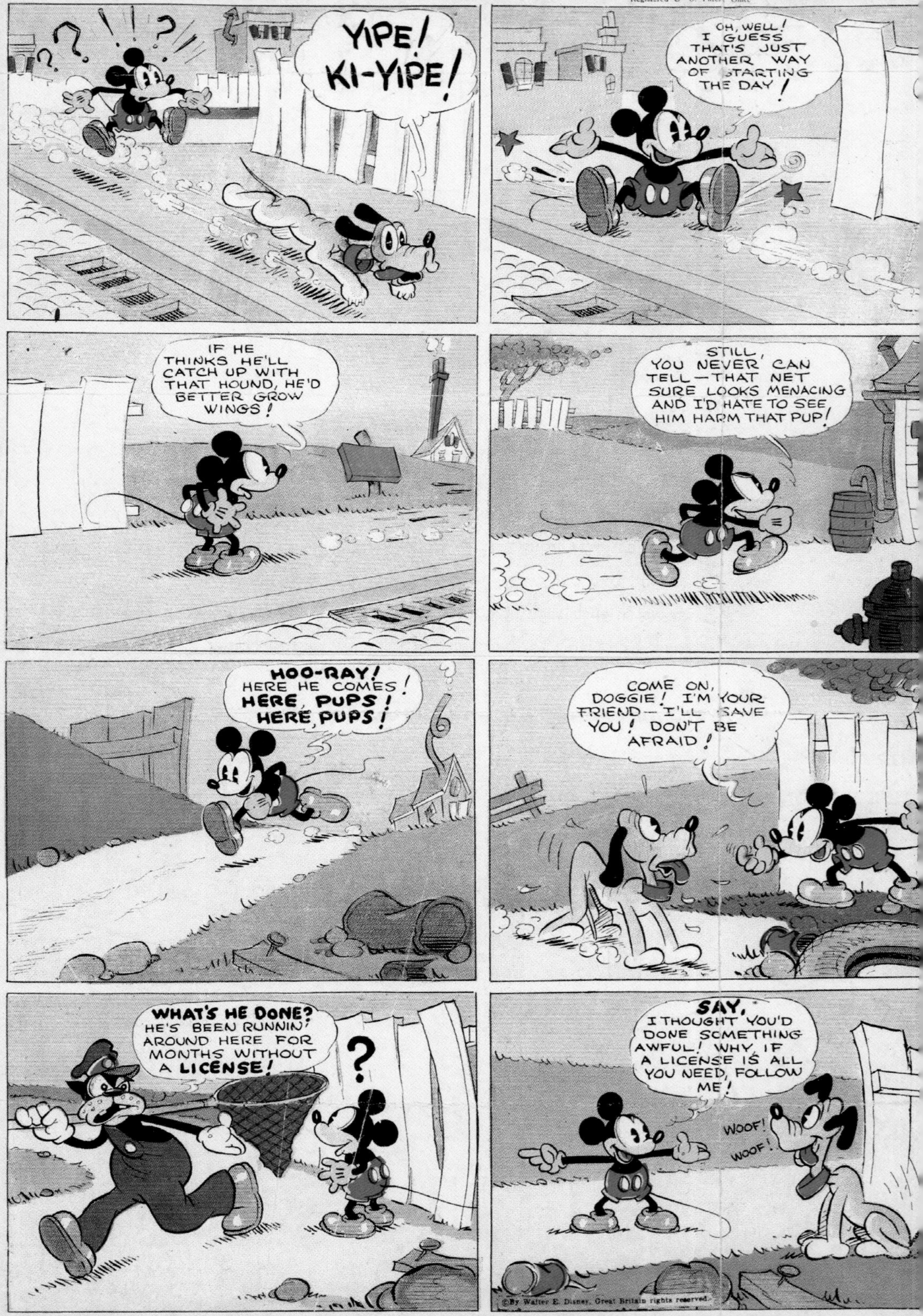

Floyd Gottfredson's work on the *Mickey Mouse* Sunday strip began with strip number two. On January 10, 1932, the *first* Sunday was this more primitive affair, written and drawn entirely by part-time Gottfredson inker Earl Duvall. Older reference books sometimes cite Duvall's strip as Pluto's comics debut, though Pluto's debut in the *daily* strip actually predated this unnamed hound's Sunday appearance by months.

Original art from the "Blaggard Castle" daily strip serial (1932–33), plotted and penciled by Floyd Gottfredson, scripted by Webb Smith, and inked by Ted Thwaites. Due to Gottfredson's workload as Comic Strip Department manager, he had to bring in other scripters, starting with Smith, though he continued to plot the serials himself.

FLOYD GOTTFREDSON'S WORLD

From the start, Disney animation had shown Mickey Mouse as a part-time authority figure, master of ceremonies for well-attended concerts and public events. How could Mickey be both this pillar of society and, in other shorts, a rambunctious youth? The films didn't deal with the discrepancy, but Gottfredson tried to build a world that did. As we have seen, the daily continuities of 1931 tried to flesh out Mickey's hometown and give him the role of public hero: by winning a boxing match, by reforming a criminal, and generally by setting the whole town talking. While Gottfredson did take care not to make Mickey into a plaster saint, the Mouse was nevertheless now a figure who could—at times—acquire believable authority in his world, the kind he often had onscreen. Of course, in comics, this authority could and did conflict with Mickey's youthful instincts. In individual mid-1930s daily-strip serials, Mickey repeatedly started out "against the world," as Gottfredson liked to put it: he was given new circumstances or a new job that shifted the weight of the world onto his shoulders—and was then forced to prove himself a hero, a survivor, a leader, or all three. When Mickey won the day, he could acquire rewards and allies who stuck

IMAGED BY HERITAGE AUCTIONS, HA.COM

with him in adventures to come. Still, achieving the honor, the privilege, and the authority didn't make Mickey a guaranteed hero. Sometimes, it made it only harder for him to live up to expectations.

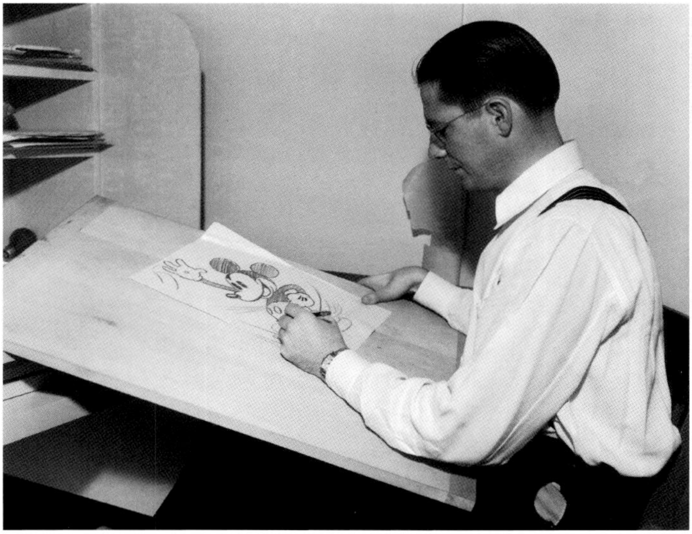

Floyd Gottfredson poses for a photo, February 21, 1933. While by this time Gottfredson's inkers put rather elongated black pupils in Mickey's eyes, Gottfredson himself, in pencil art, still gave his hero a rounder, more beady-eyed look.

A May 1932 *Mickey Mouse* Sunday strip, written and penciled by Floyd Gottfredson and inked by Al Taliaferro, shows a storytelling technique that Gottfredson's team brought to the Sunday venue. The tale of Minnie's fairground prizes features a gag that builds — and a gently ridiculous ending twist.

Mickey Mouse

Registered U. S. Patent Office.

Cover art by Enrico Pinochi for *Albi d'oro* 10 (1937), an Italian comic album reprinting the daily serial "Mickey Mouse and His Horse Tanglefoot" (1933), plotted and penciled by Floyd Gottfredson, scripted by Ted Osborne, and inked by Ted Thwaites.

The earliest issues of Nerbini's *Topolino* (1932) found cover artist Giove Toppi drawing a primitive Mickey. Just a few weeks later, an official arrangement with Disney would bring Floyd Gottfredson's work to the magazine — and to Italy — for the first time.

ITALY AND TOPOLINO

When we last checked in on Mickey's adventures abroad, Guglielmo Guastaveglia was turning out a series of original gag strips for the Italian journal *Il Popolo di Roma*. But by 1932 Guastaveglia's series had ended; most of the year transpired without any Disney comics presence in Italy whatsoever. Then suddenly Mickey returned to the country for good.

The big comeback was inauspicious at first. A new publisher, Florence-based Casa Editrice Nerbini, decided to issue a full-blown Mickey magazine without Disney or King Features involvement. The first issue of Nerbini's *Topolino*— published on December 31, 1932—was licensed and super-

C. Postale - Anno I. - N. 1.
31 Dicembre 1932. XI.
TOPOLINO
CASA EDITRICE G. NERBINI
Direttore: COLLODI NIPOTE
Abbonam. annuo L. 10
Abb. semestrale L. 5
CENT. 20
Topolino dal rinchiuso
fatto ardito, anzi gradasso
al bestione in pieno muso
scaglia dritto un grosso sasso.
L'elefante inviperito
del bernoccolo frontale
fa saltar tutto l'assito
e con furia il topo assale.
Corre corre Topolino
ma l'agguanta il pachiderma.
Un pezzetto di codino
ci rimette e non si ferma.
Corre, corre Topolino
che ha veduto di lontano
la salvezza di un buchino
in un muro suburbano.
È sparito in un baleno....
L'elefante non si arresta
e di corsa come un treno
dà nel muro con la testa.
L'elefante è lì disteso
E gli grida Topolino:
— Marameo,.. mi son difeso
Benchè sia tanto piccino.

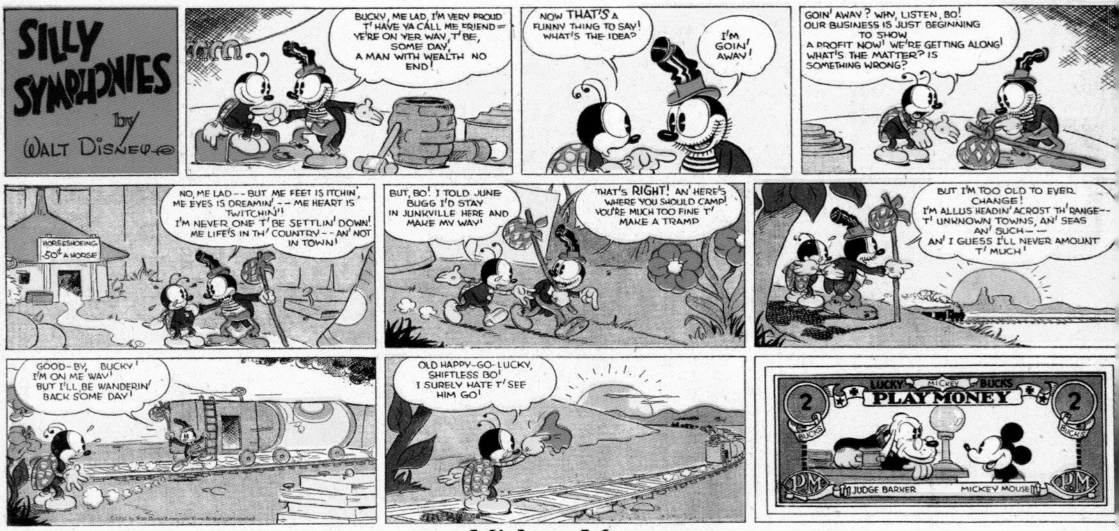

Mickey Mouse

Registered U. S. Patent Office.

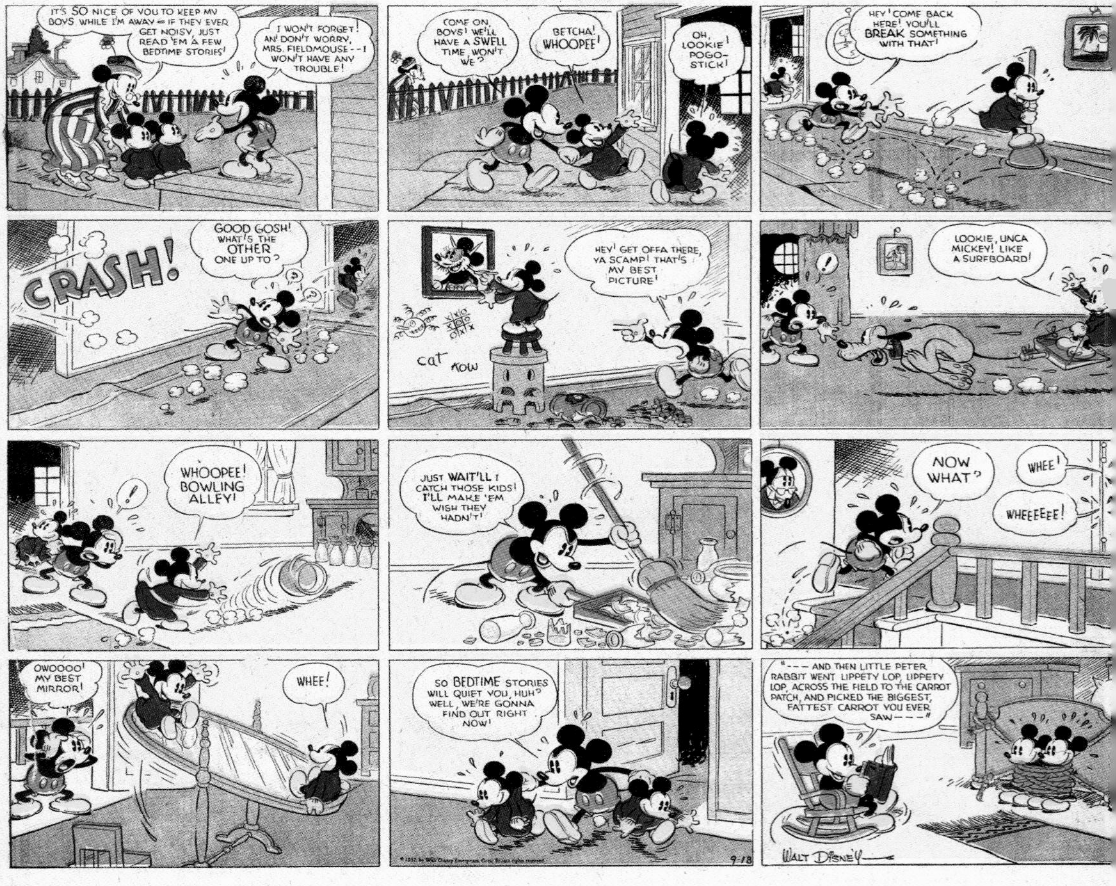

vised only by Euro International Film (EIA), Disney's local theatrical distributor. It paired Mickey with a nonhumanized elephant that he mercilessly pranked. Some Guastaveglia influence was visible; Gottfredson influence was not.

The elephant-fighting Mickey, drawn by Giove Toppi, didn't get far. King Features and Disney, unaware of EIA's involvement, objected to what they thought was an unlicensed magazine.[2] From the third issue, in an effort to mollify them, Nerbini owners Giuseppe and Mario Nerbini—father and son—replaced Toppi's Topolino with "Topo Lino" ("Lino Mouse"), an entirely different-looking rodent.

Then, however, a deal was struck. Disney reasoned that they lacked an official Italian publisher, and Nerbini seemed ideal. Its publications were intended to be educational for children—the latter due to the involvement of editor Paolo Lorenzini, grandson of *Pinocchio* creator/author Carlo Collodi. Soon Italian Disney representative Guglielmo Emanuel gave the blessing for production to continue. Nerbini became a King Features partner, allowing for a fully official use of Mickey; Disney took ownership of Nerbini's earlier mouse material—even Topo Lino—and of all Nerbini's original Disney content going forward.

Toppi and colleague Angelo Burattini continued to draw occasional Mickey strips for Nerbini. But the most prominent Disney character artist in *Topolino* was now Floyd Gottfredson, who for the first time had a regular Italian showcase for his work.

Nerbini would only publish *Topolino* for a couple of years. In theory, Paolo Lorenzini was on board with Nerbini's Disney projects; in practice, Lorenzini considered the comics medium anti-educational by nature, insisted that didactic text features appear in *Topolino*, and objected when Nerbini left those features out of a new, large-size Mickey companion series. When Nerbini launched further comics publications with no educational pretense, an outraged Lorenzini left the company.

Mickey's mischievous nephews Morty and Ferdie Fieldmouse make their debut in the Sunday strip for September 18, 1932, written and penciled by Floyd Gottfredson and inked by Al Taliaferro. Their mother, called only "Mrs. Fieldmouse" here, would later be retconned into Mickey's actual sister, Amely Mouse-Fieldmouse.

Cover art by Enrico Pinochi for *Albi d'oro* 23 (1938), an Italian comic album reprinting the Sunday serial "The Brave Little Tailor" (1938), adapted from the film short by Merrill De Maris, penciled by Floyd Gottfredson and Manuel Gonzales, and inked by Ted Thwaites.

Large-size specialty drawings by Gottfredson were created to promote the launch of the Sunday strip. The comics page that Mickey and Minnie are holding is an approximation of the strip for January 31, 1932.

The January 8, 1933, *Mickey* Sunday strip, written by Ted Osborne, penciled by Floyd Gottfredson, and inked by Ted Thwaites. Mickey's future best friend makes an inauspicious debut as "that pest, Dippy Dog"; he would respell his surname "Dawg" soon afterward, and become Goofy in the daily strip starting January 1936. Under any name, the Goof was first portrayed for comics as an annoying rube reminiscent of his earliest animated appearances.

Without him, Giuseppe and Mario Nerbini dug further into the King Features catalog, launched a non-Disney anthology comic called *L'Avventuroso*—and paid less attention to *Topolino*.

Luckily a new publisher was waiting in the wings: in 1935, Milan-based Arnoldo Mondadori began negotiating with Disney representatives. Nerbini had never held a license to publish the *Mickey Mouse* Sunday strip's Silly Symphony topper; Mondadori licensed these rights for its own Disney weekly, *I tre Porcellini* ("The Three Little Pigs"). Then Mondadori acquired a license to publish Gottfredson strips in formats—such as thick-covered albums—that Nerbini ignored. Finally Mondadori paid Nerbini off to terminate its Disney license totally, then contracted to found Edizioni Walt Disney-Mondadori ("Walt Disney-Mondadori Editions"), a new imprint under which *Topolino* was published from August 1935. The Mondadori *Topolino* was supplemented by further Disney comic books, some of which—like *Nel Regno Topolino* ("In Mickey's Kingdom")—featured original, Gottfredson-inspired cover drawings by such local artists as Antonio Rubino and Enrico Pinochi.

The seeds were being planted for an exciting new Disney comics school.

THE CONTINUING NEWSPAPER STRIP

In the mid-1930s, however, such triumphs still lay in the future—especially from the American vantage point. Webb Smith, scripter of "Blaggard Castle," had been replaced as Gottfredson's writing assistant by two new and more durable hands, Ted Osborne and Merrill De Maris. Osborne had first popped up on Disney's radar as an in-house writer and director for Los Angeles radio station KHJ; from October 1931, Disney hired

Mickey Mouse

Registered U. S. Patent Office.

WITH PILOTS DISAPPEARING ONE AFTER ANOTHER, THE WHOLE FLYING FIELD IS IN AN UPROAR OVER THE REPORT OF A HUGE SPIDER IN THE SKY!
IT'S SILLY, THAT'S WHAT IT IS! I DON'T KNOW WHAT HAPPENED TO THOSE PLANES, BUT I'M GOING TO FIND OUT!
HOW, CAPTAIN DOBERMAN?
MAIL
I'M GOING TO FLY THIS LOAD OF MAIL MYSELF! I'VE NEVE CRACKED UP YET A I'M NOT GOING TO START NOW!

NOW, TH' NEXT THING T' DO IS SHOOT OFF TH' GUNS AN' MOTORS!
SCRAM! HERE HE COMES AGAIN!

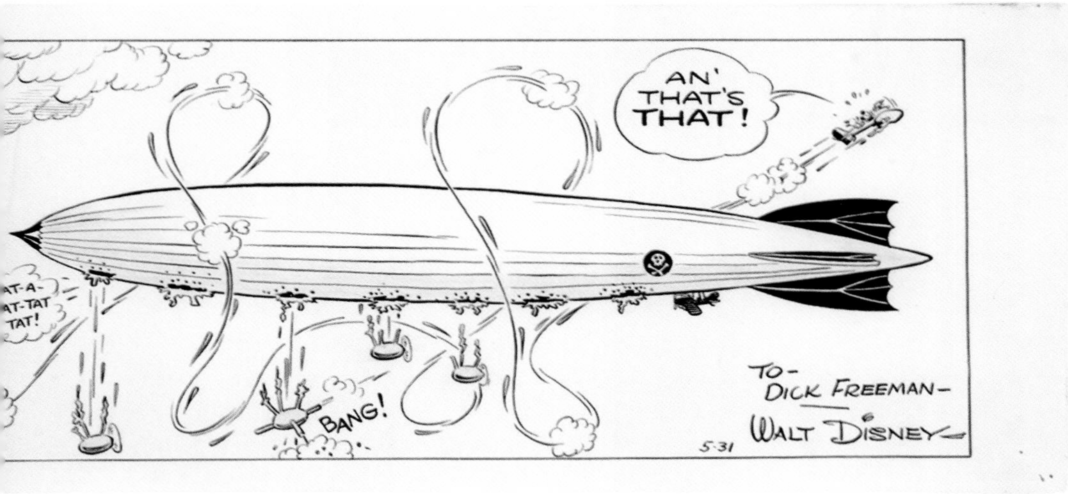

Original art from "The Mail Pilot" daily strip serial (1933), plotted and penciled by Floyd Gottfredson, scripted by Ted Osborne, and inked by Ted Thwaites. Inspired by the same-named cartoon, "The Mail Pilot" reflects Mickey's growth in comics as a complex character. At first a clumsy, boyish, and unorthodox pilot, Mickey struggles against his own immaturity, trains hard with mechanic Gloomy, and acquires the skill needed to win a difficult air battle — shooting off the guns and motors of Pete's blimp and rendering his air pirates helpless.

In France "Rumplewatt the Giant" became the feature story in the first issue of *Le Journal de Mickey*, the country's flagship Disney weekly. Launched in 1934 by Paul Winkler—owner of the French King Features representative Opera Mundi—and publisher Hachette, *Le Journal* initially differed from its British and Italian equivalents in that it featured no locally produced Disney comics. Nevertheless, the magazine cultivated a devoted French audience for American comics across the board.

Following A strip from the Sunday serial "Case of the Vanishing Coats" (1935), written by Ted Osborne, penciled by Floyd Gottfredson, and inked by Ted Thwaites. This detective story seems to have been inspired by two shelved cartoons that were in development at the time: *The Invisible Man* and *Navy Mickey*.

Osborne away—part-time at first[3]—intending for him to "develop a Mickey Mouse radio show" with KHJ colleague Dick Creedon.[4] The radio initiative didn't last long, but Osborne stuck around. De Maris, meanwhile—by Gottfredson's estimation, the more talented of the two scripters[5]—had grown up a shy introvert; having rebelled against his bossy father to become a journalist, he brought years of that experience to the Disney team.

Osborne and De Maris helped Gottfredson pilot Mickey through what comics historians often remember as his most celebrated years.

INTERLUDE: *MICKEY MOUSE ANNUAL* AND *MICKEY MOUSE WEEKLY*

As impressive as mid-1930s *Mickey Mouse* daily and Sunday strips were, and even as continental European magazines gained steam, Mickey's British comics conquests continued apace. From *Mickey Mouse Annual* No. 3 (1932), writer/artist Wilfred Haughton made a visible effort to expand the cast of characters and mimic contemporary American publications: Horace, Clarabelle, and other stalwarts appeared repeatedly and were named, albeit not always consistently at first. One of Haughton's sources was David McKay's 1931 *The Adventures of Mickey Mouse, Book 1*, a storybook in which Clarabelle is called "Carolyn" and Horace "Henry"!

By the mid-1930s a more authentic Disney cast filled the *Annual*, with Pluto, Butch, Morty, and Ferdie, and Peg Leg Pete all added to the gang. Slowly, the group began to be less a bunch of interchangeable music hall comics than a troupe of more individualized players on the American model. As such—as in Gottfredson—they became not just funny, but likeable: an increasingly endearing proxy family for readers.

A few uniquely British oddities did continue. Secondary characters, including Horace and Peg Leg Pete, could actually get killed in individual *Annual* stories—only to return later in the book, implying that they had only died in the context of the role they played in one story. Sometimes, the tempo-

LE JOURNAL DE MICKEY

L'HEBDOMADAIRE DES JEUNES
RÉDACTION - ADMINISTRATION
68, CHAUSSÉE D'ANTIN, PARIS Tél. : Pig. 94-61

PUBLICITÉ : Sté Nlle de Publicité, 11, boul. des Italiens PARIS (2e). Téléphone : Richelieu 67-60

1re ANNÉE. — No 1 LE NUMÉRO : **30** centimes 21 OCTOBRE 1934

MICKEY

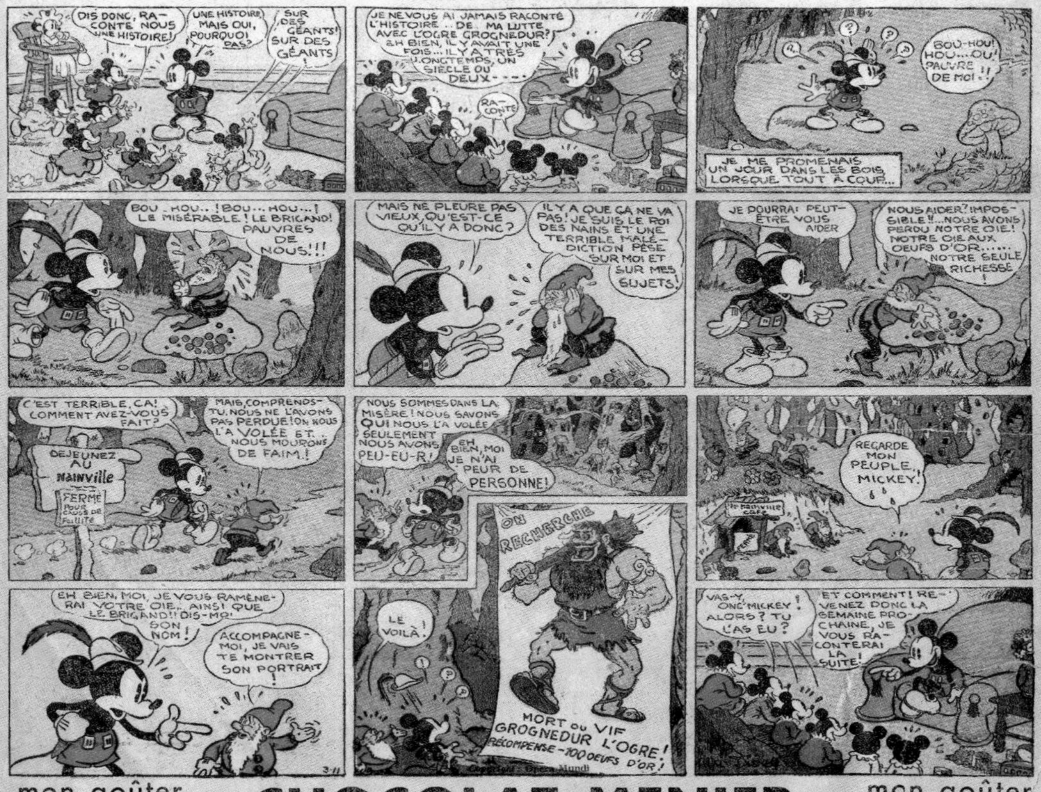

WHERE Y' BOUND DONALD?
I'M GOIN' TO MEET MY UNCLE DOWN AT HIS STORE! IT'S NEARLY CLOSIN' TIME!
AMOS P. ZOUP
CLOTHING
SHOES-TIES-SOCKS-ETC
LOOK!
JIMINY-WOW!
I'M DEAD! LEAVE ME ALONE! I'M DEAD, I TELL YOU!
NO, YOU'RE NOT, MR. ZOUP! Y' JUST GOT A SOCK ON THE COCO!
WELL, I GUESS IT COULDA BEEN LOTS WORSE!
I CAN'T AFFORD TO LOSE THAT COAT! BUSINESS IS BAD ENOUGH AS IT IS!
LIKE TO SEE 'IM COME BACK JUST LIKE TO SEE 'IM!
WELL, I'M GOIN' OU TO THE DOCTOR ABO THIS HEAD! YOU LO UP, DONALD IT'S LATE
CLUNKETY!
HATS
BUMP!
MY GOSH! WHAT WAS THAT?
SQUACK!
UP
G
S-ETC

E'S NOT REALLY
Y UNCLE, BUT
LIVE WITH
HIM!
UNCLE AMOS! UNCLE AMOS! THAT'S FUNNY!
?
?
LOOKS LIKE THE PLACE IS EMPTY!
REMEMBER, NOW! A
FELLER BUYIN' AN
VERCOAT, HIT ME
WITH A
BLACKJACK!
OH-BOY-OH-BOY! TOO BAD I WASN'T HERE-I'D A' FIXED HIM!
!
STRANGE HE DIDN'T TAKE ANY MONEY— ONLY THE OVERCOAT!
NO SALE
HE MUSTA BEEN PRETTY HARD UP, JUST TO STEAL A COAT!
I'D LIKE TO SEE 'IM COME IN AGAIN! I'D KNOCK 'IM FOR A LOOP!
K!
NLY
SH I
AD
AT--
H?
S'POSE WE LOOK AROUND? HE MAY BE HIDDEN SOME PLACE!
HATS
MAYBE THE ROBBER NEVER LEFT! HE MIGHT BE HIDIN' IN THE STORE— OVER THERE, F' RINSTANCE!
HUH? OVER THERE? OH, YEH, YEH, HE--HE COULD BE!
T'S OUT IN
THE STREET!
C'MON!
THAT NOISE WASN'T OUT HERE! IT WAS IN THE STORE!
OTHING
TIES-SOCKS-ETC
RATTLE
RATTLE
CLICK
I G-GUESS WE J-JUST IMAGINED IT! ANYWAY— W-WHY SH-SHOULD WE MAKE IT TOUGH FOR A POOR GUY THAT NEEDS AN OVERCOAT!
2-17
WALT DISNEY

The front cover of *Mickey Mouse Annual* No. 11 (1940) shows the increasingly accomplished look of Wilfred Haughton's later Disney art.

"Broadcast News," a 1934 Sunday gag written by Ted Osborne, penciled by Floyd Gottfredson, and inked by Ted Thwaites. Even as Mickey became a more mature character in adventure stories, he remained a playful, occasionally prankish fellow in Sunday strips throughout the 1930s. His most elaborate practical jokes were invariably aimed at Horace, who was just as fond of pranking Mickey.

rary "deaths" were even mocked; Haughton's strangenesses pointed up how the stories were transforming, from impersonal vaudeville farce into neighborhood plays put on by a well-loved troupe.

With *Mickey Mouse Annual* No. 7 (1936), the introduction of Donald and Goofy provided even greater opportunities for creativity. While Goofy was named as such from his print debut in Britain, Haughton drew the physically shorter "Dippy Dawg" visual design for two years. The explanation may lie in another publication that launched in 1936: *Mickey Mouse Weekly*, Odhams Press' newsstand companion to the *Annual*. Starting in *Weekly* No. 45 (1936), a long-running Haughton-drawn serial paired the Dippy-looking Goofy with Toby Tortoise as detectives: a team-up that looked most natural when the two characters were of similar height.

Haughton was never the only contributor to *Mickey Mouse Weekly*, but he did supply an elaborate, full-color rotogravure cover for each issue. British comics stalwarts such as Basil Reynolds and William A. Ward contributed interior features—and the more familiar they got with the extended Mickey stock company, the more refined their interpretations of them became. In the British comics of 1930 and 1931, Mickey had been capable of smart, foolish, heroic, or cowardly behavior as a given story required; by the late 1930s, plot was never put before character. Mickey needn't be a fight-starter when Donald was around; Minnie needn't be a slow-thinking eccentric with Goofy in the vicinity. This is not to say Mickey and Minnie became boring; in the spirit of Gottfredson, they remained plucky, determined, often bickering youths who got into no shortage of scrapes.

Back across the Atlantic, meanwhile, the scrapes were getting epic: Gottfredson by the mid-1930s had reached a peak in which legendary serials came one after the next.

SILLY SYMPHONY
by WALT DISNEY
I'M LOST! I'M LOST! OH, WHERE DID MAMA GO?
HE'S LOST!
HE'S LOST!
HA-HA!
TEE-HEE!
HO-HO!
HE MUST BE FOUND! I'LL NEVER SLEEP ALL NIGHT!
BEFORE I GO, I'D BETTER EAT A BITE!
I'LL FIND THE CHICK--- AND THEN--I HAVE A HUNCH! THAT MRS. HEN WILL ASK ME IN TO LUNCH!
I'M AWFUL TIRED— I GUESS I'M HUNGRY, TOO OH, MA! OH, MA! I WANT MY MA—I DO!
10-7

MICKEY MOUSE MOVIES
MICKEY MOUSE MOVIES
- INSTRUCTIONS -
PASTE MOVIE WHEEL ON CARDBOARD. CUT OUT WHEEL AND PAINT BACK OF IT BLACK. CUT OUT SLITS, STICK A PIN THROUGH DOT IN CENTER AND PUT PIN INTO ERASER END OF PENCIL.
TO OPERATE:— STAND BEFORE A MIRROR AND SPIN WHEEL WITH BLACK SIDE TOWARD YOU. CLOSE ONE EYE AND WATCH IMAGE THROUGH SLITS!

MICKEY MOUSE
REGISTERED U.S. PATENT OFFICE
CLARABELLE'S RADIO IS ON E BLINK AND I'M GOIN' VER TO FIX IT!
FUNNY-LOOKIN' TOOLS TO FIX A RADIO WITH!
I'LL HAVE IT O.K. IN A JIFFY, CLARABELLE!
LAND KNOWS- THEM THINGS IS ALL A MYSTERY TO ME— WELL, I BETTER GET BACK TO MY PIES!
I DIDN'T CARRY THIS HOSE AND FUNNEL ALONG FOR NOTHIN'!
I'M GOIN' NOW, CLARABELLE — IT'S ALL FIXED!
THANKS, MICKEY! WAIT A MINUTE, I'VE GOT A PIECE OF PIE FOR YOU!
NOW — IF I CAN GET IN THE BACK DOOR WITHOUT BEIN' SEEN, I'LL HAVE SOME FUN!
GOOD LAND! HE MUST HAVE BEEN IN A BIG RUSH TO GET HOME! WELL, I GUESS I'LL TRY THE RADIO!
HIS IS THE KEYHOLE-PEEPER SPEAKING! IVING YOU THE LATEST NEWS OF WHAT ND WHO -- AND SPEAKING OF WHO — E'D LIKE TO KNOW THE IDENTITY F THE LUSCIOUS BLONDE HORSECOLLAR WAS THAT WAY ABOUT LAST NIGHT---
WE'VE SEEN H.H. ABOUT TOWN WITH SEVERAL GALS THAT MIGHT--- WELL---WE NEVER SAW HIM QUITE SO GA-GA AS LAST---
THE WRETCH! I'LL TELL HIM A THING OR TWO!
HI-YA, CLARABELLE! JUST STOPPED IN TO SEE IF YOU'D GO TO A MOVIE TONIGHT! — WHY, WHAT'S THE MATTER?
YOU SHOULD ASK --- YOU FAITHLESS PHILAND--ER, PHIL- ---YOU WRETCH!
E HEAR CERTAIN ARABELLE BURNT UP UT THE WAY H.H. IS N' AND IS KELY TO E HIM--
YOU SNAKE! GO OFF WITH YOUR FLUFFY DOLLS! SEE IF I CARE!
SOMEBODY'S RAGGIN' YOU, CLARABELLE --- THAT'S NO BROADCAST!
IT'S NO SKIN OFF OUR NOSE, BUT WE HATE TO SEE NOBLE WOMAN-HOOD GIVEN THE GATE FOR---
CALLING ALL CARS! CALLING ALL CARS! GO TO THE RESCUE OF YOUNG MAN ATTACKED BY CRAZY WOMAN IN FRENZY!
WALT DISNEY
10-7

THE DETECTIVE AGENCY!
GOOFY, AND TOBY TORTOISE OPEN UP A DETECTIVE SHOP, WITH PLUTO AS THEIR BLOODHOUND—CAN YOU IMAGINE IT?
CASE No. 1. THE DISAPPEARING KIDS.
PROLOGUE
MICKEY AND MINNIE RECEIVED A NOTE FROM A MYSTERIOUS SOMEBODY, DEMANDING A BIG SUM OF MONEY TO BE PLACED ON TOP OF THE DUSTBIN BY LAST MONDAY EVENING, 8.p.m. AS MICKEY WAS BROKE, HE BROUGHT THE DUSTBIN INTO THE PARLOUR, AND IGNORED THE NOTE. ON TUESDAY MORNING ONE OF THE FAMOUS MICKEY QUINS WAS MISSING. ON WEDNESDAY ANOTHER VANISHED. ON THURSDAY YET ANOTHER!
DON'T UPSET YOURSELF MINNIE. P'RAPS THEY'RE BEING WELL CARED FOR
YES, BUT IT SPOILS THE SET, MICKEY
U MMW 45
CRASH
BANG
OH!
ANOTHER ONE TONITE —UNLESS
MICKEY! PROMISE ME YOU WON'T LEAVE ME IN THE HOUSE ALONE ALL NIGHT
I'LL BE BACK MINNIE! I'M GOING TO GET TO THE BOTTOM OF THIS AFFAIR
DETECTIVE AGENCY
CRIMES SOLVED
PUZZLES DONE
ALSO HOMEWORK
GOSH! I'LL SEE WHAT THEY CAN DO!
GOOFY!
YES SIR! AND HOW
GOSH! I GOT IT! WE'LL FIND OUT WHO NOTE THE WROTES
CLICK!
WHAT DO YOU WANT GLUE FOR?
I SAID 'CLUE' NOT GLUE
WHY HAVE WE COME RIGHT OUT IN THE COUNTRY, MILES OUT OF THE WAY, GOOFY?
THAT'S IN CASE WE'RE BEING FOLLOWED. IT WILL TIRE THEM OUT
?
NO ONE ABOUT! GOOD. NOW I CAN HAVE A QUIET SMOKE
Z Z Z
CONTINUED NEXT WEEK

FROM MAGAZINES TO COMIC BOOKS

While "Mickey Mouse Outwits the Phantom Blot," in its 1941 newsstand comic book reprint, might have functioned as the first dedicated, all-Mickey "floppy"—as ongoing comic books are called today—it was by no means the first Mickey periodical made for American newsstands. By contrast, it came on the heels of eight years of constant Mickey magazine presence—just not quite in the form of a comic book, at first.

Mickey Mouse Magazine dated back to January 1933, when Kay Kamen and United Artists publicist Hal Horne introduced it as a five-cent digest to be sold at theaters. Late in the year, a second series was designed as a premium for local dairies, who could deliver copies to ongoing milk customers. In summer 1935, Horne broke from United Artists to publish a full-size third series for newsstands. Aside from sharing content with the British *Mickey Mouse Weekly*, which began soon after, Horne's magazine joined forces with it to inspire a rush of worldwide spinoffs. Switzerland's *Micky Maus Zeitung* and Sweden's *Musse Pigg Tidningen* are two of the better known.

What was in a typical *Mickey Mouse Magazine*? Along with short, original comic strips, issue No. 5 (1936) features an editorial supposedly by Mickey ("Just Between Us"), and half- and full-page gag cartoons with Disney characters. There is a stage play for readers to put on ("Uncle Dumb's Cabin"), and a couple of stories in prose—some Disney-specific, others not.

The only problem with *Mickey Mouse Magazine* was that Horne couldn't keep it up. While it soon sold a half million copies per issue, Horne famously printed far too many more—and when this led to a money shortfall, Kamen bought out Horne's interest and took the magazine over. For a while, Kamen published it as

Page one of "The Disappearing Kids," a *Mickey Mouse Weekly* serial drawn by Wilfred Haughton. British stories of Goofy and Toby Tortoise as detectives continued into World War II. It appears Haughton resisted switching to the later, taller Goofy model for fear of confusing these stories' fans; when, in late 1937, Haughton's Goofy finally made the switch, Toby grew in height to match him.

The frontispiece from *Mickey Mouse Annual* No. 9 (1938) shows more of Wilfred Haughton's increasingly accomplished later Disney art.

Wilfred Haughton's cover for Britain's *Mickey Mouse Weekly* 1 (1936). The first issue of *Mickey Mouse Weekly* was also the first British comic to be printed in full color using the photogravure method — which offered brighter, sharper colors than the traditional lithographic process, but was prohibitively expensive barring high press runs.

Cover by Wilfred Haughton for *Mickey Mouse Weekly* 47 (1936). Donald's yellow feathers reflect his coloration in early *Mickey Mouse Magazine* and Sunday strip appearances, which themselves seem to have taken their cue from late 1934 film posters and storyboard art. Available evidence suggests that Disney considered turning Donald yellow concurrent with his move from *The Wise Little Hen* into the Mickey series — then discarded the idea.

MICKEY MOUSE
WEEKLY
Vol. 1. No. 47. December 26th, 1936
2d EVERY FRIDAY 2d
A MERRY XMAS TO YOU ALL
BANG
YOU SHOULD SEE ME DO IT WITH ONE HAND!
TOUGH, ARE YOU. WELL TRY A PIECE OF MINNIE'S PUDDING!
WHO PUT TREACLE ON MY END OF THE CRACKER?
WHAT WOULD YOU LIKE, SONNY?
AN ELASTIC TUMMY, AND SOME MORE MINCE PIES, PLEASE!
HERE'S GOOFUN!
EGGS
ARE YOU SURE YOU WON'T FALL OVER WHEN IT BANGS, TOBY?
TOBY WILL SOON BE IN THE SOUP!
WELL! HAVE YOU EVER HEARD OF A TORTOISE TURNING TURTLE, MINNIE?
I KNOW IT'S WRONG BUT I DON'T 'ORPHAN' GET A CHANCE LIKE THIS!
FUN FOR THE WHOLE FAMILY

GOOFY, DO YOU MEAN T' TELL ME YOU THINK I'M DEAD? THAT I'M A **GHOST**?
SURE! YOU AIN'T KIDDIN' **ME** NONE! G'WAN! LET'S SEE YUH FLOAT AROUND A BIT!
AW, YER CRAZY— JUST LIKE EVERYBODY ELSE IN TOWN!
ALL RIGHT! WATCH! I'LL **PROVE** THAT YUH'RE A GHOST!
...terprises, World righ

COLONEL BASSETT HAS GONE TO BED, LEAVING THE THREE GHOST HUNTERS BY THEMSELVES IN HIS HAUNTED MANSION!
9-7
GOOFY, HOW DO YA GO ABOUT **FINDIN'** THESE GHOSTS?
SHUCKS! YOU DON'T **HAFTA** FIND'EM! JUST STICK AROUND! THEY'LL BE—
HEY! WHAT HAPPENED? WHO TURNED OUT THOSE LIGHTS? **DONALD**! WHERE'S YER FLASHLIGHT?
?

Original art from the daily serial "The Seven Ghosts" (1936), plotted and penciled by Floyd Gottfredson, scripted by Ted Osborne, and inked by Ted Thwaites. "The Seven Ghosts" contrasts Donald with Mickey by portraying Donald as primarily driven by fear: a portrayal reflecting early story treatments for *Lonesome Ghosts*, which had at one point shown a cowardly Donald considering leaving Mickey's ghostbusting group.

The early series of *Mickey Mouse Magazine* usually restricted Mickey's gang to Minnie, Horace, Clarabelle, and Pluto—but when the group did expand, it was with a difference. *Mickey Mouse Magazine* seems to have been the first Disney licensed product to call Goofy by his final name—using it as early as 1934, though initially spelling it "Goofie."

Mickey Mouse Magazine, aided and abetted by its British cousin *Mickey Mouse Weekly*, inspired similar Disney children's magazines around Europe; Switzerland's *Micky Maus Zeitung*, the first dedicated Disney magazine in German, was released by the publisher Bollmann. The 1937 first issue features a reinked Wilfred Haughton cover from *Mickey Mouse Weekly* 31 (1936)—and localized versions of Donald and Horace named "Schnatterich" ("blabberer") and "Hippo."

MICKY MAUS ZEITUNG

Zürich, Mitte Januar 1937

Nr. 1 1. Jahrgang Erscheint zweimal monatlich Preis 25 Cts.

The late 1930s Mickey magazine boom anticipated the comic book explosion of the postwar years. Pictured: a young girl enjoys Mickey Mouse *Four Color* 141 (1947) in George Harris's Confectionery store, Pittsburgh, Pennsylvania, 1947.

"Kay Kamen Ltd."; from 1937, he minted a new partnership with Western Printing and Lithographing Company, leading to an influx of Western-produced content and the enduring imprint of K. K. Publications.[6]

Under any imprint, however, Western was bullish about a new medium: not children's magazines, but the burgeoning field of comic books. As Western's hold on *Mickey Mouse Magazine* grew, so did the number of Disney strip reprints per issue; and the trend was a sign of things to come. In October 1940, dropping most of *Mickey Mouse Magazine*'s editorial features and adopting a new masthead title, K. K. Publications brought out the first modern Disney comic. *Walt Disney's Comics and Stories* was here—and Gottfredson serial reprints would play a major role in its early years. Mickey Mouse, the comic *strip* adventurer, was becoming the comic *book* adventurer.

Meanwhile, of course, Mickey's strip adventures continued, with several especial classics finishing off Gottfredson's prewar golden age.

Original art from the daily serial "Island in the Sky" (1936–37), plotted and penciled by Floyd Gottfredson, scripted by Ted Osborne, and inked by Ted Thwaites. In this story Mickey's inquisitive nature leads him to fearlessly pursue an apocalyptic threat — a threat that, in the person of the mysterious Dr. Einmug, actually mocks Mickey's optimistic hopes for humanity. Yet Gottfredson also makes clear that Mickey is not misguided; at story's end, Mickey's boss Captain Doberman concedes that protecting Einmug's secrets made all the risks worth it.

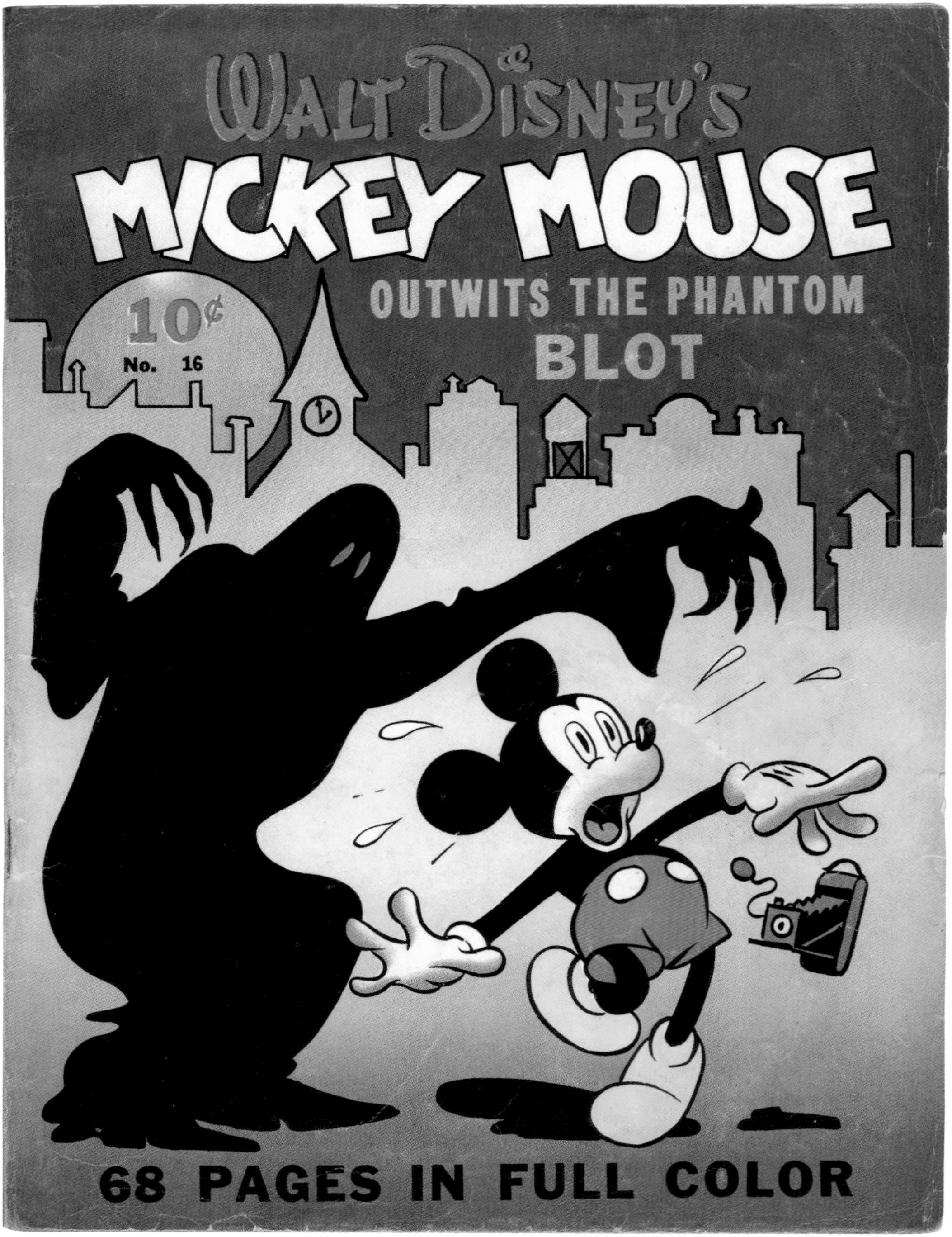

IMAGED BY HERITAGE AUCTIONS, HA.COM

The Blot was referred to as a "phantom" in Gottfredson's 1939 daily strip serial, but never alongside his name; it was this reprint in Dell's 1941 comic book *Four Color* 16 that coined the compound moniker "Phantom Blot." Issue 16 was the first of many Mickey *Four Color* issues before, in 1952, Dell published *Mickey Mouse* 28, inaugurating Mickey's ongoing series. But while the numbering followed on the preceding one-shots, Dell didn't quite count them correctly; there had been 29.

Cover art by Antonio Rubino for *Nel regno di Topolino* 21 (1936): an Italian comic album reprinting the daily strip serial "Oscar the Ostrich" (1936), plotted and penciled by Floyd Gottfredson, scripted by Ted Osborne, and inked by Ted Thwaites. "Oscar" was the first Gottfredson story to feature Goofy as Goofy — rather than Dippy — and to give him the big chin, sleepy eyes, and full wardrobe of his mature character design.

Following A 1944 *Walt Disney's Comics and Stories* reprint of the daily strip serial "Love Trouble" (1941), plotted and penciled by Floyd Gottfredson, scripted by Merrill De Maris, and inked by Bill Wright. While Gottfredson usually tried to keep his continuity consistent, "Love Trouble" saw Mortimer — previously featured in 1936 — reintroduced with a new name and a streamlined visual design. The extra work didn't go for naught; decades later, the *Mickey MouseWorks* TV cartoon would revive Mortimer again — with his original name, but drawn using this streamlined 1941 look.

MICKEY MOUSE IN "LOVE TROUBLE"
BUT, MINNIE... I THOUGHT...!
GOOD-BYE!
R-RRRRRR-ROARR
NOT TAKING MINNIE'S NEW "CRUSH" TOO SERIOUSLY, MICKEY BOUNCES BACK NEXT AFTERNOON WITH ALL HIS OLD-TIME PERKINESS!
AFTER ALL, WHAT'S THAT BOZO GOT THAT I HAVEN'T?
...EXCEPT A SPORTY CAR, AND...GOSH-DARN, HE'S HERE AGAIN! OH, WELL...!
H'LO, MINNIE... I BROUGHT Y' A LITTLE...!
OH, YES...THANK YOU!
HI Y', JASPER! BEEN ROBBIN' ASH-CANS AGAIN? HA-HA-HA!
MONTY, YOU SAY THE CLEVEREST THINGS!

MICKEY MOUSE in "LOVE TROUBLE"
IF YOU'D LIKE TO DANCE, MONTY, I HAVE SOME LOVELY NEW RECORDS!
DELIGHTED! I'LL CLEAR THE FLOOR!
!
HERE'S A PERFECTLY THRILLING RHUMBA!
THE HOTTER, THE BETTER, BABE!
OH, MONTY, YOU DANCE DIVINELY!
SO THEY TELL ME! MUST BE FROM MY TRAVELS IN SOUTH AMERICA!
YOU CUT A WICKED RUG YOURSELF, TOOTS!
OOOO-O-O ... AREN'T YOU STRONG! I ADORE MASTERFUL MEN!
CLICKETY CLACK CLICK!

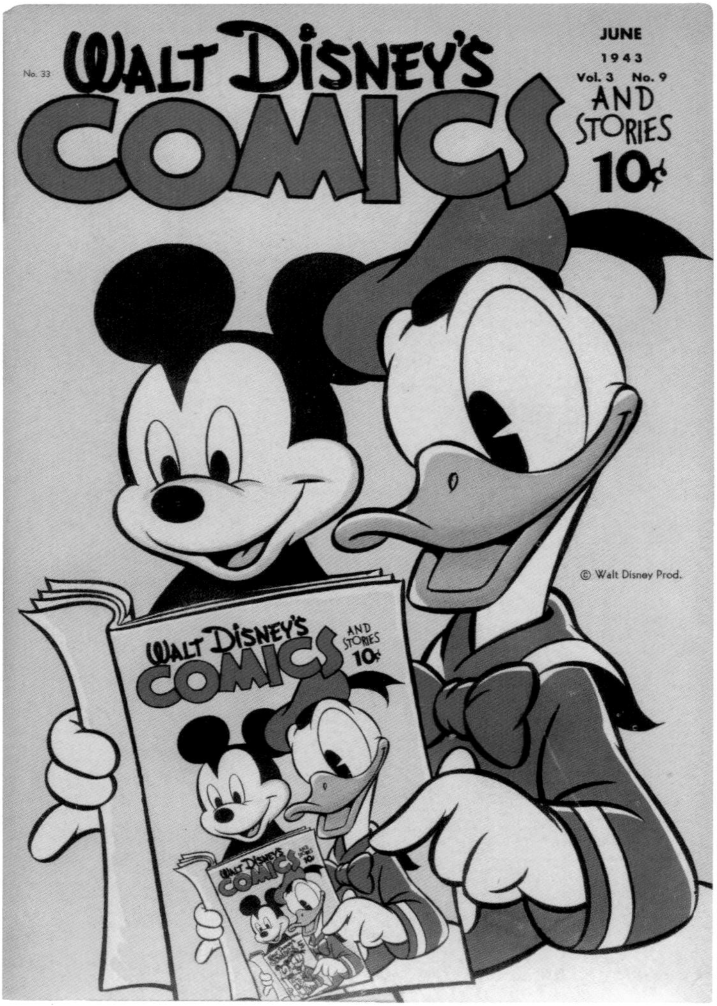

IMAGED BY HERITAGE AUCTIONS, HA.COM

Donald Duck was Disney's biggest star in the 1940s and, as such, featured without Mickey on most early *Walt Disney's Comics and Stories* covers. But now and then both big stars teamed up—for instance on the front of issue 33 (1943).

The notion of Mickey and Donald as bickering pals or even rivals, as suggested by *The Band Concert* and *Magician Mickey*, was a much more prominent theme in mid-1930s comics and especially *Mickey Mouse Magazine* than on the screen. Covers, stories, and editorial features played out the stars' amusing squabbles, not least on the football field.

Mickey Mouse Magazine

10¢

NOVEMBER
1936
VOL. 2
NO. 2

FUN FOR THE WHOLE FAMILY

MICKEY MOUSE

EXPRESSIONS

and REGULAR CAST OF CHARACTERS

THE SILVER AGE

Thousands of Eyes in the Dark
KEEP Your EYES OPEN
AWS
Remember PEARL HARBOR
© WALT DISNEY

CHAPTER SIX

Password: Mickey Mouse

Even after the war had been raging elsewhere in the world for years, even after the mounting pressure that made American involvement in the conflict seem inevitable, the United States' decisive entry into World War II produced a seismic shock at all levels of American society. Practically overnight, American life was transformed. The Disney studio was no exception; within a matter of days, peacetime productions were shelved and the studio plunged into an all-embracing program of propaganda films, public-service shorts, training films for the armed forces, and a range of other activities that would help to support the war effort.

Mickey Mouse's role in all this can be summed up quickly: it was practically nonexistent. With one notable exception—the comics, which we'll examine presently—Mickey virtually disappeared during the war years. His patriotism was never open to question, and no one who had seen *The Mail Pilot* or *Shanghaied* (or *The Barnyard Battle*, for that matter) would accuse him of running away from a fight. But by the late 1930s, Mickey's nice-guy persona was so firmly in place that he simply did not fit the role of a warrior. Mickey was a peacemaker. Donald Duck was a different story, of course; Donald sometimes seemed to be constantly at war with *everyone*, and with the official onset of hostilities he slipped into the national wartime mood without difficulty. Walt plainly told a radio interviewer in 1943 that Donald had gone to war, but Mickey had "retired" for the duration.[1]

Previous A Mickey Mouse model sheet, drawn in 1959 by Floyd Gottfredson.

The Disney studio contributed public-service and morale-boosting posters like these to the armed services, and here, as in the comics, Mickey did maintain an active presence. Note that Mickey is drawn with dimensional ears, as he was in his contemporary screen cartoons. Art attributed to Hank Porter.

Original production layout for Mickey's rare appearance in uniform in *Out of the Frying Pan into the Firing Line*.

Mickey's support of the war effort embraced a wide variety of public-service art, directed not only at the military but also at the civilian population. In this poster, Mickey, Donald, and Goofy promote the important causes of ride-sharing and gasoline conservation. Their exact occupations are not specified, but it's clear that all three are engaged in some kind of labor on behalf of the war effort; note Goofy's ID badge.

In fact, Mickey's best-remembered connection to the war—"Mickey Mouse" being the password for the invading troops on D-Day—is itself an erroneous rumor. (His name *did* serve as the password for the naval officers' invasion briefing shortly before the operation, surely a notable distinction in itself.)[2]

Mickey's withdrawal from the spotlight was not immediately obvious. Thanks to an assortment of story work beginning, in some cases, as early as 1939, Mickey continued to appear on theater screens in a full slate of cartoons throughout 1941 and well into 1942. Of course these shorts had nothing to do with the war; Mickey perhaps provided a measure of reassurance during those early months by continuing to appear in the familiar kinds of stories that audiences had come to expect. But if the story material seemed familiar, Mickey himself was moving in a remarkable new direction.

PLANES NEED GASOLINE
313
©
WALT DISNEY
SHARE YOUR CAR
FOR YOUR COUNTRY

MICKEY ON THE HOME FRONT

THE LITTLE WHIRLWIND
(February 14, 1941)

A minor gag sequence in *Playful Pluto* (1934)—Mickey's attempt to rake leaves while a little whirlwind blows them away—here becomes the basis of a complete film. It's fleshed out with a context borrowed from the unfinished *Mickey's Elopement*: Minnie, exasperated with Mickey's clowning around, promises him a slice of cake if he'll get serious and tidy up her yard. Mickey makes an effort, but once the whirlwind shows up, he hasn't a chance. Mickey's screen persona entered a new phase in this film, marked by the emphasis on his "clowning." We've observed the studio's concerted efforts to reframe Mickey as a serious, earnest citizen during the mid- to late 1930s. But Mickey did have a history of clowning in his early films, and by 1940 Walt wanted staffers to return to that lighter side.[3] With this change came a new visual design, giving both Mickey and Minnie three-dimensional ears and a loose, reckless style of motion pioneered by Ward Kimball.

Original posters for four of Mickey's 1941 theatrical cartoons. With one exception, all these films allotted more screen time to Pluto than to Mickey. Note the poster for *Lend a Paw*, which seems to depict Figaro, the kitten from *Pinocchio*.

A GENTLEMAN'S GENTLEMAN
(March 28, 1941)

On a lazy Sunday morning, Mickey gives Pluto a dime and sends him out to buy the morning paper. Pluto has a difficult time of it: first he drops Mickey's dime and goes through strenuous exertions to retrieve it; then, after he does manage to buy the paper, the wind blows it away and he must pursue the scattered sections. (Along the way, in a quiet interlude, he pauses on the sidewalk to enjoy his favorite feature of the paper: a Pluto comic strip!) Mickey's role here reinforces his new image as a comfortable suburban homeowner.

CANINE CADDY
(May 30, 1941)

Mickey tackles the game of golf, which had already served as a useful device for numerous live-action comedians and, in 1938, for Donald Duck. The film's title refers to Pluto, Mickey's caddy, who has an unusually helpful talent: having retained his lesson from *The Pointer*, he can locate the ball after a long drive and "point" to it! Presently the ball lands in a gopher hole and the film detours into another Pluto-vs.-strange-animal cartoon, the gopher leading Pluto on a chase that ravages the perfectly groomed turf of the golf course.

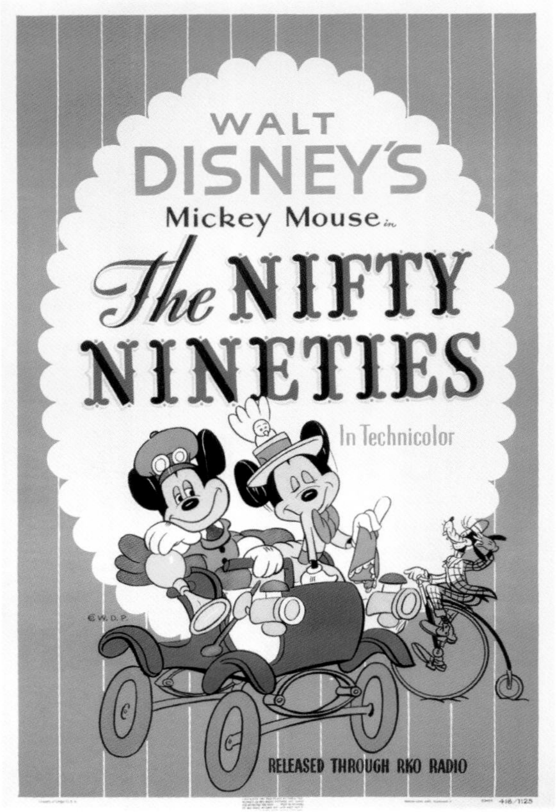

The period atmosphere of *The Nifty Nineties* was charmingly preserved in the film's poster art. The film featured animation not only by Kimball and Moore, but also by other luminaries including Walt Kelly and Les Clark.

Although Mickey is still the nominal star of the *Orphans' Benefit* remake, Donald Duck's tantrum is featured in the poster art.

THE NIFTY NINETIES
(June 20, 1941)

Mickey and Minnie are transported back to the 1890s in this offbeat short. The couple appear in period costumes, indulge in a playful flirtation in the park, enjoy a show at a vaudeville house, and take a spin in a horseless carriage. The vaudeville show includes an act called "Fred and Ward, two clever boys from Illinois"—caricatures of Fred Moore and Ward Kimball, animated *by* Kimball, performing a soft-shoe and patter routine. One gag ended up on the cutting room floor: a "Father, Dear Father" sing-along, performed in the finished film by an offscreen chorus, was originally to have been accompanied by an overemotional live singer, flooding the stage with her tears.

ORPHANS' BENEFIT
(August 22, 1941)

A planned series of remakes (see the next chapter) started with this overhaul of *Orphans' Benefit*, a "remake" so literal that it reused, and was animated to, the original 1934 soundtrack. Pencil animation from the original was simply retraced, changing the characters' appearances to fit current models, and reinked and painted in color. Riley Thomson, lately a Mickey animator, became a director via this short and *The Standard Parade*—in effect, two retracing jobs. (His subsequent directorial efforts included *The Little Whirlwind* and *The Nifty Nineties*, both of which were released *before* this picture.) Similar scene-for-scene retreads of other black-and-white shorts were planned, but someone evidently had second thoughts about the experiment, and after *Orphans' Benefit* it was not repeated.

WALT DISNEY'S
Mickey Mouse & Donald Duck
in
ORPHAN'S BENEFIT
In Technicolor
RELEASED THROUGH R.K.O. RADIO PICTURES, INC.

Walt Disney's
Mickey Mouse
in
MICKEY'S
BIRTHDAY
PARTY
TO MICKEY FROM THE GANG
© W.D.P.
In Technicolor
DISTRIBUTED BY RKO RADIO PICTURES

42/1271

LEND A PAW
(October 3, 1941)

Lend a Paw inaugurates a more conventional brand of remakes: starting with the story of *Mickey's Pal Pluto* (1933), the studio produced a new version from scratch. This time the writers revised the story in some respects, but the basic plot remained the same: Pluto helps rescue a kitten (only one this time); his jealousy gets him thrown out of the house; but when he rescues the kitten *again* he is reconciled with Mickey. If this short is less entertaining than *Mickey's Pal Pluto*, it does boast a greater concentration of personality animation and other refinements of technique, and it did win the year's Academy Award.

MICKEY'S BIRTHDAY PARTY
(February 7, 1942)

Another remake: as in *The Birthday Party* (1931), Minnie assembles a crowd of friends and throws a surprise party for Mickey. Alert viewers will note a scene of Minnie primping at the mirror, taken directly from *Mickey's Surprise Party*. Mickey's wild, loony dance scenes have long been a mystery to animation enthusiasts; surviving drafts indicated that they were composed of reused animation, but offered no details. Further investigation suggests that Ward Kimball animated Mickey's dance performance in the summer of 1940 — possibly for a planned sequence in *The Reluctant Dragon* — but that it went unused at the time, and eventually made its belated appearance in *Mickey's Birthday Party*.

SYMPHONY HOUR
(March 20, 1942)

"Mischa" Mouse's orchestra auditions for a prestigious radio program (sponsored by Pete as impresario Sylvester Macaroni) with a legitimate performance of Suppé's *Light Cavalry Overture*. On their way to the broadcast, Goofy accidentally drops all their instruments down an elevator shaft, where they are promptly smashed flat by the elevator. The musicians attempt their parts anyway on the flattened remains of their instruments, and the result is a hilarious mockery of the overture. This short preserves the musical legacy of the "Donald Duck Webfoot Sextet," a novelty ensemble that had performed on the *Mickey Mouse Theatre of the Air*.

PLUTO AND THE ARMADILLO
(February 19, 1943)

Air travelers Mickey and Pluto disembark for a short rest stop in Belém, Brazil, and Pluto, wandering into the jungle, encounters an armadillo. Essentially, this is another Pluto-meets-strange-creature short, now informed by authentic details of Brazilian geography and language. (One sight gag from Pluto's pursuit of the gopher in *Canine Caddy* is reused practically verbatim in this picture!) Mickey's scenes suggest that his tentative makeover of the early 1940s has been abandoned; in appearance and movement he seems to revert to his prewar model. In addition to this short, Mickey also appeared in prologues to some of the instructional films that the studio produced for nontheatrical distribution in Mexico and South America.[4]

The splendor of *Mickey's Birthday Party* is perfectly captured with this colorful one sheet poster. If only Mickey was to see such a perfect cake in the finished film.

By the time *Symphony Hour* was released in March 1942, the United States had joined the war effort in earnest. Belligerent Donald Duck became the wartime face of the Disney studio, appearing in public-service and propaganda shorts as well as in a series of service comedies, beginning with *Donald Gets Drafted*. Mickey, meanwhile, practically disappeared from the screen for the duration. One *very* slight exception was a public-service short, *Out of the Frying Pan into the Firing Line*, produced to encourage citizens to save and donate their used kitchen fats to help produce munitions for the war effort. This three-minute short actually featured Minnie Mouse and Pluto, but included a brief glimpse of a framed portrait, showing Mickey in uniform. For one full second, theatrical audiences saw Mickey on the screen as a G.I.

Mickey's other onscreen contributions to the cause were indirect. He appeared in recycled animation in *All Together* (1942), a public-service short encouraging Canadian audiences to buy war bonds. He also took a small part in the studio's Good Neighbor project, a government-sponsored initiative to stimulate friendly relations among North, Central, and South America.[5] In the Latin American films, once again, the Disney studio was most prominently represented by Donald Duck—but Mickey appeared in exactly one Good Neighbor short.

Pluto and the Armadillo, like Disney's other Good Neighbor shorts, was absorbed into the studio's regular program of theatrical releases.

The *Symphony Hour* poster inevitably invites comparisons with *Fantasia*.

WALT DISNEY'S
Mickey Mouse
in
Symphony hour
IN
TECHNICOLOR
RELEASED THROUGH RKO RADIO PICTURES
42/1335

In Frenchy de Trémaudan's repurposed animation from *The Band Concert*, Mickey and his band promote the sale of Canadian war bonds in *All Together* (1942).

THE VICTORY MARCH: PATRIOTIC DUTIES

Apart from film production, the Disney studio contributed to the war effort with military insignia, morale-boosting posters and ads, and other activities. Here too, thanks to Mickey's peaceful nature, his contributions were modest and indirect. The Disney artists created well over one thousand insignia designs during the war years for various branches of the armed forces. Once again the chronically hot-tempered Donald Duck led the pack, featured in more than 200 insignia designs; Mickey's appearances amounted to a fraction of that number. The Mouse was also featured on public-service posters promoting alertness and preparedness; and in a storybook, *The Victory March*, which encouraged children to buy and collect war savings stamps.[6]

COMICS CONTINUED

This 1944 publicity drawing saluting the armed forces is attributed to Hank Porter.

Following Sunday comic strip for October 13, 1946; story by Bill Walsh, art by Manuel Gonzales. Long after World War II's active hostilities ended, severe food rationing continued; here, just getting a chicken dinner becomes quite a production.

Mickey also took a leading role in another kind of march. While the Mouse may have become too much the nice guy to take part in battle onscreen—or to represent aggression on insignia—there was still a venue in which Mickey was primarily known for being a heroic, two-fisted fighter. This venue was, of course, the comics; in the pages of comic strips and books, scrapper Mickey overwhelmingly led the Disney fight against the Axis, just as scrapper Donald led that fight in films.

World War II would not directly involve the United States until late 1941, but an anti-Axis American public already looked forward to the battle against fascism. A wave of popular support for "G-men"—U.S. government special agents—had evolved from Depression-era fights against crime; by the early 1940s, the fight against foreign tyrants appealed to many average citizens the same way. In line with this, the prominence of dictatorial bad guys and overseas intrigue in Floyd Gottfredson's late-1930s *Mickey* daily strip serials directly mirrored the rise of the Axis. One might say that Gottfredson didn't wait for war to begin doing his bit. Now, with blitzkriegs actively rocking the European theater, two more important comics talents helped Gottfredson adapt Mickey to the new mood.

OF MICE AND G-MEN

War jitters echoed through Mickey's comic strip hometown as early as March 3, 1940, when up-and-coming Sunday strip artist Manuel Gonzales drew the first of many strips related to the war. In it, a cloaked Goofy rushes

MICKEY MOUSE
by
WALT DISNEY
Registered U. S. Patent Office
SCHOOL OF DRAMATICS
10-13

CLAP
CLAP
WALT DISNEY
Distributed by King Features Syndicate

In 1942 the studio produced *The New Spirit*, in which Donald Duck encouraged Americans to support the war effort with their income taxes. In this Hank Porter cover drawing for *Liberty* magazine, Mickey, Pluto, and Dumbo join in.

into Mickey's home, desperately afraid that "secret agents may be follerin' me" for the amazing invention he has just created. Testing the gadget, Mickey thinks its enormous mounted hammer must make it a giant-size nutcracker—but it proves to be an "atom-smasher"; both comical and foreboding as a hint of the era's encroaching arms race.

Soon other Gonzales-drawn Sunday strips thrust Mickey and Goofy into topical themes. In a string of episodes from January and February 1941, Goofy continues his top-secret inventing, now in the belief that he *himself* is a secret "G-man." On March 16, Goofy and Mickey experiment with genetically engineered vegetables—and create scientific miracles by accident. On the one hand, the humor shows a healthy faith in science as a bulwark against war-borne shortages; on the other, there is the unsettling awareness that the surprises of wartime technology might not all be positive.

This awareness presaged the grim shock of Pearl Harbor. By April 5, 1942, Mickey and Goofy were building bomb shelters; other Sundays saw Mickey helping Morty and Ferdie buy war bonds. "If we don't win this *war*," Morty sighs, "there won't *be* any more candy and ice cream!" In the popular imagination, the Nazis stood poised to defeat our very lifestyle. The essence of Mickey's adventurous, defiant comics persona required he fight back.

ENTER BILL WALSH

"The Black Crow Mystery" was almost the last *Mickey Mouse* adventure serial. Due to wartime paper shortages, newspaper comics began being printed at smaller sizes—and the more complex, continuity-heavy strips suffered. It was thus that the serialized *Mickey* began losing ground to its gag-a-day Disney stablemate strip *Donald Duck*.[7] Readers complained about adventure stories becoming smaller and harder to read. King Features began to rethink the *Mickey* daily. First it was converted into a *Donald Duck*-like gag-a-day — more or less; short, jokey serials still turned up.

Then along came a new ingredient. Bill Walsh, press agent for the Margaret Ettinger agency, had been writing gags for ventriloquist Edgar Bergen and the George Burns / Gracie Allen comedy team. When Disney personnel director Hal Adelquist suggested Gottfredson hire Walsh, Gottfredson jumped at the chance.[8] Walsh's sense of humor — dark, random, and wild — struck Gottfredson as an ingredient that, if added to traditional Mickey adventure stories, could win back some of their popularity.

No comics adventure took Mickey further into wartime thrills than "Mickey Mouse on a Secret Mission," which included a parodic tour of Germany and even scenes of Peg Leg Pete, now a Nazi spy, reconsidering his decision to help the enemy.

'LECTRO BOXES, ATOMS, AND VICTORY GARDENS

The world conflict weighed on many tales at the time. In Walsh's and Gottfredson's "Pluto the Spy Catcher" (1943), it's Pluto's turn to help nab a fleeing Japanese saboteur. In Walsh's and Gottfredson's "The 'Lectro Box" (1943), the wacky tale of a ray that transmutes living matter, relatively little war-related action takes place — but an enlarged germ eats Mickey's

AND HOW WILL THEY GET IT, IF THE FARMERS CAN'T GET ENOUGH HELP? YOU WON'T WIN ANY MEDALS, BUT YOU'LL BE DOING YOUR PART...
...JUST AS MUCH AS A MAN WHO RIVETS A.... A RIVET!
BY GOSH, MINNIE... MAYBE YOU'VE GOT SOMETHING!
WHY, OF COURSE... WE SHOULD'VE THOUGHT OF THAT, GOOFY! THE FARM IS JUST AS IMPORTANT AS THE MUNITIONS PLANT!
UH... COME TO THINK OF IT ...GUESS IT'S SO!
SURE, IT'S SO! AN ARMY CAN'T FIGHT, IF THEY DON'T EAT! C'MON... LET'S GET GOIN'!
AND SO, AFTER A VISIT TO THE GOVERNMENT EMPLOYMENT SERVICE OFFICE...
...BUT YOU'LL BE SO FAR AWAY!
WE HAFTA GO WHERE WE'RE NEEDED, MINNIE!
REMEMBER THAT, AT LEAST, WE'LL BE SAFE!
EAST-BOUND TRAINS
THE GOVERNMENT EMPLOYMENT SERVICE SENDS MICKEY AND GOOFY TO A SECTION OF THE MIDWEST WHERE FARM HELP IS BADLY NEEDED!
ELEV. 4232
GAWRSH! WHUT WIDE, OPEN SPACES!
RECKON YOU'RE TH' NEW HANDS SENT TO WORK ON TH' BLIMP PLACE, EH?
YEH!
GOLLY... DID Y' EVER SEE SO MUCH WHEAT IN ALL YOUR LIFE?
NEVER DID! AN' WHERE THERE AIN'T WHEAT, THERE'S CORN!
NOT AS MUCH CORN AS YE HEAR IN TH' CITY! HAW-HAW-HAW!

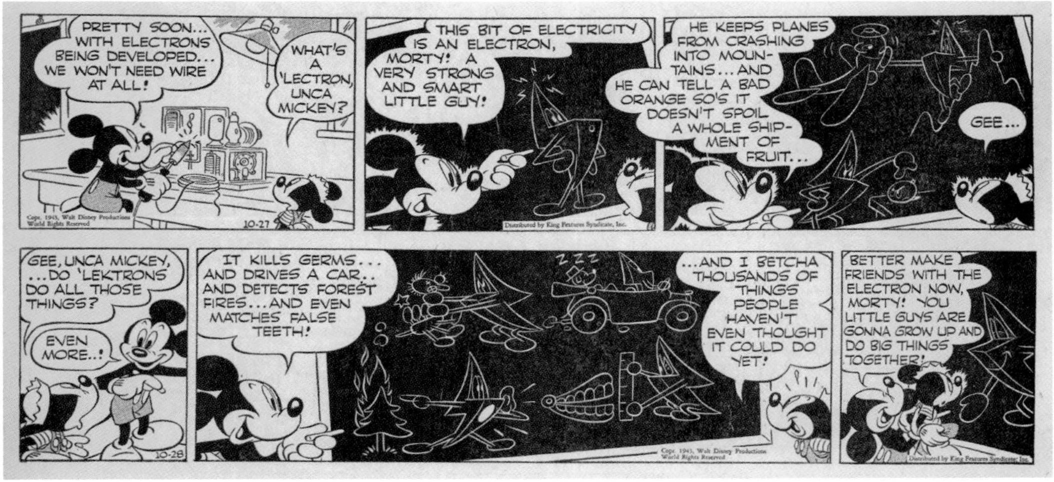

rationed steaks during a meat shortage, and the ray cannon is ultimately given over to Uncle Sam as a potential weapon of war.

Two more Mickey war stories quietly opened up a whole new front. Western Publishing, having reprinted many Gottfredson adventures in the pages of comic books, decided to produce their first entirely original Mickey comics. The Dell one-shot *Four Color* 27 featured three stories written and drawn by former Disney animator Ken Hultgren, now at work with Sangor Studios, a comics production house in New York. Two of the stories, "The Villain of the Victory Garden" and "The Seven-Colored Terror," were war-related—a sign of the times.

TUFFOLINO

Given Mickey's staunch support—and that of his creators—for the Allied side of World War II, it's striking to imagine that Mickey also eked out a comics existence among the Axis during the war; yet in some ways he did, sans authorization and with no benefit to the Disney studio. Despite Mickey's apparent popularity with many Germans, the import of American products was eventually banned in Axis territory.

The opening scenes of "The Black Crow Mystery"—here as reprinted in *Walt Disney's Comics and Stories 57* (1945)—suggest that Floyd Gottfredson's team burned to show Mickey and Goofy fighting the Axis head-on. But the team evidently concluded that within Mickey's fairly logical comics world, such a fight might not be believable. As part and parcel of this, the saboteur Crow (not seen here) ultimately proves not to be an America-hating Nazi, but just a local sociopath who hates *farmers.*

In "The 'Lectro Box," a daily strip serial from 1943, Mickey puts his optimism to work promoting the power of the electron.

This also affected Italy, where fascist leader Mussolini famously enjoyed Disney products, but was eventually coerced into overseeing their suppression.[9]

From 1942, this meant the end of authorized Disney content in *Topolino*, the ongoing Italian weekly comic. Yet, oddly enough, it didn't mean the end for Floyd Gottfredson's work. For a while, contraband American Mickey stories continued, miscredited to Italian editor Federico Pedrocchi. Then, starting in *Topolino* 478 (1942), Mickey was reincarnated as "Tuffolino," a scrappy little *human* adventurer, and the Gottfredson serial "Mickey Mouse, Supersalesman" (1941) was redrawn with Tuffolino in the leading role. It's easy to imagine that Mussolini's subjects needed such a substitute, while momentarily deprived of their beloved, daring Mickey. When war ended, happily, all sides could have him back.

Aviators on both sides of the conflict appropriated Mickey's image, with or without permission, for their planes.

In "The Seven-Colored Terror," a strikingly playful Mickey—seemingly copied from *The Little Whirlwind*-era Floyd Gottfredson strips—battles with a giant mountain lion terrorizing a mountain resort, only to learn that the animal had been guarding this government scientist and his experimental synthetic rubber.

OH, BOY! HERE ARE THE PAINTS HE USES ON THE LION! AND THIS IS THE PHOSPHORESCENT STUFF FOR THE NIGHT SCARES!
PHOSPHOR PAINT
RED
YELL
BUT, WHY? AND WHAT'S THIS CHUNK OF RUBBER MEAN? SOMETHIN' FUNNY GOIN' ON HERE!
WELL? WHAT ARE YOU UP TO?
HUH....? WHY, UH... WHAT DID Y'SAY?
YOU HEARD ME! EXPLAIN THIS INTRUSION.
N-NOTHIN' AT ALL, SIR! JUST PASSING BY... ER.. ..LOST.. STOPPED FOR DIRECTIONS...
...THOUGHT MAYBE SOMEONE...

Necco
BAR
Necco
NECCO SKY BAR
General Outdoor Adv Co
THEY'RE ALL IN IT....
Walt Disney's
NEW MUSICAL
CARTOON FEATURE
CHARLIE McCARTHY
MORTIMER SNERD
DONALD DUCK
Fun and Fancy Free
COLOR BY TECHNICOLOR
featuring
BERGEN
SHORE
RELEASED THROUGH RKO RADIO PICTURES
BONGO
LULUBELLE
GOOFY
WILLIE THE GIANT
JIMINY CRICKET
PALACE
EYEBROWS SHAPED
HAIRLINES RAISED
Electrolysis
Verna Young
TEL.
ELECTROLYSIS
Walt Disney's
Fun and
Fancy Free
COLOR BY TECHNICOLOR
DANCE PALACE
ORPHEUM
BALL ROOM
ENTRANCE
Walt Disney's
Fun and Fancy Free
BERGEN · SHORE
color by TECHNICOLOR

CHAPTER SEVEN

Mickey in the World of Features

From the beginning, the one-reel cartoon short was Mickey Mouse's natural habitat—but *almost* from the beginning, he also turned up occasionally in feature-length pictures. We've already noted his guest appearance, as early as 1931, in Douglas Fairbanks's *Around the World in Eighty Minutes*, and his later cameos in Fox and MGM features. These outside appearances were enormously entertaining, but today they are essentially curios—diverting footnotes to film history, but hardly in the same category with a starring role in a feature-length film.

One way to simulate the effect of a starring feature was to string a number of Disney shorts together in a feature-length *program*. The Carnegie Hall show of Disney shorts in December 1933 was only a beginning, and inspired the United Artists forces to suggest a Disney "revue" package of their own. Walt and Roy were enthusiastic about the idea, and proposed a "synthetic feature" in which Mickey, as a master of ceremonies, would present a show to an animated audience—the show consisting of a half dozen existing Disney shorts, their original main and end titles removed.

This project went unrealized in 1934, but all-Disney cartoon programs, *without* elaborate framing stories, continued to appear with increasing frequency at movie theaters in America and abroad. Walt later reported that his excitement at seeing such a program, at a theater in Paris in 1935, helped to reinforce his determination to proceed with production of the

The facade of New York's Globe Theatre was decorated with a spectacular display for the opening of *Fun and Fancy Free* in September 1947.

feature-length *Snow White and the Seven Dwarfs*.[1]

In the meantime, the "revue" idea lingered on at the Disney studio and resurfaced in a variety of forms: the *Academy Award Review of Walt Disney Cartoons* in 1937; a highly publicized press preview at Los Angeles' Filmarte Theatre in 1938. Some of these packages leaned heavily on the Silly Symphonies and afforded little or no visibility for Mickey himself. In 1939, however, the studio started tentative development of an all-Mickey revue, showcasing a selection of his pictures from his beginnings in 1928. For a time the proposed feature was known as *Mickey's Revival Party* and was planned for promotional showings on the occasion of Mickey's twelfth birthday in 1940. Attempting to surpass the revues that had preceded it, *Revival Party* was to have revived the framing-story concept, with extensive business of Mickey, Minnie, Donald, and company celebrating Mickey's big day at a Disney studio auditorium. The gang was to have poked fun at Mickey's past pictures as they screened them. Seeing a kiss scene in *Wild Waves*, present-day Mickey was to have goaded Minnie—"I don't get those kisses anymore"—until she planted a fresh one right on his lips.

In the end, *Mickey's Revival Party* too was abandoned. But we can be thankful it was undertaken, if only because it prompted Walt to screen an assortment of early Mickeys, some of which he had never watched since their original production. His comments, recorded and preserved for posterity, are priceless. In general, looking at animation produced a decade earlier, Walt is ruthlessly critical—*overly* critical, from today's perspective. Watching *Wild Waves*, he tells Riley Thomson: "Believe it or not, Riley, they used to laugh at it." But elsewhere, his keen eye for individual animators' strengths is in evidence. When a team member misidentifies the animator of a scene in *The Cactus Kid*, Walt quickly intervenes:

The pirate story *Morgan's Ghost* was first proposed in 1939 by writers Dick Creedon and Al Perkins. A pirate parrot, Old Yellow Beak (so christened by Walt himself), was to have led Mickey, Donald, and Goofy to a treasure island, unaware that the old lady owner of their ship was actually Peg Leg Pete in disguise. *Morgan's Ghost* was not produced as a film, but the story has special significance for Disney fans because it was adapted into a 1942 comic book story, "Donald Duck Finds Pirate Gold," written by Bob Karp and drawn by Jack Hannah and Carl Barks—in the process, doing much to launch Barks's legendary comics career.[1] Yellow Beak himself became an ongoing comics character, occasionally reappearing even in modern times.

"No, this is Fergy's [Norm Ferguson's]. You will notice the difference. Fergy had a smoothness to his [animation] as far back as this." Watching Mickey and Minnie dance together in *Mickey Cuts Up*, Walt comments: "Mickey and Minnie used to be trace-overs. Put on a skirt and Minnie's shoes [on Mickey], and it would be one action."[2]

As the screening continues, Walt begins to evince a grudging affection for some of his earlier films. Watching the cabin slide downhill in *The Klondike Kid*, he admits: "I think this was a funny thing." When the rivet gun attaches to Pete's leg in *Building a Building*, Walt volunteers: "That got a hell of a good laugh." By the time of *The Band Concert* and the subsequent Technicolor pictures, he has warmed to the quality of production: "Some of these things you see are not beyond reissue"—i.e., a fresh release in the short-subject market, independent of a revue setting. (Ultimately the studio did begin to reissue some of its Technicolor cartoon shorts, but

As *Morgan's Ghost* continues, Mickey, Donald, and Goofy battle a host of dangers, including the pirates, quicksand, and carnivorous plants. Ultimately, they succeed in locating the treasure and collaring the pirates. In this dramatic story sketch of the ending sequence, our heroes prepare to set sail for home. The 1942 comic book story "Donald Duck Finds Pirate Gold" (*Four Color* 9) recast this unproduced story with Donald Duck and his three nephews, and altered many of the details, but retained the basic plot—as well as the character of Yellow Beak.

not until 1947.) The earlier black-and-white shorts he finds unacceptable for new showings in *any* setting, unless the animation drawings are reinked and painted, possibly in color: "Get the drawings out... by the time the inking crew gets through with *Pinocchio*. That would give them a lot of stuff, keep them busy."[3] This was the beginning of the "overhaul" notion that led to the *Orphans' Benefit* remake in 1941. In the meantime, however, the idea of an all-Mickey revue program was abandoned once again.

And by this time a far more prestigious feature-length vehicle for Mickey was already in the works. We've already seen that "The Sorcerer's Apprentice" had initially been conceived as a short, but, by the time of its completion, was already planned as part of a larger "Concert Feature." Pencil animation of "The Sorcerer's Apprentice" was finished by the autumn of 1938, and at that point, production was suspended while the studio went ahead with the other segments of *Fantasia*. Multiplane elements were stored in the Ink & Paint Department "until it is decided to finish the picture."[4] Marvin Woodward, animating the penultimate scene of Mickey whacked with the broom by the sorcerer, was told:

An alternate "Mickey feature" idea was *The Emperor's New Clothes*, with Mickey, Donald, and Goofy as tailors ordered to create the eponymous garments. In the sketch, the boys' royal client marches through the town in his long johns, convinced he's wearing an invisible cloak on top. He is led by two guards and followed by an overconfident Goofy — and an increasingly nervous Mickey and Donald.

A 1941 sheet of costume suggestions for *Mickey and the Beanstalk*. Walt favored the use of special costumes for stories like this. At one story meeting for this picture, one of the writers argued against using uncharacteristic costumes. Walt stoutly defended the idea because, as he commented, "We are setting a period." He cited Mickey's appearance in *Brave Little Tailor*: "He looked very cute in that outfit he had."[2]

"The exact manner of ending our scene will depend on the decision as to how the various pictures in the Concert Feature are to be connected. For the time being, animate the scene on a still setup, six and a half field, taking Mickey out of the field after the spank."[5]

Previous A lovely background painting of Happy Valley before the harp is stolen. In the film *Mickey and the Beanstalk,* this vista is introduced gradually, starting with the green valley and adding the brook, the fields and farmhouses, and the castle one by one, as Edgar Bergen describes them on the soundtrack. The painting seen here, nearly identical, appears later in the sequence, just before the mysterious shadow approaches the castle and steals the harp.

Concept art for the harp's balcony in the opening sequence.

In the spring and summer of 1940, as *Fantasia* was taking its final shape, the "Sorcerer's Apprentice" animation drawings were taken out (now in the new Burbank studio) and inked, painted, and photographed along with the other sections of the feature. As the color scenes began to reach the screen, Walt and the directors called for changes, fine-tuning visual details. Effects animator Cornett Wood was asked to reanimate the shadows in one scene; in another, when water began to overflow the sides of Mickey's vat, the painters were asked to repaint the water cels with transparent paint. These and myriad other details in place, *Fantasia* was finally completed and readied for its New York premiere. Although the opening had been threatened by a labor dispute at the Broadway Theatre, it took place on schedule on November 13, 1940, and Mickey's most distinguished appearance to date was unveiled to the public. Of course "The Sorcerer's Apprentice" was only one of seven segments in *Fantasia*, but Mickey was the most recognizable—the *only* recognizable—animated character in the film, and a natural focus for advertising and reviews.

Today we know that *Fantasia* was released to a wildly mixed critical reaction. Responses ranged from ecstatic praise from the film critics to howls of outrage from the more conservative members of the musical world, offended at the liberties Walt had taken with sacrosanct compositions. *The New York Times* encapsulated the controversy by printing a film review and a musical review side by side on the same page. For Bosley Crowther, the *Times* film reviewer, "motion-picture history was made at the Broadway Theatre last night... *Fantasia* is simply terrific—as terrific as anything that has ever happened on a screen."[6] Olin Downes, the music critic, avowed his general admiration for Disney and acknowledged the technological advances of *Fantasia*, but called the film itself "a most forbidding example of what *not* to do with this magnificent apparatus."[7]

But even among the critics who disapproved of *Fantasia* at large, "The Sorcerer's Apprentice" evoked a measure of respect. Purists who felt that Walt had overreached himself with some of the other compositions tended to regard "The Sorcerer's Apprentice" as a more congenial match of music and animation. Critic Arthur Rosenheimer Jr. (later known as Arthur Knight) offered one flattering objection: "The extraordinary dream sequence in 'The Sorcerer's Apprentice,' with Mickey Mouse as a super-Stokowski directing the universe, is not artistically successful precisely because the delicate balance between sight and sound has been violently upset here by the overshadowing brilliance of Disney's imagination."[8] By and large, however, "The Sorcerer's Apprentice" found widespread favor as one of

Disney concept artists considered a variety of designs for the character of the singing harp. Walt was open to various concepts for the character; at some meetings he suggested a mysterious disembodied voice that warned Mickey, Donald, and Goofy to turn back—a voice that ultimately turned out to be the harp. The concept seen here was later modified, integrating the girl's body into the structure of the harp.

the more accessible sections of the feature, and served to symbolize the entire selection. When a later generation of Disney artists produced *Fantasia/2000*, "The Sorcerer's Apprentice" was the one segment of the original film to be resurrected for inclusion.

The prewar version of *Mickey and the Beanstalk* pictured the poor farmers saying grace before their meager meal, then looking up to find that Bessie the cow had eaten the last of their food while no one was looking.

Goofy sets off to market to sell the cow in a story sketch for the earliest version of *Mickey and the Beanstalk*. Some variations included not only this scene, but also scenes at the market, in which some shifty character cheated the simple-minded Goof, taking the cow and giving him "magic" beans in exchange. Yet another variation showed Mickey, not Goofy, *successfully* selling the cow to the Three Little Pigs, only to have his pay of "ten pazoozas" promptly confiscated by tax collector Pete.

By the time *Fantasia* was released to the public, Mickey was making a still more concentrated incursion into the world of features. Adapting the story of "Jack and the Beanstalk" to Mickey Mouse was not a new idea. In fact, the studio had already used the idea once: the Mickey short *Giantland* (1933) had been a loose adaptation of the tale. In the summer of 1938 Walt returned to Jack's story, picturing it as a special two-reel short with Mickey, Donald, and Goofy jointly substituting for Jack. At this time *Snow White and the Seven Dwarfs* was enjoying its spectacular worldwide success, and an apparently unlimited flood of box office returns was pouring into the studio. *Brave Little Tailor*, a one-reel Mickey short with the sumptuous production value of a feature, was being readied for release, and in the meantime the studio had embarked on the even more ambitious "Sorcerer's Apprentice." In this time of plenty, "Jack and the Beanstalk" was pictured as another exercise in extravagant production. "I think this story has great possibilities for the fantastic things," Walt said in one meeting. "I would like to see it done in a way that would really put feature quality into it."[9]

He also had specific ideas about how to achieve that quality. One was a concentration on music: "I would like to see the music worked into it—not just the score—but treat it as a semi–musical comedy and weave the music through the entire picture, as in a feature, and not bring in a song independently."[10] Key sequences were spotted as opportunities for musical numbers: Mickey, Donald, and Goofy, discovered in the castle by the giant, pretended to be toys and performed a little dance number to soothe the giant and lull him to sleep. The giant's personality came in for discussion; should he be a dimwitted giant like the one in *Brave Little Tailor* or a different type? Some of the ideas hatched at these 1938 meetings would become memorable sequences in the finished film: our heroes sleeping peacefully through the night as the beanstalk

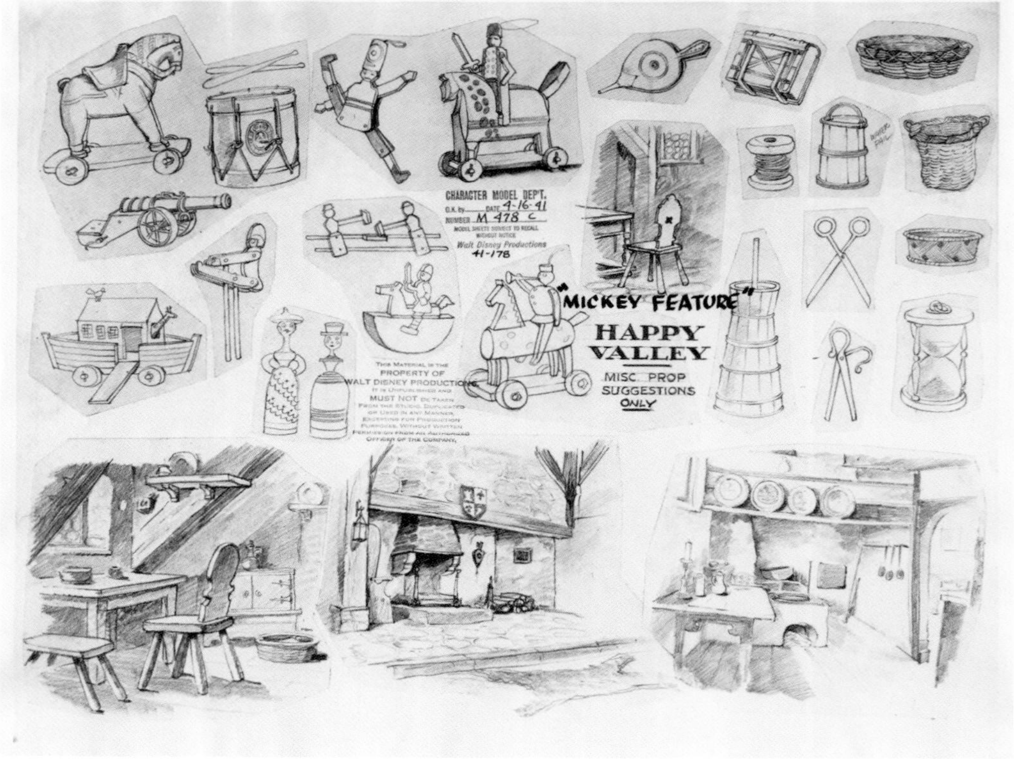

Early plans for the feature called for settings and props that were abandoned as story development continued. Note the many carved wooden toys suggested here, perhaps influenced by the studio's recent production of *Pinocchio*, with its delightful scenes in Geppetto's workshop.

grows, unaware that they're in constant danger of falling; or Mickey's suspense sequence as he tries to retrieve the key from the slumbering giant's pocket.

Other ideas were discussed at length during these meetings, then dropped. In 1938 Walt and the writers pictured Goofy as the character who would sell the cow and who would be tricked into taking a handful of beans for her. Later this role would be reassigned to Mickey. The traditional story included not only a singing harp but a hen who laid golden eggs, and at some stages of Disney story development, Clara Cluck was cast as the hen. In the finished film the hen would be cut altogether.

But as other projects proliferated at the Disney studio, this one was sidelined. "'Jack and the Bean Stalk' has been temporarily laid aside," reported *The New York Times* in the spring of 1939, "and will be resumed as soon as *Pinocchio* is out of the way."[11]

By late 1939, even before *Pinocchio* was "out of the way," Walt was giving serious thought to a prestigious starring vehicle for Mickey—not a two-reeler this time, but a full-length feature. He began to assign staff writers to develop potential feature stories for the Mouse. The already-started "Jack and the Beanstalk" was an obvious candidate for this treatment, and Walt assigned it to none other than Frank Tashlin, who had already made a name for himself at the Warner Bros. cartoon studio and would go on to carve out a distinguished career of his own in both animation and live-action films. Historian Howard Prouty has documented Tashlin's short tenure at the Disney studio (he departed in March 1941, shortly before the strike): Tashlin worked on a number of shorts but devoted most of his time to the film that would become "Mickey and the Beanstalk." In December 1939 he wrote to a friend: "Walt has given me a feature to do—with Mickey, Donald, and Goofy in it—a radical departure in their features—I'm writing the screen adaption [sic] now—am working for Walt directly with no inbetween bosses—it's a swell set-up."[12]

Another abandoned concept: Mickey petitions Queen Minnie for help. Several attempts were made to work Minnie, Pluto, and other familiar characters from the shorts into the story, but in the end this idea was discarded. As late as June 1940, when a writer asked about Minnie, Walt replied: "I don't think you will miss her."[3]

In the meantime, other events were happening that would impact the production of this and other Disney films. *Pinocchio*, the studio's most lavish film to date, was completed and opened in February 1940 to overwhelming praise from the critics—but a lackluster reception at the box office. As it moved into general release, the disappointing returns continued. Ultimately, *Pinocchio* would fail to recover its production cost during its initial release. This chilling realization cast a shadow on *Fantasia*, which was not yet finished but was being produced along the same extravagant lines as *Pinocchio*. By this time Walt and his artists had also moved into their expensive new studio in Burbank. Moreover, the war in Europe had closed off some of the lucrative overseas markets that had contributed so much to *Snow White*'s success. The new era of prosperity, which had seemed so secure only a few months earlier, was suddenly in jeopardy. Clearly, the Disney studio must act quickly to shore up its financial condition.

Walt met this emergency with a characteristically bold decision. The studio must ramp up its production schedule, *expanding* its slate of feature-length films, but including some that could be produced quickly and economically—as

A story sketch for the final version of the sequence: Mickey is chosen to take the cow to market. Perhaps to avoid depicting Mickey as overly gullible, the errand itself is not shown. We simply see Mickey, here, on his return, triumphantly displaying the magic beans.

IMAGED BY HERITAGE AUCTIONS, HA.COM

quickly and economically as the high standard of Disney quality would allow—and released to theaters without delay.

The writers rose to the challenge with a variety of "economy" feature stories, but one category was obvious: a Mickey Mouse feature. In the spring of 1940 this notion emerged in a very different light from that of 1938; now Walt embraced the idea of a Mickey feature precisely *because* such a picture could be produced so economically. The box office risk would be nil; Mickey had a worldwide following of fans who would be eager to see him in a feature-length showcase. Too, no need for a time-consuming process of character development; the shorts animators had been working with Mickey and his supporting cast for years and were already well prepared for such a project. Not only that, but several potential stories for the project were already in development. Mickey Mouse, who had given Walt his first major success a scant decade earlier, would now help him rescue his studio from financial peril.

From the beginning, Walt pictured a fantastic giant world at the top of the beanstalk: "Don't just get a castle; try for something that will fascinate the audience."[4] Background artist Art Riley obliged with this concept painting. The castle in the film has muted colors but otherwise adheres to the design seen here.

In one meeting after another, Walt hammered home the importance of getting a Mickey feature into production as quickly as possible. "The main idea is that we are trying to get a feature out of here in a hell of a hurry. . . . Our European market is shot, which you're all aware of, and we have to get something out of here that can go out and make some money on just the American market alone. There has to be something gotten out of here and we're going to do it or bust."[13] "If we can get this Mickey feature out, it is going to be a big help to the studio at this time when the war and panic are playing hell. We don't know how long it is going to continue, and the answer is a production we can get out and get on the market. If we make a Mickey feature, it will be a hell of a big help to the studio. *Pinocchio* is doing a good business, but we can't get our money out of England and France. Let's give them Mickey, the Duck and the Goof. That is what they would want to see. I want to get it in as fast as we can."[14]

The story department responded with a range of story outlines, some of which are fascinating in hindsight. Walt himself suggested that a traditional children's story like "Hansel and Gretel" might be adapted as a vehicle for Mickey.[15] Among all these ideas, however, "Jack and the Beanstalk" led the pack. Frank Tashlin's February 1940 treatment, building on the initial story work in 1938, set off a series of intensive conferences in which the story was analyzed and retooled

The T. Hee–Bill Cottrell "Sooner or Later" outline proposed some wackily whimsical additions to the story. Here, in still-prosperous Happy Valley, Goofy's inspection of eggs leads into an offbeat musical number about "The Chicken and the Egg."

For the growing beanstalk, T. Hee and Bill Cottrell proposed another musical sequence, a satiric number (the writers suggested "a parody of 'Begin the Beguine'") in which a variety of beans were personified as showgirls of different nationalities, and illustrated an international theme.

As finally developed for *Fun and Fancy Free*, and as seen in this publicity art, Willie the Giant was huge and powerful but had the mind and temperament of a child.

for immediate production. Walt was deeply involved in these conferences. At one meeting he elaborated on the idea of a modern-day framing story, describing an opening sequence in which Mickey and his pals appeared onscreen with a live-action movie executive, perhaps Walt himself. One of his comments is especially striking in hindsight: "We could use the opening business where Mickey, Don and the Goof are protesting—they're going on strike—they want to work in features... 'Disney Unfair to Short-Subject Actors.'"[16] Within a year, the studio would be assailed by real-life labor troubles that were no joking matter.

More T. Hee whimsy from "Sooner or Later": Mickey, in danger of being eaten, confounds the dim-witted giant with a frighteningly huge shadow.

As for the "Jack and the Beanstalk" story itself, Walt pressed for a very free adaptation that would play to the strengths of animation, rather than strict adherence to the traditional story. In several meetings he argued for eliminating the original ending. "Instead of going back down the vine, we could forget all that. They get rid of the giant and everything belongs to them and then they can eat and have a little banquet there on the table with these big props for the finish... They've taken over the castle—what more do they want?"[17] At another meeting he suggested a new trait for the giant, based on a plot element from another traditional tale: "This ogre in 'Puss in Boots'—he changes himself into different forms. They know that, so [in trying to escape from the giant] they have to use that as a last resort."[18] This idea would become a key sequence in the finished film. Walt distanced himself from the traditional story in other ways, too, even to changing the title: "I'd like to get away from this Jack and the Beanstalk title. It's just based on that story."[19] As an alternative, he and the writers considered "Island in the Sky"—a reference to the colossal world that the characters find at the top of the beanstalk (and, coincidentally, the title

In this 1941 model sheet, Willie has already assumed something of his final form, but other ideas will eventually be discarded. At this time, Walt and the writers considered at length the idea of the giant's pet cat, which would appear monstrously large to Mickey and his pals.

of a recent continuity in the Mickey Mouse comic strip)—but were blocked from using that title because Twentieth Century-Fox had already released a feature titled *Island in the Sky* (1938; dir. Herbert I. Leeds).[20]

One advantage of the Mickey-Donald-Goofy shorts from the beginning had been the opportunity to split up the three main characters to pursue individual story threads of their own. Scenes with fewer characters were simpler and faster to animate, and several different artists or groups of artists could work simultaneously with their respective characters, completing a film quickly and efficiently. This principle was on Walt's mind as he tackled production of "Jack and the Beanstalk"; indeed, he was counting on it. By the spring of 1940 he was assigning story teams to develop breakdown sequences for each of the main characters, detailing their adventures with the gigantic creatures and plants at the top of the beanstalk even before they approached the giant's castle. Donald Duck was pictured sneaking into a birds' nest, in an attempt to steal their food, and then being trapped there when the mother bird mistook him for one of her brood. Goofy had two possible story threads: he might encounter some giant butterflies, attach flowers to his arms as "wings," and join the butterflies in a ballet; or, alternatively, he might eat some berries that had the effect of turning him invisible. Pluto, still a member of the cast at this point, had another of his encounters with strange creatures: this time a colony of ants that were fully his own size.

Mickey's share in this adventure was his discovery of a herd of grasshoppers and his attempt to ride one of them. This idea was proposed at one meeting by Homer Brightman, and Walt immediately warmed to it: "Mickey finally gets up on him and he has a hell of a time... a grasshopper has a horse face anyway, hasn't it?"[21] As the sequence developed further, he and the writers worked to develop the comic parallels with horseback riding. At one conference specifically devoted to this sequence, Walt was at pains to keep the story grounded in Mickey's traditions; he insisted on Fred Moore's attendance at the meeting, and he linked gags and bits of business to scenes in the Mouse's earlier successes. "So he chases the grasshopper and finally catches the damn thing, then he snubs him like this... they are all built up to use that old gag."[22] The "old gag" in question

A reconstructed cel setup of the box's interior. This scene, with Mickey inside the box, never occurs in the film; but this setup does afford us a clearer view of the background painting than we get onscreen. Here we can see the treasures that Willie chooses to protect in his locked box: marbles, a top, and a pocketknife.

was from *The Cactus Kid* (and, before that, Oswald's *Sagebrush Sadie*): the protagonist lassos a runaway horse and winds the end of the rope repeatedly around a cactus, trying to stop the horse in his tracks, only to be whirled around and around the cactus himself when the horse easily pulls free.

As "Jack and the Beanstalk" was planned in 1940, these breakdown sequences would have fit easily into the film's projected running time, and they would have immensely facilitated production. "One thing we're trying to do," Walt reminded his artists, "is hold it down to one-character business, as much as possible."[23] So anxious was he to begin production that he called for animation to begin on these individual sequences even before the overall structure of the story had been finalized. "We're going to put these in work as sequences rather than build a connection. Later on we'll build the connections we need... I guarantee we'll hook them together some way."[24]

But as events unfolded at the Disney studio over succeeding months, "Jack and the Beanstalk"—sometimes, by now, titled "Slap-Happy Valley" after the characters' home village—was sidelined a second time. Walt's expanded production schedule resulted in a broad range of simultaneous projects, including the feature that would become *Dumbo*, and studio staff was spread increasingly thin. The Mickey feature did begin active production in the spring of 1941: the story crews delivered several sequences—the beanstalk's nocturnal growth, the adventurers crossing the castle moat, Mickey's efforts to steal the key from the giant—to sequence directors. The directors, in turn, assigned scenes to some key animators, including Ward Kimball, Fred Moore, and (only a few weeks before his sudden departure from the studio) Walt Kelly, but these assignments were repeatedly delayed by work on other productions. Story work and animation limped on through the spring and summer of 1941, but the manpower shortage was intensified by the onset of the studio strike. In August the cream of the story department, along with Walt and other artists, left the studio for two months in South America to pursue yet another initiative: the Good Neighbor project. Early in October Roy Disney noted privately: "The story crews [are]

A key suspense sequence in the finished film: Mickey's daring attempt to retrieve the key from Willie's pocket and rescue his friends from captivity. This was one of the earliest sequences in the film to start production; Mickey's action, climbing down the thread, was assigned to animator Ken Muse as early as April 1941.

temporarily working on the 'Mickey Feature' and 'Wind in the Willows' [then planned as another "economy" feature] pending the return of Walt from South America, at which time all or the greater part thereof will be set to work on the South American subjects."[25] Finally, in December, the attack on Pearl Harbor propelled the United States into full engagement in the war, and life at the Disney studio shifted radically overnight. As we've seen, work on practically *all* Mickey-related projects, as well as other uncompleted films, was indefinitely suspended for the duration.

"Jack and the Beanstalk" did surface in an odd way during the war years. In 1944 T. Hee and Bill Cottrell, a counterintuitive writing team if ever there was one, submitted an outline titled "Sooner or Later." Designed to salvage the already-completed animation for the Mickey feature, this treatment took Walt's original suggestion of a framing story

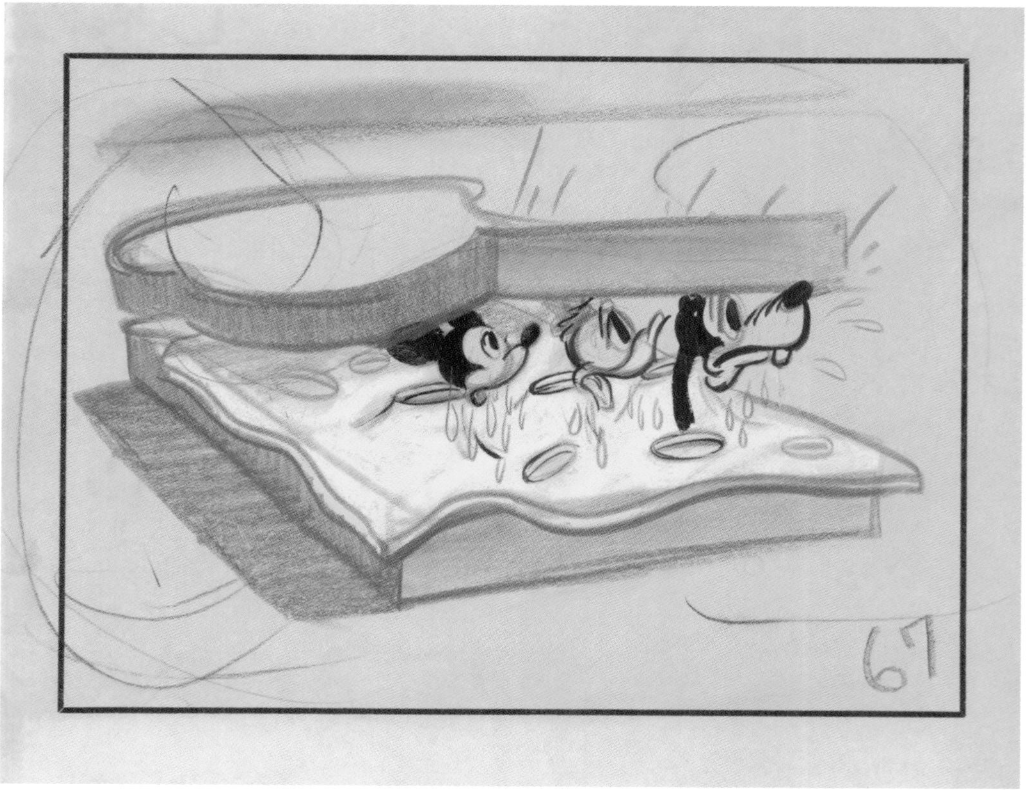

in an extreme direction: “It’s a Walt Disney satire on what Hollywood does to a famous story when they make it into a movie.”[26] Here, Hee and Cottrell suggested, Jiminy Cricket would address the audience directly, showing how a simple story like “Jack and the Beanstalk” might be transformed in Hollywood’s hands into an overblown extravaganza. The wildly satiric scenario ended with a sequence in a nightclub, “Willie’s Sky Room,” where “The Three ‘Jacks’ and Harriet, the Hot Harp” performed a gaudy musical number—accompanied by Benny Goodman in live action. Their song was a new number, “Sooner or Later” by Ray Gilbert and Charles Wolcott, hence the projected title of the film. “Earl Carroll turns green with envy, Walt Disney goes bankrupt, and we... FADE OUT.”

Needless to say, this film was not produced. The following December, however, story work on the Mickey feature was reopened, and in February 1945 production actively resumed. Ultimately, “Mickey and the Beanstalk” was produced in a form that had not been envisioned in 1941. Tentatively during the war, and wholeheartedly in peacetime, Walt had embraced the idea of combining multiple discrete, midlength segments into a single feature-length picture. Today’s Disney enthusiast knows these films as the “package features,” and they could

In these story sketches, Mickey, Donald, and Goofy, threatened by the hungry giant, make an unwise choice of hiding places. In the 1933 short *Giantland*, Mickey had hidden inside the holes in an enormous Swiss cheese, and had found himself in the giant’s sandwich; here, all three principals are in the same predicament. The scene in the finished film does not follow these sketches, but Mickey does wind up in the sandwich.

take one of several forms. Here, "Mickey and the Beanstalk" was joined with "Bongo"—yet another "economy" picture initiated before the war, based on a Sinclair Lewis short story—as the two halves of one disjointed but entertaining feature. Its title was *Fun and Fancy Free.*

And, while the lampooning excesses of the proposed "Sooner or Later" were wisely ignored, some of Hee's and Cottrell's ideas did have an impact on the new version of the story. In 1940 Walt and the writers had debated the singing harp's personality, suggesting a variety of approaches. Now, in place of Hee and Cottrell's glamorous entertainer, the harp became a lovely female character—animated by Jack Campbell, an artist who specialized in animating pretty girls—with the singing voice of Anita Gordon. Some of the comedy dialogue in "Sooner or Later" found its way verbatim into the script of the new film. Perhaps most importantly, Hee and Cottrell's suggestion of Jiminy Cricket as a master of ceremonies led to the Cricket's appearance, not just in "Mickey and the Beanstalk," but as the host of the new connecting scenes that linked the two stories together in *Fun and Fancy Free.* This was a significant development; it was the Cricket's first screen appearance since *Pinocchio*, the film for which he was created, and a story that took place in a very different animated universe. Here he fit easily and naturally into the contemporary world of *Fun and Fancy Free*, paving the way for further appearances as a continuing Disney character.

The song "Sooner or Later" was not used in the finished film, having already been diverted to another Disney film, *Song of the South*—not as a flashy production number, but as a quietly charming ballad performed by Hattie McDaniel. In its place, "Mickey and the Beanstalk" featured a new selection of songs. Walt's initial notion to produce the story as a "musical comedy" was not quite realized, but the score included two lilting songs ("My, What a Happy Day" and "My Favorite Dream") performed by the harp, and a comedy number for Donald Duck and Goofy, based on the traditional "Funiculì Funiculà." During story development, Walt had pressed for a musical theme for the growing beanstalk that might emulate the steady, insistent rhythm of Ravel's "Boléro." Composer

Two moments from the escape sequence, combined in a single image. The animation of the Duck and Goof is actually used twice in the same sequence: they lower the harp off the edge of Willie's table, and, a few moments later, repeat their action here at the top of the beanstalk.

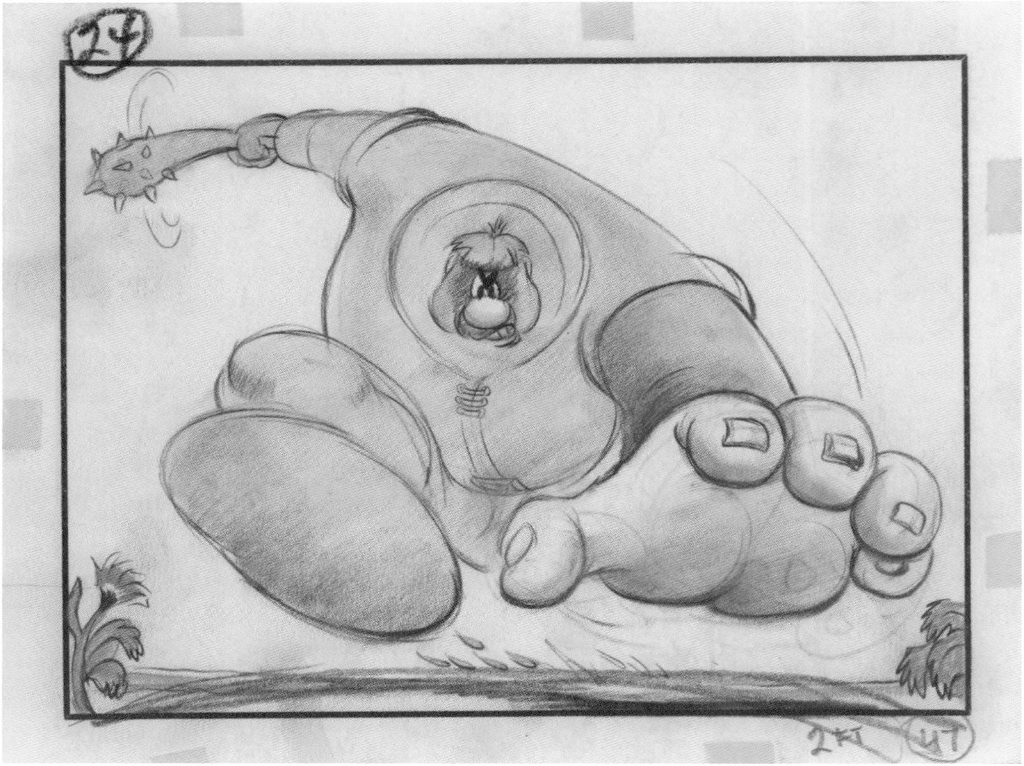

Ollie Wallace obliged with a stirring instrumental theme that was promptly dubbed “Beanero.”

Mickey Mouse was not only animated by multiple hands in “Mickey and the Beanstalk”; he also spoke with multiple voices. Walt himself had performed Mickey’s voice for the better part of the 1930s, but writer Ford Banes had started recording some of Mickey’s dialogue as early as 1939 when Walt was unavailable. In the spring of 1941, when “Mickey and the Beanstalk” was in the early stages of production, Banes recorded some provisional lines for Mickey in one sequence. But Banes left the studio later in 1941, shortly after the strike, and subsequently the sequence was completely rewritten. Walt’s next choice for a substitute Mickey voice was sound-effects wizard Jim Macdonald. “He said, ‘Do it. Just say something,’” Macdonald told Milt Gray. “So I said [in Mickey’s voice], ‘Hi, Walt, how are you?’ You know, he always had that little identifiable giggle. He said, ‘That’s fine.’ He told the directors, 'Have Jim do it, in the future. He can do it fine.'"[27] Macdonald did continue to perform Mickey's dialogue, off and on, in later years. So did Clarence Nash, best known as the voice of Donald Duck, who tested for the role of Mickey in 1949. As we'll see presently, he too went on to voice Mickey in several short subjects.

Another notable voice casting choice was the giant. The giant's personality, like the harp's, had been the subject of much speculation in early story development. In the end, the giant was named Willie and was pictured as a far more comic menace than his counterparts in *Giantland* or *Brave Little Tailor*—a towering behemoth with the mind of a toddler. The vocal role was cast with Billy Gilbert, a popular character player in movies and radio who had also performed the voice of Sneezy in *Snow White*. The latter role was linked to one of Gilbert's specialties, a well-known sneezing routine. This in turn led to a new piece of business in "Mickey and the Beanstalk": Mickey finds himself in the giant's vest pocket alongside a huge snuff box which, of course, comes open, precipitating a volley of sneezes from both Mickey and Willie.

The notion of a framing story, originally projected as a device which would show Mickey and his pals as actors assuming roles in the story, appears in a very different form in *Fun and Fancy Free*. Here, the framing story is filmed in live action and features ventriloquist Edgar Bergen and his famous dummies, Charlie McCarthy and Mortimer Snerd, as he narrates the story of "Jack and the Beanstalk" to little Luana Patten. The addition of Bergen to the cast gives the film added star power. Too, the combination of cartoons and live action that Walt had suggested in 1941 had consumed even more of his attention by the mid-1940s. Here the live performers are joined onscreen by Jiminy Cricket and, in the end, by Willie himself.

These storyboard sketches for Mickey's climactic escape suggest some visual ideas that were retained in the film, especially Mickey's narrow misses and the exaggerated low-angle perspective views of the pursuing Willie. Note, too, the footages penciled in the borders of these sketches. These are *very* short scenes, an indication of the rapid cutting planned for this climactic sequence.

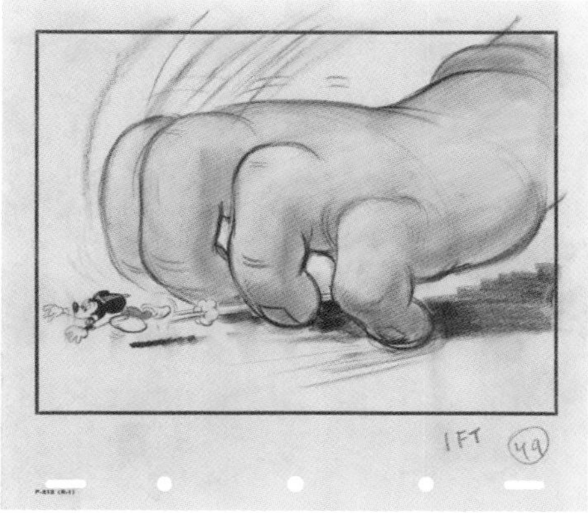

Publicity for *Fun and Fancy Free* made much of the combination of animated and live-action worlds. Here Mickey, Donald, and Willie the Giant rub shoulders (literally) with little Luana Patten and with Edgar Bergen's dummies, Charlie McCarthy and Mortimer Snerd. Note that Mickey appears with dimensional ears in this publicity drawing.

To one who knows the production history behind "Mickey and the Beanstalk," the finished film is a fascinating patchwork. The former "Slap-Happy Valley" is now simply Happy Valley, trading the slapstick tone of earlier versions for a more earnest sentimentality. Sequences started in 1941 are dusted off and completed five years later, sometimes extended with new scenes, and sometimes combined with newly hatched story material. Conversely, since this story is now *one-half* of a feature and occupies only a scant four reels of footage, some of the 1940–41 story material is excised altogether. Gone are those carefully worked out individual breakdown sequences at the top of the beanstalk; now the adventurers simply walk to the edge of the moat, appropriate a giant leaf as a boat, and start across. They encounter no mammoth creatures except a fleet of dragonflies overhead, suggesting a squadron of bombers (an allusion that the postwar audience would immediately have recognized), and a whale-sized fish that devours one of the attacking dragonflies.

As for Mickey himself, his performance here is likewise a patchwork. In some ways it functions as a time capsule, uniting the talents of two different pools of Mickey animators. Scenes started in 1941 by Walt Kelly are completed in 1946 by Hugh Fraser or John Sibley. The great Fred Moore, considered the unassailable authority on Mickey at the time production started, had—despite outstanding contributions to other films in the meantime—slipped sadly in his standing at the studio during the intervening years. In the finished film he contributes a single acting vignette to Mickey's repertoire: the character's cunning manipulation of the dim-witted giant's psychology, pretending to tell Willie's fortune by reading his gigantic palm. Else-

where, reliable Mickey animators like Marvin Woodward, Ken Muse, and Riley Thomson, familiar names among the shorts crews of the early 1940s, alternate with artists like Ward Kimball, who had been relatively new to Mickey at the time. The climactic sequence, in which our heroes do enact the traditional escape down the beanstalk, is a postwar invention and was largely animated by Woolie Reitherman—by then a long-standing member of the animation department, but one who had rarely animated Mickey before. Understandably, under the circumstances, Mickey's performance in this film is uneven. Some of his sequences offer pleasant morsels of personality animation; in others he's simply an action hero, glimpsed in long shot as he takes part in chases or escapes.

Upon its release in 1947, *Fun and Fancy Free* was greeted by mixed reviews and moderately successful box office returns. Most critics had good things to say about the film,

The New York opening at the Globe Theatre, extravagantly decked out for the occasion, in September 1947.

but few took special notice of Mickey's role in it. Instead of celebrating Mickey's postwar return to the screen in a feature-length setting, most reviewers referred to Mickey, Donald, and Goofy simply as "old troupers"[28] or "the perennial Disney favorites,"[29] and proceeded without further comment. In 1940 Walt had voiced his faith that a Mickey Mouse feature would have surefire box office appeal, but perhaps that time had passed by 1947. In any case, in 1947, no follow-up efforts were forthcoming. For the rest of Walt's life, *Fantasia* and *Fun and Fancy Free* would remain Mickey's only two starring vehicles in the feature-length arena.

Mickey, Donald, and Jiminy Cricket pose with Edgar Bergen, his dummies, and Luana Patten for a publicity shot.

The theatrical poster for *Fun and Fancy Free*, dominated by imagery from Mickey's story.

FULL-LENGTH
MUSICAL CARTOON FEATURE
Walt Disney's
"Fun and Fancy Free"
Color by TECHNICOLOR
featuring EDGAR BERGEN DINAH SHORE
Released through
RKO RADIO PICTURES, INC.
© W.D.P.

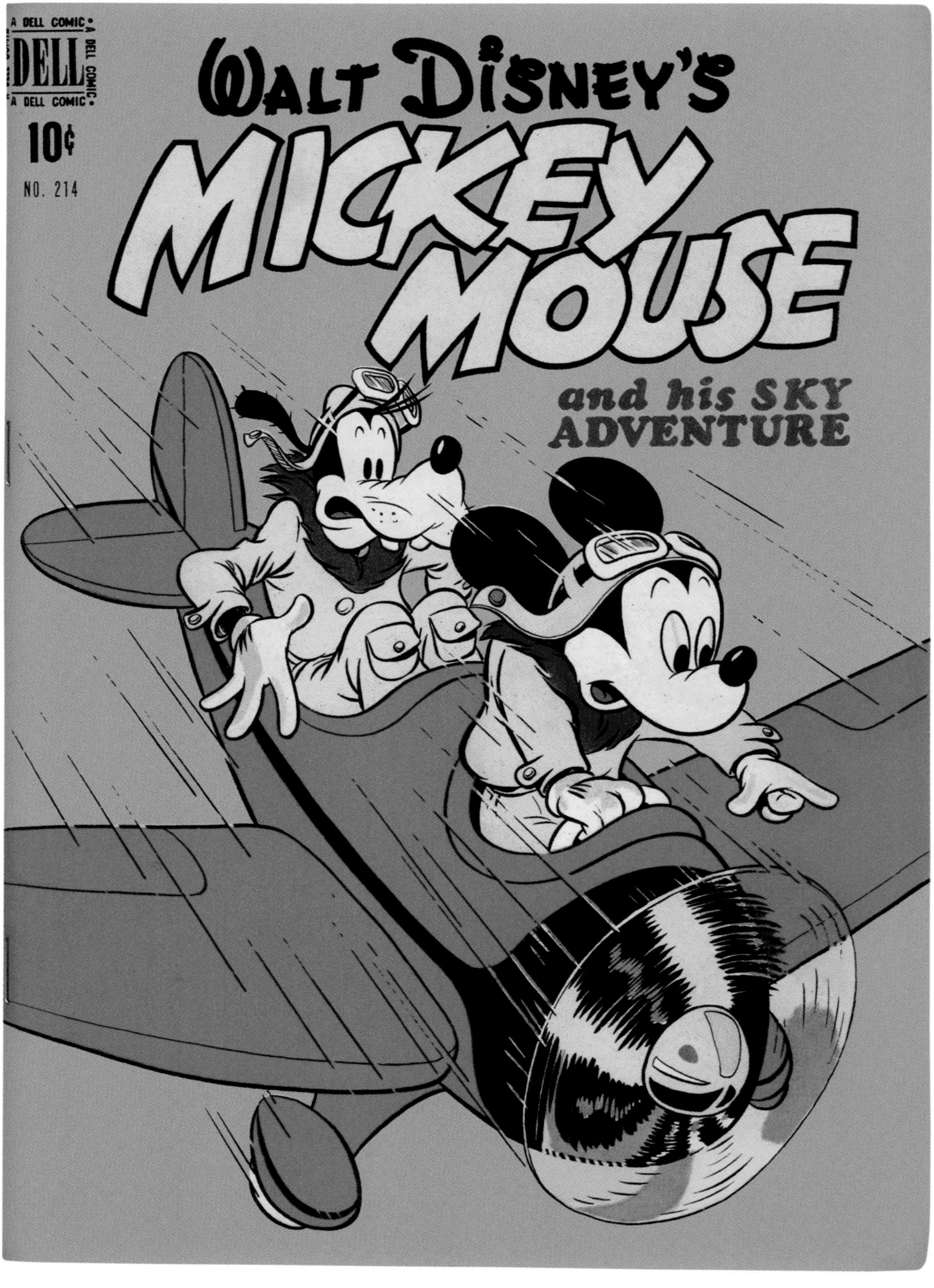
A DELL COMIC
DELL
10¢
NO. 214
WALT DISNEY'S
MICKEY MOUSE
and his SKY ADVENTURE

CHAPTER EIGHT

Modernizing Mickey

As Mickey Mouse's theatrical appearances declined in the early 1950s, there was another medium in which his star remained shining steadily. Mickey's comics "life" expanded exponentially in the postwar years, and of especial note was the manner in which the expansion took place: in which one "life" became many. Mickey began featuring in several, markedly different types of comic stories, each made for a different venue—a few outside the United States—and each with its own unique authorial and editorial direction.

WALSH, GOTTFREDSON, AND GONZALES

When we last looked in on Floyd Gottfredson's newspaper strip Mickey, the year was 1944 and he was busy battling World War II foes: the result of an intervention by new scripter Bill Walsh, as earlier serials had positioned Mickey as too young for the armed forces. But Walsh found ways to insert Mickey into war stories regardless—stories enlivened by Walsh's trademark rapid-fire random humor, as well as strikingly serious drama and macabre scares. In late 1944, Walsh began writing the *Mickey Mouse* Sunday strip as well as the daily, making the newspaper Mickey's "voice" fully his own. As if to celebrate, he dove with Gottfredson into three of the wildest daily strip serials of the 1940s.

Cover by Jim Pabian for "Mickey Mouse and His Sky Adventure" (Mickey Mouse *Four Color* 214, 1949), a Western Publishing one-shot comic. Drawn by former Gottfredson inker Bill Wright, "Sky Adventure" was a close remake of Gottfredson's own "Island in the Sky" (1937). Pabian's cover art took on a life of its own: reused on the first issue of Germany's postwar *Micky Maus Magazin*—the flagship Disney title still published there today—it has become an iconic, often-reprinted image for German comics fans.

Excerpt from "The House of Mystery" daily serial (1944–45); story by Bill Walsh, art by Floyd Gottfredson, Dick Moores, Paul Murry, and George Waiss. "Mystery" was the first Mickey comic story to feature a female villain — one who was also a scientist, reflecting women's societal advances during World War II. Likely to avoid casting female progress in a negative light, the story shows Minnie taking a heroic role in the climactic scenes, wrestling the villain down and allowing our friends to escape.

DAILY GAGS AND *FOUR COLOR* ADVENTURES

In "The House of Mystery," Walsh and Gottfredson explained their haunted house's spooks as illusions created by Drusilla's hypnotic gas; but under some circumstances, the explanation was arguably less than convincing. Critics have argued that Walsh was more interested in pouring on the ghostly gags than ensuring that they made sense.[1]

Why insert so many gags into a gothic thriller to begin with? Perhaps because King Features continued to express interest in turning *Mickey Mouse* into a gag-a-day strip;[2] indeed, "The House of Mystery" was one of the last full-fledged serials to run in the strip for a while. From mid-1945 to mid-1946, serials were dropped from *Mickey Mouse* entirely. When they came back, it was initially as just two- to three-week comedy shorts.

The strip's inconsistent format may or may not have led to concurrent changes at Disney comic-book licensee Western Publishing; but as early as 1943, with "The Seven-Colored Terror" Western had begun supplementing its Mickey strip reprints with new stories. Now, as the strip featured fewer serials, Western began producing more and more of this new material, initially for its chief one-shot series, *Four Color Comics*.

Former Disney comic-strip artists Bill Wright and Dick Moores, Gottfredson's inkers on many key 1930s and 1940s serials, began freelancing for Western, as did former Donald Duck story man Carl Barks. The enduring closeness of Wright, Moores, and Barks to Disney resulted in many of the earliest Western Publishing Mickey comics stories feeling of a piece with the Gottfredson serials that preceded them — preserving continuity, supporting cast, and the general flavor of Mickey as a gung-ho, but put-upon young adventurer and crime-buster.

Strips from "The World of Tomorrow" daily serial (1944); story by Bill Walsh, pencils by Floyd Gottfredson, and inks by Dick Moores. Peg Leg Pete's plan to replace prominent citizens with robot doubles — including Mickey's own robot twin — seems like a tired science-fiction trope today, but it was a startling new idea in 1944. Gottfredson and Walsh were inspired by the 1939-40 New York World's Fair, which took the "World of Tomorrow" as its theme; perhaps robots themselves could become the humans of tomorrow.

Following Excerpt from "The Rajah's Treasure" (Mickey Mouse *Four Color* 231, 1949); art by Bill Wright. This jewel-robbery tale arguably comes closer than any other Western Publishing story to capturing the spirit of prewar Gottfredson — with a feisty, heroic Mickey holding his own against bandits, an angst-ridden Minnie fighting to clear Mickey's name, and a fan-favorite running gag of Mickey and Minnie tied up and forced to chew through their ropes.

I SAW THE WHOLE THING FROM MY HELICOPTER, DOPE! I WAS JUST KEEPING MY EYE ON YOU... AND THAT FORTUNE IN JEWELS!
!
THE COPS WILL BE HERE SOON! MEET ME AT THE RIDGE ROUTE HIDE-OUT! AND DON'T LET ANYTHING HAPPEN THIS TIME, OR ELSE!
I'LL JUST COVER THIS WRECKED CAR SO THE NOSY COPS WON'T FIND IT!
THEN TO THE HIDE-OUT, THE RAJAH'S TREASURE...AND A LIFE OF EASE FOR YOURS TRULY FOR EVER AND EVER! HAW! HAW! HAW!
LATER...
I'M HUNGRY, MICKEY!
SO'M I!
I SURE COULD STAND A HAM SANDWICH!
BUT HERE I AM, BACK ON MY ROPE DIET! OH, WELL...
PHLLFFT!
CRUNCH!
MMMPH!
IT'S TOO LATE, MICKEY! WE'RE STOPPING!
GEE WHIZ! WHAT WILL HAPPEN NOW??
?

HERE WE ARE, BOSS! DO WE SPLIT TH' TREASURE NOW?
YEAH! DUMP IT OUT! AND LEAVE THE KIDS IN THE TRUCK! I'VE CHANGED MY PLANS ABOUT THEM!
AND WHAT ARE YOUR PLANS, YOU BIG REFUGEE FROM A PRISON CELL!
STICK AROUND, SMART GUY, AND SEE!
Later...
ALL RIGHT, SPIKE! THE TREASURE'S SPLIT! LOAD THE BAGS IN THE 'COPTER!
!
THEN PUT THE ARMORED CAR IN GEAR, AND LET IT...AND THE KIDS...GO OVER THE CLIFF!
? ! ? !
MMPH!
CHOMP!
CRUNCH

WALSH, GOTTFREDSON, AND EEGA BEEVA

If, in the mid-1940s, Western Publishing began creating Mickey comic-book comics due to a lack of new King Features serials, later years saw a different paradigm: the Gottfredson daily strip once again produced serials in force, but Western editors no longer wanted to reprint them. Though *Walt Disney's Comics and Stories* continued to feature *Donald Duck* daily strips, it ignored the daily *Mickey Mouse.* Why would that be so?

Surviving records don't seem to tell us, but published evidence suggests a possibility: in the postwar years, an emboldened Bill Walsh moved the *Mickey* daily even further into a realm of adult *noir* storytelling and wild science fiction. To Western's editors, makers of traditional kids' comics often set in the Wild West, the new serials may have felt like strange time capsules from a stranger future.

Enhancing this perception was a major new character: Mickey's time-traveler friend Pittisborum Psercy Pystachi Pseter Psersimmon Plummer-Push, nicknamed Eega Beeva, whom Walsh and Gottfredson introduced in 1947 as a deliberate attention-grabbing effort. First planned as a project for Mickey's 20th anniversary, Eega's debut became its own event, marking the strip's move back to extended-length serials—serials in which, for three years running, Eega became Mickey's permanent sidekick. Supersmart but super eccentric, the "future man" exploded into Mickey's world like dynamite: Walsh and Gottfredson clearly perceived him as the perfect vehicle for thrilling new adventures.

Cover by Harvey Eisenberg for the story "Spook's Island" (Mickey Mouse *Four Color* 170, 1947), written and drawn by Bill Wright. The locale is called Spook's Island after its resident, the trained gorilla Spooks, a 1930s daily strip character so named because Mickey originally mistook his hooting sounds for the spooky wail of a ghost.

Excerpt from "The Riddle of the Red Hat" (Mickey Mouse *Four Color* 79, 1945). By the time he produced this story for Western, Carl Barks considered Mickey "not my cup of tea"[1]—so rather than take Mickey in an original direction, Barks tried hard to follow in Gottfredson's footsteps. To do so, he imitated numerous character poses from "Love Trouble" (see Chapter 5), putting his own spin on a winsome and emotive Gottfredson-style Mouse.

WALT DISNEY'S MICKEY MOUSE, No. 79—PUBLISHED BY DELL PUBLISHING CO., INC.
149 Madison Ave., New York, 16, N. Y.

NOW TO BREAK THIS DETONATOR WIRE BEFORE..
THERE! AT LEAST WE DON'T HAVE TO WORRY ABOUT THIS ANY MORE!
SNAP!
BUT WHEN THEY DON'T HEAR ANY EXPLOSION, PETE AND TIGER WILL BE BACK HERE TO INVESTIGATE!
DYNAMITE
IT'D BE JEST LIKE THET SNEAKY DYNAMITE TUH BLOW UP ANYWAY!
NO DANGER.. BUT, SA-AY! I WONDER WHAT'LL HAPPEN IF WE SHORT CIRCUIT THIS BROKEN DETONATOR WIRE TO THE LIGHT CORD...?
AW, RATS! LET'S GET TH' BLAST OVER WITH!
OKAY! BY THIS TIME THEY'RE NOIVOUS WRECKS... HEH! HEH! ..EXPECTIN' T' GET BLOWED UP... ANY... MINUTE...
...AND THIS IS TH' MINUTE! HERE GOES!
HUH? WHAT? I DON'T HEAR... HEY! TH' LIGHTS WENT OUT!
CLUNK
HOT DIGGETY, GOOFY... IT WORKED! I BET WE SHORT-CIRCUITED THEIR WHOLE LIGHTING SYSTEM!
YEAH, BUT, MICKEY... GAWRSH, LOOKIT!
TURNIN' OFF THET ZERO-COLORED LIGHT JUST MADE US VISIBLER THAN EVER!
OH, GOSH! WE CAN'T SNEAK BY THOSE CROOKS THIS WAY!
HUMPH! THIS SHORE IS A CRAZY BIZNESS! WE TURN OUT THUH SPECIAL LIGHTS THET MAKE US VISIBLE... BUT DO WE GET INDUHVISIBLE? NO!
HMM... IN A WAY THOUGH, WE ARE INVISIBLE, GOOFY..

WALSH, GONZALES, AND THE POSTWAR SUNDAY STRIP

In mid-1955, King Features asked that the "Mickey Mouse" daily strip drop adventure serials and become a permanent gag-a-day feature; and Frank Reilly, Gottfredson's successor as manager of Disney's comic-strip department, complied. Gottfredson himself would draw this sitcom Mickey daily for two decades more, but believed his best years were behind him. "I always felt that Mickey should have [stayed] a little Chaplin Mouse against the world."[3]

For Bill Walsh the prognosis was more positive: as a gagman, he enjoyed drawing sitcom stories. Indeed, Walsh's most important stint on such material began not in 1955, but nine years earlier, when Manuel "Gonzy" Gonzales returned from World War II service and began collaborating with Walsh on the *Mickey Mouse* Sunday strip. Upon starting to draw Walsh's scripts, Gonzy found them overfilled with excessive visual detail.[4] While Gottfredson, at work on the daily strip, found it simple to condense that detail, Gonzales

Top Excerpt from "The Man of Tomorrow" daily serial (1947); story by Bill Walsh, art by Floyd Gottfredson. Some of Eega Beeva's supposed futuristic traits — being boneless, as here, or not casting a shadow — were rather inconsistently portrayed in the early comics.

Above Excerpt from "The Moook Treasure" daily serial (1950); story by Bill Walsh, art by Floyd Gottfredson. Mickey and Eega's meeting with the evil Aygotcha reveals a dichotomy that lay at the heart of many wartime comic stories.

Excerpt from "The Ghost of Man-Eater Mountain" (*Walt Disney's Comics and Stories* 129–132, 1951); story by Don R. Christensen, art by Bill Wright. The mountain's "ghost" proves to be an elaborate hoax; but the discovery of the ruse makes culprit Peg Leg Pete no less dangerous.

MICKEY MOUSE
by
WALT DISNEY
OF COURSE I DON'T BELIEVE IN GHOSTS, GOOFY... BUT THEY SAY THIS HOUSE YOU RENTED IS HAUNTED!
IT DON'T WORRY ME!
NEXT EVENING
RASP
SCREECH
I COULD LISTEN TO SINGIN' COMMERCIALS ALL NIGHT LONG!
TRY HAPPY'S HOTSY HAIR RESTORER
THE GIRLS WILL LOVE YOU MORER AND MORER
CUZZIN GOOFY... WE G
YORE TELEGRAM INVITIN
US FER A VISIT SPELL
1-25
Copr. 1953, Walt Disney Productions
World Rights Reserved

THAT NIGHT
GROAN
CLANG
WISE GUY, HUH?
I LIKE BEBOP... AS LONG AS IT'S GOOD AND LOUD!
BEBOP BEBOP BEBOP
BEBOP COOL AND CRAZY
TAIN'T NOTHIN', OUSIN WHILLIGER ...I'M LOOKIN' FORWARD TO LOTS OF YOUR MUSICAL EVENIN'S!
SHORE HOPE WE AIN'T PUTTIN' YUH OUT NONE!
YUH AIN'T PUTTIN' ME OUT!
WALT DISNEY
Distributed by King Features Syndicate

Previous Sunday comic strip for January 25, 1953; story by Bill Walsh, art by Manuel Gonzales. Numerous early 1950s Sunday strips by Walsh and Gonzales show Goofy's imagination running away with him — or maybe reality itself is warping a little? From lonesome ghosts to real-life shoe trees, the plausible impossible always seems to be lurking right around the corner from Goofy.

Paul Murry in 1951.

Excerpt from "The Last Resort" (*Walt Disney's Comics and Stories* 152–154, 1953). While Fallberg's and Murry's stories, full of stubble-faced bandits pulling shifty con jobs, relied rather heavily on Western Publishing tradition, the pair's combination of evocative art and brisk storytelling made them the baby-boom best at what they did.

on the Sunday vowed to draw "Cecil B. DeWalsh's" complex scripts exactly as provided. Backgrounds became more intricate, figures smaller, and settings richer. The overall effect was one of greater realism, which arguably made Gonzales's art a better match for Walsh's humor. Whereas Gottfredson's daily strip art was bouncy, wild, and exaggerated — leading the wackiness of Walsh's plotlines to feel expected — Gonzales created a richer, gentler world in which the outrageous retained much more ability to surprise.

PAUL MURRY AND THE COMIC BOOKS

By the mid-1950s, the domestic Mickey comics momentum lay with Western Publishing's new comic-book program; at the vantage point of that initiative stood Paul Murry.

As a storyboard artist on the shelved cartoon *Spring Cleaning*, Murry had been active at Disney as early as 1938. He trained as a Mickey specialist under Fred Moore, whom Murry called "the animator who made Mickey Mouse what he is today."[5] In 1945, Murry himself was lead Mickey animator on the picture *Squatter's Rights*; but by then, comic-strip department manager Gottfredson had already tapped him to draw Silly Symphonies Sunday pages starring José Carioca and Panchito. Murry also did some assistant penciling on *Mickey Mouse*. "I wasn't good at that point," Murry later decided.[6]

In 1946, Murry left Disney employment to become a full-time freelance cartoonist. For a while he drew both licensed Disney comics and his own Wild West–themed newspaper strip, *Buck O'Rue* (1951-52), co-created by fellow Disney alumnus Dick Huemer. But by that time, he was already returning — via Western Publishing — to Mickey.

WALT DISNEY'S
MICKEY MOUSE
IN
"The LAST RESORT"
GOSH, GOOFY... I CAN'T BELIEVE WE'VE FINALLY STARTED ON OUR FISHING TRIP! WHAT WAS THE NAME OF THAT RESORT YOU READ ABOUT, THAT SOUNDED SO GOOD?
UH... TALKIN' TREES... NO, UH... HOLLERIN' HEMLOCKS ...NO...UH...SCREAMIN' SYCAMORES... NO...UH... UH...
REG. U.S. PAT. OFF.
COPR. 1953, BY WALT DISNEY PRODUCTIONS
WORLD RIGHTS RESERVED
HERE 'TIS... IN THIS MAGAZINE... WHISPERIN' PINES!
WHAT MAGAZINE IS THAT, GOOFY?
I FOUND IT IN MUH ATTIC! IT'S THE LATEST VACATION GUIDE FOR NINETEEN-OUGHT-TWO!
VACATION GUIDE 1902
1902? GOOD GOLLY... THAT'S OVER FIFTY YEARS AGO! MAYBE THE RESORT DOESN'T EVEN EXIST ANY MORE!
WAL, I WRIT 'EM A LETTER FOR RESERVATIONS LAST WEEK!
HERE'S HOPING THEY GOT IT! IT'S TOO LATE NOW TO GET IN ANY OTHER PLACE!

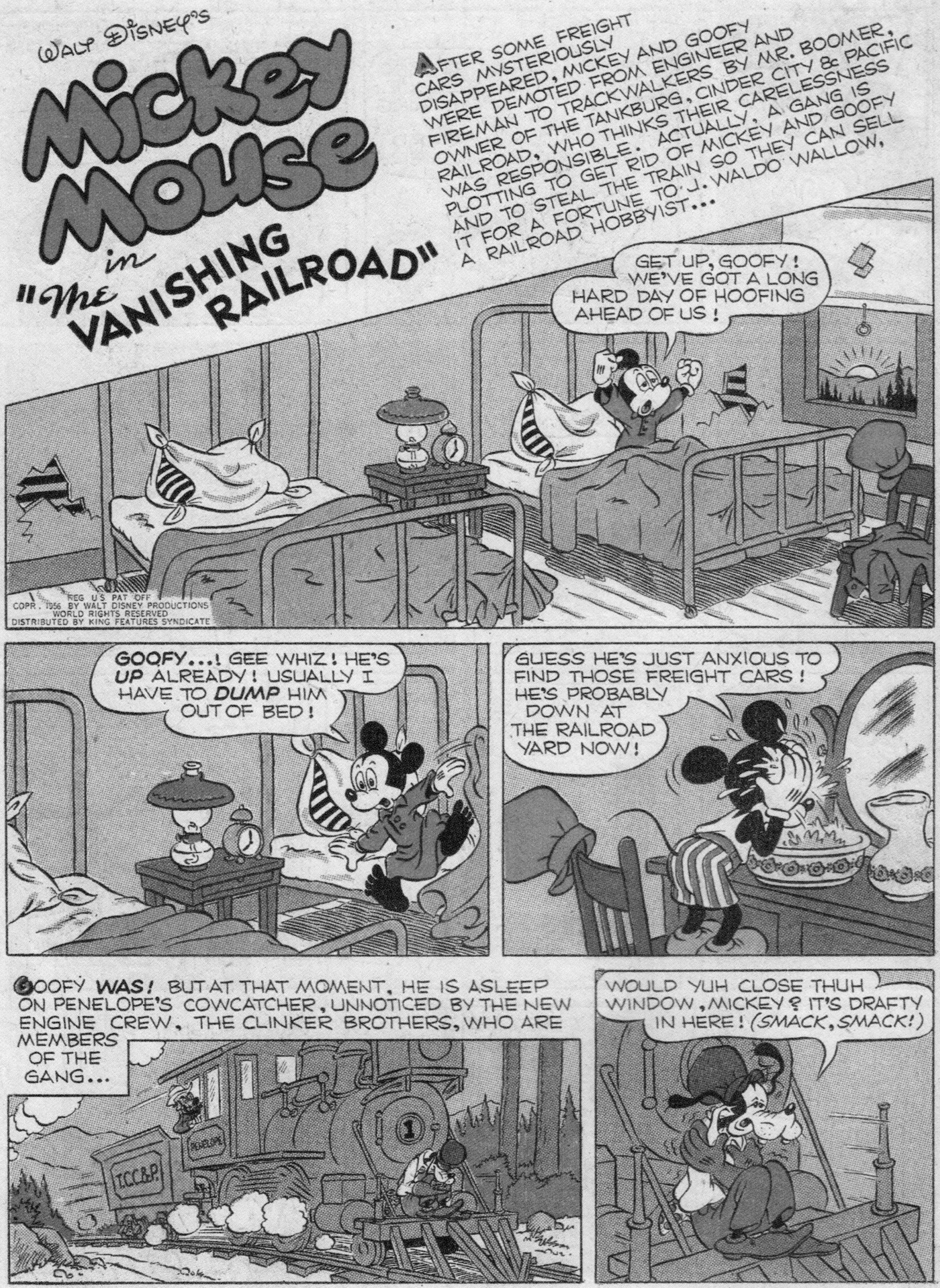
WALT DISNEY'S
Mickey Mouse
in "The VANISHING RAILROAD"
AFTER SOME FREIGHT CARS MYSTERIOUSLY DISAPPEARED, MICKEY AND GOOFY WERE DEMOTED FROM ENGINEER AND FIREMAN TO TRACKWALKERS BY MR. BOOMER, OWNER OF THE TANKBURG, CINDER CITY & PACIFIC RAILROAD, WHO THINKS THEIR CARELESSNESS WAS RESPONSIBLE. ACTUALLY, A GANG IS PLOTTING TO GET RID OF MICKEY AND GOOFY AND TO STEAL THE TRAIN SO THEY CAN SELL IT FOR A FORTUNE TO J. WALDO WALLOW, A RAILROAD HOBBYIST...
GET UP, GOOFY! WE'VE GOT A LONG HARD DAY OF HOOFING AHEAD OF US!
REG. U.S. PAT. OFF. COPR. 1956 BY WALT DISNEY PRODUCTIONS WORLD RIGHTS RESERVED DISTRIBUTED BY KING FEATURES SYNDICATE
GOOFY...! GEE WHIZ! HE'S UP ALREADY! USUALLY I HAVE TO DUMP HIM OUT OF BED!
GUESS HE'S JUST ANXIOUS TO FIND THOSE FREIGHT CARS! HE'S PROBABLY DOWN AT THE RAILROAD YARD NOW!
GOOFY WAS! BUT AT THAT MOMENT, HE IS ASLEEP ON PENELOPE'S COWCATCHER, UNNOTICED BY THE NEW ENGINE CREW, THE CLINKER BROTHERS, WHO ARE MEMBERS OF THE GANG...
T.C.C.&P.
PENELOPE
1
WOULD YUH CLOSE THUH WINDOW, MICKEY? IT'S DRAFTY IN HERE! (SMACK, SMACK!)

ENGLAND, FRANCE, ITALY — AND SCARPA

Halfway around the world, Disney comics had picked up a vast head of steam in postwar Europe. Italy's *Topolino* weekly — its Disney content reinstated after the Fascists' downfall — transmuted in 1949 from its original form, as a thin *Mickey Mouse Weekly*-like journal, into a thick, pocket-sized comics digest. Even before the switch, it had already become obvious that *Topolino*'s frequency and size required more content than Western Publishing and King Features were producing. Soon the same observation also came to publishers in Britain and France.

Having started local Disney comics production as early as 1930, Britain never entirely stopped. Odhams Press's early postwar issues of *Mickey Mouse* included many newly made strips featuring Disney feature-film stars. But little new Mickey material was included — that is, until Eega Beeva became popular with readers, just in time for Gottfredson to drop him. Odhams resolved to carry Eega onward themselves.[7] First came "Once Upon a Time," a Mickey-less tale by Ronald Nielsen, inserting him into a fairytale world. But then came several major stories set in basic Mickey daily-strip continuity. All featured a wily Eega and an eager Mickey in wacky adventures that tried — and sometimes succeeded — at carrying the Gottfredson torch.

Another try came when France got into the original Mickey comics business. The newspaper-format *Le Journal de Mickey* had been on hiatus; after the war, local Disney license rep Armand Bigle waited to effect its relaunch. First came an attempt at a more modern-format comic book, *Mickey Magazine*, published from Belgium and featuring a locally made Mickey and Donald serial. When this succeeded, *Le Journal* was revived in the same

Excerpt from "The Vanishing Railroad" (*Walt Disney's Comics and Stories* 185–187, 1956). This story displays a fascinatingly antique mood as Mickey and Goofy explore cowboy country aboard the train Penelope.

Excerpt from "The Reluctant Pirate" (British *Mickey Mouse Weekly* 642–668, 1952–53); art by Ronald Neilson. In "Pirate" and other British comics, the *Mickey Mouse Weekly* version of Eega Beeva demonstrates futuristic abilities far beyond any that Walsh and Gottfredson ever gave him. Here, Eega has transported himself and Mickey back in time simply by reaching upward and turning the comic page!

IMAGED BY HERITAGE AUCTIONS, HA.COM

format—including an even longer-lived serial, full of Gottfredson-inspired character models.

No country, however, grew a Mickey comics culture like Italy's. Even before *Topolino*'s transition to digest format, Turin-based writer Guido Martina was scripting his first Disney story, a remake of Gottfredson's "Bat Bandit." Martina, nicknamed "The Professor," was a former doctor of literature who became the most prolific Italian Disney comics writer.

But the first great Italian "maestro" was the Venetian-born Romano Scarpa. A self-taught cartoonist from childhood, Scarpa attended an art academy and opened a small animation studio before joining the Mondadori team in 1953. At the outset, Scarpa "only" drew Guido Martina's scripts; but when Gottfredson and Walsh stopped creating Mickey serials in 1955, Mondadori asked Scarpa to write and draw a series of replacements.

Mondadori didn't ask Scarpa to mimic Gottfredson's style; but Scarpa felt no other style would do. Scarpa's bouncy and dramatic art, his revivals of vintage Gottfredson costars, and his emotional, exuberant characterization of Mickey himself combined aspects of Gottfredson's self-plotted prewar stories with the Walsh-style wackiness of more recent material. Readers mistook Scarpa's product for Gottfredson's own;[8] Scarpa's Mondadori peers, most notably the artist Giovan Battista Carpi, followed in Scarpa's footsteps. A new era had arrived.

In 1949, Italy's venerable *Topolino* comic book restarted its numbering system and changed formats—from a large-size *giornale* edition to a *libretto*, or digest version. The cover art of drum major Mickey originated as a 1939 Disney promotional drawing used first for a Standard Oil tie-in.

Excerpt from "Mickey Mouse in the Delta Dimension" (Italian *Topolino* 206–207, 1959); story and art by Romano Scarpa. Floyd Gottfredson used many of his great character creations only once—including Dr. Einmug, originally the guardian of an atomic energy force. In retooling Einmug as a recurring costar, Scarpa took inspiration from the postwar nuclear-arms race, establishing that Einmug's past atomic secrets had long since gotten away from him.

A.M.
WALT DISNEY
TOPOLINO e la DIMENSIONE DELTA
(SECONDO TEMPO)
TOPOLINO RICERCA UN IGNOTO RICATTATORE CHE MINACCIA L'INTERA CITTÀ. INESPLICABILMENTE QUESTI "RITIRA" IL DENARO ESTORTO FACENDOLO SVANIRE NEL NULLA! ENTRA IN SCENA ATOMINO BIP-BIP, CHE CONDUCE TOPOLINO NELLA DIMENSIONE DELTA. QUI IL DOTTOR ENIGM LAVORA ALLA SUA SCOPERTA: INGIGANTISCE GLI ATOMI, CHE HANNO ASPETTO UMANO E PORTENTOSE PROPRIETÀ. BIP-BIP NE E' IL PROTOTIPO. ALCUNI INDIZI FANNO SOSPETTARE A TOPOLINO CHE IL RICATTATORE SIA PROPRIO IL DOTTOR ENIGM!
PROPRIO VOI, DOTTOR ENIGM! E' INAUDITO! MI SEGUIRETE ALLA POLIZIA!!
!?
BIP BIP!
SIETE IN GRAVE ERRORE, SIGNOR TOPOLINO! DEI RICATTI DI CUI DITE, IO NON NE SO NULLA!...
SARÀ MEGLIO VI SPIEGHI IL MOTIVO PER CUI VI HO FATTO VENIRE QUI! ANDIAMO NEL MIO STUDIO, PREGO!
DA QUANTO MI AVETE DETTO, CAPISCO DI AVER COMBINATO UN BEL GUAIO!
COME SAREBBE?
1

MARKET HOUSE
DISNEY

CHAPTER NINE

A Small Screen and a Great Kingdom

In the mid-1950s, just as Mickey's years on the big screen were winding down, two new developments at the Disney studio inaugurated a whole second phase of his career. One of these was Disneyland, the theme park that represented an innovative new concept in 1955. The other was television. The electronic medium had been in existence for several decades, but by the 1950s it was a widespread presence, bringing free entertainment into American homes—and threatening the motion-picture box office with a new kind of competition.

The full story of Walt's development of Disneyland has been documented elsewhere.[1] It was a project that consumed much of his attention for several years during the late 1940s and early 1950s—some of the earliest concepts date to 1948—and, from the beginning, his beloved Mickey Mouse was an integral part of this grand new enterprise. At one early developmental stage in Walt's personal correspondence the project was referred to as "Mickey Mouse Park," and from Disneyland's opening day in July 1955, Mickey was omnipresent there. Visitors arriving at the park were greeted by themed landscaping: a huge flower bed with hundreds of brightly colored flowers, forming an image of Mickey's smiling face. Once inside the gate they were apt to encounter Mickey again at parades or special occasions. Several years after the opening Mickey and other Disney characters began to circulate among the crowd and interact with the guests. At the same time, Walt was leading his studio's response to the phenomenon of

Disneyland is known to be a popular place, but Mickey has always weathered the storm of visitors. This experimental photograph by John G. Zimmerman was taken in Disneyland, Anaheim, in 1986.

Mickey, Minnie, Donald, Goofy, and many cast members gather in front of Disneyland's Main Street Station for this group photograph, taken in May 1976 by a Disney photographer.

Composed by singer-actor Jimmie Dodd as a theme song for TV's *Mickey Mouse Club*, the "Mickey Mouse March" was adapted to other uses. This 1963 performance at Disneyland is clearly inspired by the original TV animation.

television. Commercial TV had become an inescapable fact of American life, whether Hollywood liked it or not—and Walt, characteristically, embraced it with enthusiasm. As a trial run, he produced some special stand-alone programs; when they brought a strong positive response from viewers and critics, he plunged into a far more ambitious schedule of production. His studio would now produce motion pictures *and* television programming. And, once again, Mickey was an integral part of the new venture.

DISNEYLAND

Walt's vision for a weekly prime-time series was titled *Disneyland*. It was inextricably linked with his theme park, in more ways than one; the ABC network won the coveted Disney contract for this series partly by its willingness to invest in the real Disneyland. The connection between park and program was also thematic. Episodes of *Disneyland* were usually classified according to the "lands" in the park: cartoons were often linked with Fantasyland, Western adventures with Frontierland, and so on.

Mickey's place in this mixture was assumed from the outset. As early as March 1954, Walt was discussing his plan for the series' first episode: "The first half is our dream of what is going to be, and what we create for the audience, and the second half could be a tribute to the little guy who started this place. A half hour of Mickey Mouse won't be too much by the time we work it together. We could end with *Fantasia*—Mickey Mouse getting up with the immortals."[2] As the series continued, Mickey would maintain his presence in it, both in new animation and in special encores of classic shorts.

During the first two seasons of the *Mickey Mouse Club*, every Thursday was Circus Day. Walt was a lifelong circus fan and established a "Mickey Mouse Club Circus" in Disneyland, opening on Thanksgiving Day 1955. Scripted by Walt and his early Imagineers, the shows paid tribute to the small "mud show" circuses that Walt had enjoyed as a boy.

3D Jamboree, the 3-D film that attracts these young Disneyland visitors, ran from 1956 to 1964 in the Mickey Mouse Club Theater and was the only color appearance of the original *Mickey Mouse Club* cast and sets during the show's initial run. Note "Jimmy" Dodd's star billing.

MICKEY MOUSE CLUB

Roy Williams and Jimmie Dodd pose for a gag shot before a *Mickey Mouse Club* storyboard. Williams was no stranger to Disney storyboards, having moved into the story department in the mid-1930s and made his own contributions to numerous boards since then.

In addition to the weekly prime-time series, the Disney studio launched a daily children's program, and this time Mickey was the explicit star of the show. *Mickey Mouse Club* was announced as early as 1953,[3] and Walt's inspiration was clear: a return to the spirit of the original Mickey Mouse Clubs of the 1930s, now reframed in the terms of the television age. "This promotion has a wide appeal, not just to children," he said at one meeting. "We have people who were original members of the Mickey Mouse Club."[4] Early plans called for an actual "clubhouse," located at Disneyland, where park visitors could take part in the show as members of a live studio audience.[5] In the end Walt settled on a different format: the show was produced almost entirely at the Disney studio in Burbank and featured a regular cast of talented children, dubbed the Mouseketeers.

And, in the show that bore his name, Mickey Mouse was more than a figurehead. He personally appeared at the opening of each show, talking directly to the television audience and introducing the day's highlights, then returned at the end to take his leave until next time. These program openers and closers were animated by some of the studio's top artists—Ollie Johnston, Hal King, John Lounsbery—and Walt, who had long since stopped performing as the voice of Mickey Mouse, returned to provide Mickey's dialogue for the *Club*. One of the regular features of the show was the "Mousekartoon," a segment that drew on the studio's extensive backlog of theatrical cartoons. Week after week, young viewers were treated to a selection of Disney classics, including numerous black-and-white Mickey shorts that had not been shown in more than two decades.

"Who's the leader of the club?" These storyboard drawings by a Disney Studio artist anticipate all the musicality of the animated "Mickey Mouse March" sequence at the beginning of the *Mickey Mouse Club*. The popular show premiered on October 3, 1955 and aired intermittently until 1996.

Behind the scenes of the *Mickey Mouse Club*: Annette Funicello, Jimmie Dodd, and the cast pause their rehearsal of "The Mouseketeers in Paris" while Walt Disney makes a visit to the set exchanging ideas with director Sid Miller and producer Bill Walsh. Photograph taken on July 26, 1957.

Minnie underwent a similar transformation, as did Morty and Ferdie (not seen here, but referred to in internal production documents as "Marty and Morty"), whose roles marked their first screen appearance in more than a decade. Here Minnie, animated by George Nicholas, relaxes in comfort in a Rambler.

COMMERCIALS

Along with these high-profile ventures, the Disney studio also dabbled in another area of TV production: commercials. This work was not a high priority for Walt, but it did generate a healthy additional source of income for the studio. Technically, the commercials were produced by noted photographer George Hurrell and his wife Phyllis Bounds, Lillian Disney's niece, for their own independent company, Hurrell Productions; but they were produced on the Disney lot, by Disney artists, and featured Disney characters—including Mickey Mouse.[6]

In short, even without new theatrical cartoons, Mickey was everywhere in American life in the mid-1950s. His increased presence resulted in, and was compounded by, a new wave of merchandising. The *Mickey Mouse Club*, in particular, inspired a fresh crop of toys, clothing, records, Little Golden Books, and other merchandise, branded with the smiling logo of the *Club* itself.

Most of the standard Disney characters were drawn in highly stylized form for their appearances in TV commercials. Mickey, in particular, was redesigned by Tom Oreb, with a unique look, in order to distinguish him from his familiar appearances in theatrical cartoons and the *Mickey Mouse Club*.

THE MODERN AGE

Happy Birthday Mickey
MICKEY MOUSE
HIS LIFE-TIMES
JOHN HENCH

CHAPTER TEN

Pop and Nostalgia

After the wave of excitement caused by Disneyland and television, Mickey's career seemed to modulate again—sustained by the steady recycling of his earlier appearances, but with a notable lack of new ones. Television's *Mickey Mouse Club*, upon finishing its three-year run, was moved to the world of syndication. After thirty years of more or less constant exposure in popular culture, Mickey had achieved a kind of iconic status: less an active character than an emblem. In the public eye he was a symbol, signifying the Disney studio and Walt himself.

So much so that his most notable new career development in the 1960s came from *outside* the Disney studio. Avant-garde artists discovered Mickey as early as the late 1940s, but it was the pop artists of the 1960s who mounted a full-scale appropriation of his image, incorporating it into their works as a stock image—without authorization, and not always in a friendly context. So firmly was Mickey identified with Walt—and, rightly or wrongly, with a core of traditional, homespun values—that a generation of artists used Mickey's likeness to mount their own "comments" on those values.

Mickey, like Walt, was becoming increasingly often perceived as a kids' entertainer first, everything else second. As recently as 1950, the latest Mickey cartoon shorts had been promoted to adults as featuring "sophisticated touches . . . for Mickey has grown up."[1] But Mickey's *Mickey Mouse Club* role as a children's show host—in particular, running parallel

Previous Modern-day Disney animator and scholar Eric Goldberg served as 2-D animation supervisor for Mickey's retro 2013 short *Get a Horse!* "Aside from capturing Ub Iwerks's drawing style," Goldberg explained, "we were also capturing his movement style"[1]; to guide the crew, Goldberg drew this model sheet featuring a late-1928 Mickey model reenacting poses from *Plane Crazy*, *The Gallopin' Gaucho*, *Steamboat Willie*, *The Barn Dance*, *The Opry House*, and *Mickey's Choo Choo*.

Having been designated by Walt as Mickey's official portrait artist, John Hench continued in that capacity after Walt's death. Here, in Hench's 1988 entry, Mickey celebrates his continuing worldwide reach. Note the small French tricolor commemorating the beginning of construction at Euro Disney, later renamed Disneyland Paris.

The death of Walt Disney in December 1966 sparked a worldwide outpouring of emotion. His passing was marked by editorial cartoonists, many of whom spontaneously chose a weeping Mickey Mouse as the most appropriate symbol of the event. Karl Hubenthal's drawing, opposite page, perhaps summed up the moment of grief most succinctly: the whole world unites with Mickey — literally — in mourning Walt.

to Walt's host role on ABC's *Disneyland*—seemed, for contrarians, to associate Mickey and his creator with things at once childish and parental. As if forgetting Walt's and Mickey's powerful tradition of adventure, excitement, and art, a critic could call Mickey a "cross between Emily Post and Frank Merriwell."[2]

Mickey's role as Walt's representative became strikingly clear in a different way in December 1966 when the unthinkable happened: Walt Disney died. The world mourned, the studio came to a momentary standstill—and images of a weeping Mickey Mouse appeared spontaneously from around the world. The drawings captured, in their affection and emotion, the vital personality many knew Mickey could still be; a far cry from the childish figure imagined by detractors.

With the nostalgia boom of the 1970s, Mickey's status as an elder statesman took a pleasant turn. As the Marx Brothers, W. C. Fields, and other icons of Hollywood's golden age were rediscovered by popular culture, Mickey Mouse, himself a mainstay of those golden years, was likewise swept up in the wave of fresh appreciation. Now Mickey's original classic image from the 1930s became fashionable all over again—not only on T-shirts and other merchandise, but on the big screen. Classic shorts such as *The Klondike Kid* and *Shanghaied* were reissued to theaters, shown on programs with Disney features. At one time the studio would have refused even to consider theatrical reissues of the black-and-white shorts; now, from the perspective of four decades, delighted audiences discovered that Mickey's black-and-white adventures were among his very best films.

The excitement surrounding "retro" Mickey expanded with the approach of the character's 1978 fiftieth anniversary. The event fostered marketing campaigns and vast celebrations—some Disney-sponsored, others not—like none thrown for a fictional character before. A new spotlight was thrown on

L.A. HERALD-EXAMINER

Walt often said his studio's golden age was "all started by a mouse" and expanded from there. Lichtenstein's and Warhol's Mickey pop art engendered a similar effect, inspiring an ever-expanding cottage industry of modernist Mickey images. Here, a 1981 painting from Warhol's protégé Keith Haring shows Mickey zapped by another classic pop culture trope — a vintage 1930s-style UFO. In his later works, Haring would go on to caricature Warhol himself as an ersatz Mickey.

past eras of Mickey's "life": The marketing focus on Mickey's 1930s image expanded to cover new ranges of memorabilia, and the first extensive reprints of early Mickey storybooks and comics swept up a new generation of fans.

Mickey was given a star on the Hollywood Walk of Fame, making him the first cartoon character to be granted this honor. A plaque at the former Colony Theatre commemorated *Steamboat Willie*'s debut there. A Museum of Modern Art film retrospective on November 18 was only the most high-profile of many hosted around the world. Perhaps most prominently, the Library of Congress hosted *Building a Better Mouse: Fifty Years of Animation*: effectively a Disney history exhibit, curated by animation scholar Michael Barrier, but by its title acknowledging Mickey's place as an emblem—creative, adventurous, scrappy, and innovative—of the cartoon medium as a whole.

Look Mickey, a 1961 oil painting by acclaimed pop artist Roy Lichtenstein, signaled Mickey's adoption into the ranks of post-modernist muses. While designed to resemble a comics panel, *Look Mickey* is actually adapted from an image in *Donald Duck Lost and Found* (1960), a then-recent Little Golden Book written by Carl Buettner and illustrated by Bob Grant and Bob Totten.

Scenes from the film *Mickey's Christmas Carol*. Mickey was an obvious casting choice for the role of Cratchit. Scrooge McDuck was likewise suited for the leading role by more than his name; his legendary love of money, established during decades of comic books, was a trait perfectly in keeping with the traditional image of Ebenezer Scrooge.

MICKEY'S CHRISTMAS CAROL

From here it was only a step to producing new screen vehicles for Mickey. In 1983, the studio released the first new Mickey Mouse film in thirty years: *Mickey's Christmas Carol*. Inspired by a seasonal LP that had been produced by Disney's record division, this film loosely retold the story of the Dickens classic *A Christmas Carol* with a cast of Disney characters. It was an inspired idea, partly because the studio already had its own ready-made Scrooge: Scrooge McDuck, a comic-book character introduced by Carl Barks in 1947. Mickey, with his shy, unassuming personality, slipped easily into the role of Bob Cratchit, and other assorted Disney characters likewise took roles in the story. Like other film adaptations, this one took considerable liberties with the plot, and Dickens purists may have shuddered; but as a lighthearted celebration of the season, it found a warm welcome among movie audiences.

Mickey's Christmas Carol was produced during a period of turnover in the Disney animation department. A few veterans of the classic years, including some of the fabled Nine Old Men, were still at work at the studio, but many had died or retired and were being replaced by a new generation of artists. This film represented a "passing of the torch," as remnants of Walt's own handpicked animation crew — notably Eric Larson — coached the younger artists in the elements of classic Disney style. Another landmark was unrecognized at the time: *Mickey's Christmas Carol* utilized the talents of both Clarence Nash, the original voice of Donald Duck, and a young animator named Tony Anselmo, who would soon assume the role of Donald after Nash's passing.

In a cel setup from *Who Framed Roger Rabbit*, Mickey shares a cameo appearance with Warner Bros. character Bugs Bunny and with human costar Bob Hoskins, represented here by a black-and-white matte element.

WHO FRAMED ROGER RABBIT

This live-action/animation extravaganza, featuring characters from *all* the classic cartoon studios, was set in a cartoon environment that suggested the frantic, zany 1940s — not a congenial time for Mickey Mouse. Still, Mickey was far too important a character in the cartoon pantheon to be ignored altogether. In one scene in *Who Framed Roger Rabbit*, he made a cameo appearance (animated by Andreas Deja) alongside Bugs Bunny, his counterpart at the Warner Bros. cartoon studio, and human costar Bob Hoskins. Characteristically, the scene involved a deadly practical joke on Hoskins; and, characteristically, Bugs delivered the goods with sadistic glee while Mickey, the nice guy, simply looked on. He and Minnie could also be seen in the all-star wrap-up scene at film's end.

IMAGED BY HERITAGE AUCTIONS, HA.COM

THE PRINCE AND THE PAUPER

Mickey's Christmas Carol having been well received, the studio tackled another Mickey featurette with literary roots. This time he has a more central role in the story—two of them, in fact, as the two title characters in *The Prince and the Pauper*. Once again, the Disney version wanders far from Mark Twain's original, although traces of Twain's social commentary remain in the scenes contrasting the lives of peasant Mickey (trying to eke out a living under the hard, oppressive rule of the monarchy) and the Prince (never actually called Mickey onscreen; sheltered and shielded from the wrongs committed in his father's name). Still, the accent is on entertainment as the two look-alikes meet and agree to switch places. This picture features fewer of the familiar Disney characters than its predecessor, but peasant Mickey has a good friend in Goofy and a faithful dog in Pluto; Donald Duck is seen as a scheming secretary, and Horace Horsecollar as a prim and pompous royal tutor, inside the palace; and Pete, of course, is the evil Captain of the Guard who endeavors to seize control of the kingdom for himself. Too, the relatively little-known weasels from *The Adventures of Ichabod and Mr. Toad* are ideally cast as the corrupt palace guards who report to Pete. In an odd musical conceit, Verdi's "La donna è mobile," from *Rigoletto*, was adapted with gag lyrics as a vocal number by Mickey and company.

RUNAWAY BRAIN

This offbeat short, directed by Chris Bailey, represented an experimental effort to overturn Mickey's passive nice-guy image and return him to the bolder, more exciting kind of story material he had enjoyed in the 1930s. It depicts his adventures at the hands of "Dr. Frankenollie," a mad scientist who endeavors to switch his brain with that of a creature called "Julius," who looks like a three-story version of Pete. The experiment is temporarily successful: Mickey's body, housing Julius's mind, becomes a rampaging (but comical) little monster, while the monstrous über-Pete, controlled by Mickey's brain, endeavors to protect Minnie from the impostor. A massive electric shock switches the brains back again, and Mickey, back in his own body, manages to rescue Minnie from the colossal beast in an action-packed climax. Along the way, the artists squeeze in multiple in-joke references to Disney history and an assortment of horror films.

Storyboard drawing from *The Prince and the Pauper.* The Prince sulks during a boring lesson from windy tutor Horace. Onscreen, Mickey was animated by Andreas Deja in a character model reminiscent of *Fantasia*.

The poster for *Runaway Brain* makes creative use of the famous ears as a showcase for the two brains Mickey's body will host in the film. Note that the famous "sunburst" is used as a backdrop here, too, further suggesting the link to traditional Mickeyana.

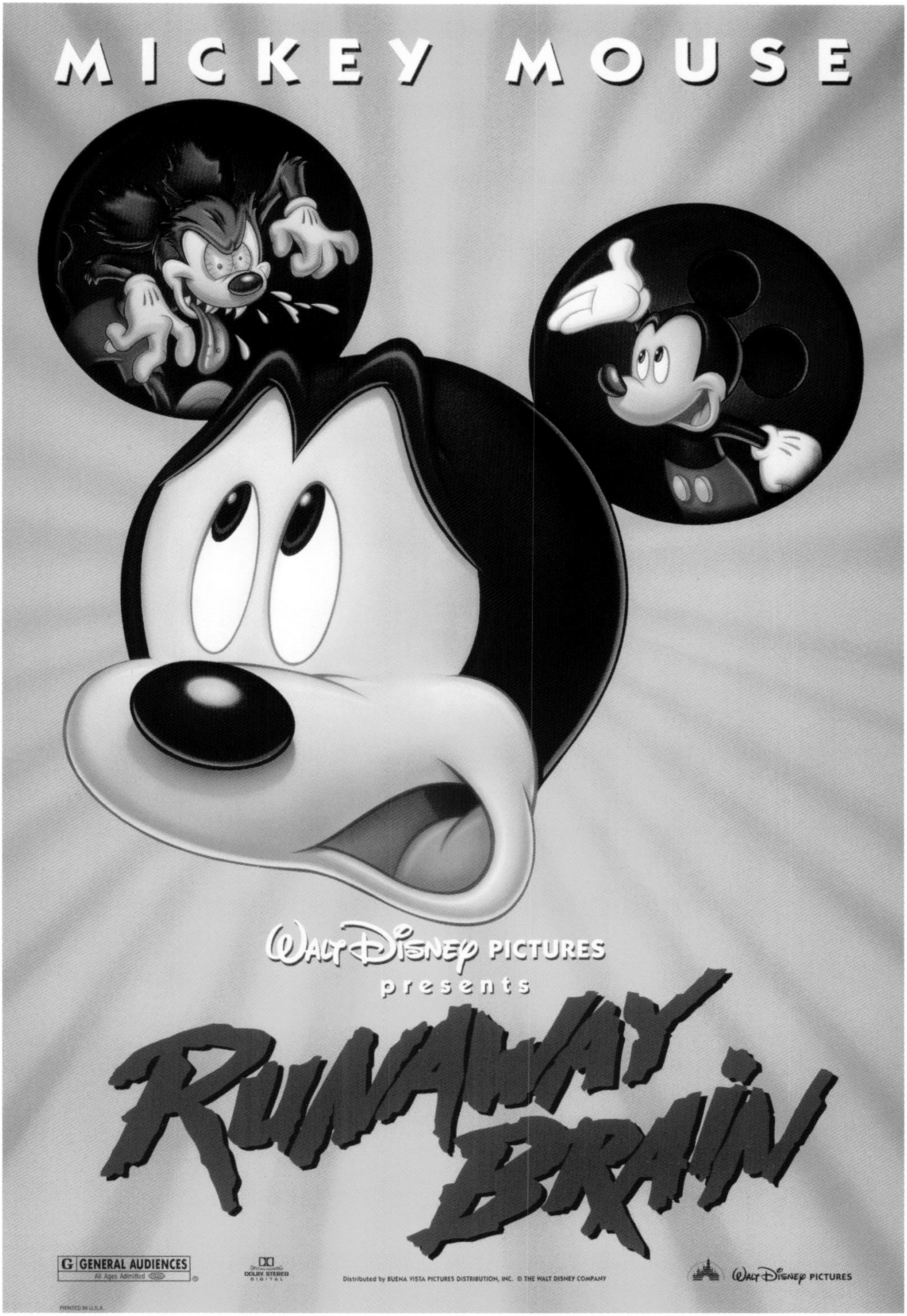
MICKEY MOUSE
WALT DISNEY PICTURES
presents
RUNAWAY BRAIN
G GENERAL AUDIENCES
All Ages Admitted
DOLBY STEREO
DIGITAL
Distributed by BUENA VISTA PICTURES DISTRIBUTION, INC. © THE WALT DISNEY COMPANY
WALT DISNEY PICTURES
PRINTED IN U.S.A.

MICKEY
JOHN HENCH '78
© WALT DISNEY PRODUCTIONS

MICKEY COLUMBUS

Alternate titles: *Mickey as Christopher Columbus*, *Christopher Mickey*. The rush to create new Mickey film vehicles in the 1980s and 1990s didn't lead to a finished product every time. Once again, as in the 1930s and 1940s, some film projects were initiated, extensively developed, and even publicly announced without actually ending up on the screen. The 1970s saw the Disney publishing department creating Goofy Classics, a series of comic albums portraying Goofy as parodic versions of Galileo, Dr. Frankenstein, and other historical and literary figures. The album *Christophorus "Goofy" Columbus* (1977), also featuring Peg Leg Pete as a bullying King Ferdinand, Clarabelle as Queen Isabella, and Columbus using a melon to demonstrate the world's round shape, seems to have inspired an early 1980s film project using Pete, Clarabelle, and the melon in the same functions.

Directed by Dave Michener and scripted by Pete Young and Steve Hulett, the aborted featurette would have seen Mickey Columbus and first mates Donald and Goofy singing "It's a Round, Round World,"[3] only to be jailed by a disbelieving Pete. Secretly freed by Clarabelle and Minnie, the boys sail to the Americas with their pet worm Alfred, who lives inside the melon. In the end, Mickey Columbus reaches his goal and tells his native hosts that the world is round, only to learn they "already know the world is round. We've got a melon of our own."

SWABBIES

This late 1980s story, directed by Darrell Van Citters and loosely spoofing the Ivan Reitman comedy *Stripes* (1981), would have seen Mickey, Donald, and Goofy as newly employed navy sailors, meeting Minnie, Daisy, and Clarabelle as Women Accepted for Volunteer Emergency Service (WAVEs) — and running into trouble with their corrupt superior, Captain Pete, and the nefarious Beagle Boys. Like the aborted *Mickey's Elopement* in 1940, *Swabbies* got quite some ways into production; it was largely recorded and in the animatic stage when it was put on the shelf. The work on *Swabbies* was handled by a special projects unit that had previously produced the TV special *Sport Goofy in Soccermania* (1987); rising studio stars such as Tad Stones *(Darkwing Duck)*,[4] Kirk Wise, and Joe Ranft were all involved with *Swabbies* in various capacities.

John Hench's Mickey portrait for 1978, the year of the Mouse's 50th birthday. For this occasion Mickey eschews his traditional shorts-and-shoes outfit and adopts "business casual" attire as he proudly shows off Epcot at Walt Disney World in Florida.

In a promotional cel for the unfinished 1980s featurette, *Mickey Columbus* holds up the world's first globe: actually a melon he has painted to demonstrate the earth's round shape. King Ferdinand, a.k.a. Peg Leg Pete, was to have taken the painted melon for a tribute, found a worm inside, and thrown Mickey in the dungeon.

Nintendo's *Mickey Mouse Game & Watch* (1981) featured a simple gag situation recalling the cartoon *Musical Farmer*: eggs roll down pipes from chickens' nests while the player, as Mickey, tries to catch them before they break.

Mickey's first text-based computer game was Sierra On-Line's *Mickey's Space Adventure* (1986). In it, Mickey and Pluto must travel the galaxy to collect the pieces of a stolen memory crystal, without which space aliens from the planet Oron stand to forget their world's history. Gameplay involved exploring planets by making quick menu-based choices—before Mickey's oxygen ran low enough to exhaust him.

VIDEO GAMES

As Mickey's new animated adventures came and went, the 1980s also saw Mickey stepping into a new medium of adventure storytelling: electronic gaming. Early efforts were primitive by later standards: Nintendo's handheld *Mickey Mouse Game & Watch* (1981) was a basic egg-catching challenge, and while Sierra On-Line's *Mickey's Space Adventure* (1986) boasted a creative kid-level sci-fi story by Roberta Williams *(King's Quest)*, its graphics were static and oddly suburban, sporting a shirt-and-jeans-wearing Mickey design derived from 1971 marketing model sheets.

Yet improvements were soon to come. The later 1980s and early 1990s found multiple Disney licensees producing more complex games—and Mickey, with his naturally rounded and compact design, proved a natural for the platform genre in particular.

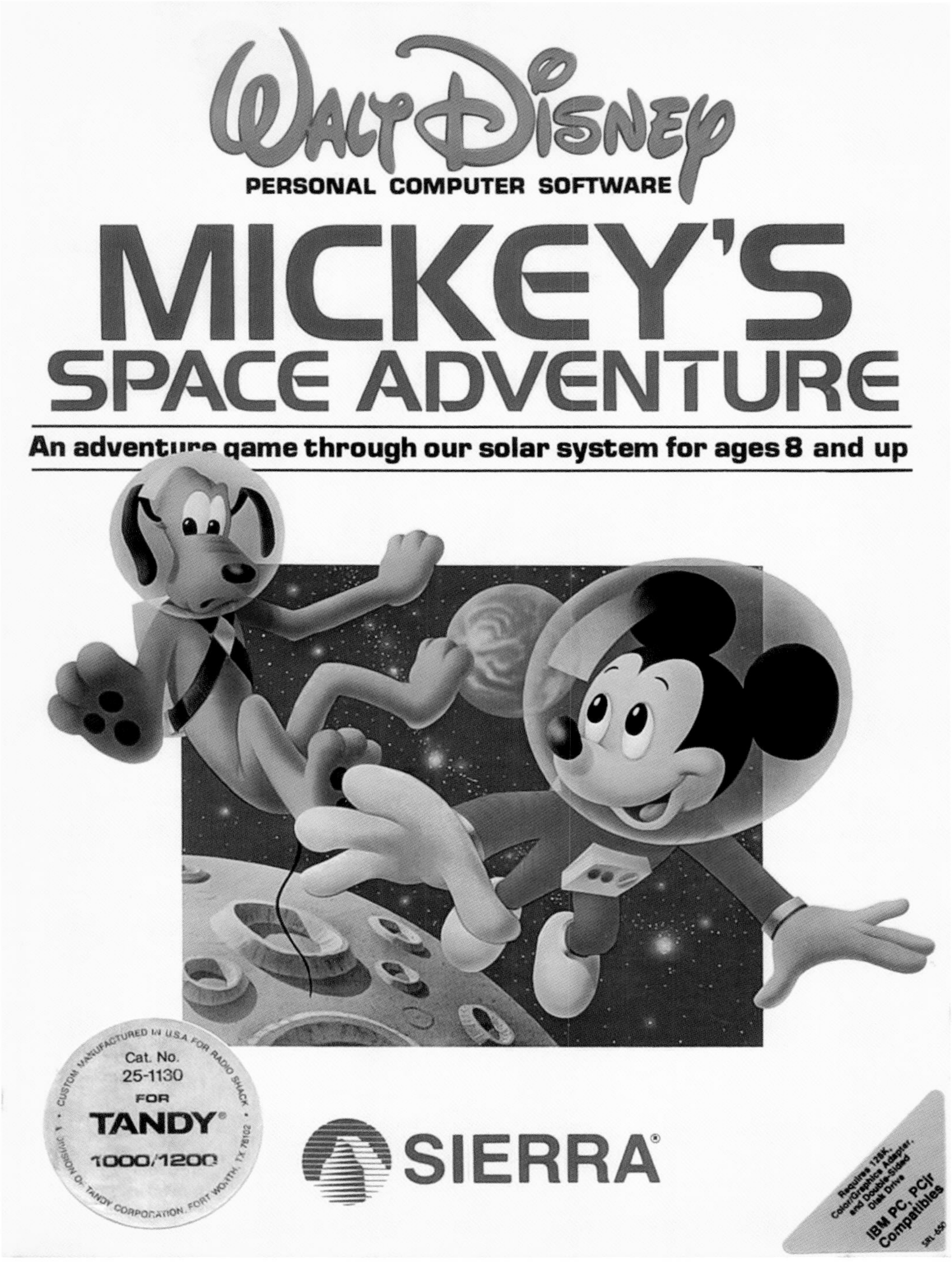
Walt Disney
PERSONAL COMPUTER SOFTWARE
MICKEY'S SPACE ADVENTURE
An adventure game through our solar system for ages 8 and up
CUSTOM MANUFACTURED IN U.S.A. FOR RADIO SHACK
Cat. No.
25-1130
FOR
TANDY®
1000/1200
A DIVISION OF TANDY CORPORATION, FORT WORTH, TX 76102
SIERRA®
Requires 128K, Color/Graphics Adapter, and Double-Sided Disk Drive
IBM PC, PCjr Compatibles

THERE WILL BE MORE NEWS ABOUT THE FABULOUS 'D&M' COMPETITION NEXT WEEK

CHAPTER ELEVEN

Cosmopolitan Mickey

There was another medium, of course, in which Mickey's fans had been provided with a steady flow of exciting adventures over the decades, and this, of course, was comics. When we last looked at Mickey's print stories in the early 1960s, more and more Mickey comics were being created directly for comic books—with British and Italian content burgeoning internationally, and domestic production ballooning. That trend has since accelerated to such a point that in many parts of the world, the name Mickey Mouse instantly brings comic books to mind.

Of course, the immense quantity of Mickey comics has not formed quite the monolith that its visibility might suggest at first. Instead, the local traditions in different countries—in different places where the stories are made—has led to a rich and fascinating mixture: to multiple storytelling schools founded on Floyd Gottfredson, on Romano Scarpa, on Carl Fallberg and Paul Murry, or on a mixture of creators. It seems fitting that a Mickey Mouse sold around the world in large cosmopolitan newsstands should be a cosmopolitan Mickey: himself a melting pot of various lands and influences.

In some respects, the Mickey Mouse of Western Publishing never developed far beyond the watershed Fallberg and Murry stories of the mid-1950s. While the greater Western creative house regularly benefited from the complex, character-driven writing of such talents as Carl Barks, John Stanley, and Don Christensen, a traditionalist faction among Western's

Excerpt from "The Man Who Wasn't There" (1974; British printing in *Donald and Mickey* 137); story by Cal Howard, art by Tony Strobl. Disney's Overseas Comics Program often set its new Mortimer Mouse stories at a new location in Mickey's town: Slim's Ice Cream, a 1950s-style malt shop where Mickey and Mortimer inevitably meet and lock horns. Slim's is run by the eponymous Slim, a masterful ice cream artisan who playfully encourages Mickey and Mortimer's bickering, runs afoul of it—or both.

Excerpts from "Return of the Phantom Blot" (*Walt Disney's Comics and Stories* 284–287, 1964); art by Paul Murry. The Blot's return led to fewer appearances by Pete, who had for years been the only recurring villain in Western Publishing's Mickey stories.

Excerpt from "Assignment Time-Lock" (*Mickey Mouse* 107, 1966). *Mickey Mouse, Super Secret Agent* stories featured Mickey and Goofy taking spy missions for "Police International." In practice, the stories were somewhat compromised by the attempt to put traditional funny animals into a realistic world.

writers and editors was famously willing to settle for repetitive plotlines and almost-interchangeable lead characters.[1]

It was thus that Mickey Mouse at Western, while still the star of good comic book stories, ended up in many that felt rather similar to each other. Mickey could be a perennial vacationer, forever encountering crooks; he could be a frazzled homeowner, "parent" to his pesky nephews and boyfriend to an atypically overbearing Minnie; or, most often, businesslike Mickey and sidekick Goofy were freelance detectives for Chief O'Hara.

Under the strictures of these story motifs, standout variety came less often due to shifts in the motifs themselves than to the imaginative trappings piled on top. As the *Leave It to Beaver* 1950s gave way to the counterculture 1960s and 1970s, Western followed the TV spy craze with tales of *Mickey Mouse, Super Secret Agent*; Western followed the rise of 1960s superheroes and supervillains by creating Super Goof and giving solo comic books to its own star villains, including the Phantom Blot.

POSTMASTER: Please send notice on Form 3579 to K.K. Publications, Inc., North Road, Poughkeepsie, New York 12602.
Walt Disney MICKEY MOUSE, No. 107, June, 1966. Published bi-monthly by K.K. Publications, Inc., North Road, Poughkeepsie, New York 12602. Second-class postage paid at Poughkeepsie, New York. Subscription price in the U.S.A. 65c per year; foreign subscriptions $1.15 per year; Canadian subscriptions 90c per year.
CHANGE OF ADDRESS should reach us four weeks in advance of the next issue date. Give both your old and new address enclosing if possible your old address label.

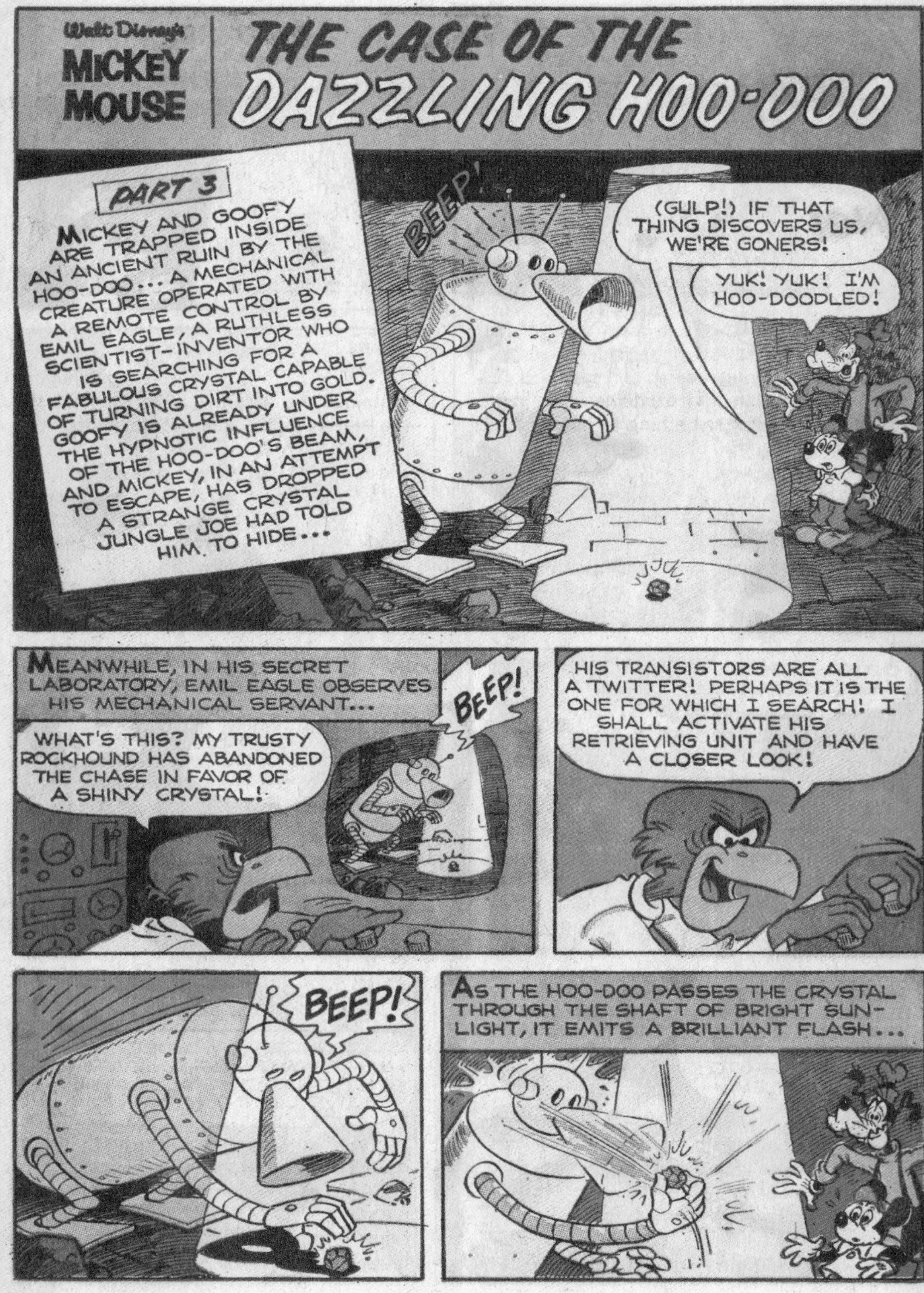
Walt Disney's
MICKEY MOUSE
THE CASE OF THE DAZZLING HOO-DOO
PART 3
MICKEY AND GOOFY ARE TRAPPED INSIDE AN ANCIENT RUIN BY THE HOO-DOO... A MECHANICAL CREATURE OPERATED WITH A REMOTE CONTROL BY EMIL EAGLE, A RUTHLESS SCIENTIST-INVENTOR WHO IS SEARCHING FOR A FABULOUS CRYSTAL CAPABLE OF TURNING DIRT INTO GOLD. GOOFY IS ALREADY UNDER THE HYPNOTIC INFLUENCE OF THE HOO-DOO'S BEAM, AND MICKEY, IN AN ATTEMPT TO ESCAPE, HAS DROPPED A STRANGE CRYSTAL JUNGLE JOE HAD TOLD HIM TO HIDE...
BEEP!
(GULP!) IF THAT THING DISCOVERS US, WE'RE GONERS!
YUK! YUK! I'M HOO-DOODLED!
MEANWHILE, IN HIS SECRET LABORATORY, EMIL EAGLE OBSERVES HIS MECHANICAL SERVANT...
BEEP!
WHAT'S THIS? MY TRUSTY ROCKHOUND HAS ABANDONED THE CHASE IN FAVOR OF A SHINY CRYSTAL!
HIS TRANSISTORS ARE ALL A TWITTER! PERHAPS IT IS THE ONE FOR WHICH I SEARCH! I SHALL ACTIVATE HIS RETRIEVING UNIT AND HAVE A CLOSER LOOK!
BEEP!
AS THE HOO-DOO PASSES THE CRYSTAL THROUGH THE SHAFT OF BRIGHT SUN-LIGHT, IT EMITS A BRILLIANT FLASH...

THE OVERSEAS COMICS PROGRAM

Western Publishing would continue producing Mickey Mouse serials for *Walt Disney's Comics* until 1971; they would produce shorter, one-part Mickey stories for another 12 years after that. But overall—due largely to rising paper costs and increased market competition—Western published fewer comic books after the late 1960s, and those that remained featured more reprints than new stories.

Western's slow decline coincided with an amazing rise in Disney comics activity around the world. In many markets—including the Nordic countries, where a Danish media company called the Gutenberghus Group began publishing Disney titles in 1948—Mickey and Donald pointedly succeeded where superheroes did not. By the late 1950s, continental Disney comics were ramping up from monthly to weekly publishing schedules, with the titles sometimes even outselling major news magazines.[2]

A side effect of ramped-up publication schedules was that Disney publishers needed new content faster than American licensees were able to serve it to them. In 1962, the Disney studio itself attempted to fill the gap. Publications director George Sherman launched the "Overseas Comic Book Program," or "Studio Program," in-house in Burbank, through which Disney would produce more than a thousand pages of original comics per year for use primarily by international publishers. Talents working with Western—notably Carl Fallberg and Paul Murry—began moonlighting for Disney; so too did Romano Scarpa and other Italian authors and artists. While some "Studio stories," as they came to be known, featured the Western-style setup of Mickey and Goofy as freelance detectives, Pete and the Blot were no longer their only foes—nor Chief O'Hara their only

Excerpt from "The Case of the Dazzling Hoo-Doo" (*Walt Disney's Comics and Stories* 330–332, 1968). Created in 1966 by writer Vic Lockman as Gyro Gearloose's unlucky rival, Evil Emil Eagle began to be portrayed as more powerful and dangerous when facing Mickey, as he does in this story.

Detail from "Trapped in Time" (*Walt Disney's Comics and Stories* 323–326, 1967); art by Paul Murry. Writers Cecil Beard and Alpine Harper ventured far from the standard formula of Mickey and Goofy as detectives: here they hide from a *real* Minotaur and its keepers, a surprising contrast from the fake monsters they unmasked in earlier stories.

boss. Other Studio stories moved even further afield; many were costume dramas casting Mickey in historical set-pieces.

The Studio stories were also called "S-coded" stories, referencing the way each was identified by a code denoting country of origin. "S" meant Disney *Studio*; as Denmark, France, and Brazil began producing material, D-, F-, and B-coded stories also emerged. Eventually, in 1990, Disney and its foreign licensees decided that the latter were producing enough original stories to fill their domestic comic books without help from Burbank.

Detail from "The Great Winks Robbery" (1975; American printing in *Walt Disney Showcase* 42, 1978). The initial *Mickey and the Sleuth* concept came from Vince Jefferds, Disney's vice president for sales promotions. Carl Fallberg and Cal Howard scripted the first few stories, after which artist Carson Van Osten scribbled rough layout drawings for each. Penciler Al Hubbard and inker Steve Steere created the final product. Later *Sleuth* stories were drawn by the Jaime Diaz Studio, a group in Argentina who handled most 1980s Studio Program art.

Original art by Paul Murry from "Desert Dilemma" (*Walt Disney's Comics and Stories* 464, 1979). While Floyd Gottfredson had often cast Peg Leg Pete as a smarter crook's sidekick, Murry's team made Pete the boss bad guy himself, often paired with a mustached weasel lackey. In later years the weasel got his own oafish helper; while today the pair are best known as Scuttle and Dum-Dum, they often went by aliases, such as this story's "Dr. Gantry" and "Galvin."

BRAZILIANS, FRENCHMEN, DUTCHMEN, AND DANES

The *Mickey and the Sleuth* and *Disney Goofy Classics* series both reflected an initiative within the Studio Program to standardize the stories' look. This standardization took place in 1971 via an extensive series of Mickey and Donald publications model sheets, in Mickey's case roughed out by Paul Murry and "finished" as final pencils by Tony Strobl.[3]

As we have noted, when Disney launched the Studio Program in 1962, overseas licensees wanted more Disney comics material to publish, but weren't in a position to make their own. Ten years on, however, publishers in Brazil, France, the Netherlands, and Denmark were actively training talent and creating new stories. The 1971 model sheets became a go-to art reference.

Plots were as important as art. Because the model sheets were drawn by Murry, local publishers looked to Murry-drawn stories for writers' references, resulting in stories that often followed the Western Publishing formulas.[4] But additional influences drifted into the works as well. At the Gutenberghus publishing offices in Denmark, staffers even tried to retool Carl Barks story formulas for Mickey—so a 1970s writers' guide could include story "variations" like these:

STORY TITLE: "DESERT DILEMMA"

PUBLICATION: WDC # 464

REGULAR COMIC LAYOUT

UN: ON MET TOUTE LA VAPEUR !
DEUX: ON SAUTE !
13
!
BRAOM !
TOUCHÉ! COULÉ!

Excerpt from "Mickey agent secret" (French *Le Journal de Mickey* 1923–1925, 1989); story by Jean-Luc Cochet, art by Cèsar Ferioli. Featuring a tougher, arguably more dangerous Pete than other French stories of the period, this 1930s-style thriller anticipated many more such "retro" Mickey adventures that Ferioli would later draw for the Danish Disney publisher.

Excerpt from "O Rapto De Herbie" (Brazilian *Mickey* 311, 1978); story by Primaggio Mantovi, art by Moacir Rodrigues and Rubens Cordeiro. When publisher Abril revived the *Mickey Mouse, Super Secret Agent* series, they followed Western Publishing's template: Rodrigues drew the cartoony Mickey and Goofy, while Cordeiro drew the realistic Herbie and his surroundings.

1. Mickey as the uncle of Morty and Ferdy [*sic*]. Just like the Donald Duck series. At home, on a fishing trip, camping, holidays in the wilderness, etc. [. . .]
2. Mickey Mouse as Minnie Mouse's boyfriend [put] to (unwanted and unwarranted) work. Shopping trips, furniture rearranging in the home, [. . .]
3. Mickey as the intelligent detective. Goofy included as an extra. Mickey is assisting the chief of police, O'Hara. Crimes of all types—from everyday ones to the most fantastic. . ."[5]

In practice, of course, unique Mickey stories could never be "just like the Donald Duck series"—because a temperamental, lazy Donald would naturally react to crises quite differently from an overwhelmed, driven Mickey. Yet quite a few stories, from Gutenberghus and elsewhere, tried to take this interchangeable approach for a while. The main thing that made Mickey special, for a plurality of writers unfamiliar with Disney history, was simply the "intelligent detective" theme. The standout Mickey stories of the 1970s,

1980s, and 1990s, then, were those in which something *beyond* that detective theme entered the mix.

Different creative teams had their own ways of adding "something beyond." Dutch publisher Oberon and its art editor, Daan Jippes, rediscovered Gottfredson's, Walsh's, and Manuel Gonzales's works. More extensive innovations came from Brazil, where Mickey talents of the 1970s and 1980s were affected—like the Dutch—by a burgeoning fandom for the past. In the early days, local publisher Abril hewed closely to the Studio stories' look and flavor. But in search of more depth and interest, Abril's team dug into preexisting Mickey lore, finding more far-flung canon to incorporate into their own.

The year 1978 saw French publisher Hachette expanding its production of original material—and along came new Mickey talents, including writer Jean-Luc Cochet and artists Claude Marin and Cèsar Ferioli. The group started out imitating the Studio Program style, but Gottfredson and Walsh influence seeped in too, Eega Beeva and all. Icing on the cake was the stories' art style, mimicking the concurrent Franco-Belgian school of humor comics.

Excerpt from "Riddle of the Runaway Sphinx" (*Mickey Mouse Adventures* [series I] 2, 1990). Mad professors Ecks and Doublex were fused into the two-headed "Dr. Doublecross" for stories in this series. Seen here: an example of their rather breathtaking handiwork.

Excerpt from "The Monastery Mystery" (Denmark, 1989; American printing in *Mickey Mouse Adventures* [series I] 8, 1991). The art for Mickey and Goofy's adventure in "Ubet" was provided by a "Tello-Team" (group of artists at Josep Tello's Spanish art studio) that included Ignasi Calvet Esteban.

IF THEY'RE THIEVES, WE MIGHT BE ABLE TO CATCH THEM IN THE ACT!
GAWRSH! IT'S SO DARK IN HERE, WE'LL NEVER SEE 'EM!
KLONK
RIGHT! ALL THE BETTER FOR US TO DO THIS!
OW!
AND LET'S NOT FORGET YOU, SHALL WE?
YEOW!
OHHH... I'D BETTER MAKE US SOME LIGHT TO SEE BY!
I'M ALREADY SEEIN' LOTSA LIGHTS AN' STARS!
OHMIGOSH! WHOEVER HIT US MUST HAVE BEEN THIEVES, GOOFY! LOOK!
THEY TOOK THUH JEWELLED FLOWER FROM THUH STATUE'S HAND!

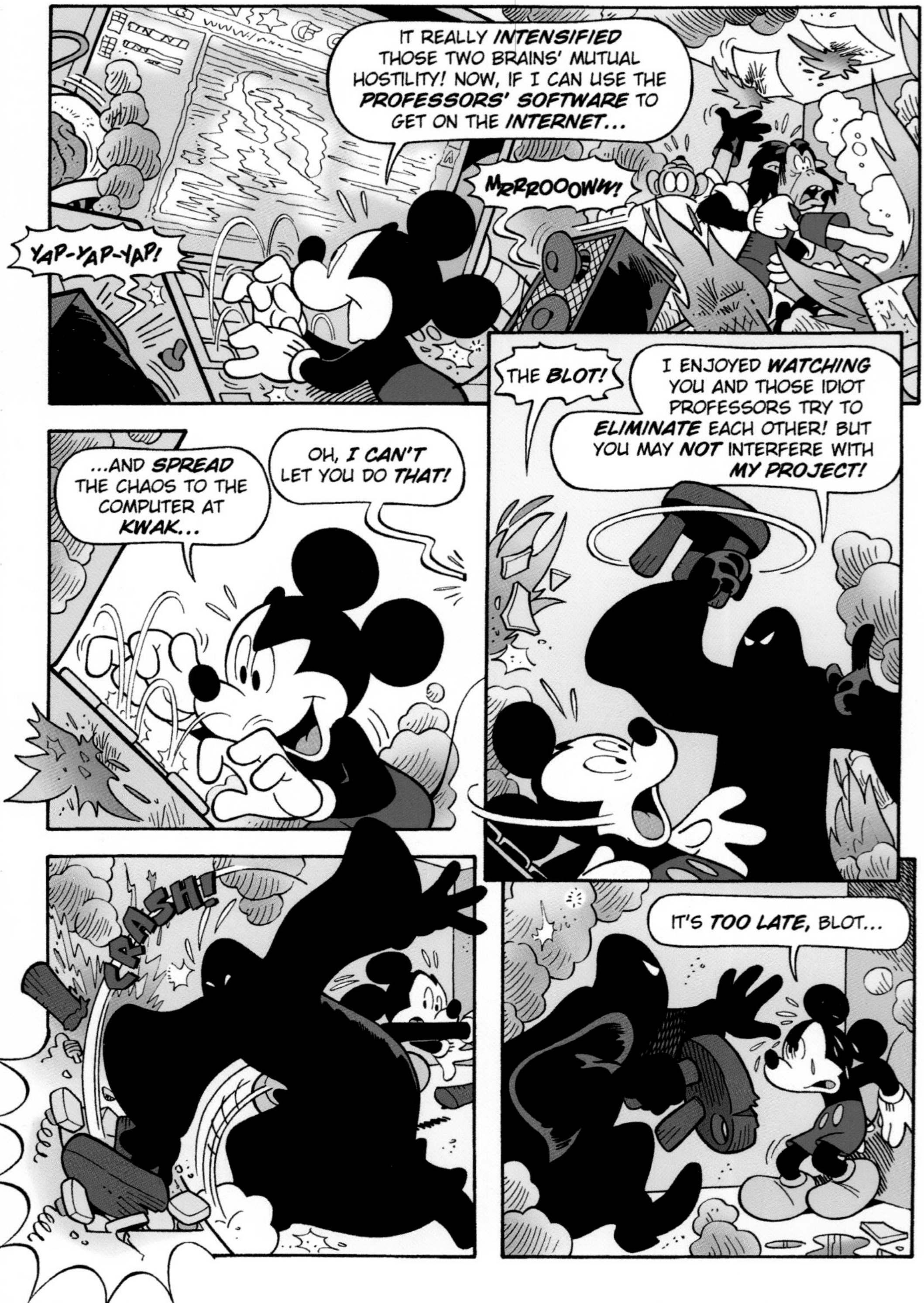
IT REALLY INTENSIFIED THOSE TWO BRAINS' MUTUAL HOSTILITY! NOW, IF I CAN USE THE PROFESSORS' SOFTWARE TO GET ON THE INTERNET...
MRRROOOWW!
YAP-YAP-YAP!
...AND SPREAD THE CHAOS TO THE COMPUTER AT KWAK...
OH, I CAN'T LET YOU DO THAT!
THE BLOT!
I ENJOYED WATCHING YOU AND THOSE IDIOT PROFESSORS TRY TO ELIMINATE EACH OTHER! BUT YOU MAY NOT INTERFERE WITH MY PROJECT!
CRASH!
IT'S TOO LATE, BLOT...

Excerpt from "Quadruple Threat" (Denmark, 2000; American printing in *Mickey Mouse Adventures* [series II] 11, 2006); story by Don Markstein, art by Joaquin Cañizares Sanchez. Modern times bring Mickey new opportunities for adventure. Confronted with a world-conquering supercomputer powered by simulated cat and dog brains, Mickey uses a Trojan computer virus to ramp up the brains' hostility—and induce them to fight like cats and dogs.

Excerpt from "A Phantom Blot Bedtime Story" (*Mickey Mouse Adventures* [series I] 8, 1991). While many stories show the Blot as a long-suffering victim in his own mind, only this one gives him a hero-worshipping daughter, a fascinating conceit never used again. The "Phantom Brat?"—so-called in an editorial feature—seems to despise Mickey too, but only due to the wicked way that the Blot characterizes him in his bedtime stories.

GLADSTONE AND DISNEY COMICS

The fan scholarship that had led international talents to discover Gottfredson and Walsh eventually affected American Disney comics. When collectors Russ Cochran and Bruce Hamilton formed Another Rainbow Publishing in 1980, their signature project was *The Carl Barks Library*, a complete anthology of Barks's Disney works. But then came Gladstone, a newsstand comics imprint developed to take over the American Disney license from Western.

Launching in 1986, Gladstone's ongoing titles reprinted Gottfredson's Mickey strip serials—and reprinted international Disney stories, including the works of Scarpa, in English for the first time. A new generation of fans discovered Mickey at his most dynamic. Editor-in-chief Byron Erickson brought aboard new Disney comics talent, such as Scrooge and Donald writer-artists Don Rosa and William Van Horn.

But no new Mickey talents . . . yet.

That situation changed in 1990, however, when Disney Consumer Products decided to publish its domestic American comic books in-house. Combining staffers from the Studio

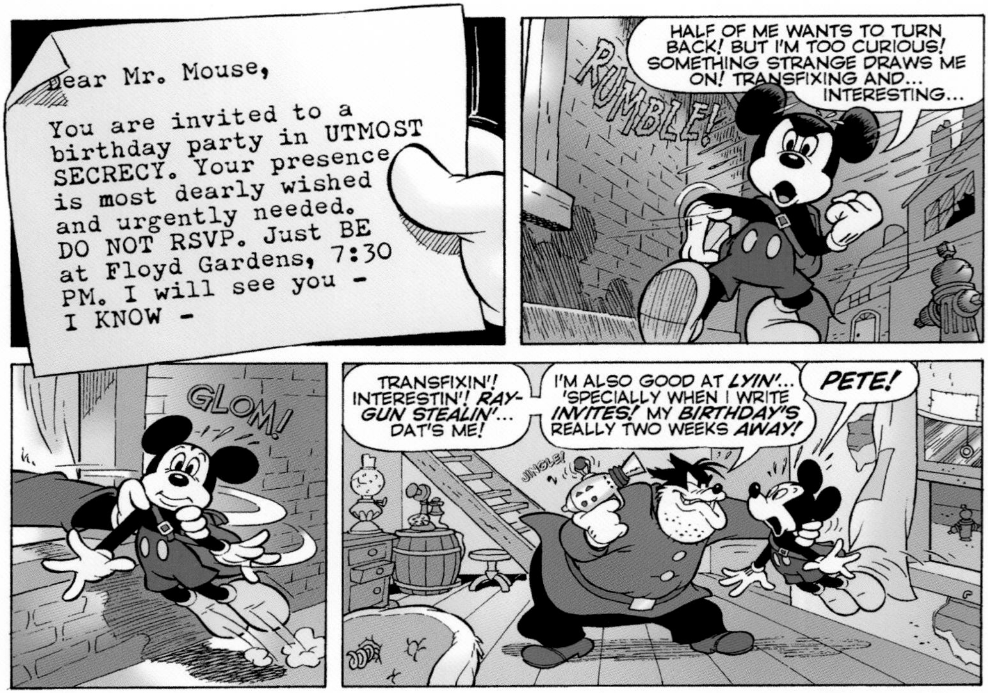

Excerpt from "History Re-Petes Itself" (Denmark, 2000; American printing in *Walt Disney's Comics and Stories* 654, 2005). Scarpa's first pages drawn for Egmont reverberate with Gottfredson inspiration — in this case, from "Mickey Mouse Sails for Treasure Island", in which a similar note lures Mickey to Mouseton's shadowy waterfront.

Excerpt from "The Treasure of Sierra Motty" (Denmark, 2003; American printing in *Mickey Mouse* 282, 2005). Artist Paco Rodriguez, better known for his tales of Mickey's nephews, Morty and Ferdie, adds amazing dynamism to a conflict between Mickey, Minnie, and Eli Squinch — and impressive detail to scenes of booby traps in an underground treasure palace.

Program with a hotbed of younger talent, the Disney Comics imprint began pumping out new stories at whirlwind speed, and a monthly title called *Mickey Mouse Adventures* was among the results. In an editorial piece, series editor David Cody Weiss presented *Mickey Mouse Adventures*' mission statement:

> *By the end of the Eighties, the Adventurous Mouse was mostly a fond memory... [but now] the new stories for Mickey Mouse Adventures harken directly back to the old-fashioned rock-'em, sock-'em thrill-a-minute adventures that made Mickey an adventure hero...*[6]

While Disney's in-house imprint only lasted a few years, the initiative brought up-and-coming talents like artist Stephen DeStefano and writers Michael T. Gilbert and Lee Nordling to Mickey for the first time. And when Disney Comics shuttered, Gilbert, DeStefano, and other former Gladstone

-:GASP!:- OR EVEN AN ENTIRE AZTEC CITY, BUILT UNDER-GROUND!
WOW! I'D LOVE TO SPEND WEEKS EXPLORING THIS PLACE! BUT FOR NOW I DON'T HAVE TIME!
THAT LIGHT AHEAD LOOKS LIKE A FLASHLIGHT! AND I BET I KNOW WHO'S AT THE OTHER END!
DRAT THIS CHEAP BOOK! I CAN BARELY MAKE OUT TH' PICTURES!
A HAT—NO, A HELMET! SO TH' PICTOGRAM IS TALKIN' ABOUT TH' CRYSTAL HELMET! TH' HELM OF MOCTEZUMA III!

Excerpt from "The River of Time" (Italy, 1998; American translation in *Mickey Mouse Adventures* [series II] 2, 2005); story by Francesco Artibani and Tito Faraci, art by Corrado Mastantuono. While this is superficially the story of Mickey and Pete salvaging the sunken *Steamboat Willie*, it is also the story of their first-ever team-up — with Pete actively wondering whether he should become Mickey's friend instead of his foe. Would Gottfredson's Mickey and Pete get this close? Maybe not, but it's a fascinating experiment.

and Disney talents were already moving on — to shape the *next* chapters in Mickey's history.

EGMONT'S "NEW MICKEY"

The ripple effect of Gladstone and Disney Comics on European comics production began in 1989. Don Rosa, Gladstone's most prominent *Uncle Scrooge* writer/artist, sought freelance work with a European Disney comics publisher, and Nancy Dejgaard, editor-in-chief of Gutenberghus in Denmark, was interested. Soon afterward, in 1991, when Dejgaard needed to hire a new Disney comics managing editor, Rosa recommended she avail herself of Byron Erickson's services.[7] It was a portentous moment.

Since the demise of the Gladstone Disney line, former editor-in-chief Erickson had worked with other comics firms. But he missed the Disney characters, in particular Mickey: whose Gottfredson and Scarpa adventures Erickson had reprinted, but whom Erickson had never been able to oversee in *new* stories. Now, taking a major editorial position in Denmark — at the creative house which, just then, renamed itself from Gutenberghus to Egmont — Erickson became a Mickey Mouse writer and, for several years, was Egmont's only Mickey editor, writing new guidelines for his team:

A boyish, exuberant little guy, [Mickey] gets easily bored with domestic life... his imaginative, inventive mind seizes on anything even the least bit out of the ordinary and follows it into a full-blown adventure...

> *Mickey is sometimes asked to help solve a particularly baffling crime by [Chief] O'Hara, but Mickey is not an all-knowing Sherlock Holmes... [he wins out] through a combination of single-minded concentration, never-say-die effort, and (sometimes) pure luck.*[8]

Joachim Stahl, editor at German Egmont subsidiary Ehapa, led a team studying reader reactions. While Donald Duck had previously been young fans' favorite, Stahl discovered that "the new Mickey stories are even more popular than Donald... Mickey is no unbearably smart super-mouse... but a likeable, clever little guy."[9]

Eventually other Egmont editors, some trained by Erickson, grounded the "new" Mickey's entire world. Erickson himself encouraged writers to feature a grimly determined Mickey in sci-fi-centric storylines. One of the present authors, David Gerstein, an Egmont editor from 1997–2004, handled stories reintroducing Gottfredson-era costars like Butch and Eega Beeva. And editor Henning Kure *(Valhalla)* jumped even further back in time: the stories his unit created, mostly for Egmont's comics pocketbooks, featured a hyper-impulsive, almost Iwerks-era characterization of Mickey, rushing eagerly into danger with the likes of giant penguins and foot-shaped space aliens.

Not every transformation lasts forever. In the late 2000s, the end of Byron Erickson's tenure as Egmont creative director also effectively ended the "new wave" of Gottfredson-inspired Mickey stories. But Mickey—the comics adventurer—would find ways of carrying on.

Excerpt from "Topolino e il mistero della voce spezzata" ("The Case of the Cut-Off Calls," Italian *Topolino* 1834, 1991); story by Silvano Mezzavilla, art by Giorgio Cavazzano. According to a survey by *Topolino* editors, readers considered this atmospheric tale by Mezzavilla, a former screenwriter, to be the finest Mickey story of its decade. In it, a late-night storm is spattering Mouseton when somehow, suddenly, everyone in town gets the same phone call at once: a voice begging for help—and only Mickey can save the day.

AL COSPETTO DELLA REGINA DELLO HEL...
COMPLIMENTI! SIETE I SOLI AD AVER SUPERATO L'ESAME NEGLI ULTIMI SECOLI E AD AVER POTUTO ACCEDERE FINO A ME!
QUALE ONORE!

MODERN ITALIAN MAESTROS

While Brazilian and Danish creative houses may no longer produce long Mickey Mouse adventures today, another country still finds an ambitious comics Mouse bounding from strength to strength. We are speaking, of course, of Italy, where the verve that fueled Romano Scarpa in the late 1950s never entirely left the scene.

One prime source of both verve and innovation throughout the late 1960s and 1970s was the artist Giorgio Cavazzano. Starting out as Scarpa's inker, Cavazzano was drawing solo stories by 1967—adopting a style of loose-limbed, abstract, emotional characters that set a new standard for his Disney contemporaries. At the same time he drew inspiration from an old master:

> *I couldn't believe my eyes: an artist could use the Mickey Mouse characters to create a very unique and intense adventurous atmosphere—without losing the Disney ambience. [. . .] Thanks to Floyd Gottfredson, I found my artistic style.*[10]

Several long costume-drama stories in the late 1980s presented Cavazzano with his first real chance to recreate that adventurous atmosphere. Fans and colleagues saw a driven, flawed Mickey as nuanced as his Gottfredson inspiration. Before long a third generation of Italian Disney writers—including Tito Faraci and Francesco Artibani—were similarly dosing their Mickey tales with fallibility, dark humor, and enthusiasm.

The 21st century has seen another popular Italian "maestro" continuing where Scarpa, and occasionally Gottfredson, left off. Andrea "Casty" Castellan has delved into Mickey

Excerpt from "Topolino e la spada di ghiaccio" (Italian *Topolino* 1411, 1982). The "Ice Sword" trilogy finds Massimo De Vita arguably at the peak of his powers. Argaar and its inhabitants follow in a famous tradition of medieval-themed novels and fairy tales; but for two generations of Italian readers, this fantasy world is still 100 percent Disney.

Detail from "Topolino e l'Atlantide continente perduto" (Italian *Topolino* 1638, 1987). In the wake of this adventure involving an asteroid strike, Italy's Mickey time travel stories became an institution: even today, Professors Spike Marlin and Zachary Zapotec have their time machine warmed up in the basement of the Mouseton Museum, ready for Mickey to investigate long-ago puzzles.

Excerpt from "The Weregoof's Curse" (Italian *Topolino* 1102, 1977); story and pencils by Romano Scarpa, inks by Sandro Del Conte. Mickey and Ellroy hit Pete, Trudy Van Tubb, and inventor cousin Portis with Portis's own species-changing serum.

Excerpt from "The World to Come" (Italian *Topolino* 2721–2724, 2008). The Rhyming Man is out to conquer the world—but after a thrilling robot battle, Mickey, Minnie, and Eega Beeva eventually confront his flying fortress in a fight to the finish.

storylines that pick up continuity from the likes of "The Delta Dimension"—while at other times introducing ongoing plot threads and costars of Casty's own. Characters like the over-eager young explorer Eurasia Toft stoke Mickey's sense of adventure, not just his quest for catching crooks. Of course, in other Casty tales, conflicts with Pete, Mortimer, and classic villains happily continue as before.

In major "event" projects from Disney Italia's own headquarters, new Mickey costume-drama stories carry on, too. Just as Mickey could live in steampunk London with the Sleuth, he can become a medieval wizard for a modern miniseries—or, as a play-acting Jim Hawkins, set out on his first-ever treasure hunt with Peg Leg Pete as a play-acting Long John Silver. Of course, we know Mickey and Pete really have a lifetime of treasure hunts—and treasured comics—behind them.

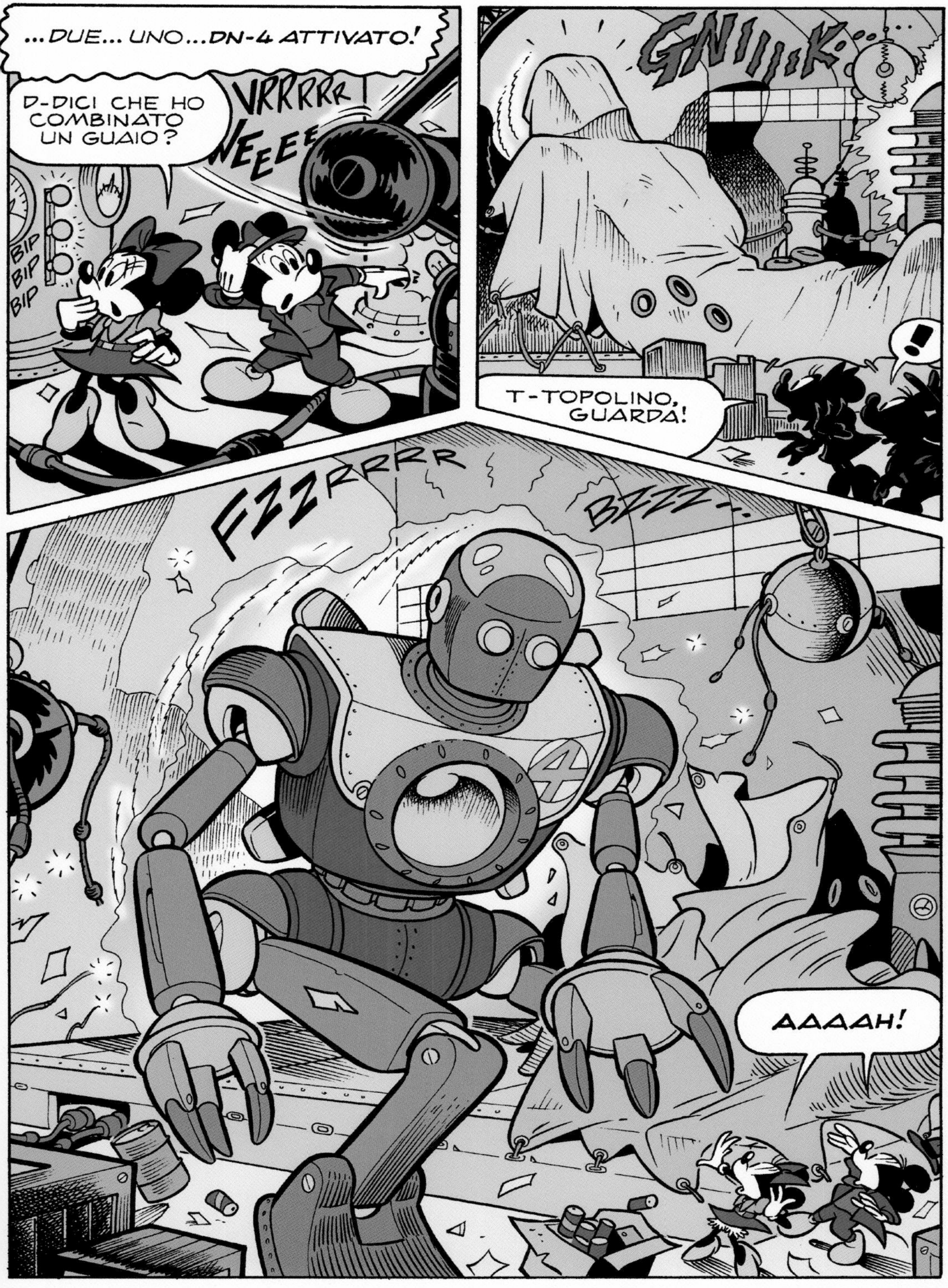
...DUE... UNO...DN-4 ATTIVATO!
D-DICI CHE HO COMBINATO UN GUAIO?
VRRRRR
NEEEE
BIP BIP BIP
GNIIIIK...
!
T-TOPOLINO, GUARDA!
FZZRRRRR
BZZZ..
AAAAH!

CHAPTER TWELVE

Twenty-First-Century Mouse

By the dawn of the 21st century, Mickey Mouse had been a phenomenon for over 70 years. Over the course of that time he had enjoyed a cartoon career of unprecedented success, branching out from his original medium into countless others, and achieving a level of worldwide recognition that surpassed that of any other pen-and-ink character. Along the way he had ridden the tide of changing fashion, emerging in a different light for each new generation—and, by 2001, had outlived almost all of the generation that had brought him to life in the first place.

But though Walt and his generation had passed on by that time, The Walt Disney Company itself was still alive and thriving and still proudly claimed Mickey as its corporate symbol and one of its greatest assets. Now a new Disney generation, primed by the efforts of the 1990s, took Mickey's career in hand. The company would continue to promote its established line of Mickey merchandise and celebrate his earlier triumphs; but in the meantime, a variety of forces within Disney would continue to seek new outlets for the famous character.

Visual development art by Jordan Lamarre-Wan from Junction Point Studios' video game *Disney Epic Mickey* (2010). A heroic Mickey clutches his magic paintbrush while dangling from the claw of the evil "Shadow Blot," a kaiju based loosely on the comics' Phantom Blot.

MICKEY MOUSEWORKS* AND *DISNEY'S HOUSE OF MOUSE

We've already seen how the Disney studio embraced the new medium of television in the 1950s and how Mickey Mouse played an important part in those efforts. By the early

Critical to the success of the early *Mickey MouseWorks* TV shorts were the voice performances by Wayne Allwine, who for this show deliberately mimicked the written cadence of Mickey's Gottfredson-era comic strip dialogue. In *Mickey's New Car*, seen here, Allwine also provided a wealth of oddball car sound effects.

21st century the television landscape had changed radically from those early days, and the studio responded with a variety of programming, some of it featuring Mickey.

This programming was inaugurated with *Mickey MouseWorks*, an aggregation of the first Mickey cartoons created by Disney Television Animation (DTVA). Initially previewed in other showcases, the series made its broadcast debut in 1999. "We've always wanted to do a [Mickey] show," Barry Blumberg, DTVA's Senior Vice President, stated during *MouseWorks*' development, "but we've never had an idea that would make everybody happy and comfortable [until now]."[1] Executive producer Roberts Gannaway told the press: "We want to remind people of who Mickey's character is, to get away from his icon-only status." *Mickey MouseWorks* would showcase Mickey's adventurous side: *Variety* noted that the series "displayed a feisty and combative stable of characters as they were in their prime."[2]

As if to help these energetic incarnations find their places in the wider Disney universe, *Mickey MouseWorks* evolved in 2001 into *Disney's House of Mouse*. This more lavish series, while featuring the same shorts as *Mickey MouseWorks*, wrapped them in framing sequences with Mickey, Minnie, and friends as hosts and performers at the House of Mouse,

a comedy club where Disney feature film characters came to unwind. Alas for Mickey's gang, landlord Peg Leg Pete owned the House of Mouse building, with the gang's tenancy contingent on the idea that "the show must go on"; if they were ever unable to perform, Pete could throw them out and raise the rent.

With their well-received use of an adventurous, funny Mickey, *Mickey MouseWorks* and *Disney's House of Mouse* led to cross-promotions with Buena Vista Home Entertainment, which derived two direct-to-video "clip show" features from the programs: *Mickey's Magical Christmas: Snowed in at the House of Mouse* (2001) and *Mickey's House of Villains* (2002). These, in turn, captured enough attention that Home Entertainment saw fit to create an entirely original Mickey feature film in 2004, aimed at the same audience.

Hansel and Gretel tells its Mickey-Minnie fairy tale in pantomime, set to the strains of Camille Saint-Saëns's "Danse Macabre." Art director Mike Moon developed the picture's unique visual style, with background painters Tim Barnes, Chris Roszak, Sy Thomas, and Don Watson producing evocative scenes of the witch's house and woods.

MICKEY, DONALD, GOOFY: THE THREE MUSKETEERS

Mickey, Donald, Goofy: The Three Musketeers concept art, early 1980s. Alexandre Dumas's original *Three Musketeers* story features the eponymous trio of Athos, Porthos, and Aramis with their wannabe-musketeer friend D'Artagnan; at Disney, an early plan was for Mickey, Donald, and Goofy to portray the big three with José Carioca as D'Artagnan. In August 1984, this version was announced as a prospective 1989 theatrical release — but ended up on the shelf for more than a decade.

Directed by Donovan Cook and developed, more or less, from various treatments created in the 1970s and 1980s, *Mickey Donald, Goofy: The Three Musketeers* was another "literary" story, following on the heels of *Mickey's Christmas Carol* and *The Prince and the Pauper*. This outing strays farther than ever from its putative source: this time, apart from its title and the convention of 17th-century French musketeers, the film has little to do with Dumas or his tale. Instead, it spins an original story of three peasants, played by Mickey, Donald, and Goofy, who as children meet the Dumas characters and grow up aspiring to be like them. Despite their appeals to Peg Leg Pete, the captain of the musketeers, their ambitions seem hopeless — not only because of their lowly social station, but also because of their bumbling inability to carry out the simplest of tasks. At length Pete assigns the three incompetents as bodyguards to Princess Minnie, hoping to get rid of them, and facilitate his own plot to kidnap Minnie, in one stroke. But the three heroes fumble their way to an almost accidental victory, vanquishing Pete and his henchmen and uniting Mickey with Minnie at story's end, while Donald and Goofy find their own happy endings. Goofy's ladylove, in a throwback to earlier times, turns out to be Clarabelle Cow, here oddly cast as a lieutenant to Pete. Even more oddly, this film expands on *The Prince and the Pauper*'s musical conceit, adapting the melodies of Tchaikovsky, Grieg, and other composers as songs for the film's narrator, a singing turtle ostensibly derived from Toby Tortoise in *The Tortoise and the Hare*.

The Wasteland of *Disney Epic Mickey* was home to sentient versions of classic Disney Parks rides, purportedly designed by Oswald. After initial designs gave the living rides a grim, scary look, this sketch for an *"It's a Small World"* spoof was the first to capture the sillier ambience that director Warren Spector wanted: "the combination of fidelity to the real ride and the whimsy of a world created from discarded stuff by a cartoon rabbit."[1]

VIDEO GAMES

As we have seen, The Walt Disney Company plunged into the world of video games from the earliest days of the infant

industry; the 1990s, in particular, featured a number of well-remembered and technically accomplished Mickey titles. Not surprisingly, Mickey has figured heavily in many more recent games as well. For a while, they were disproportionately children's games: after the popular, teen-targeted triumphs that were *Mickey Mania* and the *Illusion* series in the 1990s—all featuring Mickey's bold adventurer role—Mickey seemed to drift slowly into simpler products, such as racing, Tetris, and trivia titles.

Yet even as Mickey busied himself zooming around the racetrack in one game, in another game Mickey was on the way to regaining his throne—literally—as the adventure hero of yore. *Kingdom Hearts* (2002), the first in a famous series of role-playing games (RPGs), began with a chance meeting between Square Enix video game designer/director Tetsuya Nomura and two colleagues, Shinji Hashimoto and Hironobu Sakaguchi. Nomura was looking to feature a world-famous fantasy brand in a three-dimensional RPG; Hashimoto and Sakaguchi were in talks with Disney about an unrelated project and knew Disney to be seeking a local partner.[3] The qualifications of all three men as designers, producers, and/or

creators of the popular *Final Fantasy* games ensured that Disney would seriously consider Nomura's proposal.

As the scenario shook out, *Kingdom Hearts* stars a human boy named Sora who teams up with Court Wizard Donald and Captain Goofy in their quest to find their "lost" king Mickey. Mickey's restricted role, mandated by contractual requirements, actually gave him a *stronger* presence in this game than he might have had otherwise.[4] When the game became a best seller, Mickey was freed up for big roles in its sequels, cast as the same brave-but-irreverent battler the first game had established: as powerful and endearing as any bold adventurer Mickey before him. As one game reviewer admiringly put it, King Mickey is "less bashful . . . and more [a] glorious warrior, the type of fighter who could even take Sephiroth [*Final Fantasy VII* villain] one-on-one in man-on-mouse combat."[5]

The next step, almost inevitably, was a fully Mickey-centric fantasy game, which eventually was to become the *Disney Epic Mickey* series. In 2004, Buena Vista Games (BVG)—the Disney subsidiary that also handled Disney's end of *Kingdom Hearts* development—hosted eight college undergrads as an intern-based "Think Tank." The interns were challenged to "make Mickey Mouse cool again, preserving his family-friendly charm while also bringing him back to his more mischievous roots . . . to cater to the 'core' demographic of video gamers."[6] As participant Sean Vanaman recalled:

This publicity setup pairs a standard *Disney Mickey Mouse* publicity pose with a "Main Street" preliminary background painting for *The Adorable Couple*. In the finished cartoon, Mickey and Minnie tap-dance past a more detailed version of this cityscape while singing along with the series' theme song.

In *The Adorable Couple*, a conflict between optimistic Mickey and Minnie (seen here) and pessimistic Donald and Daisy deliberately plays the couples as comedic overexaggerations of their usual personas.

In *Wish Upon a Coin*, Mickey and Minnie sing their way through a moment of bliss by Snow White's wishing well—never guessing that they're about to be robbed by an as-yet-unseen Pete (who, upon making his appearance, momentarily starts singing, too).

We quickly found . . . a yen to steep ourselves in the complex visual and iconographic history of the Mouse himself. [Mickey was once] a mouthpiece for a creator [Walt] struggling against his own goliathan enemies as he tried to give birth to the world's first great animation studio. We liked that. We shared his spunk.[7]

The result, at this early stage, was the story of an "ink-based" Phantom Blot—in essence, a magical version of his *Mickey MouseWorks* persona—pulling Mickey into a world called Wasteland. This was a home to "forgotten" characters like Mickey's piqued predecessor, none other than Oswald the Lucky Rabbit, soon to be reacquired by The Walt Disney Company and then given a major role in this game.[8] In 2005, when acclaimed video game designer Warren Spector (*Deus Ex*) came to BVG with games to pitch, Disney "pitched me the Think Tank's concept and I was just totally blown away."[9]

Spector and his crew at Junction Point Studios spent years fleshing out the plot, adding to its cast Yen Sid, the Sorcerer from "The Sorcerer's Apprentice," portrayed here as the creator of Wasteland. In the game's backstory, a Wasteland map on Yen Sid's worktable was a portal to the real place; when a young Mickey tested out Yen Sid's magic

Drawn by John Loter, this updated version of the classic shorts' opening headshot—first featured in a 1997 marketing guide—went on to serve its predecessors' function when positioned at the start of *Mickey MouseWorks* and *Disney's House of Mouse* Mickey shorts.

Visual development art from *Mickey Mouse*. Donald and Mickey "are buddies," show-runner Paul Rudish stated in 2013, "but they . . . can bicker like brothers. Donald can be very antagonistic, and Mickey can only take it for so long."

IMAGED BY HERITAGE AUCTIONS, HA.COM

brushes on the map, he had unknowingly created a giant "Shadow Blot" that conquered Oswald's town. Now, years later, Wasteland was a dystopia; and Mickey must team up with a resentful Oswald, take the Sorcerer's magic brushes, and set things right. Released in 2010, *Disney Epic Mickey* bolstered interest in Oswald, brought new fans to Mickey—and was generally unlike any Mickey story ever told. But for fans of "self-aware" cartoon stories, it was the next best thing to another *Roger Rabbit*; its sequels, for various platforms—*Epic Mickey 2: The Power of Two* and *Epic Mickey: Power of Illusion* (both 2012)—continued its tales of "toon" war and peace for several years.

CHILDREN'S TELEVISION AND HOME VIDEO

During Walt Disney's lifetime he had maintained a strong personal concept of Mickey's personality. Seemingly contradictory character traits—the bold adventurer, contrasted with the passive nice guy—were nothing of the kind, as far as Walt was concerned; he saw them simply as facets of Mickey's complex, evolving character. In the post-Walt years, the studio's treatment of the Mouse changed dramatically. Now those varying qualities in Mickey's makeup could be isolated

Cel setup from an unidentified late 1990s short. After many years in which a polo shirt and jeans were Mickey's default wardrobe choice, the cartoons of this era—beginning with *Runaway Brain* and continuing here—marked a decisive return to the original red-shorts design.

In "The Carol of the Bells," a segment in *Mickey's Twice Upon a Christmas*, early CGI versions of Mickey and Donald watch nervously as an (offscreen) Minnie and Daisy try to outperform one another in an ice show.

Publicity still for *Mickey's New Car*, the first-premiered *Mickey MouseWorks* cartoon in 1999. There's always a great big beautiful tomorrow for Mickey and Minnie.

As ever, modern Mickey merchandise continues to blast off for the future while carrying along beloved past traditions. Decades after Ingersoll, a nostalgic 1930s-style Mickey appears on a cutting-edge 2015 Apple Watch design.

and used for a range of purposes. Mickey was, in effect, a flexible actor who could be adapted to the project at hand.

His friendly, non-threatening side was duly appropriated for toddler-friendly programming. In 1999, the direct-to-video special *Mickey's Once Upon a Christmas* featured a stylized, big-eyed Mickey and Minnie in a sentimental adaptation of O. Henry's "The Gift of the Magi." Several years later, *Mickey's Twice Upon a Christmas* turned fairly similar designs into some of the first CGI versions of Mickey and the gang. Subsequent computer-animated cable television series, including *Mickey Mouse Clubhouse*, *Minnie's Bow-Toons*, and *Mickey and the Roadster Racers*, resulted in a sub-franchise that seemed to firmly relegate Mickey to much younger audiences. That said, *Clubhouse*—created by *Mickey MouseWorks*' Roberts Gannaway—did preserve morsels of Disney history in its own way: incorporating vintage bit players, from Super Goof to Salty the Seal, into the action whenever possible. To date, *Clubhouse* and *Bow-Toons* mark the *only* animated appearances of Millie and Melody, Minnie Mouse's nieces from a handful of 1960s comics.

MICKEY MOUSE AND A TRIUMPHANT RETURN TO THE SCREEN

At the same time, other creators more aware of Mickey's pop culture standing were exploring alternate possibilities for a

more mature audience. In 2013 the studio debuted a new *Mickey Mouse* television series that in some ways reinvented Mickey and his friends. The 1950s theatrical and television cartoons had sacrificed Mickey's classic appearance for a more fashionable midcentury design mode; now the 2013 series updated the characters' design for a look more in keeping with contemporary television cartoons. On the flipside, the "updated" designs were familiar in many respects: while exaggerated, they were exaggerated *specifically from* early 1930s character models—even a pantsless Goofy and a peg-legged Pete, the first time such models were adapted for any kind of new animation.

Paul Rudish, producer and supervising director for the series, reached back to vintage designs for a reason. "As a kid, I was always into all the Disney classic *everything*," he explained in 2013. "I always responded to the black-and-white cartoons: the original introduction to Mickey."[10] While trying to be edgier and wilder than what came before, Rudish and his team—including character designer Stephen DeStefano, of 1990s *Mickey Mouse Adventures* comic book fame—worked hard to show that they knew their Mickey

WALT DISNEY'S
MICKEY MOUSE
in
"GET A HORSE!"

history. It was no coincidence, for instance, that the first season included a return battle between Mickey and the sentient hot dogs from *The Karnival Kid* (1929).[11] When other episodes repeatedly showed a tense Mickey struggling to beat the clock in time-sensitive crises, or to fight the unfair forces of fate, Rudish cited Ted Sears's mid-1930s character analysis as his raison d'être: "Mickey is most amusing when in a serious predicament trying to accomplish some purpose under difficulties."

While Disney Television Animation produced the series, with individual episodes written and devised within the studio, the actual animation was outsourced to Mercury Filmworks in Canada. Voice work, too, marked a departure; while Bret Iwan was Disney's main Mickey Mouse voice artist at this point, Rudish instead utilized Chris Diamantopoulos, who delivered a Mickey at once snappier than most and more 1930s in tone: "Walt remains the ideal Mickey," Diamantopoulos said of his chief influence.[12]

In advance of its release, *Get a Horse!* was promoted as a long-lost vintage cartoon, keeping its modern CGI sequence a surprise until the premiere. As part of the effort to make *Get a Horse!* seem antique, director Lauren MacMullan drew this vintage-style poster featuring an early 1929 Mickey model.

A promotional cel setup for *Get a Horse!* shows early-sound-era exaggeration deployed for the fun of it, with Mickey transforming his leg into a staircase for Minnie to ascend.

Mickey's official 70th anniversary portrait, painted by John Hench for Disney Art Classics in 1998. For this painting Hench added a personal touch invoking Walt himself: Mickey is seen here wearing Walt's casual orange sweater, habitually worn at work during his later years. In addition, Hench subtly suggested Mickey's age by giving him reading glasses and a slight graying at the temples.

EPILOGUE

And so, as Mickey approaches the century mark, he remains a vital, versatile, and widely loved figure in the cartoon universe. The passing decades might have rendered him obsolete, but instead they have served to add new layers of legend to his persona. Today, he is known in every country, by every generation, and in a wide variety of guises, backgrounds, and media. Surely Walt Disney never imagined such an all-encompassing worldwide mantle of fame when he first brought forth his cartoon hero, in haste and desperation, in 1928.

Then again, perhaps he did. If we've learned one thing about Walt Disney, it's that he never hesitated to dream big, to break down perceived barriers and embrace unlimited possibilities. That, indeed, was one of the key traits he passed along to Mickey Mouse. It's been remarked many times that Walt was Mickey, Mickey was Walt—and nowhere is that more evident than in the iconic scenes of Mickey eagerly improvising an airplane and taking to the skies; scaling a beanstalk and challenging a giant; donning a Sorcerer's hat and "conducting" the very courses of the stars and the planets. That joyous, wholehearted celebration of life was at the core of Walt's spirit—and the same spirit was, and still is, embodied in his most personal creation: Mickey Mouse. As long as Mickey lives, that carefree spirit will continue to venture forward, with boundless enthusiasm and great good humor, toward distant horizons we cannot yet even imagine.

GAWRSH 70!
70 HUGS

Endnotes

INTRODUCTION

1 Andy Warhol, *The Andy Warhol Diaries*, 379.
2 Story meeting notes, *Mickey's Revival Party*, June 27, 1939 (Walt Disney Archives [WDA]).
3 Paul Rotha, *The Film till Now*, 120.
4 John Updike, "The Mystery of Mickey Mouse," in Craig Yoe and Janet Morra-Yoe (eds.), *The Art of Mickey Mouse*, 8.
5 Quoted in Robert Tieman, *The Mickey Mouse Treasures*, 34.
6 Press release, Museum of Modern Art, New York, November 25, 1936.
7 Quoted in "Mouse and Man," *Time*, December 27, 1937, 19–21.
8 Quoted in Harry Carr, "The Only Unpaid Movie Star," 57.
9 Quoted in Hooper Fowler, "Interview with Hooper Fowler," in Kathy Merlock Jackson (ed.), *Conversations with Walt Disney*, 112.
10 Quoted in Tieman, 35.
11 Quoted in Katherine and Richard Greene, *Inside the Dream. The Personal Story of Walt Disney*, 40.
12 United Artists press release, April 16, 1934.
13 Quoted in Tieman, 35.

CHAPTER ONE

1 See, for example, Barrier, *Hollywood Cartoons*, 48–49; Barrier, *The Animated Man*, 55–57; Gabler, *Walt Disney*, 106–13; Thomas, *Walt Disney*, 85–88.
2 See Bob Thomas's interview with Ub Iwerks, ca. 1956, and Gottfredson to David R. Smith, July 21, 1981 (WDA). Thomas Andrae and Michael Barrier have researched the Meek connection more extensively.
3 Iwerks to George Sherman, July 30, 1970 (WDA).
4 See Barrier, *The Animated Man*, 57. Barrier based this claim on his interview with Hugh Harman, December 3, 1973, and Milt Gray's interview with Paul Smith, March 22, 1978.
5 See Dave Smith, "Ub Iwerks, 1901–1971," *Funnyworld* 14, 34; and Ub Iwerks to Bob Thomas, quoted in *Walt's People*, vol. 10, 43.
6 *Mickey Mouse* daily comic strip, April 24, 1930. At this date, the strip was still written by Walt Disney.
7 Iwerks quoted in Dave Smith, "Ub Iwerks, 1901–1971," *Funnyworld* 14, 35.
8 *Steamboat Willie* review, *Variety* ("Land"), November 21, 1928, 13.
9 Quoted in Jim Korkis, "Secrets of Steamboat Willie," Mouseplanet, https://www.mouseplanet.com/10157/Secrets_of_Steamboat_Willie (accessed September 5, 2018).
10 Memo, Walt to Roy Scott, December 23, 1935 (WDA).
11 Letter, Walt (in New York) to Ub Iwerks and Roy, September 11, 1928 (WDA).
12 See Kaufman, "The Transcontinental Making of *The Barn Dance*."
13 Letter, Walt to "The Gang," October 11, 1928 (WDA).
14 *The Barn Dance* review, *Film Daily*, February 17, 1929, 11.
15 *The Barn Dance* script, undated (WDA).
16 See "Foreign News," *Time*, July 21, 1930, 25.
17 Studio publicity drawing, "Horace Horsecollar of Mickey Mouse Fame," ca. 1933. See Gerstein and Groth (eds.), *The Floyd Gottfredson Library*, vol. 2, 236.
18 Letters, Giegerich to Walt, September 5, 1929; Giegerich to Walt, December 19, 1929; Walt to Giegerich, December 23, 1929 (all WDA).
19 Letter Walt to Giegerich, July 26, 1929; telegram, Powers to Walt, August 7, 1929 (both WDA).
20 Letter, Giegerich to Walt, December 26, 1929; telegram, Giegerich to Walt, December 27, 1929 (both WDA).
21 Telegrams, Giegerich to Walt, January 14, 1930; Walt to Giegerich, January 15, 1930 (both WDA).
22 Stalling quoted in Barrier and Gray, "An Interview with Carl Stalling," *Funnyworld* 13, 24–25.
23 Letter, Walt to Giegerich, July 30, 1929 (WDA).
24 See Munsey, *Disneyana*, 31–32 and 39–42.
25 See Storm and Dreßler, *Im Reiche der Micky Maus*, 172.
26 "Mickey Mouse, Inventor of Whiskers," *Brisbane Courier*, November 24, 1930, 14.
27 Letter, Walt to Giegerich, September 16, 1929 (WDA).
28 See Canemaker, *Paper Dreams*, 66; and Huemer, Huemeresque," *Funnyworld* 18, 15.
29 See Barrier and Gray, "An Interview with Carl Stalling," *Funnyworld* 13, 24, note 11.
30 Ibid., and letter, Wilfred Jackson to Ross Care, April 5, 1975, quoted in *Disney Legend Wilfred Jackson*, 191.
31 See "Modesty Mollified by Mickey Mouse Morality," *Los Angeles Times*, November 23, 1930, B13.
32 See "'Mickey Mouse' at Roxy," *Film Daily*, May 4, 1931, 2.
33 Jackson to Frank Thomas and Ollie Johnston, May 18, 1978, reprinted in *Walt's People* 7, 24–25.
34 Ibid. Jackson's statement is borne out by the film's cue sheet.

35 Only the previous year, astronomers had discovered the heavenly body (initially thought a planet) that would henceforth be known as Pluto.
36 Letter, Hand to J. B. Kaufman, December 30, 1980.
37 See Goessell, *The First King of Hollywood*, 420–26.
38 Ising to David Gerstein, 1991.
39 "Disney Sues To Stop Other Mouse Cartoons," *Film Daily*, 1 April 1931, 7.
40 "Says Van Beuren Mouse Came Before Disney's," *Film Daily*, 3 April 1931, 2.
41 See, for example, "Mickey's Morals," *Motion Picture News*, 15 November 1930, 27, and "The Hollywood Who's Who—and what the film famous are doing in the movie capital," *New Movie Magazine*, February 1931, 30–31.
42 Harry Carr, "The Only Unpaid Movie Star," 125.

CHAPTER TWO

1 Walt Disney, 1956 quoted in Munsey, *Disneyana*, 16.
2 See Dave Smith, interviews with Ub Iwerks, 1970–1971 (WDA).
3 See Barrier, *The Animated Man*, 21.
4 Mark Sonntag, "Carey Orr - Walt's Mentor." Tagtoonz, entry posted July 13, 2008, http://msonntag.blogspot.com/2008/07/carey-orr-walts-mentor.html (accessed October 27, 2017).
5 Letter, Giegerich to Walt, June 8, 1929 (WDA).
6 Letter, Connolly to Ub Iwerks, July 24, 1929 (WDA).
7 See Munsey, ibid.
8 Letter, Walt to Connolly, October 19, 1929 (WDA).
9 Telegram, King Features Syndicate to Walt, December 30, 1929 (WDA).
10 As first published in newspapers, the *Mickey Mouse* daily strip continuities rarely featured running titles. The "official" titles by which we refer to them in this volume were decided upon by Floyd Gottfredson, Gladstone Publishing editor Byron Erickson, and the Disney comic strip department in the early 1980s, and have for the most part been used in official documentation ever since.
11 Gottfredson to David R. Smith, quoted in *Mickey Mouse in Color*, 156.
12 William Banks Levy quoted by Wilfred Haughton and Philip Allaker, unpublished notes on Haughton's life, 1970s. The emphasis on "competent" is Haughton's.
13 Most information in this paragraph: Sergio Lama, emails to David Gerstein, 2013.
14 Mark Johnson (Archivist emeritus, King Features Syndicate), conversations with David Gerstein, December 2012. Period documentation does not survive at King, but the pattern and authorization mark match King's sublicensing of other comics features in Europe at the time.
15 Ibid.

CAPTIONS

1 Gottfredson to David R. Smith, quoted in *Mickey Mouse in Color*, 156.

CHAPTER THREE

1 "Cats & Mice," *Time*, July 21, 1930, 25.
2 Walt, *Mickey's Nightmare* story outline, undated (WDA).
3 See, for example, Maltin, *The Disney Films*, 263, and Care, "Symphonists for the Sillies," 41–42.
4 See letter, Nelson to Frank Reade, ca. March 1934, reprinted in *Walt's People* 18, 8.
5 See Kaufman, "Before Snow White."
6 See Canemaker, *Two Guys Named Joe*, 115–23.
7 See Barrier, *Hollywood Cartoons*, 120.
8 *Strange Interlude* was explicitly cited in "Mickey's Boxing Kangaroo" story outline, October 2, 1934 (WDA).
9 Letter, Lichtman to Roy, December 13, 1932 (WDA).
10 "Mickey Mouse Saves Jersey Toy Concern; Carries It Back to Solvency on His Railway," *New York Times*, January 22, 1935, 21:4.
11 "50 to 60 Makers of Novelties Join in Exploitation Campaign," *Motion Picture Herald*, October 1, 1932, 43.
12 "Cinema Topics," *South China Morning Post*, August 1, 1936, 7.
13 "Mickey Mouse Club," *Times of India*, July 29, 1933, 18.

CAPTIONS

1 Jack Kinney to J. B. Kaufman, January 20, 1985.

CHAPTER FOUR

1 Fred Moore, "Analysis of Mickey Mouse," lecture, undated but late 1935 (WDA).
2 Ted Sears, "Mickey," written concurrently with the above (WDA).
3 Rob Lawson, "Enter Donald Duck," *Glasgow Daily Record*, October 15, 1934.
4 See Weinberg, *Saint Cinema*, 329.
5 Story outline, "Mickey's Vaudeville Show," March 11, 1935 (WDA). See Gerstein, *Walt Disney's Mickey and the Gang: Classic Stories in Verse*, 58–63.
6 Mortimer is so identified in the film's original press sheet (WDA).
7 *Mickey's Circus* story meetings, October 20 and 26, 1935 (WDA).

8 Ken O'Connor to J. B. Kaufman, October 30, 1989.
9 Letter, Eugster to J. B. Kaufman, February 9, 1981.
10 "Dean's Monster Books," ad in *London Evening News*, November 5, 1930.
11 See Bruce Hamilton with David R. Smith, "The Year That Was 1930: Mouse Number Thirteen," *Walt Disney's Comics and Stories*, August 1996, 604.
12 See Alberto Becattini and David Gerstein, "Sharing the Spotlight: Roy Nelson," *The Floyd Gottfredson Library*, Vol. 1, 264.
13 See Claudine and Yves Lebrun, "Félix Lorioux: illustrateur 1872–1964," *303 arts, recherches et créations* 33, 1992.
14 Magdeleine du Genestoux, *Mickey et Minnie*.
15 Letter, Sam Lowe to Walt, April 19, 1933 (WDA).
16 "Mickey Mouse Birthday Celebrations to Mark Cartoon's 2nd Anniversary," *Columbia Showman*, [October] 1930.
17 Examples published with Troy Orr, "Master Mickey Mouse Celebrates A Gala Occasion," *Screen Mirror*, October 1930.
18 "Disney Dates Piling Up," *Motion Picture Daily*, September 25, 1935, 13.
19 Memo, Roy to Walt, September 9, 1936 (WDA).
20 See "'Mickey Mouse' is Eight Years Old," *Literary Digest*, October 3, 1936, 18.
21 "Mickey Mouse to Get Breaks For Comeback as No. 1 Star," Associated Press story, *New York World-Telegram*, April 12, 1938.
22 Frank Thomas and Ollie Johnston, *Disney Animation*, 447–48.
23 Annex sweatbox meeting, January 11, 1939 (WDA).
24 See Shamus Culhane, *Talking Animals and Other People*, 164–69.
25 See "Clock Tower" story outline, ca. August 1936 (WDA).
26 Preston Blair to J. B. Kaufman, December 6, 1987.
27 Walt in *Mickey's Parrot* story meeting, July 16, 1937 (private collection).
28 *Brave Little Tailor* review, *Film Daily*, September 16, 1938, 8.
29 Note from *Tanglefoot* story conference, May 13, 1938 (WDA).
30 See "Six Specials On Disney's Program," *Film Daily*, June 29, 1938, 1, 10.
31 Chester Cobb, "The Sorcerer's Apprentice" story outline; handwritten memo, Sears to Cobb, both undated but probably mid- to late 1936 (WDA).
32 "Stokowski Co-Star With Mickey Mouse," *Hollywood Reporter*, November 19, 1937, 1.
33 "Suggestions made during Story Meeting of Nov. 13th, not appearing in continuity," November 16, 1937 (WDA).
34 Rough Continuity, Section IV, November 19, 1937 (WDA).
35 Story Continuity as of November 30, 1937 (WDA).
36 Rough Continuity, Section Two, November 9, 1937 (WDA).
37 Joseph O'Sullivan, "100 Musicians Can't Be Wrong; New Film Breaks with Tradition," *Motion Picture Herald*, September 18, 1937, 29.
38 Bill Garity "Daily Report," January 9 [sic], 1938 (WDA).
39 Walt in *Boat Builders* story meeting, February 8, 1937 (WDA).
40 Scene instruction sheet (Marvin Woodward), scene 87, March 4, 1938 (WDA).
41 Scene instruction sheet (Woodward), scene 29, February 4, 1938 (WDA).
42 Scene instruction sheet (Grim Natwick), scene 8, February 5, 1938 (identical instructions issued to Fred Moore, April 5, 1938, both WDA).
43 Preston Blair, "The Animation of *Fantasia*," *Cartoonist Profiles*, 17.
44 Ed Love to J. B. Kaufman, August 27, 1984.

CHAPTER FIVE

1 Bill Blackbeard, "Mickey Mouse and the Phantom Artist," 38.
2 This and other details concerning the publishers Nerbini and Mondadori: Alberto Becattini, *Disney Comics: The Whole Story*, 158–160.
3 Period documents establish that Ted Osborne continued some writing work with KHJ into 1932. Confusion reigns insofar as a different Ted Osborne simultaneously began work with KHJ as an on-air actor.
4 Floyd Gottfredson to David R. Smith, quoted in *Mickey Mouse in Color* deluxe edition, 161–62.
5 See ibid.
6 See Becattini, 34–35.

CHAPTER SIX

1 See Walt in untitled Office of War Information radio broadcast, recorded August 9, 1943 (Library of Congress).
2 See United Press news item, "'Mickey Mouse,' the Password," *New York Herald Tribune*, June 8, 1944, 3. A truncated *Los Angeles Times* version of the same news item, also dated June 8, leaves out the point of the password being specifically for an invasion briefing. It seems likely that this omission led to the popular misunderstanding of Mickey's name being the password for the invasion itself.
3 Harry Teitel (i.e. Tytle) in "The Elopement" story meeting, August 27, 1940 (WDA).
4 See Kaufman, *South of the Border with Disney*, 169–71.

5 See ibid., chapter 1.
6 See Gerstein, *Mickey and the Gang*, 306–07.
7 See Mark Johnson (Archivist emeritus, King Features Syndicate), conversations with David Gerstein, 1990s.
8 See Gottfredson to David R. Smith, *Mickey Mouse in Color*, 164.
9 This paragraph and next: See Becattini, *Disney Comics*, 163–64.

CHAPTER SEVEN

1 See Walt to Pete Martin, 1956 interviews.
2 Walt in story meeting/review of 19 Disney shorts for contemplated feature, June 27, 1939 (WDA).
3 Ibid.
4 Form memo, undated, attached to scene 32.2 and other multiplane scenes in "The Sorcerer's Apprentice" (ARL).
5 Scene instruction sheet, "The Sorcerer's Apprentice," scene 92, March 21, 1938 (WDA).
6 *Fantasia* review, *The New York Times* (Crowther), November 14, 1940, 28:2.
7 Ibid.
8 *Fantasia* review, *Films* (Rosenheimer), Winter 1940, 38.
9 Walt in story meeting on "Jack in the Beanstalk" [sic], June 10, 1938 (WDA).
10 Ibid.
11 Douglas W. Churchill, "All Quiet on The Anti-Nazi, Anti-Spy Front," *The New York Times*, April 2, 1939, X:5:3.
12 Letter, Tashlin to Fred Niemann, December 4, 1939, quoted by Prouty in *Frank Tashlin*, 202.
13 Walt in "Jack and the Beanstalk" story meeting, May 14, 1940 (WDA).
14 Walt in "Men in Uniform" story meeting, May 11, 1940 (private collection).
15 See memo, Walt to Sharpsteen, May 6, 1940, subject: MICKEY FEATURE (WDA).
16 Walt in "Jack and the Beanstalk" story meeting, May 2, 1940 (WDA).
17 Walt in "Mickey Feature Overall" meeting, June 5, 1940 (WDA).
18 Walt in "Jack and the Beanstalk" story meeting, May 14, 1940 (WDA).
19 Walt in "Mickey Feature Overall" meeting, June 5, 1940 (WDA).
20 See Memo, Alma Fenter/ Harry Teitel to Walt, May 25, 1940, subject: JACK AND THE BEANSTALK - 1-130 (WDA).
21 Walt in "Jack and the Beanstalk" story meeting, May 14, 1940 (WDA).
22 Walt in story meeting on "Sequence 1132 — Mickey and the Grasshopper," June 1, 1940 (WDA).
23 Walt in "Mickey Feature Overall" meeting, June 5, 1940 (WDA).
24 Walt in "Jack and the Beanstalk" story meeting, May 14, 1940 (WDA).
25 Letter, Roy to Joe Rosenberg, October 7, 1941 (WDA).
26 This and subsequent quotes: Hee and Cottrell, "Sooner or Later" treatment, April 7, 1944 (private collection).
27 Macdonald quoted by Gray in "Jim Macdonald," *Funnyworld* 18, 21.
28 *Fun and Fancy Free* review, *Daily Variety*, August 20, 1947, 3.
29 *Fun and Fancy Free* review, *Hollywood Reporter*, August 20, 1947, 6.

CAPTIONS

1 See Barrier, *Funnybooks*, 93–96.
2 Walt in "Jack and the Beanstalk" story meeting, May 14, 1940 (WDA).
3 Walt in "Mickey Feature Overall" meeting, June 5, 1940 (WDA).
4 Walt in "Jack in the Beanstalk" story meeting, June 10, 1938 (WDA).

CHAPTER EIGHT

1 See Leonardo Gori and Francesco Stajano in *The Floyd Gottfredson Library*, Vol. 8, 80.
2 See Floyd Gottfredson, letter to Bradley Kelly, May 22, 1945 (WDA).
3 Gottfredson to Andrae, "The Mouse's Other Master," 14.
4 This and the following anecdotes (nickname for Walsh; robber encounter): Dan Gonzales, phone conversation with David Gerstein, September 24, 2013.
5 Paul Murry to Klaus Spillman, "The Man Who Drew More Tales for the Mouse," *The Duckburg Times* 16.
6 Murry to Donald and Lynda Ault, 1970s.
7 See Alberto Becattini, *Disney Comics: The Whole Story*, 145.
8 See Leonardo Gori and Francesco Stajano in *The Floyd Gottfredson Library*, Vol. 9, 269.

CAPTIONS

1 Carl Barks, letter to Michael Barrier, June 9, 1966 (private collection).

CHAPTER NINE

1 See Nichols, *Walt Disney's Disneyland*.
2 Walt in TV meeting, March 19, 1954 (WDA).
3 See Cotter, *The Wonderful World of Disney Television*, 181.
4 Walt in TV meeting, March 22, 1954 (WDA).
5 See Cotter, 181–85.
6 See Korkis, "The Secret Walt Disney Commercials," *Walt's People* Vol. 9, 218–21.

CHAPTER TEN

1. Kendis Rochlen, "It's a Comeback for Mickey Mouse," *Los Angeles Mirror*, November 18, 1950, 3.
2. Irving Wallace, "Mickey Mouse and How He Grew," *Collier's*, April 9, 1949.
3. Pete Young and Steve Hulett, "Mickey Columbus" dialogue sheet, June 18, 1984 (WDA).
4. See "Darkwing Duck: 25 Years Later," Oh My Disney (company blog), entry posted September 9, 2016, https://ohmy.disney.com/insider/2016/09/09/darkwing-duck-25-years-later/ (accessed February 9, 2018).

CAPTIONS

1. Quoted in Bill Dessowitz, "Immersed in Movies: Eric Goldberg Talks Mickey Mouse and *Get a Horse!*," IndieWire, https://www.indiewire.com/2013/11/immersed-in-movies-eric-goldberg-talks-mickey-mouse-and-get-a-horse-124631 (accessed August 2, 2018).

CHAPTER ELEVEN

1. See Dwight Decker, "Woody Woodpecker's Finest Hour," *The Comics Journal* 63, 1981.
2. In Finland, for example, the weekly *Aku Ankka* ("Donald Duck," though the anthology title also features Mickey) was the best-selling periodical of any kind as recently as 2010. See Nationalencyklopedin, "Finland: Massmedier," http://www.ne.se/finland/massmedier (accessed August 30, 2010).
3. See Paul Murry to Donald and Lynda Ault, 1970s.
4. Lars Bergström, conversation with David Gerstein, 1990s.
5. See Gutenberghus Group editors, "The Mickey Mouse [character] Group," *Anders And & Co.* writers' guide, 1970s (private collection), 18.
6. David Cody Weiss, "The Heroic Image," *Mickey Mouse Adventures* 2, July 1990.
7. See Don Rosa, "The Life and Times of Don Rosa Part 4: The Buckaroo of the Biography," *The Don Rosa Library* Vol. 4, 191.
8. Byron Erickson, "Mickey Mouse." Egmont writers' guide, ca. 1997 (private collection).
9. Joachim Stahl, "Best/worst stories of *Micky Maus*," Ehapa Verlag GmbH internal report, 2000 (private collection).
10. Giorgio Cavazzano, "From Mouseton to Casablanca," in *The Floyd Gottfredson Library* Vol. 8, 12.

CHAPTER TWELVE

1. Barry Blumberg quoted in Greg Braxton, "The Most Famous Mouse in the World Plans a Comeback," *Los Angeles Times*, November 19, 1997, section F, 2.
2. Phil Gallo, "Mickey Mouse Works," *Variety.com*, April 30, 1999, https://variety.com/1999/film/reviews/mickey-mouse-works-1117499713 (accessed April 12, 2018).
3. See Tetsuya Nomura to Satoru Iwata, "The Impact of Super Mario 64," *IwataAsks.Nintendo.com*, http://iwataasks.nintendo.com/interviews/#/3ds/creators/11/0 (accessed April 11, 2018).
4. See Tetsuya Nomura, "KHU Interview w/ Tetsuya Nomura," *KHInsider.com* (archived), https://www.webcitation.org/64xK2Fual?url=http://www.khinsider.com/content/view/42/41/ (accessed April 12, 2018).
5. Jason Schreier, "What the Hell Is *Kingdom Hearts*? A Beginner's Guide to Square Enix's RPG Series," *Kotaku.com*, https://kotaku.com/5929682/what-the-hell-is-kingdom-hearts-a-beginners-guide-to-square-enixs-rpg-series (accessed April 11, 2018).
6. Matthew Stringer, "Epic Mickey Think Tank," *Behance.net*, https://www.behance.net/gallery/7290945/Epic-Mickey-Think-Tank (accessed April 12, 2018).
7. Sean Vanaman, "Epic Mickey," *SeanVanaman.com* (archived), https://web.archive.org/web/20121129231416/http://seanvanaman.com/post/21071130597/epicmickey (accessed April 12, 2018).
8. Stringer (see note 5). The deal with NBC/Universal through which Disney reacquired rights to Oswald was completed in early 2006.
9. Warren Spector to IGN, "Epic Mickey's Warren Spector: 'Adults are the ones who have the blinders on,'" *IGN.com*, http://www.ign.com/articles/2010/10/10/epic-mickeys-warren-spector-adults-are-the-ones-who-have-the-blinders-on?page=2 (accessed April 12, 2018).
10. Paul Rudish, conversation with David Gerstein, June 14, 2013.
11. See *New York Weenie* (2013).
12. See Chris Diamantopoulos in a Reddit AMA online discussion, https://www.reddit.com/r/IAmA/comments/3psu6x/im_the_voice_of_mickey_mouse_im_moe_from_the/ (accessed April 13, 2018).

CAPTIONS

1. Warren Spector quoted in Austin Grossman, *The Art of Disney Epic Mickey*, 78.

Bibliography

ARTICLES

Joe Adamson, "With Disney on Olympus: An Interview with Dick Huemer," *Funnyworld* 17 (Fall 1977), 37–45

Thomas Andrae, "The Mouse's Other Master: Floyd Gottfredson's 45 Years with Mickey," *Nemo: The Classic Comics Library* 6 (June 1984)

Michael Barrier, "Mickey Mouse, Super Secret Agent," *The Duckburg Times* 16 (January 1, 1983), 13–14

Michael Barrier and Milt Gray, "An Interview with Carl Stalling," *Funnyworld* 13 (Spring 1971), 20–29

Cedric Belfrage, "My Love Life and Other Things, As Told by Mickey Mouse," *Motion Picture Classic*, August 1930, 68–69, 96

Bill Blackbeard, "Mickey Mouse and the Phantom Artist," in Don Thompson and Richard A. Lupoff (eds.), *The Comic-Book Book* (New Rochelle: Arlington House, 1973), 36–61

Preston Blair, "The Animation of 'Fantasia'," *Cartoonist Profiles* 49 (March 1981), 16–24

Dana Burnet, "The Rise of Donald Duck," *Pictorial Review*, October 1935, 19, 46–47

Ross Care, "Symphonists for the Sillies," *Funnyworld* 18 (Summer 1978), 38–48

Harry Carr, "The Only Unpaid Movie Star," *American Magazine*, March 1931, 55–57, 122–25

Dwight Decker, "Woody Woodpecker's Finest Hour," *The Comics Journal* 63 (1981)

Hooper Fowler, "Interview with Hooper Fowler," in Kathy Merlock Jackson (ed.), *Conversations with Walt Disney* (Jackson: University Press of Mississippi, 2006), 104–114

Milt Gray, "Jim Macdonald," *Funnyworld* 18 (Summer 1978), 21

Bruce Hamilton with David R. Smith, "The Year that Was 1930: Mouse Number Thirteen," *Walt Disney's Comics and Stories* 604 (August 1996)

Dick Huemer, "Huemeresque," *Funnyworld* 18 (Summer 1978), 15–16

Alva Johnston, "Mickey Mouse," *Woman's Home Companion*, July 1934, 12–13, 92–94

J. B. Kaufman, "Before Snow White," *Film History*, June 1993 (vol. 5, no. 2), 158–175

J. B. Kaufman, "The Transcontinental Making of *The Barn Dance*," *Animation Journal*, vol. 5, no. 2 (spring 1997), 36–44

J. B. Kaufman, "The Heir Apparent," in Daniel Goldmark and Charlie Keil (eds.), *Funny Pictures: Animation and Comedy in Studio-Era Hollywood* (Berkeley, Los Angeles, London: University of California Press, 2011), 51–65

Ward Kimball, "Ward Kimball Remembers Walt Kelly," interview by Thomas Andrae and Geoffrey Blum, in Walt Kelly, *Phi Beta Pogo*, comp. Selby Kelly and Bill Crouch (New York: Simon and Schuster, 1989)

Claudine and Yves Lebrun, "Félix Lorioux: illustrateur 1872–1964," *303 arts, recherches et créations* 33, 1992

Susan Ohmer, "Laughter by Numbers: The Science of Comedy at the Walt Disney Studio," in Daniel Goldmark and Charlie Keil (eds.), *Funny Pictures: Animation and Comedy in Studio-Era Hollywood* (Berkeley, Los Angeles, London: University of California Press, 2011), 109–126

Howard Prouty, "Documentation," in Roger Garcia and Bernard Eisenschitz (eds.), *Frank Tashlin* [festival catalogue] (Locarno: British Film Institute/Éditions Yellow Now, 1994), 185–240

Richard Schoch, "Performing Bohemia," *Nineteenth Century Theatre and Film*, Winter 2003 (vol. 5, no. 2), 1–13

Keith Scott, "Hearing Voices: Mickey Mouse, Radio Star," *Animato!* 39 (Spring 1998), 18–21

Dave Smith, "Ub Iwerks, 1901–1971," *Funnyworld* 14 (Spring 1972), 32–37, 47

Klaus Spillman, "The Man Who Drew More Tales for the Mouse," *The Duckburg Times* 16 (January 1, 1983), 17–23

John Updike, "The Mystery of Mickey Mouse," in Craig Yoe and Janet Morra-Yoe (eds.), *The Art of Mickey Mouse* (New York: Hyperion, 1991)

David Cody Weiss, "The Heroic Image," *Mickey Mouse Adventures* 2 (July 1990)

Malcolm Willits, "George Sherman: An Interview with Another One of the 'Men Behind the Mouse,'" *Vanguard* 2 (1968)

BOOKS

Thomas Andrae, *Carl Barks and the Disney Comic Book: Unmasking the Myth of Modernity* (Jackson: University Press of Mississippi, 2006)

Donald Ault (ed.), *Carl Barks: Conversations* (Jackson: University Press of Mississippi, 2003)

Michael Barrier, *Hollywood Cartoons: American Animation in Its Golden Age* (New York, Oxford: Oxford, 1999)

Michael Barrier, *The Animated Man: A Life of Walt Disney* (Berkeley, Los Angeles, London: University of California Press, 2007)

Michael Barrier, *Funnybooks: The Improbable Glories of the Best American Comic Books* (Oakland: University of California Press, 2015)

Alberto Becattini, *Disney Comics: The Whole Story* (Theme Park Press, 2016)

John Canemaker, *Paper Dreams: The Art & Artists of Disney Storyboards* (New York: Hyperion, 1999)

John Canemaker, *Two Guys Named Joe: Master Animation Storytellers Joe Grant and Joe Ranft* (New York: Disney Editions, 2010)

Ross Care, *Disney Legend Wilfred Jackson: A Life in Animation* (Theme Park Press, 2016)

Bill Cotter, *The Wonderful World of Disney Television: A Complete History* (New York: Hyperion, 1997)

Shamus Culhane, *Talking Animals and Other People* (New York: St. Martin's Press, 1986)

Neal Gabler, *Walt Disney: The Triumph of the American Imagination* (New York: Knopf, 2006)

Magdeleine du Genestoux, *Mickey et Minnie* (Paris: Hachette, 1932)

David Gerstein, *Walt Disney's Mickey and the Gang: Classic Stories in Verse* (Timonium MD: Gemstone, 2005)

David Gerstein (ed.), *The Don Rosa Library*, vol. 4 (Seattle: Fantagraphics, 2014)

David Gerstein and Gary Groth (eds.), *The Floyd Gottfredson Library,* Seattle: vols. 1 and 2 (2011), 3 (2012), 8 (2015), 9 (2016)

Didier Ghez (ed.), *Walt's People* (Xlibris): vols. 7 (2008), 8 (2009), 9 (2010), 10 (2011), and 18 (Theme Park Press, 2016)

Tracey Goessel, *The First King of Hollywood: The Life of Douglas Fairbanks* (Chicago: Chicago Review Press, 2016)

Katherine and Richard Greene, *Inside the Dream. The Personal Story of Walt Disney* (New York: Roundtable Press, 2001)

Austin Grossman, *The Art of Disney Epic Mickey* (New York: Disney Editions, 2010)

J. B. Kaufman, *South of the Border with Disney: Walt Disney and the Good Neighbor Program, 1941–1948* (New York: Disney Editions, 2009)

J. B. Kaufman, *The Fairest One of All: The Making of Walt Disney's* Snow White and the Seven Dwarfs (San Francisco: Walt Disney Family Foundation Press, 2012)

Leonard Maltin, *The Disney Films* (New York: Crown, 1973)

Russell Merritt and J. B. Kaufman, *Walt Disney's Silly Symphonies: A Companion to the Classic Cartoon Series* (New York: Disney Editions, 2016)

Mickey Mouse in Color (deluxe edition: Prescott: Another Rainbow; trade edition: New York: Pantheon), 1988

Cecil Munsey, *Disneyana: Walt Disney Collectibles* (New York: Hawthorn, 1974)

Chris Nichols, *Walt Disney's Disneyland* (Taschen, 2018)

Paul Rotha, *The Film till Now*. Revised edition (Norwich: Fletcher & Son, 1967)

J. P. Storm and M. Dreßler, *Im Reiche der Micky Maus: Walt Disney und Deutschland 1927–1945* (Berlin: Henschel, 1991)

Bob Thomas, *Walt Disney: An American Original* (New York: Disney Editions, 1994)

Frank Thomas and Ollie Johnston, *Disney Animation: The Illusion of Life* (New York: Abbeville, 1981)

Walt Disney Best Comics: Mickey Mouse [comics compilation] (New York: Abbeville, 1978)

Robert Tieman, *The Mickey Mouse Treasures* (New York: Disney, 2007)

Andy Warhol, Pat Hackett (ed.), *The Andy Warhol Diaries* (New York: Warner Books, 1989)

Herman G. Weinberg, *Saint Cinema* (New York: DBS, 1970)

Malcolm Willits, *The Malcolm Willits Collection of Mickey Mouse Paintings by Floyd Gottfredson* (Burbank: H. Lowery, 1993)

Acknowledgments

AUTHORS' ACKNOWLEDGMENTS

The authors are grateful to many people who contributed in significant ways to the writing of this book. Clearly, a work of this size and scope could never have been attempted without the assistance of some extraordinary individuals within The Walt Disney Company. Howard Green, Vice President of Communications for Walt Disney Animation Studios, has facilitated our work, as he has facilitated so many other projects, with his usual unflappable grace and expertise. This book could never have been attempted without the kind and knowledgeable help of Rebecca Cline and her skilled staff at the Walt Disney Archives. Kevin Kern, in particular, bore patiently with our presence and constant requests over the months of our research, and guided us to many important documents and other material that proved essential to our work. Additional indispensable help was provided by Maggie Evenson, Edward Ovalle, Kimi Thompson, and Kelsey Williams. Much of the book also draws on the authors' Archives research in previous years; it would be remiss not to mention the roles of Dave Smith and Robert Tieman in helping build our Mickey research files during those years. Within the Archives, the Walt Disney Archives Photo Library also proved a crucial resource in assembling this book, thanks to the kind and understanding assistance of Michael Buckhoff and Holly Brobst.

The Walt Disney Animation Research Library, under the expert guidance of Mary Walsh, bears the responsibility of maintaining the mammoth and precious library of Disney animation art. Fox Carney, Doug Engalla, Ann Hansen, and Jackie Vasquez patiently hosted both of us for months during the creation of this book, guiding us through the Library's vast holdings and making priceless selections available for these pages. At the Walt Disney Creative Resource Center, Elizabeth Spatz kindly lent her expertise in the world of licensed Mickey merchandise. Donovan Cook, Tony Craig, Eric Coleman, Todd Popp and Paul Rudish, with or formerly with Disney Television Animation, provided key insights about Mickey's latter-day television adventures. At Disney Publishing Worldwide, Jennifer Eastwood, Iliana Lopez, David Pacheco, and Ken Shue weighed in on the manuscript as it took shape, offering their counsel and knowledge.

Outside The Walt Disney Company itself, the authors are indebted to the rapidly growing community of Disney scholars, many of whom are personal friends and have specialized in particular aspects of Disney history. Some of these individuals have contributed generously of their time and expertise on specific subjects, notably Alberto Becattini, John Canemaker, Didier Ghez, Eric Goldberg, Leonardo Gori, Thomas Jensen, Mark Kausler, Stacia Martin, Kaya Özkaracalar, Hans Perk, and Keith Scott. Stefano Priarone and Fernando Ventura, in particular, provided extensive research assistance without which chapters 8 and 11 could not have come together. Equally invaluable help of a more general nature was provided by Frank Aasgård, Maggie Barnes, Michael Barrier, Jerry Beck, Joe Campana, Jacques Echegaray, Bob Foster, Jonathan H. Gray, Carole Halsted, Thad Komorowski, Sergio Lama, Paula Sigman Lowery, Russell Merritt, Erik Rosengarten, Francesco Spreafico, Steve Stanchfield, Tommy José Stathes, Joe Torcivia, and Francois Willot.

Along with these private citizens, the authors have benefited from the help of three formal institutions. One is the Margaret Herrick Library of the Academy of Motion Picture Arts and Sciences, where Laura Lee McKay, Howard Prouty, and Jenny Romero have offered the benefit of their knowledge and skill. Another is the United States Library of Congress, whose George Willeman and Mike Mashon offered access to rare film elements. The third is the Cinema-Television Library of the University of Southern California, where the irreplaceable Ned Comstock has exceeded even his own standard in the tireless pursuit of obscure historical material.

Ultimately, of course, all of us are indebted to Walt Disney and to his team of talented artists and writers who have brought Mickey Mouse to life over the span of 90 years. The authors are especially grateful to some who have graciously granted us interviews and discussed their experiences: Lars Bergström, Preston Blair, David Cody Weiss, Al Eugster, Cèsar Ferioli, Dan Gonzales, Dave Hand, Rudy Ising, Mark Johnson, Jack Kinney, Ed Love, Dorothy Compton Morton, Ken O'Connor, and Warren Spector.

At TASCHEN, we have been fortunate to work with a team of exceptional individuals, starting with Benedikt Taschen himself, whose inspiration it was to create a book of this scope for Mickey Mouse. We're grateful to Daniel Kothenschulte, a meticulous and dedicated editor who brought us on board for this project, and Anna-Tina Kessler, whose design skills have resulted in the gallery of eye-popping visuals in these pages. The book also owes much to the editorial skills of Martin Holz.

To all these people and institutions, our heartfelt thanks and our hope that their contributions are reflected in the finished book. And to Mickey himself, thanks for your untiring spirit of happiness that has kept the world smiling for nearly a century. Here's to the next century!

EDITOR'S ACKNOWLEDGMENTS

I am deeply attached to J. B. Kaufman and Dave Gerstein, whose deep love for Mickey and the art of Disney never compromised the scientific accuracy of their research.

Everyone who loves cinema owes thanks to Disney Chairman and CEO Bob Iger for his dedication in preserving the artistic heritage of Walt Disney and the artists who contributed to this unique art form. The artworks and documents within the collections of The Walt Disney Company are part of modern cultural history. The archivists at Walt Disney Archives and The Animation Research Library are researchers of the highest esteem as well as passionate Disney aficionados. Kevin M. Kern and Fox Carney spent hundreds of hours on this book, always keeping up their enthusiasm. I am deeply indebted to Michael Buckhoff at the Walt Disney Archives Photo Library, who knows a million photographs by heart and generously shared his knowledge. However, keeping such a cultural legacy alive requires talents in many fields. At Disney Publishing I would like to thank Ken Shue, Daniel Saeva, Ángela Ontiveiros, and Ashley West Leonard for their endless care with all our requests, for building bridges, and for making magic whenever we wished upon a star.

A million thanks to Carlotta Quattrocolo and Stefano Ambrosio for opening every door to the world of Disney comics. I am indebted to Howard Green and Robert Tieman.

I would like to thank Disney Legend Andreas Deja, whose dedication to sharing the secrets of classic Disney animation is invaluable.

Collectors Mike Glad, Bernie Shine, Mel Birnkrant, Alexander Braun, Philippe Videcoq, Kevin Kidney, and Timothy Hack generously allowed us to reproduce the unique Disney art in their holdings. Photographer Michael E. Stern kindly gave us access to his masterful shots of Disney artwork.

We were graciously supported by auction houses and galleries dedicated to animation art and memorabilia. I am grateful to Jeff Greer and Margaret Croft of Heritage Auctions, Alex Winter and Terence Kean of Hake's Auctions, Brian Chanes of Profiles in History, and Rob Faucette of Wonderful World of Animation Gallery.

At TASCHEN, I would like to thank Anna-Tina Kessler for her artistic skills, vision, and endless patience; Martin Holz, as editor, who always kept his cool, even in the critical stages; production manager Marion Boschka for reproducing the art with museum-like care; Erica Pak, Maurene Appelhans, and Pimploy Phongsirivech for project management; Teena Apeles, Aaron Bogart, Brandy Colbert, Thea Miklowski, and Pia Oddo for copyediting and proofreading; Pauline Lopez for photo research; and above all, a man whose deep love for Mickey and the art of Disney paved the way for this dedicated work, Benedikt Taschen.

Credits

Texts by David Gerstein and J. B. Kaufman. The opinions expressed by this book's authors do not necessarily represent the views of The Walt Disney Company.

Editor's note: Vintage artwork and comics excerpts included in this volume may contain cartoon violence and historically dated material presented in context. We caution the reader that these items reflect the era in which they were originally created.

The majority of the images included in this volume were obtained from Disney's own treasure troves. Special thanks to the Walt Disney Archives and Photo Library, the Walt Disney Animation Research Library, and the Disney Library Restoration and Preservation teams, who provided invaluable research materials and expevrtise.

IMAGE CREDITS

Karsten Bracker Collection: 142/143. Bali Collection: 348/349 (top). Courtesy Birnkrant Collection: 149, 150, 155, 255, 256 (top). Courtesy Donovan Cook: 488. Disney Consumer Products Archives: 62, 327 (bottom). Fox Photos/Getty Images: 24. Photo by Globe Photographer/The Boston Globe via Getty Images: 285. Charles 'Teenie' Harris/Carnegie Museum of Art via Getty Images: 352 (top). Photo by Douglas Miller/ Topical Press Agency/Getty Images: 50. © Estate of Roy Lichtenstein/VG Bild-Kunst, Bonn 2020: 453. Photo by NBC/NBCU Photo Bank via Getty Images: 327 (bottom). Photo by NY Daily News Archive via Getty Images: 282. Onfokus via Getty Images: 495. Photo by Popperfoto/Getty Images: 382. Photo by Edward Steichen/Condé Nast via Getty Images: 146. Courtesy German Academy of Comic Art: 336/337, 469. Courtesy Mike and Jeanne Glad: 233, 392. Keith Haring artwork © Keith Haring Foundation: 452. Richard Huemer Collection: 430. Richard W. Hall Collection, courtesy David Callahan: 145. Courtesy of Hake's Auctions, hakes.com: 49, 62, 67 (top), 67 (bottom), 64 (bottom left and right), 70, 72, 73, 94, 217, 216, 215 (top), 218, 221, 253, 272, 273. Imaged by Heritage Auctions, ha.com: front cover, 16, 13, 28, 33 (top and bottom), 52 (top), 89, 133, 134/135, 171, 186, 195, 214, 220, 230, 245, 248, 254, 256 (bottom), 278, 279, 284, 320, 326/327 (top), 331, 323, 336/337, 352/353 (bottom), 354, 358, 370, 373, 399, 405, 433, 455, 493. Janet Jamison Collection: 477. Courtesy Daniel Kothenschulte Collection: 109, 219, 236, 252, 328/329, 332, 378, 400, 401, 403, 442, 460. Mark Kausler Collection: 82, 288. LOOK Magazine, Photograph Collection, Library of Congress, Prints & Photographs Division LC-L9-60-8812, frame 8, © Earl Theisen Archives: back cover, 6. Library of Congress: 31, 32, 450. Library of Congress, Prints & Photographs Division, Harris & Ewing: LC-DIG-hec-36581: 46. Mike Matel Collection: 344. Nahmias Collection: 348/349 (bottom). National Gallery, London: 453. National Geographic Creative/Thomas Nebbia: 511. Ohio State University: 126 (top). Private Collection: 193 (bottom). Profiles in History, profilesinhistory.com: 301. RR Auction: 232. From the Bernie Shine Collection: 71, 214 (top), 198–213, 222 (objects), 224–225 (objects), 260–271, 274–277 (objects), 287, 286. Photograph by Michael E. Stern, source image © Disney: 100, 188. Courtesy Phillippe Videcoq: 177. Walt Disney Family Foundation, Gift of Diane Disney Miller: 451. Collection Walt Disney Family Foundation: 26, 27. Courtesy of John G. Zimmerman Archive: 445.

TRADEMARK NOTICES

Academy Award® and Academy of Motion Picture Arts and Sciences® are registered trademarks of the Academy of Motion Picture Arts and Sciences. Collier's® is a registered trademark of 200 Kelsey Associates, LLC. Cosmopolitan® is a registered trademark of Hearst Communications, Inc. Leica® is the registered trademark of Leica Microsystems IR GmbH. Looney Tunes® is a registered trademark of Time Warner Entertainment Company, L. P. Los Angeles Times® is the registered trademark of Los Angeles Times Communications LLC. MGM® is a registered trademark of Metro-Goldwyn-Mayer Lion Corp. The Museum of Modern Art® is the registered trademark of The Museum of Modern Art. NBC® is the registered trademark of NBC Universal Media, LLC. New York Post® is the registered trademark of NYP Holdings, Inc. The New York Times® is the registered trademark of The New York Times Company. Oscar® is a registered trademark of the Academy of Motion Picture Arts and Sciences. RCA® is a registered trademark of Audiovox Corporation. Rube Goldberg® is a registered trademark of Rube Goldberg Inc. Technicolor® is a registered trademark of Technicolor, Inc. United Artists® is the registered trademark of United Artists Corporation. Universal® is the registered trademark of Universal Fluid Heads (Aust.) Pty. Limited. Universal® is a registered trademark of Universal City Studios, Inc. Variety® is a registered trademark of Reed Properties Inc. Walter Lantz® is the registered trademark of Walter Lantz Productions, Inc. Warner Bros.® is a registered trademark of Warner Bros. Entertainment Inc.

Page 1 A 1929 publicity pose shows Mickey as he would continue to appear in his early black-and-white shorts: complete with rubbery limbs and eyes with a slice cut out of them like a piece of pie — a style fondly nicknamed "pie-eyes."

Page 2 In the 1940 feature *Fantasia*, Mickey played what many consider his grandest role as "The Sorcerer's Apprentice." The story was based on J. W. Goethe's poem, but the scene of Mickey conducting the stars was Walt Disney's own invention. This iconic painting by Al Dempster, based on the scene, was created for a 1957 record album.

Page 5 Mickey and Pluto pay Minnie a visit as Christmas carolers, while Horace and Clarabelle provide their musical talents too: special art created for Disney's 1931 studio Christmas card.

Page 6 It had been more than two decades since Walt Disney introduced Mickey to the world when this portait was shot in the early 1950s. Yet the doll that seamstress Charlotte Clark designed in 1930 remained unsurpassed.

Opposite A 1963 publicity photo captures Walt amid an impressive array of past awards, many given to the studio founder himself — such as a large Oscar with seven small Oscars, received for *Snow White and the Seven Dwarfs*. Also spotted in the scene are examples of the Mousecar and Duckster, character-shaped trophies awarded by Disney for exemplary work or service.

Following A March 1939 "special black and white stock shot of Mickey for general use," described as such in Disney's publicity department logbooks.

Front cover Mickey Mouse, as drawn by Les Clark for a 1929 stock one-sheet poster announcing releases from Celebrity Productions, an entity formed by distributor Pat Powers to handle sales of the Disney cartoons. Imaged by Heritage Auctions, ha.com.

Back cover This publicity picture — picturing the original Mickey Mouse, as he appeared in the 1930s, posing with Walt Disney two full decades later — suggests something of Mickey's enduring appeal to many generations.

EACH AND EVERY TASCHEN BOOK PLANTS A SEED!
TASCHEN is a carbon neutral publisher. Each year, we offset our annual carbon emissions with carbon credits at the Instituto Terra, a reforestation program in Minas Gerais, Brazil, founded by Lélia and Sebastião Salgado. To find out more about this ecological partnership, please check: www.taschen.com/zerocarbon
Inspiration: unlimited. Carbon footprint: zero.

To stay informed about TASCHEN and our upcoming titles, please subscribe to our free magazine at www.taschen.com/magazine, follow us on Instagram and Facebook, or e-mail your questions to contact@taschen.com.

Concept, composition, and design by TASCHEN GmbH

TASCHEN GmbH
Hohenzollernring 53, D-50672 Köln
www.taschen.com

Printed in Bosnia-Herzegovina
ISBN 978-3-8365-8099-1

©
W.D.P.